Praise for *Dark*

"The urge to find meaning and value through connecting with creation likely constitutes a deep and enduring human need. This important book provides insight regarding how a profound sense of relation to nature offers many in the modern world a vehicle for attaining this spiritual wholeness akin to what has been historically associated with established religion. In this sense, *Dark Green Religion* offers both understanding and hope for a world struggling for meaning and purpose beyond the isolation of the material here and now."

Stephen Kellert, Tweedy Ordway Professor of Social Ecology,
Yale University School of Forestry
and Environmental Studies

"In this thought-provoking volume, Bron Taylor explores the seemingly boundless efforts by human beings to understand the nature of life and our place in the universe. Examining in depth the ways in which the most influential philosophers and naturalists have viewed this relationship, Taylor contributes to the construction of sound foundations for the further development of thought in this critically important area, where our depth of understanding will play a critical role in our survival. This important book should be widely studied and will be greatly appreciated by those who take the time to savor its intellectual depths."

Peter H. Raven, President, Missouri Botanical Garden

"A fascinating analysis of our emotional and spiritual relationship to nature. Whether you call it dark green religion or something else, Bron Taylor takes us through our spiritual relationship with our planet, its ecosystems and evolution, in an enlightened and completely undogmatic manner."

Claude Martin, Former Director General,
World Wildlife Fund

"An excellent collection of guideposts for perplexed students and scholars about the relationships between nature religions, spirituality, animism, pantheism, deep ecology, Gaia, and land ethics—and for the environmentalist seeking to make the world a better place through green religion as a social force."

Fikret Berkes, author of *Sacred Ecology: Traditional Ecological Knowledge and Resource Management*

"In this exceptionally interesting and informative book, Bron Taylor has harvested the fruits of years of pioneering research in what amounts to a new field in religious studies: the study of how religious and spiritual themes show up in the work of people concerned about nature in many diverse ways. Taylor persuasively argues that appreciation of nature's sacred or spiritual dimension both informs and motivates the work of individuals ranging from radical environmentalists and surfers, to ecotourism leaders and museum curators. I highly recommend this book for everyone interested in learning more about the surprising extent to which religion and spirituality influence many of those who work to protect, exhibit, or represent the natural world."

Michael E. Zimmerman, Director, Center for Humanities and the Arts, University of Colorado at Boulder

Dark Green Religion

For Maynard:
on the occasion of
the 2012 IRAS

Dark Green Religion

Nature Spirituality and the Planetary Future

Bron Taylor

meeting at Lake George,
New York, July/Aug 2012.
Persevere in all your
own good works

Bron Taylor

UNIVERSITY OF CALIFORNIA PRESS

Berkeley / Los Angeles / London

University of California Press, one of the most distinguished university presses in the United States, enriches lives around the world by advancing scholarship in the humanities, social sciences, and natural sciences. Its activities are supported by the UC Press Foundation and by philanthropic contributions from individuals and institutions. For more information, visit www.ucpress.edu.

University of California Press
Berkeley and Los Angeles, California

University of California Press, Ltd.
London, England

Library of Congress Cataloging-in-Publication Data
Taylor, Bron Raymond.
Dark green religion : nature spirituality and the planetary future / Bron Taylor.
p. cm.
Includes bibliographical references and index.
ISBN 978-0-520-23775-9 (cloth : alk. paper)
ISBN 978-0-520-26100-6 (pbk. : alk. paper)
1. Nature—Religious aspects. 2. Nature worship. I. Title.
BL65.N35T39 2010
202'.12—dc22 2009009180

Manufactured in the United States of America

18 17 16 15 14 13 12 11 10 09
10 9 8 7 6 5 4 3 2 1

This book is printed on Cascades Enviro 100, a 100% post consumer waste, recycled, de-inked fiber. FSC recycled certified and processed chlorine free. It is acid free, Ecologo certified, and manufactured by BioGas energy.

For the elders
and compadres
found in these pages . . .
for my beloveds
Beth Ann
Anders, Kaarin, and Kelsey . . .
and for all
who in their own ways
revel in
defend
and worship
the chorus of life

Contents

Preface

Dark green religion is like a phantom. It is unnamed and has no institutions officially devoted to its promotion; no single sacred text that its devotees can plant in hotel rooms in hopes of reaping a future harvest of souls; no identified religious hierarchy or charismatic figure responsible for spreading the faith, ministering to the faithful, or practicing its rituals.

Yet with alertness and the right lenses, the apparition appears.

It can be found in the minds and hearts of individuals who invent and are drawn to organizations that express its central convictions and moral commitments. It has charismatic figures and bureaucratic hierarchies devoted to its globalization. It is reinforced and spread through artistic forms that often resemble, and are sometimes explicitly designed, as religious rituals. It seeks to destroy forms of religiosity incompatible with its own moral and spiritual perceptions. It is considered dangerous by some, while others see it as offering salvation.

Dark green religion—religion that considers nature to be sacred, imbued with intrinsic value, and worthy of reverent care—has been spreading rapidly around the world. I label such religion "dark" not only to emphasize the depth of its consideration for nature (a deep shade of green concern) but also to suggest that such religion may have a shadow side—it might mislead and deceive; it could even precipitate or exacerbate violence.

Whether beneficent, dangerous, or both, such religion is becoming increasingly important in global environmental politics. It motivates a wide array of individuals and movements that are engaged in some of the most trenchant environment-related struggles of our time. It increasingly shapes the worldviews and practices of grassroots social activists and the world's intelligentsia. It is already important in global environmental politics. It may even inspire the emergence of a global, civic, earth religion.

• • •

In 1859, Charles Darwin published *On the Origin of Species,* shattering traditional explanations of the fecundity and diversity of the biosphere. Religion would never be the same. Where this cognitive shift has been mostly deeply made, traditional religions with their beliefs in nonmaterial divine beings are in decline. Where traditional religions have not declined significantly, and to the extent their practitioners encounter societies that have adopted an evolutionary worldview, such conventional religions find themselves on the defensive. Yet the desire for a spiritually meaningful understanding of the cosmos, and the human place in it, has not withered away. Some find ways to graft evolutionary understandings onto long-standing religious traditions. Yet increasingly, new perceptions, both explicitly and implicitly religious, have filled the cultural niches where traditional religious beliefs have come to be seen as less plausible. This book provides detailed evidence that many of the innovative responses to the Darwinian revolution are forms of dark green religion.

After wrestling with the terms critical to its analysis and rattling assumptions about what counts as "religion," *Dark Green Religion* explores the early roots of dark green religion, especially in Europe and the United States. I focus especially on the century and a half since Darwin published his treatise. I analyze, as do most scholars, the material products emerging from the individuals and groups I study—writings, art, music, crafts, as well as newer modes of communication such as photography and motion pictures. In many cases I discuss, I have also interviewed the producers and personally viewed the productions, and so am able to provide a "you were there" intimacy unavailable from archival research alone.

Readers will not only learn afresh about streams of dark green religion in Europe that influenced America, they will also discover the spiritual dimensions of easily recognized environmental saints such as Henry David Thoreau, John Muir, Aldo Leopold, Rachel Carson, and many others. But this essential backdrop, while sometimes surprising, is just the beginning. We will also consider whether radical environmentalism is a dangerous example of dark green religion . . . the sport of surfing a new, global manifestation of it . . . motion pictures, documentaries, and theme parks an influential expression of it . . . scholars and scientists key producers of and inspiration for it . . . and the United Nations its global champion. By the end of this global tour, readers can evaluate whether, in this age of globalization, such spirituality is rapidly spreading, viruslike, and if so, what its impact might be. In short, our journey will enable readers to consider whether the emergence and global diffusion of dark green religion is a harbinger of hope, or a portent of doom.

Readers' Guide

While this is a scholarly book, I have taken care to write it so that it is accessible to a general readership. Along the way I define and explain terms and analytical perspectives. Those who wish to get quickly into the substance of the study may elect to skim the first chapter. But such readers should note that the operative definition of religion in this work does not presume a belief in nonmaterial spiritual beings; otherwise, some of the analysis might be confusing. The flexible definition of religion underlying the book allows discussion of some phenomena that otherwise might not be included.

This book provides wildly diverse and fascinating examples, as well as substantial detail, about "dark green religion." The detail is necessary because a key part of my argument is that this kind of "nature religion" is far more prevalent and important than is commonly recognized. Graphics, music, and video at www.brontaylor.com complement this book. This online material will give readers a more visceral feel for dark green religion than can be provided through words alone. At this website I also provide detailed additional notes, for which there was insufficient space in this book. Specialists and researchers will find much in these notes of interest. There are also additional specific acknowledgments there, which I regret having to relegate to the online reference. Finally, these online notes point to many background readings from the *Encyclopedia of Religion and Nature,* which enrich what I present here. Many readers would benefit from having it handy.

My objective is to provide readers with the lenses needed to see dark green religion for themselves, to recognize its growing importance, and to consider its implications.

CHAPTER I

Introducing Religion and Dark Green Religion

This chapter explores terms that are central to this study: *religion, spirituality, nature religion, green religion*, and *dark green religion*. Although this sort of linguistic labor may seem most pertinent to those with backgrounds in anthropology and religious studies, it should be even more valuable to those with little background in the academic study of religion. The rationale for this starting point is simple: terminology matters. It shapes methods and focuses attention in illuminating ways. Terminology also carries assumptions that may occlude phenomena that might well be relevant to any given inquiry. It is important in this investigation, therefore, to reflect critically on the terms employed.

What, for example, is the difference between religion and the absence of religion—or between religion and spirituality—or between what I am calling nature religion, green religion, and dark green religion? Where are the boundaries between them? Do such distinctions illuminate or confuse our understanding of the world we inhabit?

Religion and Family Resemblance Analysis

There has been much debate, of course, about the origin, definition, and utility of the word *religion*. One of the reasons for this lack of consensus is the difficulty of agreeing on what characterizes "religious" phenomena. Does religion have a *substantive* essence? Or does it *function* typically or universally in certain ways? Since people began thinking analytically about religion, many competing definitions have been offered. No consensus has emerged, however, including as to whether any specific traits or characteristics are essential to the phenomena. Such questions are certainly relevant to discussions surrounding what I am calling dark green religion. Are specific things essential to it, such as beliefs about supernatural or nonmaterial beings, as some scholars contend? Or is a nebulous sense that "nature is sacred" sufficient to justify using the term *religion?*

Unfortunately, selecting the earliest uses of the word does not set us on uncontested terminological ground.[1] In the last analysis, observers must choose the lenses, the definitions, that they think will best guide their inquiries and illuminate the phenomena they seek to understand.[2] As good a starting place as any is the scholarly work that has traced early forms of the idea of religion to the Latin root *leig,* meaning "to bind" or "tie fast," or *religare,* which could be rendered "to reconnect"—from the Latin *re* (again) and *ligare* (to connect). Examining such roots in the context of contemporary understandings, we might conclude that religion has to do with that which connects and binds people to that which they most value, depend on, and consider sacred.

Yet there are dangers in specific definitions, especially for those who seek to understand the phenomena and compare different types of it in various times and places. As the anthropologist Benson Saler put it, "Explicit definitions are explicit heuristics: they guide or impel us in certain directions. By doing so they tend to divert our attention from information beyond the channels they cleave, and so choke off possibilities."[3] It is important, therefore, both to recognize the danger of explicit definitions (they might lead us to ignore important phenomena or dynamics) as well as their value (they might focus analytic attention and yield insights).

Taking into account the dangers and value of definitions, Saler and others advocate looking at "family resemblances" or taking a "polyfocal approach" to the study of religion, exploring, analyzing, and comparing the widest possible variety of beliefs, behaviors, and functions that are typically associated with the term. The heart of such an approach is to (1) note the many dimensions and characteristics of religious beliefs and practices; (2) reject a presumption that any single trait or characteristic is essential to religious phenomena and refuse to become preoccupied with where the boundaries of religion lie; and (3) focus instead on whether an analysis of religion-resembling beliefs and practices has explanatory power.[4]

Analyzing family resemblances is valuable despite the absence of any clear, essential, universal trait that everyone will agree constitutes religion's essence. Such an approach to conceptualizing religion leaves in play and open to contestation the definition of religion, and even challenges whether choosing a definition is important. Finally, it insists that the critical thing is to learn interesting things about human beings, their environments, and their earthly coinhabitants.[5] With this strategy for analyzing religion (and religion-resembling phenomena) in place, a few other terms critical to this study require elaboration.

Spirituality

In contemporary parlance people increasingly speak of spirituality rather than religion when trying to express what moves them most deeply; and many consider the two to be distinctly different. Most of the characteristics scholars associate with religion, however, are found whether people consider themselves spiritual or religious. From a family resemblance perspective, therefore, there is little *analytical* reason to assume these are different kinds of social phenomena. It is important, however, to understand what most people understand the distinction to entail, especially because the term *spirituality* is more often than *religion* associated with nature and nature religions.

In common parlance, *religion* is often used to refer to organized and institutional religious belief and practice, while *spirituality* is held to involve one's deepest moral values and most profound religious experiences.[6] But there are additional ideas that are more often associated with spirituality than religion. Spirituality is often thought to be about personal growth and gaining a proper understanding of one's place in the cosmos, and to be intertwined with environmentalist concern and action.[7] This contrasts markedly with the world's predominant religions, which are generally concerned with transcending this world or obtaining divine rescue from it.

Although those who consider themselves spiritual but not religious generally consider spirituality to be superior to religion, *spirituality* is also a term increasingly used by traditionally religious people. They use it similarly to how the "spiritual but not religious" crowd speaks of the sacred importance of everyday life. Thus, spirituality can also be understood as a quest to deepen, renew, or tap into the most profound insights of traditional religions, as well as a word that consecrates otherwise secular endeavors such as psychotherapy, political and environmental activism, and one's lifestyle and vocational choices. Such understanding of the term fosters a "rethinking of religious boundaries."[8]

Unless one considers belief in divine beings or forces to be essential to a definition of religion, most contemporary spirituality can easily be considered religious. Those who have studied contemporary spirituality find a common feature of it to be a sense that nature is sacred and that ethical responsibilities naturally follow such a realization. Who are the individuals and groups that have such perceptions? Anna King pointed in the right direction when she urged scholars to look for spirituality not only in small, marginalized religious sects but also in "movements such as Amnesty International [and] Greenpeace." Empirical studies have begun to demonstrate that many people in advanced industrial cultures resonate deeply with what could be called nature spirituality or nature religion. Some of these people view the world as full of spiritual intelligences with whom one can be in relationship (an animistic perception), while others among them perceive the earth to be alive or even divine (a more pantheistic belief).

In an analysis of a large social-science database generated in 2000, for example, James Proctor examined the relationship between religion and trust in various forms of authority. He found two sources of authority most prevalent: traditional religious authority (grounded in what he labeled theocracy) and religious ecology (which he called ecology, as shorthand). In both Europe and North America, large numbers of people express "deep trust in nature as inherently spiritual or sacred," Proctor discovered, and in many countries, such religiosity is even more prevalent than in the United States. He concluded, "Institutional religion is inextricably bound up with relations of trust in authority, and thus is functionally similar to [political] regimes rarely understood as religious. *We should therefore be cautious in bounding the domain of religion too narrowly.*"[9]

This assertion is pertinent to my current objective, which is to rattle assumptions as to what counts as religion in order to awaken new perceptions and insights. Are the people whose spirituality is intertwined with environmental concern, or who perceive and trust in nature and understand it to be sacred, engaged in nature religion?

Nature Religion

Nature religion is most commonly used as an umbrella term to mean religious perceptions and practices that are characterized by a reverence for nature and that consider its destruction a desecrating act. Adherents often describe feelings of belonging and connection to the earth—of being bound to and dependent upon the earth's living systems.[10]

Over the last few centuries a number of phrases have been used to capture the family resemblance of nature religions, including *natural religion, nature worship, nature mysticism,* and *earth religion.* Meanwhile, words have been invented to reflect what is taken to be the universal essence of such religiosity, such as *Paganism, Animism,* and *Pantheism.* In both popular and scholarly venues the term *nature religion,* which began to be employed regularly at about the time of the first Earth Day celebration in 1970, is used increasingly to represent and debate such nature-as-sacred religions.

The idea of nature religion has a long history that parallels important watersheds in the study of religion. Indeed, the most common contemporary understanding of nature religion resembles the nature-venerating religiosity described in E. B. Tylor's *Primitive Culture* (1871), Max Müller's *Natural Religion* (1888), James G. Frazer's *The Worship of Nature* (1926), and Mircea Eliade's *Patterns in Comparative Religion* (1958).[11] Despite changes in scholarly fashions, there have been important continuities in both popular and scholarly contestations over nature religion. The most common debate has been between those who consider nature religions to be religiously or politically primitive, regressive, or dangerous, and those who laud such religions as spiritually perceptive and ecologically beneficent.

Negative views of nature religions likely originated with Abrahamic religious traditions, which have long had antipathy toward pagan and polytheistic religions. Throughout their histories, the Abrahamic religions often sought to force nature religions and the peoples who practiced them into decline or extinction through conversion, assimilation, and sometimes through threats and violence. Such persecution was often justified in religious terms, including through beliefs that assimilation was spiritually beneficial.

The tendency to view the practitioners of nature religions as primitive (though not always dangerous) intensified as Occidental culture placed increasing value on reason and as many thinkers became less religious. The German philosopher Georg Wilhelm Friedrich Hegel

(1770–1831), for example, advanced an idealistic philosophy that viewed nature religions as failing to perceive the divine spirit moving through the dialectical process of history.

More important for the historical study of religion in general and scholarly reflection on nature religion in particular was the influence of Charles Darwin's (1809–1882) theory of evolution.[12] Generations of scholars came to view nature religions as grounded in primitive misperceptions that natural forces are animated or alive. John Lubbock cited as an example Darwin's observation that dogs mistake inanimate objects for living beings, and Lubbock surmised that religion had its origin in a similar misapprehension by primitive humans.[13] E. B. Tylor, whom many consider to be the father of anthropology, would coin the term *Animism* for the attribution of consciousness to inanimate objects and natural forces, asserting that this misapprehension was grounded in the dream states and sneezing of "primitive" or "savage" peoples, and arguing that this kind of perception is the root of human religious consciousness.[14] Not long afterward, Max Müller, considered by some to be the father of the academic study of religion, traced the origin of Indo-European religion to religious metaphors and symbolism grounded in the natural environment, especially the sky and sun.[15]

Both classical Paganism and polytheistic religions involved supplication to or veneration of celestial bodies and other natural entities and forces. According to Sir James Frazer, belief and ritual related to the sun, the earth, and the dead were especially common in the worldwide emergence and ancient history of religion.[16] The idea of religion as involving nature-related beliefs and practices became widely influential, as did Frazer's "worship of nature" rubric to describe such religions:

> [By] the worship of nature, I mean . . . the worship of natural phenomena conceived as animated, conscious, and endowed with both the power and the will to benefit or injure mankind. Conceived as such they are naturally objects of human awe and fear . . . To the mind of primitive man these natural phenomena assume the character of formidable and dangerous spirits whose anger it is his wish to avoid, and whose favour it is his interest to conciliate. To attain these desirable ends he . . . prays and sacrifices to them; in short, he worships them. Thus what we may call the worship of nature is based on the personification of natural phenomena.

This early nature religiosity, Frazer thought, was replaced first by polytheism and then by monotheism as part of a "slow and gradual" process that was leading inexorably among civilized peoples to the "despiritualization of the universe." Most scholarly observers during the nineteenth and early twentieth centuries agreed that monotheistic religions, or no religion, would eventually supplant nature religions. They assumed that although nature religions might be regressive, they were not dangerous, at least not to cultural and material progress.

More recently, however, a chorus of voices have suggested that some nature religions are indeed dangerous. In *Nature Religion in America* (1990), for example, Catherine Albanese broadly defined nature religion to include cases in which nature is an important symbolic resource but is not itself considered sacred. She argued that many forms of nature religion mask an impulse to dominate both people and nature, citing as evidence how the "religions of nature," which had prominent adherents among the most influential of figures during the formation of the United States, justified the subjugation of both the natural world and the continent's aboriginal peoples. Albanese's assertions caused consternation among many who had a positive attitude toward nature religions. She also blurred the boundaries as to what counts as religion by considering examples that did not always, at first glance, appear religious, such as the macrobiotic dietary movement.[17]

At about the same time, a number of studies found worldview affinities and historical connections between some nature religions (especially northern European Paganism and various pagan revival movements) and racist subcultures and political movements, including extremist environmentalism. Among the most influential studies were those by Anna Bramwell. She argued that the environmental movement, which can be traced roughly to the middle of the nineteenth century, represents an entirely new "nature worshipping" ideology that, while it can be fused to many ideologies, has often had strong affinity with racist ideologies and political movements (such as Nazism) and programs (such as eugenics) that reject Enlightenment rationality in favor of a romantic, agrarian ideal.[18]

Of course, historical understandings of nature religion are contested. Many other scholars consider such religions to be spiritually perceptive, humane, and ecologically beneficent. Historical studies of such spiritual beliefs and practices demonstrate not only fear of and hostility toward them but also their persistence and diversity. In a seminal study of such religiosity in the Occident, the geographer Clarence Glacken argued that an organicist worldview, which believes the world to be alive, interdependent, and sacred, was one of the two most prevalent, long-standing general ways people have oriented themselves to nature and religion and have understood how religion and culture are related. Urging his readers not to "forget the echoes of the primordial Mediterranean world: its age-old veneration of Mother Earth" or its "astrological paganism," Glacken's work helped pave the way for the scholarly pursuit of nature religion. Other studies, such as by Donald Worster, underscored that, whereas belief in specific earthly and celestial nature gods may have declined or disappeared, the perception that nature's places and forces are alive and sacred—the underlying perception that gave rise to classical Paganism and other nature religions—has not withered away. Even in the modern West, such perception has been resilient, even episodically threatening the hegemony of the monotheistic consensus and, later on, challenging secular, science-based worldviews.[19]

Early Exemplars: Spinoza and Rousseau

Two thinkers writing at the dawn of the Age of Reason, the Jewish philosopher Baruch (or Benedictus) Spinoza (1632–1677) and the French social theorist Jean-Jacques Rousseau (1712–1778), are worth spotlighting as examples of the resilience of nature religion. They were also inspirational figures to dark green religion.

Spinoza articulated a sophisticated organicism, or monistic pantheism, that influenced generations of future nature religionists.[20] Those embracing or influenced by such philosophy include some of the greatest theologians and philosophers of the nineteenth and twentieth centuries: Friedrich Schleiermacher and Albert North Whitehead (and his progeny of "process" philosophers and theologians who have expressed either pantheistic or panentheistic worldviews), as well as leading proponents of "deep ecology" such as Arne Naess and George Sessions.[21] The affinity of the deep ecologists for Spinoza makes sense, for if every being and object is a manifestation of God or God's activity, then everything has value, which presents a fundamental challenge to the prevailing anthropocentrism.[22] (Although deep ecology is not equivalent to dark green religion, they have many affinities.)

Rousseau's religious thought and political philosophy became even more influential than Spinoza's pantheistic philosophy in promoting nature religion. Most important for the present purpose is that Rousseau rejected Europe's Abrahamic orthodoxies in favor of a deistic "natural religion" in which God's existence could be perceived in the order of nature. For Rousseau, natural religion and an epistemological turn to nature could lead the way to a life free from the alienation and materialism of Western civilization.[23]

Rousseau's memoir *Reveries of a Solitary Walker* (1782), written in the last years of his life, provides insight into his deepest feelings. In it he described a series of long walks, noting that although he had loved being in nature as a free and natural young man, during that stage of his life he had "hardly ever contemplated [nature] otherwise than as a total and undivided spectacle."[24] Walking and writing as an old man, in contrast, he was focusing like a naturalist on "the details of the great pageant of nature." A number of remarkable passages conveyed his mystical sense of oneness with nature and the cosmos in a way that presaged future forms of nature religion:

> The more sensitive the soul of the observer, the greater the ecstasy aroused in him by this harmony. At such times his senses are possessed by a deep and delightful reverie, and in a state of blissful self-abandonment he loses himself in the immensity of this beautiful order, with which he feels himself at one. All individual objects escape him; he sees and feels nothing but the unity of all things. His ideas have to be restricted and his imagination limited by some particular circumstances for him to observe the separate parts of this universe which he was striving to embrace in its entirety.

Passages like this and in his well-read novel *Julie, or the New Heloise* (1761) were especially responsible for kindling the nature-revering romantic movements in Europe and North America.[25] Rousseau also articulated many of the key ideas typically found in dark green religion, including a critique of materialism as a distraction from what makes people truly content or happy, namely, intimate contact with and openhearted contemplation of nature, which was itself an epistemological principle;[26] a belief that indigenous peoples lived closer to nature and were thus socially and ecologically superior to "civilized" peoples and from whom civilized people had much to learn;[27] a conviction that people in the state of nature and uncorrupted by society have a natural predisposition toward sympathy and compassion for all creatures and a corresponding conviction that a good society would cultivate and not destroy such affections; and finally, belief in an expansive self in which one's own identity includes the rest of nature and a felt unity with and empathy for it.[28] This latter sentiment anticipated and spurred similar ones among romantic movement figures and, much later, among proponents of deep ecology.

In related ways, Spinoza and Rousseau contradicted claims that nature-based religions, as opposed to "revealed" religions, were primitive and dangerous. They asserted that nature religion offers instead an attractive antidote to the West's spiritual malaise, social violence, economic inequality, and callousness to nonhuman nature: a harmonious future characterized by fulfilling relationships among the earth's diverse forms of life.

Green and Dark Green Religion

It is important to distinguish between green religion (which posits that environmentally friendly behavior is a religious obligation) and dark green religion (in which nature is sacred, has intrinsic value, and is therefore due reverent care). These two forms are often in tension and sometimes in direct conflict. Exploring their similarities and differences further sets the stage before turning in the following chapters to the diverse examples of four types of dark green religion.

Rousseau is an especially important early exemplar of dark green religion. But his writings did more than encourage the emergence and proliferation of diverse forms of dark green religion (although they were not called by that term). His explicit and implicit criticisms of revealed religions, including his belief that they distort human societies into forms that detract from the freedom and well-being of all natural beings, eroded support for such religions and have continued to gain traction ever since. In some cases, Rousseau's critiques caused soul searching and reform movements within the criticized religions. Since the 1960s this reformist trend has become so pronounced that some scholars and laypeople have come to speak about "the greening of religion" or "religious environmentalism," by which they mean religions that are becoming more environmentally friendly.[29] In this work I speak of green religion or the greening of religion when discussing religious environmentalism or its development.

Much of this innovation was precipitated by criticisms that echoed those made by Rousseau, the most famous of which was articulated by the historian Lynn White Jr. in 1967. White contended that Christianity bore a heavy burden for the environmental crisis, arguing the following:

1. Christianity but not Asian religions promoted a dualistic attitude between people and nature that fostered exploitation: "Christianity, in absolute contrast to ancient paganism and Asia's religions . . . not

only established a dualism of man and nature but also insisted that it is God's will that man exploit nature for his proper ends."

2. Paganism and Animism (typically associated with indigenous peoples) were more environmentally friendly than Christianity, a religion that made people callous toward nonhuman creatures: "By destroying pagan animism, Christianity made it possible to exploit nature in a mood of indifference to the feelings of natural objects."
3. Christianity was "the most anthropocentric religion the world has seen" and as a result helped precipitate the environmental crisis.[30]

White thought that Western people, even those who were no longer religious, were deeply conditioned by Christianity's anthropocentrism and irreverence toward nature. Although he averred that animistic indigenous cultures and religions originating in Asia were more naturally inclined toward environmentally beneficent attitudes and behaviors, he doubted such religions would appeal to many Westerners, so he proposed that they seek inspiration from the ecologically holy (if somewhat heretical) St. Francis of Assisi. White believed that St. Francis's spiritual biocentrism provided an antidote to the West's pernicious anthropocentrism.[31] Drawing on St. Francis, White argued that humility is a virtue "not merely for the individual but for man as a species." Moreover, "More science and more technology are not going to get us out of the present ecologic crisis until we find a new religion, or rethink our old one."[32] For White, religion was the decisive variable that had fueled but could now reverse environmental decline, especially if it rejected an instrumental and anthropocentric worldview in favor of religious biocentrism.

Although White was not alone in articulating such views, he did so in a prominent venue (the widely read journal *Science*) and at an auspicious cultural moment—the apex of the 1960s cultural upheavals. This period was characterized by growing receptivity to the religious beliefs and practices of indigenous and Asian peoples at the same time that many were rejecting mainstream Western religions. Fused with intensifying environmental alarm, this religion-related ferment provided fertile cultural ground for a robust debate about the relationships between people, religion, and nature.

Christians and some others in the Abrahamic traditions who encountered such views tended to respond in one of four ways: either apologetically, arguing that properly understood their traditions were environmentally sensitive; or confessionally, acknowledging guilt (at least in part) and undertaking internal religious reform to make their religions environmentally responsible. These two responses were a part of the greening of Christianity that has been underway since the late 1960s.[33] The third response was indifference, viewing the criticisms and environmental concern as of minor or no importance to their religious faith; and a fourth type was hostility, seeing such a concern as antithetical to Christianity. These latter two responses ironically provided evidence for White's thesis.

These four types of response came from both laypeople and scholars. Scholarly experts began probing sacred texts for their environmental values, and some laypeople began to organize to encourage the greening of their traditions. Before long, the soul searching that White's thesis precipitated within Occidental religions spread to religions originating in Asia. This occurred, in part, because of scholarly reactions to White's thesis, including an important paper published by the geographer Yi-Fu Tuan shortly after White's. Tuan challenged the idea of a naturally environmentalist Asia by arguing that in China there was massive deforestation long before it could have been corrupted by an anti-environmental Christian civilization.[34] After Tuan, more scholars began to ask why environmental decline had been so pronounced in Asia if, as many believed, the religions there were environmentally friendly. Just as White's thesis had precipitated apologetic, confessional, indifferent, and hostile reactions within the world's Abrahamic traditions, the diverse reactions to White's thesis triggered similar responses among religionists and scholars engaged with Asian religions.

In the case of both Western and Asian religions, religious studies scholars played a significant role in the efforts to understand the environmental strengths and weaknesses of their traditions. Scholars of religion have often played twin roles as observers and participants in the religions they study, so it is unsurprising that in the face of newly perceived environmental challenges they would rethink the ethical responsibilities of the traditions they know best. Quite a number of them, indeed, became directly involved in efforts to push the traditions they were analyzing toward ethics that make environmental sustainability a central objective.

The greening of the world religions is not, however, the focus of the present volume, except to the extent that such green religion is also *dark:* on the one hand, perceiving nature as sacred and due reverent care; and on the other, arousing the concern that inheres in all holistic ethics—that the well-being if not rights of individuals could be endangered by efforts to ensure the flourishing of some supposedly sacred whole.

CHAPTER 2

Dark Green Religion

Since the publication of Rachael Carson's *Silent Spring* in 1962, environmental alarm has intensified and become increasingly apocalyptic. Meanwhile, nature-related religion has been rekindled, invented, spread, and ecologized.[1] A great deal of this religious creativity has been *dark green,* flowing from a deep sense of belonging to and connectedness in nature, while perceiving the earth and its living systems to be sacred and interconnected. Dark green religion is generally deep ecological, biocentric, or ecocentric, considering all species to be intrinsically valuable, that is, valuable apart from their usefulness to human beings. This value system is generally (1) based on a felt kinship with the rest of life, often derived from a Darwinian understanding that all forms of life have evolved from a common ancestor and are therefore related; (2) accompanied by feelings of humility and a corresponding critique of human moral superiority, often inspired or reinforced by a science-based cosmology that reveals how tiny human beings are in the universe; and (3) reinforced by metaphysics of interconnection and the idea of interdependence (mutual influence and reciprocal dependence) found in the sciences, especially in ecology and physics.

This chapter presupposes that clear understanding of dark green religion emerges best by examining four main types of it, while providing concrete examples of each. In this and in subsequent chapters I focus especially on examples drawn from what I call the *environmentalist (or environmental) milieu,* namely, contexts in which environmentally concerned officials, scientists, activists, and other citizens connect with and reciprocally influence one another. I have adapted "environmentalist milieu" from the British sociologist Colin Campbell's notion of the "cultic milieu." He used the phrase to describe sectors in Western societies in which socially deviant, countercultural knowledge—both spiritual and scientific/quasi-scientific—are brought together by their carriers and proponents, incubating, cross-fertilizing, reproducing, and spreading. Within the countercultural, cultic milieu, individuals and groups are remarkably receptive to each other's ideas, and they generally understand themselves to be in resistance to the cultural mainstream.[2] The result is an eclectic *bricolage*, by which I mean an amalgamation of bits and pieces of a wide array of ideas and practices, drawn from diverse cultural systems, religious traditions, and political ideologies. In a bricolage these various ideas and practices are fused together, like a bricklayer or mason piecing together a wall or building with mortar and stone. As this and the subsequent chapters demonstrate, there is a global environmentalist milieu in which shared ideas incubate, cross-fertilize, and spread. It is a process characterized by hybridization and bricolage.

Commonly, dark green religious and moral sentiments are embedded in worldviews and narratives that are believed to cohere with science—but they are also often grounded in mystical or intuitive knowledge that is beyond the reach of scientific method. To perceive how dark green religion emerges, diversifies, and spreads, it is important to understand the basic processes within this creative, increasingly global milieu. Such an understanding also helps to explain why, even when certain types and tendencies of dark green religion can be identified, the boundaries between them remain permeable, blurred, and perpetually shifting—much like the boundaries of religion itself.

Four Types of Dark Green Religion

Although they all have historical antecedents, I perceive four main types of dark green spirituality that have been flourishing since the first Earth Day in 1970 (see table 1).

The first two types are forms of Animism (see middle column, reading down), one supernaturalistic and the other naturalistic. The second two types I refer to as Gaian Earth Religion (right column, reading down), a shorthand way to suggest holistic and organicist worldviews. As with Animism, one form of Gaian Earth Religion is spiritual or supernaturalistic, which I call Gaian Spirituality (in the row labeled "Su-

TABLE 1

	Animism	Gaian Earth Religion
Supernaturalism	Spiritual Animism	Gaian Spirituality
Naturalism	Naturalistic Animism	Gaian Naturalism

pernaturalism"); the other is naturalistic, which I have called Gaian Naturalism (in the row labeled "Naturalism"). The blurred lines between the four types indicate permeable boundaries; the types represent tendencies rather than uncomplicated, static, and rigid clusters of individuals and movements.

Animism is etymologically rooted in the Latin word *anima,* meaning life, breath, and soul. Today it commonly refers to perceptions that natural entities, forces, and nonhuman life-forms have one or more of the following: a soul or vital lifeforce or spirit, personhood (an affective life and personal intentions), and consciousness, often but not always including special spiritual intelligence or powers. Animistic perceptions are often accompanied by ethical mores specifying the sorts of relationships that human beings should have, or avoid having, with nature's diverse forces and beings. Sometimes Animism involves communication and/or even communion with such intelligences or lifeforces, or beliefs that nature's intelligences and forces are divine and should be worshipped and/or beseeched for healing or other favors. Animism generally enjoins respect if not reverence for and veneration of such intelligences and forces and promotes a felt kinship with them. Put simply, Animism has to do with the perception that spiritual intelligences *or* lifeforces animate natural objects or living things. With the term *spiritual intelligences,* I especially seek to capture the beliefs of those for whom there is some immaterial, supernaturalistic dimension to the Animistic perception. This is the form of dark green religion I have labeled *Spiritual Animism.* With the expression *lifeforces,* I focus especially on those who are agnostic or skeptical of any immaterial dimension underlying the life-forms or natural forces they wish to understand and with whom they may also seek to communicate. This is the form of dark green religion I have labeled *Naturalistic Animism.* In both cases, *Animism,* as I am configuring the term, involves a shared perception that beings or entities in nature have their own integrity, ways of being, personhood, and even intelligence. Animism postulates that people can, *at least by conjecture and imagination,* and sometimes through ritualized action and other practices, come to some understanding of these living forces and intelligences in nature and develop mutually respectful and beneficial relationships with them.[3]

Gaian Earth Religion, in my lexicon, stands firmly in the organicist tradition. It understands the biosphere (universe or cosmos) to be alive or conscious, or at least by metaphor and analogy to resemble organisms with their many interdependent parts. Moreover, this energetic, interdependent, living system is understood to be the fundamental thing to understand and venerate. Such a perspective takes the whole, usually but not always understood scientifically, as a model. Gaian Earth Religion thus defies the naturalistic fallacy argument in ethics (the assertion that one cannot logically derive a value from a fact) by suggesting that nature itself provides models and natural laws to follow. Furthermore, Gaian Earth Religion relies on metaphors of the sacred to express its sense of the precious quality of the whole. What I term *Gaian Spirituality* is avowedly supernaturalistic, perceiving the superorganism—whether the biosphere or the entire universe—to have consciousness, whether this is understood as an expression or part of God, Brahman, the Great Mystery, or whatever name one uses to symbolize a divine cosmos. Gaian Spirituality is more likely to draw on nonmainstream or nonconsensus science for data that reinforces its generally pantheistic (or panentheistic) and holistic metaphysics. It is more open to interpretations commonly found in subcultures typically labeled New Age. The form of dark green religion I call *Gaian Naturalism,* on the other hand, is skeptical of supernaturalistic metaphysics. It is more likely to restrict its claims to the scientific mainstream as a basis for understanding and promoting a holistic metaphysics. Yet its proponents express awe and wonder when facing the complexity and mysteries of life and the universe, relying on religious language and metaphors of the sacred (sometimes only implicitly and not self-consciously) when confessing their feelings of belonging and connection to the energy and life systems that they inhabit and study.

This typology is based on close observation of the diverse expressions of green and dark green religion both in the United States and abroad. Extended analysis of each of the four types will clarify my classifications and reveal that some actors and movements have affinity with more than one type of dark green religion.

Living Examples of Dark Green Religion

SPIRITUAL ANIMISM AND GAIAN SPIRITUALITY

Exemplars of Spiritual Animism and Gaian Spirituality include three green thinker/activists whose spiritual paths involved serious encounters with Buddhism: Gary Snyder, Joanna Macy, and John Seed. All three also identify with deep ecology.

An American Buddhist-Animist. Many from the 1960s generation will remember Gary Snyder as one of the "Beat poets" from the second wave of the San Francisco poetry renaissance during the 1950s and 1960s, and as the model for the character Japhy Ryder in Jack Kerouac's famous *Dharma Bums.*[4] What distinguished Snyder and fellow poets Michael McClure and Kenneth Rexroth from the rest of the beat movement was a deep sensitivity to nature and a perception of its sacredness and intrinsic value, making Snyder and kindred spirits excellent exemplars of dark green religion.

Gary Snyder gained widespread attention after winning a Pulitzer Prize in 1974 for *Turtle Island,* a book of poetry and prose in which he articulated many of the major themes of his life work.[5] These included the possibility of animistic perception and the promotion of the green social philosophy known as bioregionalism, which seeks to decentralize political decision-making processes so that, as much as practical, they take place within the contours of specific ecological regions.

Extended time as a child in the Pacific Northwest's great forests evoked in Snyder a profound reverence for wild nature and a concern about its destruction, themes that would become central in his life work. "From a very early age," he wrote, "I found myself standing in an indefinable awe before the natural world. An attitude of gratitude, wonder, and a sense of protection especially as I began to see the hills being bulldozed down for roads, and the forests of the Pacific Northwest magically float away on logging trucks."[6] This wonder was related to what, for Snyder, has been an enduring, animistic perception. During a 1993 interview, he called himself a "Buddhist-Animist," reflecting his long-standing identity as a "fairly orthodox Buddhist" as well as his belief that the world is full of spiritual intelligences: "I was born a natural animist. It wasn't a moral or intellectual thing, from early childhood, I felt the presence of other beings, and I enjoyed being out in the woods right back of our farm . . . I think most kids are natural animists."[7]

Given this animistic perception, Snyder was drawn to and studied anthropology related to American Indian cultures, but he discovered that they were largely inaccessible to non-Indians. As he put it with regard to Hopi culture, "Its content, perhaps, is universal, but you must be Hopi to follow the Hopi way."[8] So he elected to study Zen Buddhism in Japan, which he did for twelve years beginning in 1955. In Buddhism, Snyder found a metaphysics of interdependence and also kinship ethics with the nonhuman world that he thought had many affinities with American Indian spirituality and resonated with his own animistic perceptions.

After returning to the United States and being influenced by the subcultures of San Francisco, which he described later as rich "with anarchist and Wobblie connections and full of antiauthoritarian leftists," he began integrating animistic nature religion into a new bioregional spirituality. He hoped this kind of hybrid of nature religion and place-based activism would reconnect humans to nature and nudge them toward more ecologically sustainable spiritualities and political arrangements. Snyder's influence soon spread beyond Beat subcultures into the broader U.S. counterculture and environmentalist milieu. This was in part because he was offering something innovative, both in terms of spirituality and politics, to a culture that was alienated from nature and anxious for a political alternative to an impersonal and technocratic nation-state.

Snyder also proved adept at integrating ideas with tropes that would resonate with many Americans. When the term *deep ecology* was introduced in America, for example, Snyder embraced it as embodying spiritual and political beliefs and ideals he had long held.[9] Yet he maintained a Buddhist identity and contended in discussions with deep ecology proponents that Zen Buddhism expressed deep ecological ethics with unsurpassed philosophical sophistication. In 1973 he called himself "a practicing Buddhist, or Buddhist-shamanist," and twenty years later said he was a "fairly orthodox Buddhist" and "Buddhist-Animist."[10]

Snyder's enduring animist identity is as central as Buddhism to his religious identity. When I asked him in 1993 about interspecies communication, which he had periodically alluded to in his writings, he recalled an experience with a woman named Ella, an Irish mystic he knew during the 1950s, who once accompanied him on a walk in Northern California's (John) Muir Redwoods. Hearing the song of a yellow crown warbler, Ella turned to him and reported that this song was a special gift to her from that bird. Reflecting on this and my follow-up question about what animist perception was like, Snyder answered:

> It's not that animals come up and say something in English in your ear. You know, it's that things come into your mind. . . . Most people think that everything that comes into their mind is their own, their own mind, that it comes from within. . . . Well, some of those things that you think are from within are given to you from outside, and part of the trick is knowing which was which—being alert to the one that you know was a gift, and not think, "I thought that." Say [instead], "Ah, that was a gift!" . . . I have a poem about magpie giving me a song ["Magpie's Song"].

Snyder ended this reflection saying this was just one example. I have never found a more forthcoming statement by Snyder about his actual animistic experience. As with others, he has also made statements that cohere with more than one type of dark green religion, in his case, with Gaian Spirituality.

Since religion is defined as much by what is dismissed as by what is endorsed, recognizing Snyder's criticisms of monotheistic religions further illustrates his worldview. Reflecting on the metaphysics of interconnection, for example, Snyder commented:

> Interrelatedness is a common-sense observation. We should remind ourselves that ordinary working people, traditional people . . . notice that things are connected. What's not common is the mind-body dualism that begins to come in with monotheism. And the alliance of monotheism with the formation of centralized governance and the national state, that's what's unnatural, and statistically in a minority on earth. The [most common] human experience has been an experience of Animism. Only a small proportion of people on earth have been monotheists. . . . Everybody else in the world is a multifaceted polytheist, animist, or Buddhist who sees things in the world [as alive].

In this dual critique of monotheism and nationalism, Snyder combined animistic spirituality with his anarchistic, bioregional politics—views prevalent but not all encompassing in the milieu of dark green religion. For Snyder, however, monotheism and authoritarian nationalism "do seem to go together."

With Snyder's animistic perceptions in mind, it is easy to understand why he liked Christopher Stone's widely discussed argument that trees should be represented in democratic processes and the courts.[11] About this argument Snyder commented that he had long resonated with the "animistic idea that you can hear voices from trees," adding that this makes for an easy transition to the idea that all "nonhuman nature has rights." Snyder came to understand that his own role as a poet was to promote such rights and to bring nonhuman voices "into the human realm."[12]

For Snyder, these are sacred voices. Still, he has cautioned against regularly using the word *sacred,* fearing that overuse could devalue what it signifies. Yet his work unambiguously conveys his reverence for life. Indeed, a central theme in Snyder's writings is the sacramental nature of life itself, and even the process of eating and being eaten: "Eating is a sacrament. The grace we say clears our hearts and guides the children and welcomes the guest, all at the same time. . . . To acknowledge that each of us at the table will eventually be part of the meal is not just being 'realistic.' It is allowing the sacred to enter and accepting the sacramental aspect of our shaky temporary personal being."[13]

In both his spirituality and critical perspectives on Western societies and their destructiveness, Snyder has promoted ideas typical of dark green religion. Chief among these is the intrinsic value of nature: "Biological diversity, and the integrity of organic evolution on this planet, is where I take my stand."[14] But he has also been an important spokesperson for the view that the world's dominant theistic religions are inferior to nature religions and place-based spiritualities. Like many involved with dark green religion, he expresses an ethics of kinship with all life, which produces a preference for vegetarianism and a penchant for political resistance to life-threatening forces. Snyder has thus contributed to the spread of bioregionalism, deep ecology, and even radical environmentalism. But his greatest legacy may be in his contributions to the revival of Animism in Western societies.

Views such as Snyder's raise a fundamental epistemological question: if Animism is best kindled in childhood through ready access to nature, as it was for Snyder, then how in an increasingly urbanized world can this life-saving perception be encouraged?

Snyder's prescription is bioregional "reinhabitation"—carefully learning the local lore, plants, and animals that are found in particular places. When one does this mindfully, he believes, appropriate lifeways that respect the place can be (re)discovered. By going "back to the land," people can rediscover their affective connections to nature. Another way to facilitate such felt connections, Snyder says, is through "poetry and song."[15] These can be increasingly integrated into rituals that promote reverence for specific places and their inhabitants. Snyder and the others in his intentional community, located in the foothills of California's Sierra Nevada, have worked on this for a generation. Their ritualizing draws on many traditions, including Buddhism, contemporary Paganism, and American Indian cultures. Snyder thinks that after many years experimenting with nature-related ritual they are "just beginning to get it right."

Ritual Innovators. Joanna Macy, an American scholar and practitioner of Buddhism, and John Seed, an Australian Buddhist who founded the Rainforest Information Centre, have been on a kindred religious path. Unlike Snyder, who is not known for disseminating the ritual forms he and his community have been developing, Macy and Seed have labored to spread globally their ritual processes, believing that they reconnect people to the earth and its diverse inhabitants.

Their best-known ritual process is the Council of All Beings, which has inspired further experimentation with nature-focused ritual. The "sacred intention" of such rituals has been to reawaken understandings of spiritual realities that people today rarely perceive but that they believe animate nature in its many expressions. There are a variety of rituals that constitute the Council of All Beings, many of which are said to derive from indigenous cultures, because "rituals affirming the interconnectedness of the human and nonhuman worlds exist in every primitive culture."[16] But the heart of this often multiday council process is newly invented. It involves participants being instructed to go out into nature until they feel or perceive they are being chosen *by* some natural entity to speak *for* it in the upcoming gathering. This time period is sometimes likened to the vision quest practiced by some American Indian societies. Afterward, participants make costumes to facilitate their transformation and prepare for the rite. Then they assemble in their posthuman personas, having allowed themselves to be imaginatively or spiritually possessed by the consciousness of nonhuman entities—animals, plants, fish, rocks, soils, and rivers, for example.

The assembled council then discusses the current state of the world, verbalizing the anger, confusion, and pain that they feel as a result of being so poorly treated by human beings, and their profound grief over the rapid decline of the natural world they love. After this, some representative humans are brought into the circle to face their accusers. Eventually, the generous non–human beings offer support, and sometimes their special powers, to the humans in their midst. This is to help these compassionate humans to more effectively defend and heal the Earth. The ritual ends in various ways, sometimes in ecstatic dance celebrating interspecies and interplanetary oneness.

As is usually the case with any ritual, the experiences people have during the council varies. Some participants report being possessed by and speaking for the spirits of nonhuman entities. For such participants, the experience seems to fit what I am calling Spiritual Animism—and it seems to resemble the experiences of some indigenous shamans who move between human and nonhuman identities and worlds, and also what some New Age spiritual leaders describe as channeling the spirits of other beings. Other participants in the council may speak for DNA or energy pulses permeating the universe, or of the pain felt by Gaia from mining or the pollution of her waters. One of the central intentions of the council rituals, according to its creators, is to help people to "hear within themselves the sounds of the earth crying."[17] For such participants, both those possessed and those who hear the plaintive cries of a sentient, sacred earth, the experience fits what I am calling Gaian Spirituality. For others, speaking for nonhuman life-forms is considered more an act of moral imagination than of being called or possessed by spiritual intelligences or a sentient earth. For such activists, the council is a kind of ritualized performance art in which participants act out what they surmise it must feel like to be a nonhuman entity. Such participants understand that they are engaged in a creative act rather than making a mystical connection with spirits in nature. This latter type of understanding can be understood as a form of Naturalistic Animism or Gaian Naturalism.

NATURALISTIC ANIMISM AND GAIAN NATURALISM

Naturalistic Animism involves either skepticism or disbelief that some spiritual world runs parallel to the earth and animates nonhuman natural entities or earth herself. But those engaged in it nevertheless express, at minimum, kinship with and ethical concern for nonhuman life. Moreover, for many naturalistic animists, understanding and even communion with nonhuman lifeforms is possible. According to the historian Donald Worster, this kind of felt kinship, and the biocentric ethics that tends to accompany it, can be grounded in evolutionary theory. Worster cited Charles Darwin himself to illustrate: "If we choose to let conjecture run wild, then animals, our fellow brethren in pain, diseases, death, suffering and famine—our slaves in the most laborious works, our companions in our amusements—they may partake [of] our origin in one common ancestor—we may be all netted together."[18]

Darwin clearly believed that a kinship ethic can be deduced from knowledge of our common ancestor and awareness that other animals suffer and face challenges, as do we. This kind of conjecture represents an empathetic form of analogical reasoning as well as an act of moral imagination—this is typical of those engaged in Naturalistic Animism. Animism understood in this way can be entirely independent of metaphysical speculation or supernaturalistic assumptions.

In the last paragraph of *On the Origin of Species,* Darwin also spoke about the evolutionary process in a way that I think expresses the form of dark green religion I am calling Gaian Naturalism:

> It is interesting to contemplate . . . that these elaborately constructed forms, so different from each other, and dependent on each other in so complex a manner, have all been produced by laws acting around us. . . . There is grandeur in this view of life, with its several powers, having been originally breathed into a few forms or into one; and that, whilst this planet has gone cycling on according to the fixed law of gravity, from so simple a beginning endless forms most beautiful and most wonderful have been, and are being, evolved.[19]

Even though Darwin lost faith in a superordinate divine, creative force, here he spoke in an evocative way that could be read, in concert with his kinship-promoting passages, as expressing a reverence for life. We shall never know for sure whether Darwin would acknowledge such reverence were he alive today.[20] But many scientists and other readers have subsequently understood these passages in precisely this way, in the way I am calling Gaian Naturalism. Moreover, through interviews with environmentalists and scientists, and analysis of widely scattered environmental writing, I have found many similar examples.

Kinship feelings are certainly common among those who endorse evolutionary theory's supposition of common ancestors, including among ethologists, who study animal behavior, and cognitive ethologists in particular, who are especially interested in animal consciousness, communication, and emotions. Such Naturalistic Animism is easy to find among those who study primates, elephants, and other animals (especially mammals). (For simplicity I use the word *animals* to refer only to nonhuman ones, even though humans are also animals.) Katy Payne, an acoustic biologist, for example, has scrutinized elephant communication and concluded that attentive humans can communicate with elephants.[21] Increasing numbers of scientists are arriving at similar conclusions, finding communicative and affective similarities between humans and other animals.[22] A sense of delight, wonder, appreciation, and reverence for Gaia, often combined with terminology that speaks of the earth as sacred, has been often expressed by scientists and others who are skeptical if not dismissive of beliefs in a divine creator or other nonmaterial divine beings.

An Ethologist and Primatologist. The American biologist-ethologist Marc Bekoff is a well-known contemporary proponent of Naturalistic Animism. He argues that cognitive ethology and everyday observation of animals prove they have rich affective lives and can communicate with humans in many ways, including by expressing their desires, pleasures, aversions, pain, and grief. He also believes they have traits that resemble morality, if not also spiritual experiences or precursors to them. Bekoff draws on both anecdotal reports from scientists as well as methodologically rigorous research in making such assertions.[23] While acknowledging that interpretation can be difficult, Bekoff claims that the pathway to communication with animals is through their eyes. Here, his animistic perception becomes clear: "Eyes are magnificently complex organs that provide a window into an individual's emotional world. As in humans, in many species eyes reflect feelings, whether wide open in glee or sunken in despair. Eyes are mysterious, evocative, and immediate communicators. . . . Personal interpretation or intuition plays a role, and yet there is no more direct animal-to-animal communication than staring deeply into another's eyes."[24]

Bekoff traced his ability to understand the meaning in animal eyes to an occasion when he had to kill a cat as part of a doctoral research project. When he went to pick up the animal, whom he considered intelligent, he faced a piercing, unbreaking stare, which he took to communicate, "Why me?" These eyes brought Bekoff to tears, for they "told the whole story of the interminable pain and indignity [the cat] had endured"; afterward, Bekoff "resolved not to conduct research that involved intentionally inflicting pain or causing the death of another being." Bekoff buttressed his own anecdotes of communicative experiences with animals by drawing on similar reports by other scientists, which often also had to do with eye contact.[25]

I musingly think of such experiences as eye-to-eye epiphanies—and have found many examples of them in animistic, dark green spirituality, including in the life and work of the famed primatologist Jane Goodall.

One of Goodall's most profound experiences of interspecies communication began with eye-to-eye communication with a dominant male chimpanzee she named David Greybeard. She felt as though he had invited her to follow him, one day, waiting for her to catch up. Recalling the event some four decades later, she wrote that when she "looked into his large and lustrous eyes, set so wide apart; they seemed somehow to express his entire personality. David taught me that so long as I looked into his eyes without arrogance, without any request, he did not mind. And sometimes he gazed back at me as he did that afternoon. His eyes seemed almost like windows through which, if only I had the skill, I could look into his mind."[26] This eye-to-eye connection led to other forms of nonverbal communication, such as when they communicated trust through touch, "a language far more ancient than words, a language we shared with our prehistoric ancestor, a language bridging our two worlds. And I was deeply moved." Goodall believes, based on such experiences, that communication and communion can be enhanced through nonverbal communication: "It is all but impossible to describe the new awareness that comes when words are abandoned. . . . Words are a part of our rational selves, and to abandon them for a while is to give freer reign to our intuitive selves."

It is not surprising that Goodall and Bekoff became close friends and collaborators, given the similarity of some of their experiences with animals. They both like and commonly discuss, for example, the story of a chimpanzee named JoJo, which has the potential of becoming a new, sacred story of human/animal connection. In a section titled "The Power of Eyes" in *The Ten Trusts,* a book they coauthored, Goodall explained that JoJo was unfamiliar with chimpanzee ways because he had been orphaned young and grew up in a cage. Eventually he was transferred to a zoo, where he was threatened by more aggressive chimpanzees, from whom he fled in terror, falling into the surrounding water-filled moat and beginning to drown. Within moments, a man risked his own life, ignoring the threatening chimpanzees and the terrified protests of his own family, and jumped into the enclosure and made repeated, eventually successful efforts to save JoJo.

According to Goodall, when asked what made him do it, the visitor answered, "I happened to look into his eyes, and it was like looking into the eyes of a man. And the message was, 'Won't *anybody* help me?' " Goodall commented: "I have seen that appeal for help in the eyes of so many suffering creatures. . . . All around us, all around the world, suffering individuals look toward us with a plea in their eyes, asking us for help. And if we dare to look into those eyes, then we shall feel their suffering . . . [and reach] out to help the suffering animals in their vanishing homelands. . . . Together we can bring change to the world, gradually replacing fear and hatred with compassion and love. Love for all living beings."[27] Bekoff, who provided his own examples of eye-focused communication, and who acknowledges that reading emotions in eyes requires intuition and personal interpretation, nevertheless insists that "even when we can't measure their meaning, it is the eyes that most evocatively convey sentience."[28]

In their individually authored books and lectures, Bekoff and Goodall repeatedly urge people to learn from animals by humbly opening their minds and hearts to them. If people would only learn to enter imaginatively into the worlds of other creatures, "billions of human and animal beings would be spared untold misery and suffering."[29] In this idea of animal teachers, there is at work a kind of empathetic and animistic moral imagination.

An Animist Missionary. By early in the twenty-first century, through hundreds of lectures each year around the world and empowered by her designation as a United Nations Ambassador for Peace in 2002, Goodall had become the world's foremost Animist missionary. The genesis of her spirituality appears to be largely naturalistic, through direct observation and experience, although her views are more anecdotal than some scientists find credible. She certainly agrees with Bekoff that ethology and especially "our understanding of chimpanzee behavior . . . has blurred the line, once seen so sharp, between humans and the rest of the animal kingdom." From this follows, "a new sense of responsibility."[30] But this new perspective does even more. The kind of communicative encounter Goodall had with David Greybeard provided not only a feeling of connection with another being but it convinced her that she belonged to a something greater, a sacred, interdependent universe: "Together the chimpanzees and the baboons and monkeys, the birds and insects, the teeming life of the vibrant forest . . . the uncountable stars and planets of the solar system formed one whole. All one, all part of the great mystery. And I was part of it too."[31]

I once made a presentation to a student conference held by Goodall's Roots and Shoots program, during which she graciously agreed to an interview. Included in the conversation were Mary Lewis, Goodall's assistant, and Dana Lyons, an environmental balladeer who was performing at the conference and had collaborated with Goodall in projects involving music and storytelling. During the interview I followed up on a number of themes Goodall regularly explores in her books and presentations. Having noticed the kind of statement quoted above about being part of the Great Mystery, I asked her if she had been inspired by Thomas Berry (1914–2009), a Catholic priest who urged that we consider the scientific story of the universe, and of biotic evolution, as a sacred story. Berry became one of the most influential proponents of dark green religion and in his own right is an excellent exemplar of Gaian Spirituality. Goodall expressed affinity for his thought, but added, "I can't say I was influenced because I came to him afterwards, but I love what he writes."[32]

Goodall's spirituality is eclectic and thus is difficult to pigeonhole. She indicated in her spiritual autobiography that she had many enchanted moments in nature as a child, which cultivated the "sense of wonder, of awe, that can lead to spiritual awareness." She added that her grandmother wished "to make sure our beliefs weren't limited to the animistic worship of nature and animals," however, and encouraged her to also believe in God.[33] Goodall has retained her theism, but her views seem far from her grandmother's orthodox Christian theism. This can be seen at many points, including where Goodall expresses affinity with beliefs that can be characterized as panentheistic, pagan, and animistic, as well as beliefs about out-of-body experiences and reincarnation.[34]

Her pantheistic and animistic feelings can be seen in her writings about becoming "totally absorbed into this forest existence" during her years in Gombe.[35] Her assessment that there is no substitute for direct, personal experience with nature resonates with dark green religion:

> I was getting closer to animals and nature, and as a result, closer to myself and more and more in tune with the spiritual power that I felt all around. For those who have experienced the joy of being alone with nature there is really little need for me to say much more; for those who have not, no words of mine can ever describe the powerful, almost mystical knowledge of beauty and eternity that come, suddenly, and all unexpected . . .
>
> The longer I spent on my own, the more I became one with the magic forest that was now my home. Inanimate objects developed their own identities and, like my favorite saint, Francis of Assisi, I named them and greeted them as friends. . . . In particular I became intensely aware of the being-ness of trees.

When reading this I was taken by how spiritual power, which animates all things, is immanent and intimately felt. I was particularly interested in her statement about the personhood of trees, for I knew from Lyons that their collaboration began because Goodall was moved by "The Tree," a song Lyons wrote and later published as a children's book.[36] Lyons wrote the song at the end of a multiday campout under an ancient Douglas fir. As the song came to him, he had the feeling that the tree was giving him the song, that it was that tree's song. Given his scientific bent, Lyons recalled later that he initially "only light-heartedly believed it."[37] He later became convinced when Native American elders who heard the song told him that, indeed, it was the tree's song. Translated from Tree-speak into first-person English, the song is about the tree's fear as loggers draw near as well as its anguish about the destruction of the tree's beloved forest and forest friends.

I asked Goodall why she resonated with Lyons's song and spoke of the personhood of trees. As a child, she answered, she always had a deep connection with trees, climbing up a special one in her garden, "near the sky and the birds and the wind." She then described visiting central Africa's Goualougo Triangle during a trip sponsored by the National Geographic Society. It "was the first time I had been in a forest that had never been lived in nor logged," she noted. "That was a spiritual experience."

After she related another story of being in a templelike forest, I asked her, "Have you had experiences like Dana . . . [when] you feel almost the energy of the individual trees that seem to be wanting to communicate?" She answered emphatically, "But I felt that *all the time*. That's why I was always putting my hand on the tree and feeling the sap like blood coming up." This was why she loved Fangorn (the tree-being or ent, whose informal name was Treebeard) in J. R. R. Tolkien's *Lord of the Rings* novels. She likened the ents to some of the great Greek myths in which nature is full of spiritual personalities. I have heard such affinity for Fangorn and the ents expressed on numerous occasions within the environmentalist milieu and especially among those involved in dark green religion.

In conversations like these, Goodall and others express themes common in dark green religion, including that nature is sacred and full of intelligences that can be experienced through the senses but that are often only dimly perceived by those in modern societies. During our interview, for example, she spoke at length about a "brilliant" hand-raised Congo African gray parrot named N'kisi, who lives in New York City with an artist, knows nearly one thousand words, and uses them appropriately in fully grammatical sentences. According to Goodall, N'kisi even initiates conversations; and those who have studied the bird have documented her uncanny telepathic ability, which, Goodall said, one peer-reviewed article concluded had been proven scientifically.[38]

During another part of our conversation, Goodall favorably mentioned Alexandra Morton's book, *Listening to Whales*, commenting that this woman was "passionate about whales" but "decided she had to go the scientific route and the whole book, although it's not meant to be, is a fight between what she knows about the whales and her determination to stay in the scientific method. At the end she breaks out. She can't help it." By breaking out, Goodall meant breaking past the scientific taboo about anthropomorphizing, but more importantly, beyond reductionist science that ignores the spiritual dimensions of life. Goodall respects science and her fame is grounded on her scientific advances. But for Goodall, not everything can be perceived through scientific lenses. She thinks, for example, that quantum mechanics supports "the idea that there is intelligence behind the universe. So that particular branch of science, which seems so very unspiritual to start with, ends up coming right back around" to spirituality.

In another example of her nature spirituality, after the death of her husband, Goodall sought "healing and strength in the ancient forest" and "the serenity that had come from living, day after day, as part of the natural world."[39] A few years later she was deep in the forest with the chimpanzees when the weather changed rapidly, leading to one of her most profound experiences, which she considered truly mystical: "Lost in awe at the beauty around me, I must have slipped into a state of heightened awareness [when] . . . that *self* was utterly absent: *I and the chimpanzees, the earth and trees and air, seemed to merge, to become one with the spirit power of life itself.* The air was filled with a feathered symphony, the evensong of birds."[40] Lingering long afterward, she understood the place where it occurred as sacred.

Most Western scientists do not speak in this way. It is equally unorthodox in Western religion to speak of the "spirit power of life" or to consider natural places to be sacred. But for Goodall, these perceptions and experiences were not to be feared or rejected, for if we recognize that intact natural places are sacred places and "reestablish our connection with the natural world and with the Spiritual Power that is around us . . . then we can move . . . into the final stage of human evolution, spiritual evolution."[41] This is one of Goodall's central themes and the ground of her hope for the world.

An important aspect of this needed spiritual evolution is that all people should gain a perception that Goodall believes is common among indigenous people: that animals have spirits that should be respected. Her criticism of Western reductionism is perhaps most clear when she indicates her belief that animals have souls: "Many theologians and philosophers argue that only humans have 'souls.' My years in the forest with the chimpanzees have led me to question this assumption."[42] She has also speculated on what seem to be waterfall dances among chimpanzees, suggesting that they reflect the kind of ecstatic experiences in nature that may resemble or be a precursor to a kind of animistic, pagan religion.[43]

Goodall thus believes there is more sentience and intelligence in nature than most modern people perceive. Indeed, individual creatures, and even groups of them, can have important things to tell us, if we would only listen. One story she now commonly tells enthusiastic audiences exemplifies this perception: On the day bombs began falling in Baghdad, in March 2002, as Britain and the United States began their war to topple the Iraqi regime, Goodall was staying with a friend on the Platte River in Nebraska. There, the largest migration of sandhill cranes in decades was underway. During our conversation, she described watching the cranes dance for nearly two hours:

> If you think of them [cranes] as a symbol of peace, at first it was just wonderful, but then I began to think, you know, are they telling me something? Because animals do come and tell you something if you listen to them. And then the message that evening that, you know, in spite of all that we've done, that there was still enough food here to sustain twelve million birds to get enough body fat to fly off to Siberia and Alaska without stopping to feed again. You know, so this was a call to action. We must preserve what's left. . . . We've got to work doubly hard to keep the planet safe so that when peace comes we are ready for it. That was the main message of the cranes that day.

Lyons then asked if the message was "from the animal kingdom," and Goodall assented, "It came from the animal kingdom." This kind of perception, that animals come as oracles, providing wisdom, hope, or presaging an important event, is one I have periodically encountered among those engaged in dark green religion.

Goodall's own religious bricolage resembles many others in modern, multicultural contexts. It is also an example of the ways in which individuals within the environmentalist milieu piece together their spirituality from diverse encounters and readings. Goodall's spirituality also illustrates how the lines can be blurred among the four types of dark green religion. Early caregivers encouraged her childhood receptivity to animals and penchant for understanding them as valuable, sentient creatures, which enabled her to perceive things about chimpanzees that others could not. The genesis of her worldview seems to lie primarily in her own naturalistic, animistic experiences. But to her ethology-grounded understanding of the emotional lives of animals, she added a belief that animals have souls and can communicate with human beings. Moreover, she has an affinity for Gaian Spirituality, with her oceanic experiences of oneness with the universe during intimate times in nature, which led her to consider the universe and earth in general, and especially the wild places where special revelations occur, as sacred places.

Goodall, like many involved in dark green religion, is thus developing a hybridized spirituality that draws on both science and personal spiritual experience that includes animistic perceptions, holistic metaphysics, and a belief that there is some superordinate intelligence animating the universe.

An Interpreter of Wolves and Mountains. Many consider the American Aldo Leopold (1887–1948) to be the greatest ecologist and environmental ethicist of the twentieth century. Also one of the country's first foresters, Leopold expressed at an affective level something that may be unavailable from science alone, namely, a deep emotional connection to and reverence for the earth. Leopold is best known today for his "land ethic," which many consider to be the foremost expression of an ecocentric ethic. The most famous passages in this ethic follow:

> All ethics so far evolved rest upon a single premise: that the individual is a member of a community of interdependent parts. . . .
>
> The land ethic simply enlarges the boundaries of the community to include soils, waters, plants, and animals, or collectively: the land.

> In short, a land ethic changes the role of *Homo sapiens* from conqueror of the land-community to plain member and citizen of it. It implies respect for his fellow-members and also respect for the community as such.

> It is inconceivable to me that an ethical relation to land can exist without love, respect, and admiration for land, and a high regard for its value. By value, I of course mean something far broader than mere economic value; I mean value in the philosophical sense.

> A thing is right when it tends to preserve the integrity, stability, and beauty of the biotic community. It is wrong when it tends otherwise.

> I have purposely presented the land ethic as a product of social evolution because nothing so important as an ethic is ever "written." . . .
>
> The evolution of a land ethic is an intellectual as well as emotional process.[44]

For Leopold, the perceptual shift needed for the land ethic must be grounded both in science and our deepest emotions. But he felt that people had become so separated from and ignorant of the land community that they no longer had a "vital relation to it." Developing any ethic depends on changing our "loyalties, affections, and convictions," but it was difficult to promote a land ethic because "philosophy and religion have not yet heard of it." Making the point three decades before Lynn White, Leopold forthrightly asserted that Western religion was to blame: "Conservation is getting nowhere because it is incompatible with our Abrahamic concept of land. We abuse land because we regard it as a commodity belonging to us. When we see land as a community to which we belong, we may begin to use it with love and respect."[45]

Leopold clearly sought to awaken a reverence for life. One way he did this was to draw on Darwinian cosmogony, an evolutionary understanding of how the world came to be the way it is. With reasoning similar to Darwin's, Leopold thought this would evoke kinship feelings, a sense of ethical responsibility toward all life, and a corresponding wonder toward nature: "It is a century now since Darwin gave us the first glimpse of the origin of species. We know now what was unknown to all the preceding caravan of generations: that men are only fellow-voyagers with other creatures in the odyssey of evolution. This new knowledge should have given us . . . a sense of kinship with fellow-creatures; a wish to live and let live; a sense of wonder over . . . the biotic enterprise."[46] In Leopold's perceptions we see the main elements of dark green religion: a critique of Abrahamic religion and a feeling that all species have a right to be here, a sense of belonging and connection to nature, and a consecration of the evolutionary story. This passage echoes Darwin's expression of evolutionary kinship and wonder at the grandeur of the evolutionary process.

Indeed, for Leopold, the evolutionary story is not *only* a scientific narrative, it is an *odyssey*—an epic, heroic journey—and for many, this assumes a sacred, mythic character. In 1978 E. O. Wilson first used the phrase "Epic of Evolution," calling it "the best myth we will ever have" to capture the feelings of awe, wonder, and grandeur that scientific observers of nature often feel.[47] Wilson's phrase sounds very much like the "odyssey of evolution" that Leopold wrote about in the 1940s. By the late twentieth and early twenty-first century, new forms of religious creativity emerged that promoted the Epic of Evolution and the so-called Universe Story as new sacred narratives for humankind. But Leopold told another story in *A Sand County Almanac*, in an essay titled "Thinking Like a Mountain," which over the past several decades has been exceptionally influential within the environmentalist milieu.

It is a story steeped in irony because, as a young man and one of the first foresters in America, with pen and gun, Leopold participated in a nearly successful campaign to eradicate wolves from North America.[48] But he had a change of heart precipitated in part by an experience (probably in 1909) when he and his Forest Service comrades shot a mother wolf they spotted when surveying timber in New Mexico. Three and a half decades later, in 1944, Leopold wrote what are now among the most famous lines in American environmental literature:

> We reached the old wolf in time to watch a fierce green fire dying in her eyes. I realized then, and have known ever since, that there was something new to me in those eyes—something known only to her and to the mountain. I was young then, and full of trigger-itch; I thought that because fewer wolves meant more deer, that no wolves would mean hunters' paradise. But after seeing the green fire die, I sensed that neither the wolf nor the mountain agreed with such a view.[49]

Although one can surmise what might be a wolf's point of view regarding death by gunfire, more is needed to understand what Leopold meant by the mountain's point of view. It is valuable to know, for example, that while serving on a Wisconsin wildlife commission Leopold had been harshly criticized by both hunters and deer lovers for his belief that the health of the land depends on the presence of wolves.[50] One can imagine that this controversy was well in his mind when he wrote poignantly about the many meanings people and other living things invest in the wolf's infamous howl, adding mysteriously that underneath lies a deeper meaning known only to the mountain itself. After this passage, Leopold discussed how devastating game animals like deer can be when not checked by predators, concluding, "I now suspect that just as a deer lives in mortal fear of its wolves, so does a mountain live in mortal fear of its deer."[51]

Leopold was writing metaphorically, of course, when he argued that the land knows that its well-being depends on the flourishing of all native lifeforms, using this as a pedagogical tool to suggest that an ecologically informed people can learn this too. But Leopold's epiphany involved more than grasping the value of the predators he had once persecuted; it reflected his deepening ethical holism and his long-term reverence for wildlands. Indeed, Leopold concluded this now famous essay drawing on Henry David Thoreau, who was probably the most important architect and inspiration for dark green religion. Writing during the depths of World War II and reflecting the hope for peace, Leopold noted that for many creatures "too much safety seems to yield only danger in the long run. Perhaps this is behind Thoreau's dictum: In wildness is the salvation of the world. Perhaps this is the hidden meaning in the howl of the wolf, long known among mountains, but seldom perceived among men."[52]

This "green fire" story has become one of the most beloved narratives for environmentalists. Wallace Stegner, a famous American writer and environmentalist, made this explicit when he called *Sand County Almanac* a "holy book."[53] He was not alone in this feeling: on many occasions within the environmental milieu I have heard Leopold's writings called "sacred texts," not incidentally in the same way some speak also of the writings of Thoreau, John Muir, and sometimes Edward Abbey. Leopold's green fire story expresses the "live and let live" philosophy he developed over a lifetime closely observing and loving nature.

Yet his holism was not hatched through ecological observation alone. It was nurtured by the metaphysics of Peter Ouspensky, a Russian philosopher who had articulated an organicist notion of a living earth and whom Leopold had avidly read. As Leopold's biographer Curt Meine put it, Ouspensky's philosophy "dovetailed well with Leopold's field-based appreciation of the complex interrelations of the landscape of the American Southwest."[54] Leopold's blending of intuition and science is clear in some of his most often-quoted statements:

> The land is one organism. Its parts, like our own parts, compete with each other and co-operate with each other. The competitions are as much a part of the inner workings as the co-operations. You can regulate them—cautiously—but not abolish them.
>
> The outstanding scientific discovery of the twentieth century is . . . the complexity of the land organism. . . . If the land mechanism as a whole is good, then every part is good, whether we understand it or not. If the biota, in the course of aeons, has built something we like but do not understand, then who but a fool would discard seemingly useless parts? To keep every cog and wheel is the first precaution of intelligent tinkering.[55]

> Possibly, in our intuitive perceptions, which may be truer than our science and less impeded by words than our philosophies, we realize the indivisibility of the earth—its soil, mountains, rivers, forests, climate, plants, and animals, and respect it collectively not only as a useful servant but as a living being, vastly less alive than ourselves in degree, but vastly greater than ourselves in time and space—a being that was old when the morning stars sang together, and when the last of us has been gathered unto his fathers, will still be young.[56]

Meine also noted both Leopold's lifelong reticence to speak about his spirituality and how he was much more forthcoming in his final published book about his affective connections to nature and the ethics that flowed from them. Meine recorded that late in Leopold's life he was pressed by his youngest daughter about his religious beliefs. She told Meine, "he believed there was a mystical supreme power that guided the universe but to him this power was not a personalized God. It was more akin to the laws of nature. He thought organized religion was all right for many people, but he did not partake of it himself, having left that behind him a long time ago. His religion came from nature, he said."[57] Leopold's son corroborated this view: "I think he, like many of the rest of us, was kind of pantheistic. The organization of the universe was enough to take the place of God, if you like. He certainly didn't believe in a personal God, as far as I can tell. The wonders of nature were, of course, objects of admiration and satisfaction to him."[58]

Considering Leopold's regard for animals and the possibility he expressed of communicating with them, of sensing something meaningful in a wolf's eyes, it seems possible that Leopold manifested perceptions like those I am calling Naturalistic Animism. At the same time, with regard to his holistic view of ecological systems and of the universe as a whole, Leopold's perceptions seem to reflect Gaian Naturalism. So does his metaphorical suggestion that the mountain has its own point of view. His holism was deeply grounded in a naturalistic understanding of the processes by which the universe and biotic evolution unfolded. Like others involved in dark green religion, Leopold also had an activist side; in 1935 he was one of seven prominent cofounders of the Wilderness Society, an organization whose mission is itself an expression of the idea that nature has intrinsic value.

A Devotee of Gaia. The independent British environmental scientist, James Lovelock, can be credited with resurrecting Gaia, the Greek goddess of the earth.[59] He did this by adopting her as the namesake for his now famous Gaia theory, which asserts that the biosphere functions as a self-regulating organism, maintaining the conditions necessary for all the lifeforms it contains. As he put it in 2006, "I have for the past forty years looked on the Earth through Gaia theory as if, metaphorically, it were alive at least in the sense that it regulates climate and composition of the Earth's surface so as always to be fit for whatever forms of life inhabit it. . . . I am continuing to use the metaphor of 'the living Earth' for Gaia; but do not assume that I am thinking of the Earth as alive in a sentient way."[60]

Because many who encountered the theory took it in an overtly religious direction (some concluded that Gaia theory vindicated pantheistic or panentheistic beliefs), Lovelock emphasized that for him Gaia is a metaphor, not a sentient god. Lest anyone misconstrue him, Lovelock declared, "I am a scientist and think in terms of probabilities not certainties and so I am an agnostic." Such statements indicate that Lovelock unambiguously represents what I am calling Gaian Naturalism, for he wishes to ensure that everyone understands that his epistemology and worldview is scientific.

While concerned that religious interest in his theory might hinder understanding and further exploration of his hypothesis, Lovelock nevertheless grew to appreciate the impulse to consider the Gaian system in religious terms. In this he agreed with his friend and mentor Crispin Tickell, who wrote in the foreword to Lovelock's *Revenge of Gaia*, "If we are eventually to achieve a human society in harmony with nature, we must be guided by more respect for it. No wonder that some have wanted to make a religion of Gaia, or of life as such. This book is a marvelous introduction to the science of how our species should make its peace with the rest of the world in which we live."[61]

While Lovelock may not consider himself conventionally religious, he has nevertheless expressed many convictions that cohere with beliefs typically found among dark green religionists and that signal that he would welcome a new, science-based nature religion. Proponents of dark green religion, for example, are typically critical of Abrahamic religions, which are accused of being arrogant and anthropocentric. Lovelock agrees: "Our religions have not yet given us the rules and guidance for our relationship with Gaia. The humanist concept of sustainable development and the Christian concept of stewardship are flawed by unconscious hubris. We have neither the knowledge nor the capacity to achieve them. We are no more qualified to be the stewards or developers of the Earth than are goats to be gardeners."[62]

Lovelock's prescription is that "those with faith should look again at our Earthly home and see it as a holy place, part of God's creation, but something that we have desecrated." He recognizes that some "church leaders are moving towards a theology of creation that could include Gaia" and are "troubled by its desecration"; and he lauded Anne Primavesi for her book *Gaia's Gift,* which "shows the way to consilience between faith and Gaia." But while he encourages people of faith to integrate a reverence for Gaia into their theology and concern for all life into their ethics, he does not think one needs a theistic grounding for such reverence and ethics. Far more important is a recognition that we belong to and are dependent upon Gaia, for "the well being of Gaia must always come before that of ourselves: we cannot exist without Gaia [and if we do not come to realize this] we will, by thinking selfishly only of the welfare of humans and ignoring Gaia, have caused our own near extinction." For Lovelock it is a sense of belonging and connection with the earth that is the most critical recognition of all: "Most of all we should remember that we are a part of Gaia, and she is indeed our home."[63]

Lovelock often sounds like those proponents of deep ecology who—beginning with Arne Naess—argue that a hubristic anthropocentrism is the key driver of environmental decline. Like them, Lovelock believes that most environmentalists share the culture's deeply seated and environmentally destructive anthropocentrism: "Environmentalism has rarely been concerned with this natural proletariat, the underworld of nature; mostly it has been a radical political activity, and, not surprisingly, Rachel Carson's message was soon translated, at the dinner tables of the affluent suburbs and universities, from a threat to birds into a threat to people."[64] The current crisis is related to and compounded by, Lovelock thinks, the disconnection from and lack of love for nature typical of urbanized humankind:

> Over half the Earth's people live in cities, and they hardly ever see, feel or hear the natural world. Therefore our first duty if we are green should be to convince them that the real world is the living Earth and that they and their city lives are a part of it and wholly dependent on it for their existence. Our role is to teach and to set an example by our lives. . . .
>
> We need most of all to renew that love and empathy for nature that we lost when we began our love affair with city life.[65]

It is not surprising that Lovelock would express affinity with deep ecology since these ideas cohere well with the philosophy. Indeed, Lovelock praised deep ecology proponents Arne Naess and *The Ecologist* founder Edward Goldsmith for their efforts to reconnect citified people to nature.[66]

If reconnecting people to nature is critical, then the question of means naturally arises. Lovelock notes that what people believe is quite malleable, and therefore we could "make Gaia an instinctive belief by exposing our children to the natural world, telling them how and why it is Gaia in action, and showing that they belong to it." He also suggests that scientists should not be too quick to reject religious metaphors in this educational quest. "There is a deep need in all of us for trust in something larger than ourselves," Lovelock avers, offering this personal testimony: "I put my trust in Gaia." Indeed, Lovelock thinks religious metaphor may be unavoidable: "We have to use the crude tool of metaphor to translate conscious ideas into unconscious understanding. Just as the metaphor, a living Earth, used to explain Gaia, was wrongly rejected by reductionist scientists, so it may be wrong of them also to reject the metaphors and fables of the sacred texts. Crude they may be, but they serve to ignite an intuitive understanding of God and creation that cannot be falsified by rational argument."[67]

Yet it seems clear that what Lovelock would most like to see is not an ecologized theism but a Gaian religion of nature. A good example can be found in his 2001 comments about a speech given by then-president Vaclav Havel of the Czech Republic: "When he was awarded the Freedom Medal of the United States . . . [Havel] took as the title for his acceptance speech, 'We are not here for ourselves alone.' He reminded us that science had replaced religion as the authoritative source of knowledge about life and the cosmos but that modern reductionist science offers no moral guidance. He went on to say that recent holistic science did offer something to fill this moral void. He offered Gaia as something to which we could be accountable." Lovelock concluded, "If we could revere our planet with the same respect and love that we gave in the past to God, it would benefit us as well as the Earth." And although a faith-based approach is not Lovelock's preference, he added, "Perhaps those who have faith might see this as God's will also."[68]

For Lovelock, then, a proper understanding of the human place in the Gaian system is akin to Leopold's exhortation that people understand themselves as "plain members and citizens" of the biotic community—a phrase that resembles Lovelock's idea of belonging to and depending on Gaia.[69] Moreover, when people understand their proper place, Lovelock believes, they will revere rather than consider themselves superior to other life-forms and will strive to create a world where all can flourish.

All of this fits quite well with my model of dark green religion, and it also raises the specter of a shadow side of such nature spirituality. On the one hand, Lovelock's notions might worry those who view deviation from their preferred theism as an aberration from eternal religious truths and their corresponding ethics. On the other hand, the kind of ethical holism advocated by Lovelock might lead to violations of individual rights. It is not difficult to identify passages in Lovelock's writings that those who prioritize individual rights and liberties would find troubling. For example: "We are part of the Gaian family, and valued as such, but until we stop acting as if human welfare was all that mattered . . . all talk of further development of any kind is unacceptable."[70] Some would criticize this statement, and Lovelock's expressed aversion to both Christian stewardship and the humanistic idea of sustainable development, as evidence of indifference to human needs.

Equally likely to engender criticism are the following passages in which Lovelock argues for a dramatic reduction in human numbers and that the freedoms typically expected in democratic societies may need to be curtailed in order to heal the Gaian system:

> The root of our problems with the environment comes from a lack of constraint on the growth of population. There is no single right number of people that we can have as a goal: the number varies with our way of life on the planet and the state of its health. . . .
>
> Personally I think we would be wise to aim at a stabilized population of about half to one billion, and then we would be free to live in many different ways without harming Gaia.[71]

Whenever someone urges a dramatic reduction in human population, others worry or expect that draconian means to achieve the envisioned reductions will follow. Lovelock thinks people may already be moving voluntarily in the right direction, but warns, "In the end, as always, Gaia will do the culling and eliminate those that break her rules." Then he expresses doubts that democracies "with their noisy media and special-interest lobbies" will act fast enough. Here, he is arguing that if we continue to exceed the planet's carrying capacity, Gaia will eventually and necessarily take her revenge.[72]

Those who encounter Lovelock's critiques of humanism and sustainable development, and assertions that some reduction in currently enjoyed freedoms may be needed to heal Gaia, conclude that he is espousing ecofascism. Some philosophers would add that this is unsurprising, for the violation of individual rights is the bedfellow of ethical holism. In 2007 I heard from colleagues who listened to Lovelock's inaugural lecture as the first holder of the Arne Naess Chair at the University of Oslo. One of them was disturbed by what he took to be Lovelock's antihumanistic views, citing Lovelock's belief that a large proportion of the human population was likely to die during the twenty-first century because of climate change and the limited aid that affluent countries would be able to render.

Lovelock would likely rejoinder that such criticisms are based on the kind of anthropocentric humanism that precipitated the environmental crisis in the first place. Moreover, he thinks that a proper scientific understanding of the human place in nature demonstrates that the supposed opposition between the needs of humanity and the well-being of nature is patently false. In a passage defending the deep ecologists who have faced similar criticisms, he wrote, "Our task as individuals is to think of Gaia first. In no way does this make us inhuman or uncaring; our survival as a species is wholly dependent on Gaia and on our acceptance of her discipline."[73]

In summary, Lovelock provides an example of both Gaian Naturalism and of how difficult it is for nature-loving scientists to speak personally about their respect for nature without using religious terminology (in a way reminiscent of how ethologists have difficulty speaking about the animals they study without using anthropomorphic language). In a concluding passage from an essay titled "Gaian Pilgrimage," Lovelock expressed his feeling of belonging to and reverence for the biosphere:

> Four billion years of evolution have given us a planet unsurpassed in beauty. We are a part of it and through our eyes Gaia has for the first time seen how beautiful she is. We have justified our ancient feeling for the Earth as an organism and should revere it again, and what better way to do it than by a pilgrimage. Gaia has been the guardian of life for all of its existence; we reject her care at our peril. . . . If you put trust in Gaia, it can be a commitment as strong and as joyful as that of a good marriage, one where the partners put their trust in one another and since they are, as Gaia is, mortal, their trust is made even more precious.[74]

The fusion of Gaia as worthy of reverence and trust with a naturalistic acknowledgment of her mortality may not fit easily into traditional definitions of religion, which often require belief in immortal divine beings. This melding, however, is a wonderful example of Gaian Naturalism. One need not believe in nonmaterial divine beings to have religion, for there are no better roots for the word than the ancient ones having to do with being tied fast or connected. The felt sense of dependence, connection, and belonging to nature that Lovelock expresses is also commonly felt and articulated by multitudes of environmentalists, conventionally religious and not. Combined with Lovelock's environmental advocacy, it is clear that he provides a good example of a kind of dark green religion.

• • •

My objective in this chapter has been to examine dark green religion within the environmentalist milieu through various lenses. The examples illuminate the types of dark green religion I identify—Spiritual Animism, Naturalistic Animism, Gaian Spirituality, and Gaian Naturalism—while also demonstrating that the boundaries between them are complicated and fluid. Yet the general impulse to perceive nature as sacred, valuable as a whole as well as in its parts, but also imperiled and in need of reverent care, has been found throughout.

My expectation is that the trope *dark green religion,* and the fourfold typology involving naturalistic and supernaturalistic Animism and Gaian Religion, will have explanatory and interpretive power. If so, then readers acquainted with environmental literature, movements, and politics should be able to readily think of their own examples of people, movements, and practices that fit one or more of the types.

My experience has been that working through terms such as *religion, spirituality, nature religion, green religion*—and coming to understand what appear to be different but sometimes overlapping types of dark green religion—can clarify how we understand a host of complicated social phenomena. In the subsequent chapters I do not belabor this schema, tediously noting every time something akin to an animistic perception, Gaian worldview, or a dark green idea is expressed. Instead I explore the roots, sometimes surprising manifestations, and growing influence of contemporary nature spirituality.

CHAPTER 3

Dark Green Religion in North America

Writing a history of dark green religion raises many questions about what individuals and groups to include: Do they have to clearly state that they consider nature to be sacred and intrinsically valuable? Were they inspirations to it but not fully a part of it? Should indigenous peoples or people engaged in religions that originated in Asia be included? Instead of setting out to write a comprehensive history of the phenomena, which would pose these and other insurmountable questions, I have opted for a descriptive and analytic strategy that looks for patterns and resemblances without laboring obsessively to demarcate boundaries. There is, however, a historical *dimension* to this study. This chapter examines some of the critical figures, especially from the mid-nineteenth to the early twentieth centuries, who were responsible for the emergence and subsequent strength of dark green religion in North America.

The Interrelatedness of European and North American Attitudes and Practices toward Nature

Ralph Waldo Emerson, Henry David Thoreau, and John Muir are often and properly credited with catapulting nature-related spiritualities into prominence in North American life and environmental politics; this chapter provides a fresh reading of their contributions. But this holy trinity did not drop from heaven or spontaneously generate. Instead, these figures emerged from and were shaped by cultural currents even as they followed their own unique trajectories. Exploring the cultural milieu that gave rise to these giants will make it easier to understand them, their widespread influence, and also the twists and turns of dark green religion that followed. This requires a brief look at the ways in which Europeans encountered and made sense of American Indian societies and their religious practices.

From the beginning of European contact with North America, the religious narratives immigrants brought with them shaped their relationships with and impacts on the land and its first peoples. Conversely, the land and its native peoples had an impact on these immigrants and their perceptions, narratives, and cultures. Scholars who study religion and nature in North America since the arrival of Europeans generally provide the following account.

European Americans were deeply conditioned by attitudes typical of the continent from which they had come. Their perceptions and feelings regarding nature were often characterized by fear and hostility, or at least by deep ambivalence toward the wild landscapes that differed so greatly from the domesticated agricultural and pastoral ones they had left behind. In the region the new arrivals labeled New England, these attitudes were decisively shaped by Christianity, especially Puritanism. American Indians were often considered physically and spiritually dangerous, even in league with Satan. The early colonial leader and minister William Bradford, for example, described his first impressions of the landscape as "a hidious & desolate wilderness, full of wild beasts & willd men."[1] Few of European heritage had affinity with the continent's native peoples, who generally respected and valued the land and its denizens more than the colonists.

In other parts of North America, Spanish explorers and friars founded missions and settlements in what would become Florida, Mexico, and the American Southwest. These newcomers held many of the same ambivalent views about the North American landscape and its inhabitants. With notable exceptions, such as the Spanish Dominican priest Bartolomé de las Casas, they generally sought to convert both the land and native populations from "savage" to "civilized."[2] Such beliefs played an important role in the often-violent subjugation of the continent's indigenous peoples.

Native Americans had dramatically different orientations to and perceptions about the natural world than those found among Europeans at the time of contact. Religious historian Catherine Albanese lists some religious beliefs common to North America's first peoples: a fundamentally relational universe, a belief that nature is inhabited with other-than-human persons, a sense of kinship with such presences and a corresponding "ethos of reciprocity," mythic narratives that included birth-out-of-nature origin accounts, rituals to restore harmony with nature, a belief in shape-shifting (i.e., humans and animals are able to change physical forms with one another), and an understanding that primary foods had sacred origins.[3] For these reasons, Native American religions are often said to hold nature sacred or to be place-based spiritualities. In contrast, the cosmology and theology of Christianity in general, and Puritanism in particular, reinforced the tendency among European settlers to consider land, not as something sacred and worthy of reverence, but as a resource to be exploited for both material and spiritual ends. For such Christians, both of these ends had to do with glorifying and satisfying a deity who resided beyond the earth and who thus should not be too closely identified with it.

Such views did not have a monopoly, however. Some early colonial writings presented a contrasting view that one could learn about this deity through nature and that people could grow spiritually through the challenges and dangers posed by natural processes. For some early settlers, nature was not only a material inheritance or a dangerous place. It was also a spiritual gift from God.

During the first half of the eighteenth century, Puritan ministers such as Cotton Mather and the famous theologian and revivalist Jonathan Edwards, for example, promoted a Platonic doctrine of correspondence, in which nature on earth was seen as corresponding to divine realities. Expounding upon the traditional Christian doctrine that the book of nature complemented the book of scripture, Mather encouraged people to take walks in nature's "public library." While most famous today for his fire and brimstone sermons, Edwards was also keenly interested in science and viewed it as one way to observe the divine signs in nature. The literary historian John Gatta even concluded that Edwards anticipated Aldo Leopold's biocentric land ethic when he wrote, "A thing appears beautiful when viewed most perfectly, comprehensively and universally, with regard to all its tendencies, and its connections with everything it stands related to."[4] For Edwards, the natural world was not merely a commodity but had inherent worth because it reflected the glory of God.

This sort of thinking comes close to dark green religion but shrinks from the idea that nature is itself sacred; in good theistic fashion, the sacred is reserved for God alone and his heavenly realm. Nevertheless, given the influence of figures like Edwards and Mather, their hints about reverence for nature likely helped prepare the American soil for an appreciation of the natural world. This appreciation would grow wildly, particularly in transcendentalism and the variety of nature religions that would follow. In any case, it is apparent that nature in early European American culture was invested with complicated religious meanings.[5]

Most historiographies suggest that attitudes in North America did not shift toward nature appreciation until this had first occurred in Europe, beginning with ferment precipitated by the writings of Jean-Jacques Rousseau and the philosophers Edmund Burke and Immanuel Kant, all of whom had published their most important works in the middle of the eighteenth century.

Although Burke is best known for his counter-revolutionary writings against the French revolution, his *Philosophical Enquiry into the Origin of Our Ideas of the Sublime and Beautiful* is a remarkable work that deserves consideration as one of the earliest examples of the scholarly study of religion. One can perceive his conservative political philosophy within its pages—but it is primarily a work that purports to explain how the affective states that he referred to as the sublime and the beautiful arise from the human experience in nature. In a nutshell, he argued that the experience of the sublime is evoked by and thus associated with the feeling of "Astonishment" that comes from encounters with great and terrifying power: "The passion caused by the great and sublime in *nature,* when those causes operate most powerfully, is Astonishment; and astonishment is that state of the soul, in which all its motions are suspended, with some degree of horror. In this case the mind is so entirely filled with its object, that it cannot entertain any other [thing]. . . . Astonishment, as I have said, is the effect of the sublime in its highest degree; the inferior effects are admiration, reverence and respect."[6] In his views about "inferior effects" we can see how Burke linked the experience of astonishment, and its aftermath, to the perception of the holy, whether conceived of as a sacred place, object, or divinity.[7]

Most important for the present purpose is the epistemological premise Burke articulated through his observations: the sacred is experienced especially in wild, untamed nature, for example, in powerful oceans, dangerous dark forests, and encounters with fierce, wild animals:

> Whatever therefore is terrible, with regard to sight, is sublime too, whether this cause of terror, be endued with greatness of dimensions or not; for it is impossible to look on any thing as trifling, or contemptible, that may be dangerous. There are many animals, who though far from being large, are yet capable of raising ideas of the sublime, because they are considered as objects of terror. . . . The ocean is an object of no small terror. Indeed terror is in all cases whatsoever, either more openly or latently the ruling principle of the sublime.[8]

Moreover, the angry cries of animals "may be productive of the sublime" and the least-tame and most-powerful animals evoke the sublime. Beauty, on the other hand, Burke associated with mere pleasures and with the emotion commonly called love: "The sublime and beautiful are built on principles very different, and that their affections are as different: the great has terror for its basis; which, when it is modified, cause that emotion in the mind, which I have called astonishment; the beautiful is founded on mere positive pleasure, and excites in the soul that feeling, which is called love."[9]

From this passage it is easy to see why there would be tension between Burke and Rousseau. On the one hand, "Rousseau . . . heaped such praise on the sublimity of wilderness scenes in the Alps that it stimulated a generation of artists and writers to adopt the Romantic mode."[10] But unlike Rousseau, who found a close association between beauty and the sublime in nature, Burke found natural beauty (and its associated emotion, love) different from and inferior to astonishment and the sublime. This difference also reflects their political disagreements. While Rousseau believed that in a true state of nature there is sublime harmony, equality, beauty, and contentment, for Burke the natural state was one in which the powerful (people and animals) inevitably evoked feelings of the sublime in others and thereby easily and properly ruled over them.

There are, nevertheless, important affinities between these otherwise competing visions. Both Rousseau and Burke are Enlightenment figures who started not with religious revelation but with sensory experience and observation. As Adam Phillips put it with regard to Burke, "In Burke's *Enquiry* . . . we find the beginnings of a secular language for profound human experience: in rudimentary form an erotic empiricism."[11] The same could be said of Rousseau, and even of Kant, whose own book on beauty and the sublime seems a derivative of Burke's (published seven years earlier).[12] This turn toward the sensuous experience in nature as the key to both secular and sacred knowledge became central to the romantic movement, which then fertilized the ground for many subsequent forms of nature religion in the West.

These eighteenth-century figures were extremely important to subsequent developments related to nature religion and dark green religion. They represented an epistemological turn toward viewing nature itself as the source for the direct human apprehension of the sacred. Moreover, they raised a set of related issues that would be dramatically contested during the following generations: *In political philosophy*—is one form of political organization "natural" and somehow consecrated by its embeddedness in nature, properly understood? And *in environmental ethics*—are some organisms more valuable than others? Although none of these figures promoted what in contemporary parlance would be called intrinsic value theory (in accord with Western culture at the time, they were anthropocentric), they opened the door to considering that wild nature and wild creatures have special value and deserve respect. In this, they countered much that was typical of the Scientific Revolution, at least in its mechanistic form as led by Francis Bacon (from the early seventeenth century), which viewed nonhuman organisms as having only instrumental value for human beings.

Indeed, from the late eighteenth century in western Europe, ideas about the sublime and the beautiful in nature—and related political and ethical ideas—were fully in play within the romantic movements growing rapidly there, and were finding expression in philosophy, poetry, visual art, and music. These powerful movements have too many dimensions to do more than identify a handful of the most influential writers, in addition to Burke and Rousseau: Goethe, Shelling, Blake, and Wordsworth. More important is that this broad movement grew as people were increasingly alienated from rural landscapes during the Industrial Revolution; and that unease was in part grounded in growing concern about the negative effects of industrialization and a corresponding nostalgia for a time when people were closer to nature. While often represented as a rebellion against Enlightenment thinking in favor of an interior spirituality and affective connection to nature, the priority of direct experience that these romantic movements represented actually had affinity with the empirical emphasis of Enlightenment epistemologies, which subverted faith in divinely revealed religions. Romanticism also fueled the democratic and republican impulse, as problematic and violent as this sometimes was.

Nineteenth-Century Developments in North America

By the early nineteenth century, romanticism began to influence significantly the literate classes in America as they became acquainted with romantic writers and artists, some of whom visited America to experience wild nature in all of its sublime power.[13] These writers and artists reshaped the perceptual horizons of the urban intelligentsia, many of whom took to romantic ideals with an enthusiasm equal to their European counterparts. That Americans could see wild landscapes retreating rapidly also contributed to the impulse, while imbuing American romanticism from early on with a deeper environmental concern than romanticism in Europe. An appreciation for the sacred dimensions of nature rapidly gained momentum; and this development had many sources.

Deism—based on Christian teachings purged of their supernatural elements and traceable to mid-seventeenth-century Europe—for example, has long contributed to nature religion in America. Deists understand God to be revealed exclusively through the laws of nature. The deistic third president of the United States, Thomas Jefferson, exemplifies how deistic thinking contributed to the sense of the land's sacredness. His *Notes on the State of Virginia* (1785) linked the "sacred fire" of liberty to people's connection to the land. Additionally, in the late eighteenth and early nineteenth century, a number of prominent figures from the Religious Society of Friends (popularly known as the Quakers) conveyed their own perceptions of nature's sacredness and articulated a kinship ethic with nonhuman creatures.[14]

Many famous nineteenth-century Americans promoted the idea of the sublime in nature. The art of Thomas Cole and the Hudson River School painters depicted wildlands as mysterious, sacred places. The poet William Cullen Bryant's "A Forest Hymn" (1825) exalted the Creator's hand that could be found in the very forests that most European Americans had previously found perilous. Walt Whitman, an even more famous poet, wrote in *Leaves of Grass* (1855), "This is what you shall do: love the earth and sun and animals," articulating an early, religious kinship ethic.[15] The novelist James Fenimore Cooper, in his five-part Leatherstocking tales (1826–1841), not only expressed reverence for nature, but an appreciation for Native American lifeways, understood to be dependent on and embedded in nature. Cooper's perspective later became typical of much environmentalist thinking, especially the dark green sort; but this stance was also evident in early calls for nature preservation, such as when in 1832 George Catlin, "an early student and painter of the American Indian," was the first to promote setting aside large national parks that would include both wild natural beauty as well as Indians. Susan Cooper, James Fenimore Cooper's daughter, added her own contributions, including in *Rural Hours* (1850), which the historian Lawrence Buell has called "the first major work of American literary bioregionalism."[16] She articulated a number of the views then being advanced by Henry David Thoreau, such as a preference for natural over domesticated landscapes and a deep, affective connection to the land.[17]

Better known are developments that gained momentum in the second half of the nineteenth century, some of them precipitated by the transcendentalists, led by Ralph Waldo Emerson and advanced influentially through his essay "Nature" (1836). Emerson articulated, in sometimes novel ways, a number of themes that would appear repeatedly in nature religions and dark green religion, including a mystical/pantheistic sense of belonging to nature, animistic perceptions, an epistemological call to experience nature directly, a belief that all natural objects can awaken reverence, a critique of the shallow and myopic human cultures that do not have such understandings, and a claim that spiritual understanding in nature comes more easily to children than adults. The following passages from the first section of "Nature" convey these themes and Emerson's style in expressing them:

> The stars awaken a certain reverence, because though always present, they are inaccessible; but all natural objects make a kindred impression, when the mind is open to their influence.
>
> To speak truly, few adult persons can see nature. Most persons do not see the sun. At least they have a very superficial seeing. The sun illuminates only the eye of the man, but shines into the eye and the heart of the child. The lover of nature is he whose inward and outward senses are still truly adjusted to each other; who has retained the spirit of infancy even into the era of manhood. . . .
>
> In the woods, too, a man casts off his years. . . . Within these plantations of God, a decorum and sanctity reign, a perennial festival is dressed, and the guest sees not how he should tire of them in a thousand years. In the woods, we return to reason and faith. There I feel that nothing can befall me in life,—no disgrace, no calamity (leaving me my eyes), which nature cannot repair. Standing on the bare ground,—my head bathed by the blithe air and uplifted into infinite space,—all mean egotism vanishes. I become a transparent eyeball; I am nothing; I see all; the currents of the Universal Being circulate through me; I am part or parcel of God.
>
> The greatest delight which the fields and woods minister is the suggestion of an occult relation between man and the vegetable. I am not alone and unacknowledged. They nod to me, and I to them. The waving of the boughs in the storm

is new to me and old. It takes me by surprise, and yet is not unknown. Its effect is like that of a higher thought or a better emotion coming over me, when I deemed I was thinking justly or doing right.[18]

Emerson shared Edmund Burke's belief that the sublime is to be found in wild nature but rejected Burke's contention that such encounters were tethered to fear and horror. In this, Emerson exhibited the sentimental view of nature that characterized most post-Burkean romanticism.

Some interpreters assert that Emerson's Platonic idealism led him to view nature more as the pathway to spiritual truth than as a spiritual end, making environmental concern difficult to achieve.[19] Yet Emerson contributed decisively to the dramatic rise in nature spirituality in the latter decades of the nineteenth century, and it is hard to imagine what contemporary nature religion and environmentalism would look like without him. Emerson's influence on Henry David Thoreau and John Muir has certainly been well documented, but they were, by most accounts, more interested in nature *itself* than was Emerson. The present question, however, is whether Thoreau and Muir are more suitable exemplars of dark green religion than Emerson. A further question is whether they set in motion trends that precipitated such spirituality.

The answer to the first question turns on two main issues: (1) Did Thoreau and Muir come to understand nature as sacred and/or its creatures as beings with whom one could be in a consecrated relationship? That is, did these thinkers embrace a pantheistic, animistic, or otherwise pagan spirituality, moving beyond a view of nature as spiritually important only as a means of understanding truths beyond it? (2) And did Thoreau and Muir exhibit a biocentric perspective with a corresponding kinship ethic?

Henry David Thoreau: Exemplar of Dark Green Religion?

Definitive answers in the case of Thoreau are complicated because he died at forty-four years of age (in April 1862), when he was in the middle of many scientific and literary projects. Most provocatively, his thinking was in transition, having read Darwin's *Origins of Species* in February 1860 (it was published in London on 24 November 1859). Although Thoreau clearly found Darwin's theory compelling, he had little time to fully assimilate its implications. Nevertheless, it is possible to identify in Thoreau's writing at least eight themes that would become common in dark green religion. These are documented in the Thoreau excerpts, provided in the appendix, which I recommend reading concurrently with the summary of the following eight themes:

The simple, natural, and undomesticated (free) life. Thoreau's loyalty was more to nature in general, and wild nature in particular, than to the city and what he considered the banalities and evils common in human societies. This includes his notion that wild animals and plants are preferable to domesticated ones and that citified humans are inferior to those who are in touch with their animal nature and in communion with the wider natural world. Most people, he thought, are desperate to be free from the meaningless and trivial prison that characterizes most human civilization; but they do not even know what they need or are missing, for they toil in meaningless pursuit of material things. If they become perceptive they will see that in wildness is the salvation of people and the rest of nature. With such recognition they can work with rather than against nature—which is in the interest of all life and nature herself.

The wisdom of nature. For Thoreau, wisdom and knowledge come through direct experience of nature. Thoreau's embrace of his animality is the basis of his epistemological sensuality. In places, however, he expressed a puritan distaste of sexuality, which he viewed as unimportant compared to the pursuit of the proper way to live in the world. Yet he craved direct, visceral, and personal contact with all of wild nature; he sought to belong to it and to understand his embeddedness in it, even though in some of his writings he is inconsistent in this regard. Thoreau thus held in creative tension an empirical understanding of nature (which grew in importance over time) combined with an intuitive, personal, and affective relationship with the natural world. He strongly opposed any kind of positivistic reductionism that would hinder communion between people and natural forces and beings.

A religion of nature. Thoreau's thinking can be considered religious in view of his emphasis on the sense of belonging to nature, but many other dimensions to his thinking and life practice also can be seen as religious. He related experiences and perceptions that could variously be called pagan (or heathen), pantheistic (or organicist)—including notions of the sublime in nature—and animistic (although some of these terms can only be applied after the fact because they had yet to be coined when Thoreau was alive, such as with Animism). Additionally, he made it clear that he was post-Christian, indicating at one point that he had much to learn from Indians (and implicitly from their spirituality and life practices) but nothing to learn from missionaries or even from Christ.[20] He expressed neither a fear of death nor belief in an afterlife, apart from delight with the idea of being reunited with nature in a fitting homecoming. Indeed, in his most mature thinking Thoreau seemed convinced that there was a divine dimension to the universe and that science alone could not and never would be able to account fully for the sacredness of nature or our affective and spiritual lives in nature, even though he appeared to believe that the actual characteristics of the divine forces of nature were beyond human ken. Despite acknowledging the mysteries of life to the end of his own, he maintained a strong faith and trust in nature, metaphorically expressed in his last manuscript when he confessed "faith in a seed," namely, that life would continue to renew itself.[21]

Laws of nature and justice. Thoreau expressed outrage over slavery early in his life and considered the U.S. government evil for allowing it. He also disapproved of U.S. imperial ventures and expressed sympathy for the plight of American Indians. He encouraged civil disobedience and resistance to laws he thought unjust, arguing that they were unnatural and illegitimate. His criticism of government was so strong that many subsequently considered his social philosophy libertarian if not anarchistic. Thoreau cannot accurately be said to be either, in part because he rejected what he considered to be status-seeking and pretentious philanthropy (which he clearly considered most political activity to represent), and in part because he was not optimistic enough about human nature to endorse utopian hopes and expectations. Indeed, he was impatient with impractical, philosophical hairsplitting and more interested in real-world change than in utopian social philosophy; instead, he signaled the possibility of a harmonious existence with nature if people would learn *from* her and, through simple and wise living, act in concert *with* her. His central recognition was of the interdependence (and mutual dependence) of all aspects of nature.

An ecocentric moral philosophy. Contemporary scholars debate the extent to which Thoreau achieved a biocentric or ecocentric point of view. Partisans of ecocentrism can cite many more passages in which such moral sentiments are eloquently presented, however, than there are passages inconsistent with such a perspective. It seems clear that Thoreau expressed a sense of love and kinship with wild nature that moved dramatically toward life-centered ethics: he rejected the prevalent, anthropocentric notion that the proper role of humanity was to dominate nature; he urged vegetarianism with increasing intensity (while sometimes celebrating the wildness involved in killing and eating animals); and he attacked hubris, including the homocentric belief that humans could "improve" the land. Closely related was his criticism of the commodification of land, and he spoke approvingly of Native American societies that held land and waters in common.

Loyalty to and the interconnectedness of nature. All of the above contribute to understanding the interconnectedness of everything in nature and to deep feelings of belonging and connection to her. Such perceptions and feelings corresponded to an epistemological and political turn to the local—to the bioregion—and to all of its inhabitants. Moral and spiritual growth comes from a long-term engagement with nature that is both open-hearted and empirical. This depends on a reorientation of observations and loyalties concerning the nature to which a person has access, namely, to the local bioregion. When this occurs people understand they belong to nature and are mutually dependent on her—and that defending and protecting nature and wild animals is critically important to human well-being. When people understand these interconnections, human pettiness and repressive behavior will decline. To Thoreau, recognizing one's place in nature also meant an appreciation for one's own eventual reuniting with the earth after death.

Moral evolution: the necessity of human moral/spiritual/scientific growth. Thoreau had a complicated moral anthropology that was related to all of the above points. In many ways he was disaffected from mainstream society and preferred solitude in and communion with nature. He nevertheless also sought and maintained close friendships throughout his life and clearly enjoyed nontrivial human sociality. At the same time he thought that most people were shallow and hubristic, that many perpetuated or were indifferent to injustice, and that few had insight into reality or how to live properly. Those with more distance from what he considered superficial and unhealthy civilized lifestyles potentially had more legitimacy, but even this approval was a reserved one. He believed, for example, that some rural people, and especially indigenous peoples, had a depth of insight and wisdom unfamiliar to most Europeans (especially in recognizing the spiritual dimensions and value of wild nature). But despite being drawn to native people (he studied them in depth and sought out their company), he could also be condescending, viewing them as superstitious and unscientific, unable to provide a model for civilized humanity. Nevertheless, at various points Thoreau indicated that he thought European Americans could learn from them how to develop kinship with nonhuman living things; and he believed that if this were to occur, it would lead people to design townships with sensitivity to nature, to give up eating animals, and to otherwise protect and restore the natural environment.

Ambivalence and enigma. By and large, the trajectory of Thoreau's writings pointed beyond anthropocentrism and Western dualism toward a metaphysics of interconnection and belonging. Thoreau mused in ways both animistic and pantheistic, expressing a reverence for life and intimating a biocentric kinship ethics. He also expressed respect for the animistic (and sometimes pantheistic) spiritualities of American Indian and Asian cultures, as he understood them. Yet some of his writings suggest he had not consistently adopted such views and was skeptical even about animistic and pantheistic experiences of his own that had moved him greatly. At times Thoreau appeared torn between his scientific and spiritual epistemologies of nature. Ultimately, however, he valued and sought to integrate both into his worldview. He did not wish to dismiss his most intimate experiences in nature, including his animistic ones. This helps explain why he never embraced without qualification positivistic science. If his writings exhibit ambivalence, enigma, and some inconsistency, they also reveal an ambivalent resolution in his fusion of spiritual and scientific perspectives.

• • •

For three reasons, I have provided detailed documentation for the just-summarized themes in appendix A: First, because of Thoreau's importance. He is properly considered to be the most important innovator of American environmental thought.[22] Second, despite the substantial attention he has received, his religiosity is poorly understood—and the only way to appreciate it fully is to read the critical passages, which the appendix provides in one place. Third, the appendix allows readers to evaluate my interpretation by reviewing the passages upon which it is based.

Given Thoreau's intellectual dynamism and ambivalence about certain matters, it is not surprising that he would be interpreted differently. Catherine Albanese, for example, concluded that Thoreau retained a transcendentalist perspective throughout his life despite becoming more comfortable with nature itself than did Emerson. Transcendentalism expressed a perennial religious dilemma in a distinctly American form, she argued, the philosophical tug-of-war between an understanding "of matter as 'really real,' the embodiment of Spirit and the garment of God, and—on the other hand—a view of matter as illusion and unreality, ultimately a trap from which one needed to escape." According to Albanese, in the end "Thoreau *did* move further than the older, more conservative Emerson toward the spiritual paganism of one kind of nature religion. But he never fully got there. . . . Thoreau had not found the world illusory . . . but . . . he had found it penultimate."[23] If she is correct and nature was penultimate for Thoreau, he could hardly be the true intellectual godfather of deep ecological biocentrism, as many today claim.

Albanese found support for her conclusion in Donald Worster's statement that Thoreau vacillated "between pagan naturalism and a transcendental moral vision."[24] But she did not also cite Worster's next sentence: "What remains is to suggest that these polarities could become complementary views rather than simple opposites." Nor did she mention that he afterward quoted passages in which Thoreau indicated that he "reverenced" both his mystical spirituality and his "primitive savage life." Indeed, Worster has underscored his belief that "pagan animism" was a central aspect of Thoreau's religiosity, averring that Thoreau maintained this perception simultaneously with his neo-Platonic/idealistic, transcendental beliefs.[25] Lawrence Buell also seemed to agree with Albanese's interpretation when he wrote that she "rightly insists that although Thoreau moved further toward 'spiritual paganism' than Emerson, 'he never fully got there,' at least not by the time *Walden* was completed." However, Buell's last clause was a significant qualification, which he followed by observing that Thoreau's "personal intimacy with nature continued to grow, notwithstanding his increasingly scientific approach to nature study."[26]

Others familiar with Thoreau have been less reluctant to consider him as a pagan or deep ecologist. Emerson himself seemed to recognize Thoreau's ecocentrism when he paid "tribute to him as the attorney of the indigenous plants."[27] The scientist Joseph Wood Krutch, who would achieve near-canonical status within the growing pantheon of twentieth-century nature writers (and dark green religion proponents), praised Thoreau's "reproach to anthropocentrism." Krutch was, moreover, certain that Thoreau "would have opposed the later desacralization of wilderness," and he also perceived in Thoreau's writings both animistic and pantheistic themes.[28] The philosopher/historian Max Oelschlaeger agreed, concluding that Thoreau anticipated a biocentric perspective and achieved an almost mythic, organicist, and animistic consciousness, which Oelschlaeger also speculated was common among

Paleolithic hunter-foraging peoples (and presumably also among contemporary indigenous peoples).[29]

In *The Rights of Nature*, Roderick Nash made a similar point, citing as evidence of Thoreau's antianthropocentrism his 1852 statement, "There is no place for man-worship," and quoting a number of passages that express kinship with nonhuman animals. "Thoreau was not only unprecedented in these ideas," Nash concluded, "he was virtually alone in holding them."[30] Additionally, Thoreau biographer David Robinson was one of many who concluded that Thoreau's perceptions have affinities with deep ecology.[31]

Answering several additional questions might account for some of the differences in interpretation. Was Thoreau gravitating more toward the naturalistic than the transcendentalist pole of his spirituality in his final years? If so, was this in part due to his reading, barely two years before his death, of Darwin's *Origin of Species*? Should Thoreau be considered an early exemplar and inspiration for dark green religion? Like all people, of course, Thoreau was a creature of his time and social milieu; what seem to be unique ideas often have identifiable precursors. He was certainly influenced by Euro-American nature romanticism and agrarian literature, social justice–oriented liberal Christianity and transcendentalism, and what he learned of Asian and American Indian religions. Yet in a novel way he integrated such influences with scientific knowledge as well as with his personal and sometimes mystical experiences in nature. The outcome was, I think, an early expression of dark green religion, perhaps the earliest that can be clearly identified in American literature.

In considering Thoreau as a dark green religionist, one can find evidence of both Naturalistic Animism and Gaian Naturalism. These naturalistic spiritualities grew stronger during his final years as his interest in philosophical abstraction and transcendentalism weakened.[32] Given Thoreau's strong and clear turn toward a sensuous (scientific) epistemology, had he lived longer and had more time to assimilate the Darwinian worldview, I think that he would have continued to gravitate toward a more naturalistic nature spirituality.

In analyzing where Thoreau might best be located on the ecospiritual and moral spectrum, this question is provocative: To which social groups would Thoreau have been drawn had he been living and writing around and after the first Earth Day in 1970? During his time there was no neopagan, deep ecology, radical environmental, or green anarchist movement; there was only at most an inkling of an environmental movement. Had he lived during a time characterized by greater social support for feelings and ideas like his, he likely would have been engaged with and expressed affinity for such related movements, just as he did with the transcendentalists, the closest social group available during his time. Had he lived in the second half of the twentieth century instead of the mid-nineteenth, I would not be surprised to hear Thoreau call himself a pagan, given his periodic sympathetic references to pagan writers and myths and his animistic and pantheistic perceptions; nor would I be surprised if he called himself a deep ecologist or radical environmentalist, given that he wrote some of the earliest and strongest antianthropocentric statements in American letters, while also expressing at least protobiocentric sentiments.[33] These leanings were also combined with a strongly articulated rationale for resisting social and environmental evils, which could easily be drawn upon as a rationale for radical tactics.

More important than these conjectures is how Thoreau has been understood by thinkers and activists during and since his own time. Thoreau has become something of a Rorschach test for people—he is taken as an exemplary social-justice advocate, antiwar crusader, abolitionist, conservationist, deep ecologist, radical environmentalist, and even as an anarchist. These interpretations are often a projection by the interpreters who wish to consider him one of their own. One thing is clear: many who have been engaged in the production and spread of dark green religion have taken inspiration from Thoreau and consider him an ecospiritual elder. Certainly, deep ecologists and radical environmentalists have enthusiastically embraced him. On a number of occasions in green enclaves I have heard activists speak of Thoreau's writings as sacred texts; writings by others evoke similar reverence, typically those by John Muir and Aldo Leopold but also increasingly those of Rachel Carson, Joseph Wood Krutch, Edward Abbey, Loren Eiseley, and a number of others. Analysis of these figures and their influence could be possible with all environmental writers who appear to be on the way to canonization.

An analysis of dark green religious leadership would also observe the ways in which those moved by Thoreau's writing often make pilgrimages to the sites where he lived or traveled. The pilgrims seek to enter imaginatively into his spiritual and moral world and to pay their respects to if not venerate their prophet-saint.[34] The Thoreau scholars among them might even be considered priests of Thoreauvian religion. (I am aware that this analytical lens could also be turned on me to suggest that I am another scholar engaged in canon formation, both with regard to Thoreau and the other luminaries I spotlight in this book.) Such observations indicate that while Thoreau has typically been considered an *intellectual* elder of the environmental movement, he has also played a pivotal role as a *spiritual* elder, which helps account for the persistence of his influence.

To provide just two more examples of how interest in Thoreau's life and teachings resembles the kind of religious productivity that often surrounds charismatic religious leaders: Many volumes have been devoted to Thoreau's works and commentary on them. This resembles the intensity of effort that Christian biblical scholars and theologians have put into understanding that tradition's sacred texts. Intense exegetical work suggests that there is something special if not sacred about a text. For a second example, Robert Richardson Jr., one of many devoted Thoreau scholars, concluded his introduction to a volume that published for the first time many of Thoreau's most mature writings with words that show the ongoing salience of the Thoreauvian pilgrimage. After noting that Thoreau once told a dear friend, "When I die you will find swamp oak written on my heart," Richardson wrote, "On my next visit to Walden Pond, I think I will put an acorn instead of a stone on the growing cairn that marks the place where he lived."[35] This expressed intention is beyond scholarship—Richardson planned to participate in a popular ritual of veneration and commemoration.

After Henry David Thoreau (AHDT)

The Western calendar divides history into periods before and after Christ. If the many interpreters who consider Thoreau a watershed figure are correct, then the extensive attention I have devoted to him is merited. A demarcation of time, such as AHDT, might amusingly make the point.

There have been other seminal figures in the historical emergence and fecundity of dark green religion, of course. In the remainder of this chapter I discuss John Burroughs and John Muir. They were both influenced by Thoreau and represent two main streams of dark green religion that flowed from him. The first involves a bioregional impulse, the quest to return to and commune and live in harmony with nature in a particular ecoregion. The second involves an activist impulse, whose chief moral priority is to engage in political action to prevent the desecration of nature.

I devote less space to the American naturalist and essayist John Burroughs (1837–1921), because although he was popular in his time his influence did not endure to the extent of Emerson, Thoreau, and Muir. Consequently, Burroughs has been less of a canonical figure in the minds of those engaged in dark green religion. Nevertheless, he was a remarkable figure and one who might well be poised for cultural resurrection.

Growing up in the Catskill Mountains, Burroughs was deeply influenced by Emerson as well as by the poets Wordsworth and Whitman, who became friends. After completing seminary and securing a job as a U.S. Treasury Department bank examiner, in 1871, Burroughs began publishing a steady stream of essays. In 1874, while still working in New York City, he purchased a farm. By 1886 he withdrew entirely from urban life, focusing much of his writing on his new life as a farmer and promoting a simple, agrarian life. In this, Burroughs was exemplary of the Arcadian impulse in American culture and a progenitor of bioregionalism. This Arcadian vision is rooted in the idea that rural and pastoral landscapes are idyllic places where communities flourish. Burroughs was also deeply influenced by Darwin and took a dramatic turn toward a naturalistic form of dark green religion, while retaining traces of a mystery-infused Pantheism (or Panentheism), which suggests that he never rejected his Emersonian roots. He seemed to retain a belief (or hope) that a divine consciousness remained mysteriously behind the natural world that he considered sacred.[36] In this he was complicated and contradictory, which he acknowledged in his later works.[37]

Whatever ambiguities and seeming contradictions one discovers in his writings, a number of themes emerge that clearly express dark green perception. Among these is a rejection of theistic religion and anthropocentrism; a feeling of delight, wonder, reverence, and belonging to nature as well as ecological appreciation for all natural processes—we should even gladly accept death as a wellspring of life.

> When we come to see that the celestial and the terrestrial are one, that time and eternity are one, that mind and matter are one, that death and life are one, that there is and can be nothing not inherent in Nature, then we no longer look for or expect a far-off, unknown God.[38]

> Nature exists for man no more than she does for monkeys, and is as regardless of his life or pleasure or success as she is of fleas. . . . [While] man is at the top in his own estimation . . . Nature values him only as manure—squanders him as recklessly as autumn leaves.[39]

> We must get rid of the great moral governor, or head director. He is a fiction of our brains. We must recognize only Nature, the All, call it God if we will, but divest it of all anthropological conceptions. Nature we know; we are of it; we are in it.[40]

> The forms and creeds of religion change, but the sentiment of religion—the wonder and reverence and love we feel in the presence of the inscrutable universe—persists. . . . If we do not go to church so much as did our fathers, we go to the woods much more, and are much more inclined to make a temple of them than they were.
>
> . . . Death is a phase of life, a redistribution of the type. Decay is another kind of growth.[41]

Like so many before and since, however, Burroughs did not find it easy to accept the evolutionary and "animal origin of man." But once he did, he integrated evolution into a post-theistic nature religion, writing, "It seems to me that evolution adds greatly to the wonder of life, because it takes it out of the realm of the arbitrary, the exceptional, and links it to the sequence of natural causation."[42] Not incidentally, here Burroughs echoed the heart of Darwin's conclusion to *Origin of Species.*

According to Rebecca Gould, who has written about Burroughs and the nature-oriented spiritualities of the American back-to-the land and homesteading movements that he helped inspire, Burroughs's dilemma represented "the competing influences of Emerson and Darwin on his own view of nature [and also] . . . gave voice to the cultural anxieties of his age, anxieties about having to choose between outmoded Christian doctrine and a secularized world without meaning."[43] This is certainly true, as is her judgment that homesteading movements are engaged in "a post-Enlightenment historical process, one more far reaching than is often assumed" wherein people turn "to nature for moral authority and spiritual renewal." Gould views Burroughs as an especially good example of this stance because he "was quite intentionally . . . relocating religion" in nature itself. Burroughs has this in common with what I am calling dark green religion, a religion that challenges conventional definitions and that represents a much more widespread religious shift than is usually recognized.

Gould also examined how Burroughs became a popular figure and his farm a pilgrimage site. This dynamic resembles Thoreauvian pilgrimages, as when several decades after Burroughs lived, two prominent vegetarians and socialists, Helen and Scott Nearing, left urban life to return to the land, first in Vermont and later in Maine.[44] As Gould put it: "Like Burroughs in his time, the Nearings became representative symbols for the spiritual benefits of living close to nature and away from a materialist society. Helen's Theosophical background (which included a belief in reincarnation and a reverence for the sacred in nature) and Scott's early Social Gospel . . . shaped their back-to-the-land experiments, which centered on organic gardening, strict vegetarianism, pacifism, anti-materialism and a staunch work ethic." Many who flocked to the Nearings' homestead during the 1960s and 1970s "continued to live rurally and practice relative self-sufficiency through growing their own food and producing local crafts."[45]

Gould aptly labeled stories about homesteading and the decision to do so—by Burroughs, the Nearings, and their followers—as "conversion narratives."[46] Research exploring back-to-the-land and bioregional movements makes it clear that what people in such movements convert *to* is one or another form of dark green religion.[47] The streams of dark green religion that flow from Thoreau through Burroughs and the Nearings continued in the bioregional movement after Earth Day.[48] A related channel flows from Thoreau through John Muir and his progeny, who instead prioritized the preservation of nature over simple rural living.

Muir is better known in American culture today than Burroughs, the Nearings, or other bioregional figures and movements, in part because he founded the Sierra Club in 1892, which has become one of the world's most influential conservation organizations. No one was more instrumental in inaugurating the era of environmental activism than Muir.

John of the Mountains

Born in Scotland in 1838, John Muir immigrated to rural Wisconsin as a youngster. In 1861 he enrolled at the University of Wisconsin, where he developed an interest in geology and natural science. Muir subsequently enjoyed brief success as an inventor and manufacturing foreman before suffering an eye injury that temporarily blinded him. Nearly losing his sight convinced him he should pursue his deeper longings for nature. When sufficiently healed, he began long wanderings that were prompted in part by transcendentalist writings (including Emerson and Thoreau) and by the German explorer and naturalist Alexander von

Humboldt (1769–1859), whose pathbreaking analyses help account for Muir's keen awareness of ecological interdependence.

Thus inspired, Muir became an adventurer, naturalist, writer, and eventually the driving force behind the Sierra Club, which promoted the preservation of wilderness and provided the underlying philosophy that, at least in theory, would shape the management strategies of the National Park Service in the United States. This philosophy was in turn incorporated into international national parks movements in subsequent generations. Despite his important role in shaping the national parks model domestically and internationally, Muir's sense of the sacredness of nature as the ground for environmental protection may be his most enduring legacy.

Although there are, as with Thoreau, contending interpretations of Muir's spirituality, the preponderance of evidence suggests that Muir's tendencies were first and foremost animistic and pantheistic. His prose is indebted variously to transcendentalism and romanticism (nature as sublime weaves throughout his descriptions of dramatic natural areas, intimate beautiful places, and scenes involving weather-related transitions). He also regularly invoked God in his writings, including expressions of gratitude to the Deity for nature's beauty, which some readers have interpreted as evidence of theism.[49] A more likely interpretation is that Muir thought it politically useful to use language that would be compelling to the various publics he sought to enlist in the cause of environmental protection, which included romantics, transcendentalists, and theists. Two seminal studies portray Muir as more pagan than theistic.[50]

Certainly Muir's writing often viciously (and humorously) attacked the Christian thinking prevalent in his day. Although neither *anthropocentrism* nor *biocentrism* had been coined, he clearly had contempt for the former and affinity with the latter. Indeed, while Muir echoed most of the themes articulated earlier by Thoreau, his biocentric moral sentiments were more consistently and clearly expressed than Thoreau's. Muir heaped scorn, for example, on the arrogant human "conceit" that the world was made entirely for man, an idea Muir associated with Christianity. He promoted the sense of kinship he felt with all forms of life by writing about other species as "peoples," such as of "precious plant peoples" and even "insect peoples."[51] By portraying them as persons, Muir subtly implied that human persons have obligations to them. Muir likened wildlands to sacred places, sometimes calling them holy and often using the romantic trope "sublime" to express the same idea.

This linking of wildness with sacredness led Muir to contrast wild places with civilized and domesticated spaces, viewing humans and their domesticated animals as agents of desecration. He evocatively expressed a deep sense of belonging, connection, and loyalty to nature (even at times intimating a greater loyalty to nature than to human society). He spoke regularly of feeling "Nature's love" from mountains, waterfalls, plants, birds, and other animals, which may explain why he also believed in the healing power of wild places. Muir found a divine harmony in nature that was absent in human civilization and articulated many now-famous and often-quoted aphorisms of metaphysical and ecological interdependence. He also wrote of dramatic, ecstatic experiences in nature that, like much mysticism, erased his perception of individuality and intensified his feelings of being a part of a great cosmic whole, such as when he felt rescued by a mysterious natural force while engaged in dangerous mountaineering. Such experiences gave his life meaning and reinforced his sense of the sacred power of nature, even suggesting an organicist perception that the earth is alive and the idea that interspecies communication is possible. Muir's enthusiasm about a Yosemite earthquake is telling. He wrote in a letter to Emerson that its rumblings "are the first spoken words that I have heard direct from the tender bosom of mother earth."[52] These perceptions can be summed up in what may be his most famous aphorism: "When we try to pick out anything by itself, we find it hitched to everything else in the universe." But equally representative is the next, more animistic line, which is far less often quoted: "One fancies a heart like our own must be beating in every crystal and cell, and we feel like stopping to speak to the plants and animals as fellow mountaineers."[53]

Despite the pantheistic and animistic perceptions that are apparent to the alert reader, Muir also seemed to express, or at least to consider, an entirely naturalistic nature religion, one that is reminiscent of Thoreau's later thinking. Like Thoreau (and Burroughs), Muir understood death not as something to be feared or escaped but rather appreciated as a part of nature's beautiful cycle.

Muir's biocentrism is evident in his earliest writings. Although his feelings of connection to nature had roots in his childhood, his nature mysticism apparently crystallized in an epiphany he had when he was twenty-five years old (in 1864). Encountering a rare white orchid, *Calypso borealis,* he exclaimed, "I never before saw a plant so full of life; so perfectly spiritual, it seemed pure enough for the throne of its Creator. I felt as if I were in the presence of superior beings who loved me and beckoned me to come. I sat down beside them and wept for joy."[54] According to Stephen Fox, "years later [Muir] ranked this encounter along with meeting Emerson [in Yosemite in 1871] as the two supreme moments in his life," which suggests the long-term influence of the transcendentalists as well as Muir's central epistemological premise: that one must seek spiritual experience and wisdom directly in wild nature.[55]

The development of Muir's nature-grounded spirituality was further recorded in journal entries penned during his long walk to the Gulf of Mexico in 1867 (posthumously published as *A Thousand Mile Walk to the Gulf*) and during his first encounter with California's most spectacular mountains in 1869 (recalled in *My First Summer in the Sierra*).[56] Passages from both books—along with essays first written a little later, published originally between 1875 and 1882 and then printed together in *The Mountains of California* (1894)—provide a feeling for Muir's passionate and often humorous style as well as for the substance of his religious environmental ethics.

The essay "Cedar Keys," written at the end of Muir's walk to the gulf near where the Suwannee River meets Florida's Gulf Coast, expressed many of the views for which he would eventually become famous. In what was then a stunning and direct rejection of anthropocentrism he wrote: "The world, we are told, was made especially for man—a presumption not supported by all the facts. A numerous class of men are painfully astonished whenever they find anything, living or dead, in all God's universe, which they cannot eat or render in some way what they call useful to themselves."[57] He then lampooned those who believed that the Creator made everything for people, asking, "Why does water drown its lord? Why do so many minerals poison him?" He continued sardonically: "In the same pleasant plan, whales are storehouses of oil for us, to help out the stars in lighting our dark ways until the discovery of the Pennsylvania oil wells." Then he concluded with his definitive evidence: "venomous beasts, thorny plants, and deadly diseases of certain parts of the earth prove that whole world was not made for him [man]."[58]

After citing additional examples to debunk anthropocentric conceit, Muir expressed a contrasting spirituality, one that involved kinship with nonhuman organisms and animistic perceptions regarding many of them. He even suggested an ethics in which one's sense of self extends affectively beyond one's own human body in a way that presaged Arne Naess's notion of the deep, ecological self. Muir's reflections also anticipated the idea of a sacred "Universe Story," popularized in the late twentieth and early twenty-first centuries foremost by the Catholic priest and "geologian" Thomas Berry.[59] For example, Muir wrote:

> Why should man value himself as more than a small part of the one great unit of creation? And what creature of all that the Lord has taken the pains to make is not essential to the completeness of that unit–the cosmos? The universe would be incomplete without man; but it would also be incomplete without the smallest transmicroscopic creature that dwells beyond our conceitful eyes and knowledge.
>
> From the dust of the earth, from the common elementary fund, the Creator has made *Homo sapiens*. From the same material he has made every other creature, however noxious and insignificant to us. They are earth-born companions and our fellow mortals. The fearfully good, the orthodox, of this laborious patchwork of modern civilization cry "Heresy" on everyone whose sympathies reach a single hair's breadth beyond the boundary epidermis of our own species. Not content with taking all of earth, they also claim the celestial country as the only ones who possess the kind of souls for which that imponderable empire was planned. . . .
>
> Plants are credited with but dim and uncertain sensation, and minerals with positively none at all. But why may not even a mineral arrangement of matter be endowed with sensation of a kind that we in our blind exclusive perfection can have no manner of communication with?[60]

This passage also reveals his animistic perception.

Another sentence, originally in a section of Muir's journal that became "Cedar Keys," suggested not only biocentrism but discomfort with human beings and their societies: "I have precious little sympathy for the myriad bat eyed proprieties of civilized man, and if a war of the races should occur between the wild beasts and Lord Man I would be tempted to side with the bears."[61] This passage was abandoned before publication. Perhaps Muir or an editor thought it would be too controversial, that it would distract readers from Muir's already radical environmental message. The passage displaced humanity from the seat of exclusive moral consideration and would have directly challenged what Muir considered to be hubristic "ecclesiastical fires and blunders." Indeed, apparently feeling that he had prevailed against such errors, Muir concluded in his published account, "I joyfully return to the immortal truth and immortal beauty of Nature."[62] This hints at a naturalistic spirituality and suggests that, for Muir, nature was sufficient as a sacred source.[63]

By 1869, Muir was recording in his personal journal most of the remaining perceptions and convictions that would propel him to prominence in America's fledgling environmental-protection movements. In eventually published journal passages that recounted his first summer in the Sierra Nevada, for example, Muir described the mountains as "The Range of Light" and places in it as "holy" and its trees "sublime," even labeling its stone cliffs "altars" and speaking of "stone sermons" that revealed divine truths.[64] About Yosemite (which became a national park), Muir wrote, "No words will ever describe the exquisite beauty and charm of this Mountain Park—Nature's landscape garden at once tenderly beautiful and sublime." And in a passage focusing on Cathedral Peak, one of the most impressive granite spires in Yosemite, Muir wrote:

> No feature, however, of all the noble landscape as seen from here seems more wonderful than the Cathedral itself, a temple displaying Nature's best masonry and sermons in stones. How often I have gazed at it from tops of hills and ridges, and through openings in the forest on my many short excursions, devoutly wondering, admiring, longing! This I might say is the first time I have been at church in California, led here at last, every door graciously opened to the poor lonely worshiper. In our best of times everything turns into religion, all the world seems a church and the mountains altars.[65]

This was for Muir a lasting perception. A few years later, writing about the alpenglow of the High Sierra evening, Muir wrote similarly:

> Now came the solemn, silent evening. Long, blue, spiky shadows crept out across the snow-fields, while a rosy glow, at first scarce discernible, gradually deepened and suffused every mountain-top, flushing the glaciers and the harsh crags above them. This was the alpenglow, to me one of the most impressive of all the terrestrial manifestations of God. At the touch of this divine light, the mountains seemed to kindle to a rapt, religious consciousness, and stood hushed and waiting like devout worshipers. Just before the alpenglow began to fade, two crimson clouds came streaming across the summit like wings of flame, rendering the sublime scene yet more impressive; then came darkness and the stars.[66]

This was in a passage describing his long "first assent" to the summit of Mount Ritter, one of the tallest and most imposing peaks in the Sierra Nevada. The following day, scrambling up a talus slope toward a glacial lake nestled below Ritter and its slightly lower cousin Mount Banner, he came across cassiope, a rare alpine flower, that moved Muir much like *Calypso borealis* had earlier: "I met cassiope, growing in fringes among the battered rocks. . . . No evangel among all the mountain plants speaks Nature's love more plainly than cassiope. Where she dwells, the redemption of the coldest solitude is complete. The very rocks and glaciers seem to feel her presence, and become imbued with her own fountain sweetness."

Here and elsewhere in *The Mountains of California,* Muir repeated the idea of nature as a personal, loving, redemptive, and healing presence. This seems prescient given the next part of the story when, after ascending the glacier and then working his way up the dangerous north face of Ritter, he became stuck, unable to ascend or descend, with a dawning realization that his doom had become inevitable:

> When this final danger flashed upon me, I became nerve-shaken for the first time since setting foot on the mountains, and my mind seemed to fill with a stifling smoke. But this terrible eclipse lasted only a moment, when life blazed forth again with preternatural clearness. I seemed to suddenly become possessed by a new sense. The other self, bygone experiences, Instinct, or Guardian Angel,—call it what you will,—came forward and assumed control. Then my trembling muscles became firm again, every rift and flaw in the rock was seen as through a microscope, and my limbs moved with a positiveness and precision with which I seemed to have nothing at all to do. Had I been borne aloft upon wings, my deliverance could not have been more complete.

Muir was describing an experience reported by some mountaineers, surfers, and other adventurers, whose sense of self diminishes or seems to disappear entirely during practices that involve mortal danger.[67] These people sometimes describe moments of extraordinary clarity as they engage in their practice, in which time slows down and it seems as if an extraordinary force is flowing through them, taking away their agency. Those with such experiences often struggle, as Muir did, to find words to describe what they felt or encountered—they may call it nature, or the universe, or the lifeforce, or God—and it is not unusual for them to attach profound spiritual and moral meaning to such experiences. Such experiences sometimes evoke feelings of connection to nature and perceptions of its sacredness.

This experience of redemption by the mysterious forces of nature helps to explain why Muir's text is replete with passages about nature's love and healing power. Nature's love is expressed, for example, by plants and animals as well as by entities most Westerners would consider inanimate, such as waterfalls. Writing about high mountain passes, Muir urged people not to fear them for they "are full of the finest and most telling examples of Nature's love; and though hard to travel, none are safer." Indeed, Muir argued, such places are redemptive both spiritually and physically.[68]

The perceptions of love and healing coming from nature, as well as the belief that there is no more fitting and authentic death than in a wild place, are typical of dark green religion. Muir also regularly expressed a spirituality of belonging and kinship, another key marker of such religion. During his first summer in the Sierra, Muir referred to its entire high country as "the Sierra Cathedral," likening it metaphorically to Sinai and thus to divine revelation. But the Sierra Nevada's revelation differed from Sinai's: "The Sierra Cathedral, to the south of camp, was overshadowed like Sinai. Never before noticed so fine a union of rock and cloud in form and color and substance, drawing earth and sky together as one; and so human is it, every feature and taint of color goes to one's heart, and we shout, exulting in wild enthusiasm as if all the divine show were our own. More and more, in a place like this, we feel ourselves part of wild Nature, kin to everything."[69] This passage followed a paragraph that exulted in the cycles of life and death in which all living things are intertwined.[70]

This linking of ecologies and metaphysics of connection with an appreciation for the cycles of life, including the regenerative role of death, is common in dark green religion. In mainstream culture, it can also be controversial, and the expression of it subversive. I think Muir intended it that way in an early essay, "Wild Wool," which he did not include when, decades later, he prepared the manuscript for his book on his first Sierra summer. The immediately preceding quotation (with gentler prose) replaced this earlier, more overtly subversive (and heretical) expression of what is essentially the same idea:

> To obtain a hearing on behalf of nature from any other stand-point than that of human use is almost impossible. . . .
>
> No dogma taught by the present civilization seems to form so insuperable an obstacle in the way of a right to understanding of the relations which culture sustains to wildness, as that which declares that the world was made especially for the uses of man. Every animal, plant, and crystal controverts it in the plainest terms. Yet it is taught from century to century as something ever new and precious, and in the resulting darkness the enormous conceit is allowed to go unchallenged.
>
> I have never yet happened upon a trace of evidence that seemed to show that any one animal was ever made for another as much as it was made for itself. Not that nature manifests any such thing as selfish isolation. In the making of every animal the presence of every other animal has been recognized. Indeed, every atom in creation is said to be acquainted with and married to every other,

but with universal union there is a division sufficient in degree for the purposes of the most intense individuality; and no matter what may be the note which any creature forms in the song of existence, it is made first for itself, then more and more remotely for all the world and worlds.

Were it not for the exercise of individualizing cares on the part of nature, the universe would be felted together like a fleece of tame wool. We are governed more than we know, and most when we are wildest. Plants, animals, and stars are all kept in place, bridled along appointed ways, *with* one another, and *through the midst* of one another—killing and being killed, eating and being eaten, in harmonious proportions and quantities. And it is right that we should thus reciprocally make use of one another, rob, cook, and consume, to the utmost of our healthy abilities and desires. Stars attract each other as they are able, and harmony results. Wild lambs eat as many wild flowers as they can find or desire, and men and wolves eat the lambs to just the same extent. This consumption of one another in its various modifications is a kind of culture varying with the degree of directness with which it is carried out, but we should be careful not to ascribe to such culture any improving qualities upon those on whom it is brought to bear.[71]

Although Muir did not call this ecological cycle of eating and being eaten, killing and being killed, a sacrament (as Gary Snyder did generations later), he did in his own way treat it as a sacred process, even though he understood it to be entirely natural. For Muir "divinely common" processes are nevertheless miraculous: "The natural and common is more truly marvelous and mysterious than the so-called supernatural. Indeed, most of the miracles we hear of are infinitely less wonderful than the commonest of natural phenomena, when fairly seen."[72] A few years after writing this, Muir confided to one of his dearest friends that he had lost his ability to hear the earth's voices, as he had during his first years in the mountains.[73] In another suggestive passage, after speaking again about sublime wildness and how nature kept him safe by "a thousand miracles," Muir wrote of "glorying in the eternal freshness and sufficiency of Nature."[74] These passages are among those that lead me to conclude that Muir may well have left behind any vestige of a supernaturalistic worldview, finding nature itself to be absolutely sufficient for his spiritual and religious needs.

• • •

Thoreau, Burroughs, and Muir are prototypical of the forms of dark green religion that followed. Although lauded by those who feel affinity with them, these three men have also been considered dangerous or misguided. Thoreau and Burroughs were criticized for their supposed lack of commitment to democratic polity.[75] Muir's occasionally misanthropic statements, his indifference to the injustices faced by the urban poor, Indians, and African slaves, have also drawn harsh criticism.[76] So has the national parks model that Muir inspired, which has often displaced indigenous peoples from their lands, a pattern for which some explicitly blame Muir.[77] Those engaged in salvation-oriented religions have also considered the forms of nature spirituality expressed by these figures to be a spiritual path to nowhere, or worse. So for some, dark green religions cause real harm and danger.

Whatever one concludes about these seminal figures, their lives pose possibilities and templates for thinking about the nature-related spiritualities that would follow. The next generations have included both charismatic figures and social movements, and the ideas experimented with and promoted by them have increasingly been reflected in American culture at large. Indeed, dark green religion has grown to such an extent that it would take many volumes and authors to explore all of its manifestations. Instead of attempting such a systematic history, I turn to case studies of the irruption and growing, global influence of dark green religion.

CHAPTER 4

Radical Environmentalism

On 22 December 2005, William C. Rogers pulled a plastic bag over his head and asphyxiated himself. He had been arrested seventeen days earlier, suspected with eighteen others of involvement in the Earth Liberation Front (ELF), a radical environmental group responsible for setting a series of fires and causing tens of millions of dollars in damage at logging companies, Forest Service offices, genetic-engineering research facilities, automobile dealerships, and corrals where captured wild horses were held, awaiting slaughter.[1] The targets were scattered across the western United States and included an exclusive ski resort lodge that was under construction in Vail, Colorado, which was destroyed by fire in 1998. The arsonists hoped to keep the resort from expanding into habitat considered by wildlife biologists to be critical for the endangered lynx and to deter other projects that would destroy the homes and lives of ELF members' nonhuman kin.

Before his suicide, Rogers learned that he had been betrayed by several of those once in his ELF cell. Aware that his crimes were considered terrorist acts and facing life in prison, he left these words for his comrades: "Certain human cultures have been waging war against the Earth for millennia. I chose to fight on the side of bears, mountain lions, skunks, bats, saguaros, cliff rose and all things wild. I am just the most recent casualty in that war. But tonight I have made a jail break—I am returning home, to the Earth, to the place of my origins." He signed it "Bill" and dated it "21 December, winter solstice."[2]

Since 1990 I have been researching and writing about radical environmental movements; one of my contacts supplied me with the words from this suicide note. I knew Rogers from several conversations at radical environmental gatherings and campaigns during the mid-1990s. Those who knew him recall an intelligent, quiet, and unassuming man who had a deep feeling of connection to and kinship with all life, who wished to save everything and every place that was still wild, who disliked the domestication of any living thing. I remember thinking that his suicide note resembled Muir's musing about siding with the bears if a battle were to erupt between them and "Lord Man." When I learned of Rogers's death, I thought that in a tragic way it made sense: how could someone who devoted his life to the liberation of wild creatures allow himself to be incarcerated for life? His final words about returning to the place of his origins also made sense, for it was ultimately an expression of belonging to the earth.

The Bricolage of Radical Environmentalism

Rogers's life and death provides an ominous pathway into considering radical environmentalism as a form of dark green religion and as a bricolage of diverse religious, political, and scientific beliefs. That Rogers exemplifies this process is apparent from the paper trail he left behind: two photocopied compilations of essays, poetry, art, and cartoons that he prepared for activists.

The first of these compilations he distributed without reservation. He drew the title, *Mountains and Rivers Compel Me: A Deep Ecology Reader for Forest Activists,* from the Chinese painter/poet, Shih-t'ao. Inside the book he included the entire, animistic sentence from the poet: "Mountains and Rivers compel me to speak for them; they are transformed through me and I am transformed through them."[3] Also on the cover was a drawing inspired by J. R. R. Tolkien's *Lord of the Rings,* a series of novels in which, near its climax, the massive, ancient tree-beings known as ents rose up to resist the destruction of their precious forest.[4] The back cover had an image of the "green man," a pagan symbol of connection to the earth that survived Christianization in carvings on churches and cathedrals.[5] Rogers signed the introduction to his compilation using his nom de guerre, Avalon, which he took from a bestselling *Mists of Avalon.*[6] This novel recast the Arthurian legend as a struggle between druidic, earth-revering, and goddess-worshipping pagans against an invading patriarchal, nature-destroying, Christian culture. Rogers explained that his purpose in producing the compilation was to help activists reject "human chauvinism" and cultivate a "biocentric perspective."

Rogers gave me the second compilation in the remote Cove-Mallard wilderness in Idaho, the site of a multiyear campaign of resistance to logging. Sporadic incidents of sabotage had occurred, targeting the equipment of loggers and law enforcement officers; and many arrests had been made. During the summer of 1996, hundreds of activists arrived to join the blockade of a logging road, working arduously to make it impassible by digging trenches and building structures with the trees already cut down during the road's construction.[7] That summer, late one night after a long conversation, Rogers went to the back of his truck and returned with a copy of his second anthology. This one he did not distribute widely. I had the impression that during our conversation he had been sizing me up, deciding whether I was trustworthy.

When I saw the front cover I understood why: it was emblazoned with a howling, arched-backed, black cat, along with the anthology's title, *Beware! Sabotage!,* accompanied by these words, "We never sleep . . . we never forget." The back cover stated simply, "If you're not outraged, you're not paying attention." Inside was a primer on "monkeywrenching," also known as "ecotage" in movement parlance. These terms refer to the sabotage of facilities or equipment that cause environmental destruction. The manual also reprinted articles about pagan and indigenous cultures and a great deal of poetry and prose about and promoting compassion toward nonhuman beings. But it also included (1) articles challenging what some considered an anthropocentric nonviolence code common in radical environmental subcultures;[8] (2) practical sections describing how to procure, use, and deploy incendiary devices and firearms; and (3) additional articles pondering whether the time had come to use explosives or commit assassinations, implying that such a time was at hand, since nonviolent tactics had not halted the destruction of Mother Earth.[9] If such sentiments are a form of dark green religion, then obviously, it can have a dangerous expression.

• • •

Contemplation of and debates about illegal and possibly violent tactics were certainly not new to radical environmentalism. Many of the above-mentioned practices had been introduced and contemplated by the western writer Edward Abbey (1927–1989), often through the characters in his novels, who represented a variety of perspectives, including about violence and spirituality. Abbey's most widely read work, *Desert Solitaire* (1968), for example, expressed a deep reverence for wilderness in general and desert ecosystems in particular. It also cryptically referred to "rumors from the underground" of a growing, illegal resistance to the greedy and desecrating, industrial-corporate nation.[10] This reference was to a number of little-publicized campaigns, beginning in the 1950s, wherein environmentalists turned to sabotage as a means to thwart enterprises destroying the wildlands they loved. In 1975, Abbey published *The Monkey Wrench Gang*, basing the novel's characters on people he knew within the fledgling underground resistance. The novel was a ribald tale about environmental saboteurs seeking, ultimately, to dynamite Arizona's Glen Canyon Dam and liberate the Colorado River imprisoned behind it.[11] Both *Desert Solitaire* and *The Monkey Wrench Gang* struck a chord with a range of nature lovers who thought that Abbey had given expression to their love of nature and outrage at its destruction. Both books had an unanticipated impact, helping to inspire the formation of Earth First! in 1980, the first radical environmental organization officially devoted to civil disobedience and sabotage as means of environmental resistance.

That Rogers was one of the many who had been influenced by Abbey was clear in both of his own collections, but especially in *Beware! Sabotage!* Each of its sections were introduced with passages from *The Monkey Wrench Gang*, which was called "absolutely essential reading for the ecosaboteur." Seven other books were also listed, along with one by Dave Foreman, the most charismatic of Earth First!'s cofounders. With *Ecodefense*, Foreman had produced the movement's first sabotage manual, describing how to destroy bulldozers, topple billboards, "inoculate" trees by driving metal or ceramic spikes into them (in the hope of making it unprofitable to log them), and avoid arrest.[12] Critics assailed such tactics as terrorism.[13] The second edition of *Ecodefense* began with a foreword by Abbey, who asserted that since wilderness is our home, defending it "by whatever means are necessary" is morally justifiable, just as it would be to defend loved ones during a home invasion. Rogers considered *Beware! Sabotage!* a complimentary sequel to *Ecodefense* but acknowledged that it was "more militant." *Beware! Sabotage!* also articulated themes common in radical environmental enclaves, including that wildlands are sacred places worthy of defense, while claiming that environmentalists and Native Americans have been developing alliances to defend such places.

The Radical Environmental Worldview

Although Rogers's sabotage manual was more radical than *Ecodefense,* for the most part his two compendiums reflected the main tenets of the radical environmental worldview. They also illustrate why radical environmentalism is an excellent exemplar of dark green religion.

Certainly one characteristic typical of radical environmentalism is its critique of Abrahamic anthropocentrism, which is believed to separate humans from nature. We have already encountered such critiques in the elder statesmen of American environmentalism, and such views are also expressed in other venues and genres, including novels and fantasy literature. It can be seen, not only in *The Mists of Avalon* (and in Rogers's affinity for it), but in the articles and images Rogers chose to reproduce and disseminate, as well as in the bricolage that characterizes the global environmental milieu.[14]

The sources of radical environmentalism are stunningly diverse and are further evidence of this bricolage. These sources include the following:

Environmental philosophers: Especially those promoting Leopold's land ethic, such as J. Baird Callicott; those promoting primal spiritualities, such as Max Oelschlaeger; and proponents of deep ecology, including Arne Naess, Michael Zimmerman, Alan Drengson, George Sessions, Bill Devall, Dolores LaChapelle, John Seed, David Rothenberg, Andrew McLaughlin, and Fred Bender.

Native American scholars: Most notably Vine Deloria, who influentially accused Christianity of waging a genocidal war against Indians and nature and argued that only indigenous wisdom could save the planet.

Environmental historians: Especially Donald Worster, who contributed heft to the story of environmental decline in Western history, critiquing its legitimation by a religion-infused, imperialistic, and capitalistic ideology, punctuated by resistance from those with organicist and Arcadian visions; and Roderick Nash, whose books on the American attitudes and practices toward wilderness, and explorations of the gradual extension of "rights" to nature, subtly promoted the intrinsic rights of nature and criticized the pursuit of "progress" as inherited in the West.

Environmental scientists and *conservation biologists:* Especially those who built bridges with environmental activists in the cause of biodiversity conservation, such as David Ehrenfeld, Michael Soulé, and Reed Noss, all of whom were important in the founding of the Society for Conservation Biology and its journal and who expressed affinity with deep ecology and/or radical environmentalism.

Anarchistic critics, including social ecologists and bioregionalists: Such as Lewis Mumford, Murray Bookchin, John Clark, Brian Tokar, and Janet Biehl.

Critics of technology: Such as George Friedrich Juenger, Martin Heidegger, Jacques Ellul, Bruce Foltz, Langdon Winner, Jeremy Rifkin, and Jerry Mander.

Ecofeminists: Such as Susan Griffin, Carolyn Merchant, Riane Eisler, Marija Gimbutas, Vandana Shiva, Charlene Spretnak, Janet Biehl, and Carol Warren, who generally view the domination of women and nature as linked.

Anthropologists: Such as Marshall Sahlins, Loren Eiseley, and Stanley Diamond, who have influenced many movement intellectuals by urging a positive appraisal of "primitive" cultures and by arguing that foraging and small-scale societies were morally, ecologically, and even psychologically superior to modern ones.

Ecopsychologists: Including Paul Shepard, although he was surprised to be so labeled, and also Theodore Roszak, Roger Walsh, Joanna Macy, Warwick Fox, and Chellis Glendinning, some of whom have been influenced by the above anthropologists and all of whom trace environmental degradation to unhealthy and unfulfilled mental states, while emphasizing the importance of ritual and earth-based spiritualities to the healing of both people and the planet.

Contemporary pagans: Including Starhawk and Margo Adler, who through their influential books hoped to turn the neopagan movement in an activist direction.

"New science" theorists and religionists: Alternately referred to as "new physics," "systems theory," or "complexity" theorists, as well as "Gaia theorists", these people represent diverse schools of thought that nevertheless, in their own ways, promote kinship ethics and a metaphysics of interdependence.

Science-infused metaphysics have often been borrowed by ecocentric environmental ethicists, ecofeminists, ecopsychologists, and deep ecology proponents, as they seek to correct what they consider to be the errors of mechanistic and dualistic Western religions and sciences, supplanting such views with perspectives that recognize the interrelatedness of reality and nature as a process or cybernetic system—a perspective said to root humans in nature rather than place them above it. Also noteworthy in this regard is the adoption of the deep ecology rubric by a number of counterculture gurus and theorists who have led the way in fusing "new science" with earth-friendly spiritualities. Many of these individuals were involved in early experimentation with hallucinogens or with ritual processes designed to create transpersonal religious experiences; and most of these people before the 1990s were involved in New Age rather than environmentalist subcultures, but are now reaching out to radical greens. These figures and institutions include Fritjof Capra and his Elmwood Institute, Stanislov Grof, James Hillman, Ralph Metzner, the Institute for Noetic Sciences, Andy Fisher, and Naropa University. These diverse streams of thought have influenced many radical environmentalists—more than is commonly recognized—which contributes to the overall diversity of the movement.

Such a robust bricolage of sources has contributed to the growth and development of dark green religion among radical environmentalists, even as many of these people and organizations are exemplars of dark green religion in their own right.[15] Social contexts characterized by such hybridity are fluid in nature and thus easily shape-shift into new forms. Radical environmentalism, then, like many other expressions of dark green religion, has figures and forms that are both obviously religious and that only resemble religious characteristics without being self-consciously religious. Moreover, radical environmentalism appropriates and reflects a diversity of political ideologies and strategies, from those that are more passive and/or spiritual, to those that are politically focused and aggressive; from those that are radically leftist, to those that are radically right wing, libertarian, and even anarchistic.

Mountains and Rivers was not large enough to capture all of the diversity and influences that careful observation discovers in the environmentalist milieu and among radical environmentalists. But it did make references to many of them, including the most important movement elders, most notably Thoreau, Muir, Leopold, and Abbey, but also various activists and writers who expressed affinity with deep ecology and had became influential after Earth Day in 1970. Such individuals include Dolores LaChapelle, Joanna Macy, John Seed, Gary Snyder, and David Abram, several of whom were already introduced. A range of novelists and naturalists were also cited.

Foreman's Synthesis

By reprinting in *Mountains and Rivers* the first chapter from Foreman's *Confessions of an Eco Warrior*, which began with Thoreau's famous aphorism, "In wildness is the preservation of the world," Rogers invoked the movement's saints and simultaneously conveyed what may be its central tenet.[16] Foreman traced environmental decline to the advent of agriculture and the Neolithic revolution, explaining that this inaugurated a ten-thousand-year blitzkrieg against the earth's foraging peoples and its biological diversity. Foreman drew this cosmogony foremost from Paul Shepard (1926–1996), an endowed professor of natural philosophy and human ecology at California's Pitzer College, whose publications argued that foraging societies—with their pantheistic and polytheistic spiritualities, close connections with animals, and rich forms of ritualizing—promoted emotional health and were environmentally sustainable.[17] Foreman continued that agriculture's war on nature and foraging peoples was now so advanced that it had come to threaten the evolutionary process itself, a perspective he buttressed by citing Michael Soulé, a prominent and respected ecologist who cofounded the Society for Conservation Biology. This provides one example of how the strongly apocalyptic worldview common among radical environmentalists is fueled by a certain reading of the environmental sciences.

Foreman, drawing on Shepard and others, linked the devastating rise of agricultural civilizations to the emergence and spread of otherworldly and anthropocentric religions as well as to humanism, which eventually followed.[18] As Foreman put it in an early Earth First! publication, "Until the paradigm of Western Civilization is replaced by another worldview"—and here he alluded to the goddess religions of the ancients and to Native American worldviews—"until children see wisdom alone on a mountain rather than in books alone," the restoration of earth-harmonious communities will be impossible.[19]

Not incidentally, elsewhere in his collection, Rogers recommended Daniel Quinn's novel *Ishmael*. In it and its sequel, *The Story of B*, Quinn articulated the most prevalent cosmogony found within radical environmental subcultures.[20] In the initial novel, a burnt-out environmentalist was tutored, telepathically, by a gorilla named Ishmael. Ishmael taught that the fall from an Edenic state of harmony with nature was precipitated by the domestication of plants and animals and the concomitant advent of agriculture, which went hand-in-hand with world-denigrating religions. Totalitarian agricultures then spread globally, destroying biologically diverse ecosystems and animistic foraging cultures wherever they went. In Quinn's reading, the religions of imperial agricultures, whether Abrahamic or Vedic, all promise divine rescue *from* this world, instead of promoting feelings of reverence toward and belonging to nature. Edward Abbey articulated a similar view about the ecologically devastating mistake represented by agriculture and otherworldly religions.[21]

In the excerpt reprinted by Rogers, however, Foreman then offered John Muir's views as an antidote to destructive, anthropocentric, otherworldly worldviews: "There is another way to think about man's relationship to the natural world, an insight pioneered by . . . John Muir and later by the science of ecology. This is the idea that all things are connected, interrelated, that human beings are merely one of the millions of species that have been shaped by the process of evolution for three and a half billion years. According to this view, all living beings have the same right to be here." Here, Foreman (and Rogers) not only declared an ecological metaphysics of interconnection but a kinship ethic grounded in recognition that all life shares a common ancestor. To make this point Foreman again borrowed from Muir, who as shown in the previous chapter, referred disdainfully to the arrogant attitude of "Lord Man." Foreman urged his readers to reject such arrogance—to humble themselves—and *become* "the rain forest, the desert, the mountain, the wilderness in defense of yourself. It is through becoming part of the wild that we find courage far greater than ourselves, a union that gives us boldness to stand against hostile humanism, against the machine, against the dollar, against jail, against extinction for what is sacred and right: the Great Dance of Life." Foreman followed this with Aldo Leopold's story about shooting the wolf, focusing on its climax where Leopold repented his anthropocentrism "after seeing the green fire die." Foreman then exhorted: "Green fire. We need it in the eyes of the wolf. We need it in the land. And we need it in our own eyes."[22]

The opening chapter from Foreman's book, prominently featured in Rogers's compendium, provides a synthetic overview of radical environmental themes. The notion that wildness constitutes the best aspects of nature and people, and that domestication must therefore be resisted, was prominent in Thoreau, Muir, Shepard, and Abbey; and such perceptions have become common among environmentalists, both radical and mainstream.

Foreman's justifications for earth defense were based not only on an extrapolation from kinship ethics; they were also premised on the idea that humans are a part of nature and therefore nature defense is a form of self-defense. Foreman was likely influenced in this area by John Seed.[23] Seed wrote that activism can promote a spiritual consciousness beyond anthropocentrism such that the notion, "I am protecting the rainforest," could develop into an understanding, "I am part of the rainforest protecting myself. I am that part of the rainforest recently emerged into thinking." The idea that human consciousness is the universe reflecting on itself may have first been expressed by Pierre Teilhard de Chardin in the 1930s in a book only published posthumously.[24] Indeed, Teilhard's thought anticipated Gaia theory and can be seen as a form of Gaian spirituality.

Foreman clearly agreed that a spirituality of belonging and connection was much needed as a means to encourage a biocentric perspective. Unlike Teilhard and Seed, however, Foreman's approach went in a nonsupernaturalistic direction, especially after his flirtation with more spiritual forms of Paganism in the early to mid-1980s. During an interview, for example, after mentioning that he often spoke of nature as sacred and had argued repeatedly that, if humans are to live in harmony with the wider community of life, they must "resacralize" their perceptions of the earth, I asked him what he meant by sacred. He answered:

> It's very difficult in our society to discuss the notion of sacred apart from the supernatural, I think that's something that we need to work on, a nonsupernatural concept of sacred; a nontheistic basis of sacred. When I say I'm a nontheistic pantheist it's a recognition that what's really important is the flow of life, the process of life. . . . [So] the idea is not to protect ecosystems frozen in time . . . but [rather] the grand process . . . of evolution. . . . We're . . . just temporary manifestations of this life force, which is blind and nonteleological. And so I guess what is sacred is what's in harmony with that flow.[25]

Abbey's Archetypal Naturalism

This expression of Gaian Naturalism has affinities with the worldview and perceptions of Edward Abbey, who influenced a broad spectrum of environmentalists. In an essay reprinted in Rogers's *Mountains and Rivers,* for example, Abbey's pantheistic and organicist beliefs are on display, as well as some (at least youthful) perceptions about the possibility of communicating with trees and animals.[26]

Most of Abbey's religion-related thoughts, however, were fully formed when he penned *Desert Solitaire,* which became one of the most beloved texts among radical environmentalists, at least during the 1970s and 1980s. In it Abbey called himself an "earthist," a "pagan Gentile," and he spoke glowingly of the "increasingly pagan and hedonistic" American population that is "learning finally that the forests and mountains and desert canyons are holier than our churches."[27] He also described a mystical experience of unity with nature during an extended time in canyons near Arizona's Havasu Indian Reservation.[28] But in conversations with friends and based on his own spiritual experiences and experimentations, he wondered what constituted true spiritual insight and how one arrived at it. Marveling at a favorite desert landscape, for example, he wondered:

> Is this at last *locus Dei?* There are enough cathedrals and temples and altars here for a Hindu pantheon of divinities. Each time I look up at one of the secretive little side canyons I half expect to see not only the cottonwood tree rising over its tiny spring—the leafy god, the desert's liquid eye—but also a rainbow-colored corona of blazing light, pure spirit, pure being, pure disembodied intelligence, *about to speak my name.*

In the very next paragraph, however, he pointedly rejected such supernaturalism:

> If a man's imagination were not so weak, so easily tired, if his capacity for wonder not so limited, he would abandon forever such fantasies of the supernatural. He would learn to perceive in water, leaves, and silence more than sufficient of the absolute and marvelous, more than enough to console him for the loss of ancient dreams.[29]

Nearing death twenty years later, Abbey underscored the point in a new preface to the 1998 edition:

> *Desert Solitaire,* I'm happy to add, contains no hidden meanings, no secret messages. It is no more than it appears to be, the plain and simple account of a long sweet season lived in one of the world's most splendid places. If some might object that the book deals too much with mere appearances, with the surface of things, and fails to engage and reveal the patterns of unifying relationships that many believe form the true and underlying reality of existence, I can only reply that I am content with surfaces, with appearances. I know nothing about *underlying reality,* having never encountered any. . . . Appearance *is* reality, I say, and more than most of us deserve. . . . Come home for God's sake, and enjoy this gracious Earth of ours while you can. . . .
>
> Throw metaphysics to the dogs. I never heard a mountain lion bawling over the fate of his soul.

As he put it in the original text, "The earth which bore us and sustains us [is] the only home we shall ever know, the only paradise we ever need."[30]

Both in the original and emphasized as he faced death, Abbey rejected all supernatural metaphysics—but his Gaian Naturalism is evident. For Abbey, there are important teachings from all types of wilderness, but the desert speaks the paramount wilderness lesson most clearly through its indifference to humanity: that human beings are neither the apex of creation nor the only valuable creature.[31] For those who are honest and willing, Gaia can speak clearly—as nature did to Muir on his walk to the Gulf of Mexico—overturning anthropocentric hubris and teaching that the world was not made for man.

Abbey sought communion not only with Gaia; he also expressed views that cohere with what I am calling Naturalistic Animism. In one poignant passage, for example, he described his eye-to-eye encounter with a great predator, a mountain lion. This occurred after he spotted and then followed its fresh tracks, hoping to see the elusive creature. After describing how he was attracted to the lion but also felt fear when he finally saw it, he wrote:

> I felt what I always feel when I meet a large animal face to face in the wild: I felt a kind of affection and the crazy desire to communicate, to make some kind of emotional, even physical contact with the animal. After we'd stared at each other for maybe five seconds—it seemed at the time like five minutes—I held out one hand and took a step toward the big cat and said something ridiculous like, 'here, kitty, kitty.' The cat paused there on three legs, one paw up as if he wanted to shake hands.

Abbey eventually retreated, after realizing that he was "not yet quite ready to shake hands with a mountain lion," but then he mused, writing to readers whom he assumed would share his longing for contact and communion with nonhuman others: "I want my children to have the opportunity for that kind of experience. I want my friends to have it. I want even our enemies to have it—they need it most. And someday, possibly, one of our children's children will discover how to get close enough to that mountain lion to shake paws with it, to embrace and caress it, maybe even teach it something, and to learn what the lion has to teach us."[32]

Like Thoreau on Katahdin, Abbey craved intimate contact and communion with wild nature in its various manifestations, believing that the earth and its denizens had much to teach, and that undomesticated humans were the ones most likely able to learn. Unlike some of the more spiritually animistic individuals engaged in dark green religion, however, Abbey was tentative about such communicative possibilities, even though he pursued and craved them.

As unusual as Abbey's views might seem, even the most striking themes he articulated had been expressed earlier by the writers he praised most highly. He especially lauded Thoreau, Mary Austin, Joseph Wood Krutch, Farley Mowat, and Gary Snyder for not only seeking to understand but to save nature.[33] He also articulated the central affective feeling and ethical sensibility present in dark green religion—a feeling of belonging to nature and kinship with its diverse lifeforms, and a corresponding sense of responsibility for their well-being.

To gain such perception, one must get away from the distractions of civilization, Abbey believed. He wrote in *Desert Solitaire,* for example, that when he could get away from the artificial lights of civilization he felt "part of the environment" and experienced, "a mighty stillness [that] embraces and includes me; I can see the stars again and the world of starlight. I am twenty miles or more from the nearest fellow human, but instead of loneliness I feel loveliness. Loveliness and a quiet exultation."[34]

Here is Gaian Naturalism in a form that, when considering the entire body of Abbey's work, can be seen as tinged with a Naturalistic Animism and a deep sense of felt communion with all life. While for Abbey such perception leads to the defense of wilderness and wildlife, this does not require a vegetarian or vegan ethics. After killing a rabbit on one occasion, instead of feeling guilt, Abbey exulted, "No longer do I feel so isolated from the sparse and furtive life around me, a stranger from another world. I have entered into this one. We are kindred all of us, killer and victim, predator and prey."[35]

The very process of eating other organisms, and eventually being eaten by them, is a part of the reality of life that binds Abbey to it. Abbey's spirituality of belonging and desire for intimacy with nature thus involved an attitude toward death that is uncommon among those who seek divine rescue from this world. Instead, Abbey saw death as a transformation to be appreciated and embraced, in part for the new life it gives, in part for the reality of belonging it inescapably conveys.[36] As shown earlier, the embrace of a natural death and the life-renewing transformations it brings has been a recurring theme since Thoreau and Muir, and has even been discussed explicitly as a sacrament by Gary Snyder.

Apocalypticism and Hope

Many individuals or groups can have perceptions of the kind attributed to these radical environmentalists without a similar political radicalism, of course. What often makes religions politically rebellious and sometimes violent is a millennial or apocalyptic expectation, which is often combined with a belief that it is a religious duty to resist or usher in the impending end, or to defend sacred values in the face of an unfolding cataclysm. Thus, what separates radical environmentalism from many other forms of dark green religion is apocalypticism. But it is an apocalypticism that is radically innovative in the history of religion—because it is the first time that an expectation of the end of the known world has been grounded in environmental science.[37]

An apocalyptic perspective was certainly central in Rogers's compilations. In *Mountains and Rivers* he introduced one section with these words: "We are in the midst of a crisis. . . . But has the reality of mass species extinction really sunk in? . . . It is not enough to acknowledge the severity of the situation on an intellectual level. We must continually allow ourselves to feel grief and to feel rage. Emotions are the source of one's empowerment and the gateway to a deeper connection with other beings. . . . let down your emotional armor and allow yourselves to feel." Much of the compendium assumed that cataclysmic decline of the earth's ecosystems was already unfolding. It also promoted "compassion for all beings" and expressed anger at, and resistance to, those responsible for the destruction.

There are differences, complexities, and ironies in radical environmental apocalypticism. While all the nuances cannot be teased out here, an article published in *Earth First!* by James Barnes exemplifies the movement's apocalypticism. His perspective is based on population science and the idea of carrying capacity, that the population of an organism will collapse if it grows numerically such that its individuals cannot find enough calories to survive or reproduce, or if it produces lethal amounts of toxic waste. Radical environmentalists (and many scientists) think this process is already underway, reducing human numbers in many regions. "There is hope—but not for us," wrote Barnes, as a pithy way to express the impending doom. Barnes acknowledged that a global human population crash is not inevitable but thought it unlikely that humans will "gracefully reduce" their numbers. So for Barnes and many radical environmentalists, pessimism and optimism are two sides of the same tragic coin: "We're going to have to get used to the idea that, for us at least, everything is not going to be all right. . . . One way or another . . . humans will be far less numerous than at present. The rest of the biosphere, what's left of it, will take a quick breather."[38] For those who most value the diversity and resilience of the earth's living systems, like Barnes, this is a hopeful expectation, that nature's laws will eventually reduce the numbers of organisms, like humans, who consume too many calories or produce too much waste.

The inseparability of pessimism and optimism, and ambivalence about the coming catastrophe, can be found in the earliest of radical environmental elders. Indeed, from early on, the movement's hope, its ironic and fragile optimism, was forged in despair. As Edward Abbey put it in *Earth First!* in 1986:

> I predict that the military-industrial state will disappear from the surface of the Earth within fifty years. That belief is the basis of my inherent optimism, the source of my hope for the coming restoration of higher civilization: scattered human populations modest in number that live by fishing, hunting, food-gathering, small-scale farming and ranching, that assemble once a year in the ruins of abandoned cities for great festivals of moral, spiritual, artistic and intellectual renewal—a people for whom the wilderness is not a playground but their natural and native home.[39]

Radical environmental apocalypticism, then, is deeply ambivalent about catastrophe. Disaster is imminent, it involves the desecration of a sacred world, and it must be resisted. Yet the decline of ecosystems and the collapse of human societies may pave the way back to an earthly paradise.

This kind of thinking, as Barnes intimated, would be difficult to swallow for those he calls "exceptionalists," by which he means people who think that *Homo sapiens* is somehow exempt from nature's laws. Certainly, radical environmentalists have been denounced as uncompassionate social Darwinists who are unconcerned about human beings. Whether these criticisms have merit, however, turns on the facts, for there is nothing *necessarily* uncompassionate about observing that negative consequences follow from believing one is exempt from natural laws. Those engaged in carrying-capacity analysis argue that the compassionate path is to warn humankind of the suffering that will intensify if fertility rates are not reduced.[40]

The scientifically based apocalypticism of radical environmentalism is also sometimes fused with or supplemented by religious prophesy, which often offers hope. Rogers's first compendium, for example, revisits a

Native American prediction that multiethnic "Warriors of the Rainbow" would arise to "make the Earth green again . . . and create [a] New Eden."[41] It also mentions a Tibetan myth regarding Shambhala warriors who would arise during a time of great danger, averting a cataclysm. Both of Rogers's compilations end with poetry that anticipates a reharmonization of life on earth after a period of great darkness, suffering, and struggle. Such prophecies and narratives, as well as other "ecotopian" (environmentally utopian) literature, are often drawn into the radical environmental milieu. They function to inspire activists and provide hope that somehow life might flourish, despite the present difficulties and long odds.

The analysis in this chapter thus far has focused on naturalistic forms of radical environmentalism and the science-based apocalypticism common within it. For a more complete picture of radical environmentalism as an exemplar of dark green religion, however, its experiential dimension requires more attention. Some radical environmentalists have extraordinary experiences and perceptions, which are also characteristics of dark green religion in other contexts.

Cultivating Perception

Rogers certainly presented the work of radical environmentalists who fit both naturalistic and more spiritual or supernaturalistic forms of nature spirituality, both Gaian and animistic. He included prose and poetry from Gary Snyder, Joanna Macy, and John Seed, for example, whose nature-related spirituality and innovative ritual practices are particularly good examples of the more overtly spiritual manifestation of dark green religion. Moreover, these authors all have expressed sympathies for radical environmentalism, share many of its perceptions, and have influenced its participants. Rogers quoted, for example, from Macy's "Bestiary," a poem she included in the book introducing the Council of All Beings; the council itself is a process that can be understood as a "ritual of inclusion," designed to evoke or deepen kinship feelings with nonhuman organisms.[42] But other writers and poets that Rogers featured wrote of mystical experiences encountering a divine life-force in the earth, or of animistic encounters with the spiritual intelligence of nonhuman beings or entities.

Rogers quoted a poem by Mark Davis, for example, which drew on Buddhist themes and promoted "compassion for all beings." Davis had been arrested along with four others in 1988 and charged with several acts of ecotage. These included an effort to thwart the expansion of a ski resort in Arizona's San Francisco Mountains—an area considered sacred by many Hopi and Navajo Indians. Writing from a federal penitentiary, Davis explained what precipitated the ski-resort sabotage: "Certainly there was some outrage involved at the blatant disregard of agreements with the Hopi and Navajo tribes, anger at the destruction of hundreds of acres of irreplaceable old growth forest for the new ski runs, and indignation that the Forest Service was subsidizing a private company with public dollars. But the bottom line is that those mountains are sacred, and that what has occurred there, despite our feeble efforts, is a terrible spiritual mistake."[43] The religious motivations behind Davis's extralegal activities are illuminated in his poem and this statement, motivations Rogers found inspirational. Indeed, just like any other religious tradition, radical environmentalism has its heroes and saints. Davis became one. So now has Rogers.

Of all of those featured in Rogers's compilation, none got more ink than David Abram. Abram, as a slight-of-hand magician, used his skills to facilitate encounters with indigenous magic practitioners in Indonesia and Nepal in the early 1980s. These experiences decisively shaped his thinking and later scholarly work (he earned a doctorate in cultural ecology and philosophy in 1993). In the mid-1980s Abram encountered radical environmentalism by chance, when he happened to camp near an early Earth First! rendezvous. Abram appreciated their earthly spirituality and biocentric ethics and soon was reporting in the pages of *Earth First!* on the meetings of the North American Bioregional Congress, a kindred movement expressing dark green religion that he had been deeply involved with from its inception. About this time he also began publishing a number of articles that would influence radical environmentalists and many others in the environmentalist milieu.[44]

The articles Rogers included were two of Abram's most influential. They explained how he had come to an animistic perception and provided theoretical grounding for his belief that the entire world was alive and seeking relationship and communion. In "The Perceptual Implications of Gaia," Abram championed James Lovelock's Gaia theory.[45] After summarizing the hypothesis, Abram argued that, upon further analysis, this atmosphere-focused theory shows that humans are inside of Gaia and belong to her, and that such *perception,* at variance with most Western philosophical and scientific thought, can provide a basis for a deep sense of communion and identification with nature and even with the universe itself. As Abram put it: "Perception is communication. It is the constant, ongoing communication between this organism that I am and the vast organic entity of which I am a part. In more classical terms, perception is the experience of communication between the individual microcosm and the planetary macrocosm. . . . Perception, then—the whole play of the senses—is a constant communion between ourselves and the living world that encompasses us."[46]

To substantiate his idea of an ongoing, reciprocal relationship and communion between human and nonhuman entities, Abram drew on his experiences with indigenous shamanism and understandings of their ecological roles, enhanced especially by the work of the French phenomenological philosopher Maurice Merleau-Ponty and the American perceptual psychologist James J. Gibson. According to Abram, they viewed the "surrounding physical world as an *active* participant in our perceptual experience." Abram argued that their research into perception undermined "the traditional mind-body" dualism that prevents us from recognizing (as indigenous shaman generally do) that everything is alive. When we overcome dualistic perceptions and cultivate a sensitive awareness of relationships with all of our surroundings, Abram averred, "birds, trees, even rivers and stones begin to stand forth as living, communicative presences." Moreover, such epistemology is "consonant with the Gaia hypothesis, and with the Gaian implication that perception itself is a communication, or communion, between an organism and the living biosphere."[47]

Abram concluded this remarkably innovative essay by linking Lovelock's Gaia hypothesis with the perception common in many religions, that the holy is manifest in wind or breath:

> [Gaia is] a reality that encompasses us, a phenomenon we are immediately in and of . . . it is our own body, our flesh and our blood, the wind blowing past our ears and the hawks wheeling overhead. Understood thus with the senses, recognized from within, Gaia is far vaster, far more mysterious and eternal than anything we may ever hope to fathom. . . . The most radical element of the Gaia hypothesis . . . may be the importance that it places on the air. . . . In Native American cosmology, the air or the Wind is the most sacred of powers. It is the invisible principle that circulates both within us and around us, animating the thoughts of all breathing things as it moves the swaying trees and the clouds. And indeed, in countless human languages the words for spirit or psyche are derived from the same root as the words for wind and breath. Thus in English the word spirit is related to the word respiration through their common origin in the Latin word spiritus, meaning a breath, or a gust of wind. Likewise our word psyche, with all its recent derivations,

has its roots in the ancient Greek psychein, which means to breathe or to blow (like the wind).[48]

This is an example of Gaian spirituality that hints at the kind of communication and communion involved in animistic spiritualities.

The second Abram article reprinted by Rogers, "The Ecology of Magic," made Abram's understanding of animism more explicit, which is particularly interesting because it coheres with perceptions increasingly articulated by religion scholars, ethnobiologists, and anthropologists (especially specialists in ecological anthropology). Abram asserted that shamans are the ecologists of tribal societies. Contrary to early anthropological assessments of them, shamans were not encountering "supernatural" entities; they were simply engaging the mysterious powers, beings, and forces of nature itself. The shaman's "magic," which for Abram was really about animistic perception, involved "heightened receptivity to the meaningful solicitations—songs, cries, gestures—of a larger, more-than-human field. . . . Magic, then in its perhaps most primordial sense, is the experience of living in a world made up of multiple intelligences, the intuition that every natural form one perceives—from the swallows swooping overhead to the fly on a blade of grass and indeed the blade of grass itself—is an experiencing form, an entity with its own predilections and sensations."[49]

Abram wrote of living with indigenous people in Bali, where his hosts presented food to the "spirits" on the ground around the corners of their buildings, and he observed ants arriving to receive the gifts. This seemed to encourage the ants to not enter the building, Abram commented, adding that "my encounter with the ants was the first of many experiences suggesting to me that the 'spirits' of an indigenous culture are primarily those modes of intelligence or awareness that do not possess a human form."[50] Abram then gave examples of how he came, during that time in Bali, into a deep awareness of the animate earth and intelligence of all of the things in it. In a passage reminiscent of the eye-to-eye epiphanies described previously, but with a new, communicative twist, Abram wrote:

Gradually, other animals began to intercept me in my wanderings, as if some quality in my posture or the rhythm of my breathing had disarmed their wariness; I would find myself face-to-face with monkeys, and with large lizards that did not slither away when I spoke, but lean forward in apparent curiosity. In rural Java I often noticed monkeys accompanying me in the branches overhead, and ravens walked toward me on the road, croaking. While at Pangandaran, a peninsula jutting out from the south coast of Java . . . I stepped out from a clutch of trees and discovered I was looking into the face of one of the rare and beautiful bison that are found only on that island. Our eyes locked. When it stared, I stared back; when it shifted its shoulders, I shifted my stance; when I tossed my head, it tossed its own in reply. I found myself caught in a nonverbal conversation with this Other, a gestural duet with which my reflective awareness had very little to do. It was as if my body were suddenly being motivated by a wisdom older than my thinking mind, as though it were held and moved by a logos—deeper than words—spoken by the Other's body, the trees, the air, and the stony ground on which we stood.

Shortly after this, Abram noted with anguish that upon his return to North America it was difficult to maintain the intimate relationships and animistic perceptions he had established while in Asia. Yet he continued to cultivate such consciousness both personally and for others through his writings and other activities, including by founding the Alliance for Wild Ethics in 2006 and creating a website for it.

The entry to this remarkable website begins with a phrase first published in Abram's *Spell of the Sensuous,* a book that became popular within the North American environmentalist milieu: "We are only human in contact, and conviviality, with that which is not human."[51] This sentence, which so succinctly expresses Abram's animistic spirituality, then floats as if magically across the screen. Then, as one enters the site, an image inspired by shamanism and the rock art of ancient aboriginal people appears. In nimble computer animation, a human form merges with a tree, upon which a bird alights. These words then appear: "The Alliance for Wild Ethics: Awakening to Wonder." With its evocative words, images, and music, this creative web art is designed to evoke worldly wonder. Exploring the website further reveals that Abram's intention was not merely to promote wonder but also animistic perception. In a section that describes the animistic mission of the society, Abram is shown in a video clip in a "conversation" with a river, waving his arms as if in ecstatic relation to it. The video ends with Abram bowing to the river with hands in a "prayer pose" or "namaste," which in South Asian culture signifies at least deep respect if not reverence for the divine essence in the one faced. Indeed, in an interview, Abram explained that he considers everything to be alive, even a rock, although "its pulse may move a lot slower than yours or mine."[52]

Not incidentally, the interviewer was Derrick Jensen, a radical environmentalist who has written some of the movement's most apocalyptic and anarchistic books, as well as ones that promote the kind of animistic perception that some radical environmentalists consider endemic within indigenous cultures and available to all who cultivate their innate communicative abilities. In *A Language Older than Words,* for example, Jensen described experiences communicating with nonhuman animals, tracing the perceptual ineptness of most Westerners to Cartesian dualism and instrumental science. He then contrasted Western obliviousness to the intelligences in nature with the kind of perception common among Native Americans, quoting Jeannette Armstrong, whom he described as a friend and traditional Okanagan Indian: "Attitudes about interspecies communication are the primary difference between Western and indigenous philosophies," she told him. "Even the most progressive Western philosophers still generally believe that listening to land is a metaphor. [But] it's not a metaphor. It's how the world is." Jensen replied, discussing his experience of hearing a tree: "I noticed an old pine tree on the corner, as I had noticed it many times previous, and I thought, 'That tree is doing very well.' Immediately I heard a response that did not pass through my ear but went directly to the part of my brain that receives sounds. I heard a completion of my sentence that changed its meaning altogether: 'for not being in a community.' I looked around, and though there were other trees nearby, this was not a full tree community." After describing various experiences of interspecies communication, Jensen then told Armstrong that he was learning that communication with nonhuman beings was easy. She answered, referring to the hundreds of years since European arrival in the Americas, "Yeah. That's what we've been trying to tell you now for 500 years."[53]

Along with critics like John Zerzan, Jensen was promoting "anarcho-primitivism," a type of radical environmentalism that, like most forms, considers foraging societies superior to agricultural and pastoral ones; but it adds an anarchist and primitivist ideology that envisions and seeks to hasten the collapse of nation-states and all industrial civilizations.[54] In two related volumes titled *Endgame,* Jensen promoted this ideology: he argued that modern civilizations destroy indigenous peoples and nature but that they will soon collapse because they are ecologically and therefore socially unsustainable. Reciting the radical cry also voiced by Abbey and Rogers before him, that the resistance to ecocide must deploy "whatever means necessary," Jensen justified violent resistance, even quoting Ward Churchill, whose argument that pacifism is "pathology" was previously discussed: "We must seek nothing less than the dismemberment and dissolution of every statist/corporate entity in the world. All of them. No exceptions."[55] Despite his apocalypticism, or perhaps because of it, Jensen expressed hope for the future of the earth—as well as his conviction that the quicker the collapse the less suffering there would be for all living things. This was, as well, a part of his rationale for violence—in the long run, effective violence would yield less suffering. Meanwhile, he repeatedly urged his readers to listen to the land and its denizens, even in planning revolutionary strategy. To reinforce his belief that this was important strategically, he often quoted Native Americans as they expressed their own animistic perceptions. A good example appears near the end of *Endgame,* where he urged his readers, "If you want to know what to do, go to the nearest mountain, the nearest native tree, the nearest native soil, and ask what it needs. Ask it to teach you. It knows how to live there . . . it will teach you.[56]

Jensen's form of radicalism has affinities with Rogers's as well as with Abram's. The discussion between Abram and Jensen made it clear that, although Abram has not issued a clarion call to violent ecological resistance as did Jensen, he agreed with the declensionist cosmogony, which links ecological degradation to agriculture, with its social hierarchy, technological fetishism, sky gods, and repression of pagan animism. Abram also introduced an innovative theory: that alphabetic language was a critically important factor, if not the most important precipitating variable, in the decline of animistic perception and the increasing disconnection of humans from nature.[57] But in responding to Jensen's question about what motivates his writing and speaking, Abram clearly articulated a feeling common among radical environmentalists: "My work is motivated in great measure by my sense of loss, by the spreading destruction and desecration of so much earthly beauty. By the accelerating loss of other species—the extinction of so many other styles of sensitivity and sentience . . . I'm trying to understand how it's possible that a culture of intelligent critters like ourselves can so recklessly and so casually destroy so much that is mysterious and alive, and in the course of it destroy so much of ourselves and our own capacity for wonder."[58]

This is an excellent example of dark green religious sentiment. But more than suggesting that radical environmentalism is a good exemplar of dark green religion, I can show that there is a permeable border between this sort of radical environmental spirituality and that which appears in the wider environmental milieu; for Abram's animistic writings struck not only a chord among Rogers, Jensen, and radical environmentalists. The "Ecology of Magic" article was initially published in *Orion* magazine, which itself promotes reverence for life through nature-related essays, poetry, and art (especially photography). In 2008 the magazine included on its board of directors one of the leading figures in religious environmentalism, the scholar Mary Evelyn Tucker, who has devoted herself to facilitating the greening of the world's major religious traditions. Pierre Teilhard de Chardin and Thomas Berry, two figures who have urged people to understand the scientific narrative of cosmological and biological evolution as a sacred story inseparable from God himself, were very influential on both Tucker and her husband John Grim, a scholar of indigenous traditions, who partnered with her in creating the Forum on Religion and Ecology.[59] *Orion*'s board of advisors and regular contributors include a long list of nature writers who promote through their writing and lives various versions of dark green religion: Gary Snyder, William Kittredge, Barry Lopez (whose work Bill Rogers also included in his compendium and who wrote a remarkable essay that fits the "naturalistic animism" type introduced in this book),[60] Peter Matthiessen, Bill McKibben, W. S. Merwin, Gary Paul Nabhan (an ethnobiologist who has argued that indigenous traditions and religions are, generally speaking, reservoirs of ecologically beneficent perceptions and practices),[61] Richard Nelson (a scholar of Native American cultures), Scott Russell Sanders, Mitchell Thomashow, Terry Tempest Williams (whose essays Rogers included in one of his compendiums), Edward O. Wilson, and Ann Zwinger. These names would be familiar to anyone immersed in nature writing since Earth Day in 1970.

The origin of *Orion* is equally telling: it was created in 1982 by a nonprofit foundation that sought to "change environmental consciousness" and affirm "the contribution [that American] Indian culture can still make to our understanding of nature and ourselves."[62] The magazine's first editor even asserted that its goal was to help people develop a "personal bond with nature."[63] This spiritual goal and *Orion*'s conservationist agenda became all the more clear when an environmentalist Orion Grassroots Network was established in 1997 to promote personal and ecosocial transformation. So, when Rogers selected Abram's essay from *Orion,* he was drawing from a deep well of dark green spirituality that had long been flourishing in North American nature writing. An entire scholarly discipline of "ecocriticism" has emerged to explore this literature, which could certainly be analyzed in depth for expressions of dark green religion.

Perception and Direct Action

It is not just *theorists* of radical environmentalism who have the kinds of experiences and perceptions involved in dark green religion; so do many frontline activists. Sometimes such experiences occur even while activists are engaged in direct-action resistance to those they believe are desecrating the earth.

One example can be seen in the longest antilogging occupation/trespass of a tree in the history of direct-action environmentalism. On 10 December 1997 a young minister's daughter climbed a giant redwood that had earlier been occupied and named "Luna" by Earth First! activists. Julia "Butterfly" Hill, who took her middle name from her childhood connection with butterflies, intended to extend their desperate effort to prevent Luna and the surrounding trees from being logged. Hill soon felt a connection with Luna and ended up more than two years aloft in her branches, enduring winter storms, frostbite, and a broken toe before descending. She did so only after negotiating an agreement with the logging company that left Luna standing as well as a two-hundred-foot buffer of surrounding trees.

The photogenic Hill and her arboreal campaign became a global media event as, in scores of interviews with reporters from around the world, she spoke of her spirituality and reverence for life. Hill also explained that, although she had grown up in Arkansas, she had been sent "by the spirit" to the redwoods via a wilderness vision quest, which she took after a life-threatening injury convinced her of the meaninglessness of her prior existence. Hill's greatest epiphany, however, came immediately after arriving in the redwoods: "The first time I entered into a redwood forest . . . I dropped to my knees and began crying because the spirit of the forest just gripped me."[64] She became even more connected during her tree sit. As the *San Francisco Examiner* reported:

> Julia "Butterfly" says she is so attuned to her host that she believes she has felt its tears with her bare feet and body. Butterfly [reported], "I was scared at first, and then I just started paying attention to the tree, drawing strength from the tree," she said. "I could see all her scars and wounds, from fires and lightning strikes. I was making a spiritual connection. . . . Eventually, I took my shoes off so I could feel the tree and started free climbing around," she said. When Pacific Lumber started logging the steepest part of the ridge and hauling logs out by helicopter, "I found myself crying a lot and hugging Luna and telling her I was sorry. . . . Then, I found out that I was being covered by sap pouring out of her body from everywhere, and I realized, 'Oh, my God, you're crying too.'"[65]

This article included Hill's animistic assertion that trees "know how to communicate feelings." The reporter also noted that Hill, with the exception of wearing wool, was a "vegan," consuming neither meat nor other animal products, in order to reduce animal suffering. In the years after her famous tree sit, Hill continued her work, blending activism with a fervent belief that activists must come from a loving place if they are to be effective.[66]

Hill was far from the only activist to report personal connections to nature during direct-action protests. Five years before Hill's experience, Alisha Little Tree told me of bonding with a redwood that she occupied during an eleven-day tree sit to prevent logging. Sitting on a massive redwood tree stump along a river in Northern California's Sinkyone Wilderness, she explained how her perceptions changed as a result of that experience:

> I stopped being a vegetarian after that tree sit because I connected with that tree so intensely . . . it has really changed my whole reality. Now I'm thinking of beings not as conscious creatures, but as life-force. There's a really strong life-force in all of us, and in this forest in these trees. Connecting to the tree is not [hesitating], it's like just being [pausing], it's not like you talk to the tree, because it can't hear, but there's this feeling, I don't know how to describe it, [it is], like a deep rootedness, very powerful, not superior to us, but certainly not inferior to us and more primitive or less evolved than us.[67]

When asked why this experience led her to renounce vegetarianism, she replied, "Because I just started to appreciate the incredible life-force in plants . . . and the line between animal and plants blurred. It's all just different forms of life-force." Little Tree and many other activists speak of epiphanies in nature, of feeling intensely the life-force that infuses and imbues all living things with value and that evokes feelings of awe and reverence.

Graham Innes, an Australian radical environmental activist, while buried up to his neck in an Australian logging road during a campaign to prevent logging there, had an experience that he felt connected him directly to the earth. He reported later "a slow dawning of awareness of a hitherto unknown connection—Earth bonding [when the Earth's] pulse became mine, and the vessel, my body, became the vehicle for her expression . . . it was as though nature had overtaken my consciousness to speak on her behalf."[68]

Other activists report experiencing the earth's sacred energies or life-force, or communication with nonhuman beings, during environmentalist campaigns. Some even engage in what they call "magical direct actions," where the goal is to seek, explore, and direct the sacred energy of the forest (itself an expression of the earth's energy) toward specific ends. In marked contrast to Jensen's angrier expressions, such action may involve activists even reaching out to their most bitter adversaries through a kind of *prayer-as-energy-manipulation* that seeks to focus, in an ecologically positive and healing way, what some of them consider to be the loving energy of the universe.

During the summer of 1997, for example, I spoke with three men involved in the direct-action defense of the Headwaters redwood forest in Northern California. A young man calling himself Reverend Fly spoke about some intense conflicts in the woods, asserting that "because we're unpredictable," the cops and loggers "are really scared of us. We walk and get there before they do in their trucks. They know how strong we are. . . . They know our motives come from another energy level. They don't grock [understand] that [we act] from love."[69]

In describing the spirituality of their activism, the men recounted conflicts in the woods as well as ritual circles at their activist encampments and how these helped them get in contact with the spirit or consciousness of the forest. Reverend Fly explained, "What we know about redwoods is that they sprout; they hold on to each other." Redwoods are "part of this continuous, sprouting, living being, or consciousness, that once covered millions of acres. And all of this knowledge has been chewed up and chased into small pockets." He then described experiences with other activists, including how during a meditative circle in the redwoods among "the tall ferns" the forest "echoes like a cathedral." On one such occasion, he recalled:

> I don't know what kind of woo [movement parlance for spirituality, in this case spiritual practice] we'd been engaged in at the time, but suddenly, this cold, icy breeze came through the camp, washed over our knees, and we heard a long rolling moan, and every one stopped talking—then afterward—we said—"did you hear that? That was no breeze." I didn't try to give it a name. There's lot of old energies, old pain, there, that I can't name. Their memory is fucking old. And lots of the spirits that have dwelled there a long time—they have a lot to say.

Another activist in the small circle that day went by the earth-name Goat. He used to be a Greenpeace direct-action expert but left that organization to pursue a more spiritual approach. Responding to Fly, he said, "I felt such [deep, forest] consciousness in that group—heavy consciousness. We were addicted to it. Talking about conjuring about things—we were even praying for [Charles] Hurwitz," referring to the Texas tycoon who controlled Maxxam Corporation and Pacific Lumber, the logging company they were fighting. Their activism was all about love and healing, Goat elaborated. "In the circle we'd sing out, 'We love you Hurwitz—we'll take you in here any time.' It was amazing, there was a pretty pure love and intent." Clearly, for these forest defenders, redwood forests are transformational and time in them is sacred. They believed that if they could somehow get their adversaries into the forest, they would be changed forever. As Fly put it, "Nobody can go in there and not be transformed."

For these activists, cultivating and promoting such spirituality is not narcissism, as some radical environmentalists have claimed—it is activism. Goat asserted that in Europe, spirituality changed consciousness fast enough to save the whales. When asked what he meant by spirituality, he answered, "It is honoring the universal power, the flow, the power far beyond me, [the power] that I exist in." Asked for his understanding, Fly replied that spirituality is "when I know what the trees are saying, when I know what my friends are thinking [its when] I and the people I'm with open ourselves to other energies or to a higher vibrational level. People call them all sorts of things, Ghosts. Fairies. Telepathy. It has [convinced me we are not] separate from each other, and from the rocks, and everything else."

Like all good mystics, Fly cautioned, "The more words I put on this the farther we can go from the reality I refer to." He then offered his spiritual prescription: what we need to do is "just sit down, shut up, breathe, have eye contact, touch . . . ," and falling silent, he put his hands on the earth.

Biocentric Religion

A concluding example underscores that radical environmentalism has sympathizers around the world among people who could never imagine lawbreaking to defend nature.

Paul Watson cofounded Greenpeace in 1972, leaving it in 1977 to create the more aggressive Sea Shepherd Conservation Society, which campaigns to defend marine life and ecosystems by trying to directly thwart those who hunt whales, dolphins, seal pups, and other marine creatures. Watson and his comrades sometimes use risky tactics, placing their bodies and boats between hunters and the hunted and otherwise interfering with the whalers, sometimes even sinking the whaling ships (while docked) or trying to disable whaling vessels by ramming them with their own ships.

Born in Toronto, Canada, in 1950, as a youth Watson felt his closest friends were the animals who lived nearby, and he has written that by age fifteen his earth consciousness was so intense that he "pledged allegiance not to Canada, the Church, or humanity, but to nature."[70] But one adulthood experience, during a confrontation with a Russian whaler in 1975, is especially noteworthy. After failing, in rolling seas, to prevent the harpooning of a huge sperm whale, Watson would later recall:

> The whale wavered and towered motionless above us. I looked up . . . into a massive eye the size of my fist—an eye that reflected back intelligence, an eye that spoke wordlessly of compassion, an eye that communicated that this whale could discriminate and understand what we had tried to do. . . .
>
> Ever so slowly, the whale fell back into the sea. As I watched the massive head sink beneath the swells, the flicker of life extinguished in the whale's eye. . . . On that day, I knew emotionally and spiritually that my allegiance lay with the whales first and foremost, over the interests of those humans who would kill them.[71]

Watson's version of the story is reminiscent of the experiences others, including Aldo Leopold, who report being transformed through empathic, eye-to-eye contact with animals.

Roaming the seas to prevent the slaughter of marine life is an expensive endeavor. To mount his campaigns, Watson has garnered donations from around the world as well as volunteers who pay their own way to be crew on his dangerous voyages. Watson attributes his success to his strategy of generating massive media coverage by engineering and recording confrontations, and using celebrity supporters to help publicize campaigns. He even became a celebrity himself when, in 2008, the cable television station Animal Planet began broadcasting *Whale Wars,* a series chronicling his ongoing antiwhaling campaign.[72] Watson believes, however, that he must do more than gain media attentions or prevail in specific confrontations; he must contribute to the kind of dramatic transformation of consciousness that radical environmentalists generally believe must occur if we are to reharmonize life on earth.

I once asked Watson to elaborate on his moral and religious beliefs, about which he had spoken from time to time but never expressed in writing.[73] His response in "A Call to Biocentric Religion" provides an excellent summary of the kind of dark green religion prevalent in radical environmental subcultures. Watson began by urging people to abandon the world's dominant religions, claiming that they promote and justify violence, bigotry, and anthropocentrism and focus "exclusively on the superiority and divinity of the human species." On the contrary:

> What we need if we are to survive is a new story, a new myth, and a new religion. We need to replace anthropocentrism with biocentrism. We need to construct a religion that incorporates all species and establishes nature as sacred and deserving of respect.
>
> Christians have denounced this idea as worshipping the creation and not the Creator. Yet in the name of the Creator, they have advocated the destruction of the creation. What is true however is that we can know the creation; we can see it, hear it, smell it, feel it and experience it. We can also nurture and protect it. . . .
>
> I reject the anthropocentric idea of custodianship. This is an idea that once again conveys human superiority, and quite frankly, we have always been lousy custodians.
>
> Religions are based on rules, and we already have the rules in place for the establishment of a religion based on nature. These are the basic Laws of Ecology. . . .
>
> The first is the Law of Diversity. The strength of an ecosystem is dependent upon its diversity. The greatest threat to the planet's living species in the present is the escalating destruction of biological diversity. The primary reason for this can be found in the next three laws.
>
> The second law is the Law of Interdependence. All species are interdependent upon each other. As Sierra Club founder John Muir once said, "When you tug on any part of the planet, you will find it intimately connected to every other part of the planet."
>
> The third law is the Law of Finite Resources. There are limits to growth in every species because there are limits to carrying capacity of every ecosystem.
>
> The fourth law of ecology is the Law that a Species must have Precedence over the interests of any individual. . . . This means that the rights of a species to survive must take precedence over the right of any individual or group to exploit the species beyond the law of finite resources.
>
> What does this mean for humanity? . . . [That] the protection, conservation, and preservation of the Earth should be the foremost human concern. We must look upon the Earth, her ecosystems and species as sacred. . . .
>
> We must develop a philosophy where a redwood tree is more sacred than a human-made religious icon, where a species of bird or butterfly is of more value and deserving of more respect than the crown jewels of a nation, and where the survival of a species of cacti or flower is more important than the survival of a monument to human conceit like the pyramids.
>
> With the laws of ecology as a foundation for a new biocentric, ecocentric worldview, we can then look at providing a sense of identity. Religious identity

has been primarily tribal, dividing people into groups or cults at odds with each other. A biocentric identity is something completely different because it is all encompassing.

An acceptance of interspecies equality allows a sense of planetary belonging. To be part of the whole is to be free of the alienation caused by an individual species like our own becoming divorced and alienated from the biospheric family of life.

With this revolutionary approach to forming a new religion, we have rules and we have a sense of belonging. Since the membership is multi-species and encompasses all ecosystems, there is no need for a church. The planet becomes its own church and the philosophy is uncontainable.

Watson continued by saying that a new story, "a reason to live and create and nurture" is needed as a ground for such a biocentric religion, and he asserted that many indigenous nations have such stories. The common thread in them is an "understanding of the connectedness of all things" and that all "the living beings of the past remain connected to the living beings of the future through the living beings of the present." This understanding of "Continuum," he said, is the key to a biocentric religion:

Born of the Earth, we return to the Earth. The soil beneath our feet contains the material reality of the ancestors of all species. Without the collective, expired lives of the past, there would be less soil. For this reason, the soil itself is our collective ancestry, and thus the soil should be as sacred to us.

The water of the Earth is the blood of the planet and within its immensity will be found the molecules of water, which once enlivened the cells of our ancestors of all species. The water you drink once coursed through the blood of the dinosaurs, or was drunk by Precambrian ferns, or was expelled in the urine of a mastodon. Water has utilized the lives of all living things as part of its planetary circulatory system. All life contains water. Therefore water is sacred.

The air that we breathe has passed through countless respiratory systems and thus has been chemically stabilized by plants and animals. Without the lives that have gone before, there would be no air to breathe. The life of the past has nurtured the atmosphere. Therefore the air is sacred.

In fact, the air, the water, and the soil form the trinity of sacredness in a biocentric perspective.

Our lives in the present should be sacred to the living beings of the future.

Watson concluded that by rejecting tribalism and anthropocentrism, and adopting a biocentric religion that understands and lives within the laws of ecology, "we will find ourselves on a planet living harmoniously with millions of other species who we can, and should, call fellow Earthlings."

This was a truly remarkable statement, first of all, because Watson recognized that religion is invented for specific purposes, something few religious practitioners themselves ever realize. It is also noteworthy as perhaps the best extant insider-penned summary of radical environmental religion. Watson's statement represents, moreover, another example of a self-conscious effort to ground religion and ethics in nature, both in one's personal experience *of* nature and in an understanding of its laws through science. It is also worth noting that Watson quoted John Muir in his statement, writing at the very time he was serving on the Sierra Club Board of Directors. This suggests that dark green religion, which finds perhaps its most fervent proponents in deep ecological and radical environmentalist subcultures, enjoys support in politically moderate sectors of the global environmentalist milieu as well.

The Shadow and Radical Environmentalism

Of course, radical environmentalists have been both feared and harshly criticized, and these critiques have religious, secular, and ethical dimensions. In the culture at large it is not uncommon to hear devotees of Abrahamic religions denouncing the environmental radicals and others engaged in nature-focused religion, casting them as spiritually dangerous and heretical, idolatrous in their worship of the creation rather than God. Politicians, law-enforcement officials, scholars, and many ordinary citizens decry what they judge to be illegal, violent, and antidemocratic tactics. Agents of the Federal Bureau of Investigation have asserted that radical environmentalists and animal rights activists (which they conflate) pose the foremost threat of domestic terrorism. Some antiterrorism researchers, novelists, and screenwriters ponder whether ecoradicals will deploy weapons of mass destruction to precipitate the collapse of civilization and reduce human numbers to a carrying capacity the earth can support. Still others fear that nature religions, including radical environmentalism, are ultimately misanthropic and harbor fascistic designs.[74] Given the incendiary tactics and rhetoric sometimes deployed by such activists, these fears are understandable. Yet given mounting evidence of the precipitous decline in earth's life-support systems, the apocalyptic expectations that fuel environmental resistance are also understandable.

The heart of dark green religion does not lie, however, in the tactics and strategies engaged in or supported by its various participants; among radical environmentalists and others engaged in dark green religion, there are diverse views about what is permissible and impermissible with regard to whether and when lawbreaking or violence should be risked and is morally acceptable.[75] The heart of dark green religion is to be found in the belief that everything in the biosphere is interdependent, intrinsically valuable, and sacred.

By now it should be clear that dark green religion exists, has many forms, and is increasingly global. But is it only found within environmentalist and conservationist subcultures? Or is it escaping such enclaves and providing a religious and ethical alternative more widely? Whether one is sympathetic toward dark green religion or fearful of it, these are important questions. Posed differently: how long is the shadow of dark green religion?

CHAPTER 5

Surfing Spirituality

On a sunny November day in 1997, I played hooky from a conference in San Diego, California. The surf was up and I was soon chatting with a young woman at a surf shop, deciding which board to rent. When she learned I was formerly an ocean lifeguard from the region, transplanted to Wisconsin, she exclaimed, "Whoa dude, no amount of money is worth living away from Mother Ocean."

The Hollywood motion picture *Point Break* (1991) was a campy thriller in which a band of surfers funded their global surf quest by robbing banks. Early in the film Keanu Reeves, acting as FBI Special Agent Johnny Utah, went to buy a surfboard as the first step in his effort to penetrate the surfing "tribe" and find the robbers. Utah explained to the teenager-clerk that he always wanted to learn to surf. The teenager replied, "It's never too late." Utah protested, "But I'm only twenty-five." The young evangelist responded, "I hope you stay with it, surfing's the source, it'll change your life, I swear to god." The movie continued with religious themes woven throughout. The leader of the bank-robbing surfers, for example, was named Bodhi—and this bodhisattva proclaimed a mystical gospel of surfing.

As surfing author Matt Warshaw put it, and as anyone experienced with surfing cultures can attest, surfing "is based in sport, but can drift into art, vocation and avocation, even religion."[1] Jay Moriarity in the *Ultimate Guide to Surfing* wrote similarly, that surfing is art, sport, and "SPIRITUAL because it's just you and Mother Nature."[2] In 2005 Brad Melekian even suggested that "surfing may be the next world religion."[3]

• • •

It does not take long in surf culture to see its spiritual nature. Melekian astutely observed that surfing resembles religion in important ways and he promoted surfing as a legitimate spiritual path. He contended, as well, that surfing can make one more compassionate toward both people and nature.

As the sport has spread so has this form of aquatic nature religion. In June 2006, I found a book in an Istanbul bookshop, translated from German into English by a German publisher. It began with the claim that surfing "has a spiritual aura that you only get once you've experienced it" and it "never will lose its soul and spirit, because the magic that envelops you when surfing is far too powerful."[4]

The ideas introduced in this chapter—that there is a mysterious magic in surfing that can only be apprehended directly through the experience; that surfing fosters self-realization; that commercialization of the practice is a defiling act but that even such acts cannot obviate its spiritual power; that surfing can lead to a life characterized by compassion toward other living beings—have been expressed repeatedly and increasingly within surfing subcultures. Indeed, a significant and increasing part of the evolving, global surfing world can be understood as a form of dark green religion, in which sensual experiences constitute its sacred center. These experiences, and the cultural enclaves in which people reflect upon them, foster understandings of nature as powerful, transformative, healing, and sacred. Such perceptions, in turn, often lead to ethical action in which Mother Nature, and especially its manifestation as Mother Ocean, is considered sacred and worthy of reverent care. Many surfers also develop feelings of communion and kinship with the nonhuman animals they encounter during their practice. These experiences sometimes take on an animistic ethos and lead surfers to activism on behalf of marine ecosystems and particular species.

Soul Surfing

Some of those who experience surfing as religious call themselves *soul surfers*, a term that can be traced to the 1970s in both the United States and Australia.[5] There is neither definitive data on the number of surfers globally nor on the proportion of surfers who consider their practice to be spiritual or religious.[6] That many surfers do regularly discuss the spiritual dimensions of their sport does, however, suggest that a significant proportion of the global surfing community considers surfing to be a religious practice.

The *Ultimate Guide to Surfing,* for example, asserted that surfing is "a powerful, elemental activity" involving "the pure act of riding on a pulse of nature's energy," which brings contentment and also the "magic that only comes from spending time on the moving canvas."[7] Explaining what this has to do with "soul," Chris Gallagher added that the key is how the experience connects the surfer to nature, its energies, and its wild creatures, expressing the spirituality of belonging and connection that typifies dark green religion.[8] Another soul surfer claimed that surfing "puts you one with nature, clears your soul of bad vibes, and can make you a more humble person."[9]

Yet surfers are also known for sexism, territoriality and even violence, as practitioners battle to get the best wave or prevent newcomers from paddling out in places they consider special.[10] Is it possible, then, that surfing fosters territorial feelings toward sacred places in which only some people are considered worthy to enter, and others are infidels or desecrating agents who must be excluded and suppressed?

By examining surfing subcultures with the lenses typically deployed by scholars of religion, the question of whether soul surfing fosters humility and connection with nature or exclusionary attitudes and behaviors can be clarified. Such analysis explores the role of myths, symbols, leaders, texts, technologies, and institutions, as well as devotee beliefs and practices, including those having to do with natural forces and living things.

Origin Myths

Few elements of a religious worldview are more critical than cosmogony—the narrative understanding about how the world came to be. Among soul surfers there is no common story about the origins of the biosphere. There is, however, significant agreement regarding how surfing emerged, assumed a religious character, was suppressed for religious reasons, and began a revival in the early twentieth century.

Glenn Hening, who in 1984 founded the environmentalist Surfrider Foundation and assembled the team of surfer visionaries who would develop the organization, began during the late 1980s to explore the possibility that ancient Peruvians were the first surfers, basing his speculations on their art and architecture, which he began to learn about during a surfing trip.[11] Ben Finney, a Southern Californian surfer, ocean lifeguard, and anthropologist, found evidence of ancient Peruvian wave riding that used small reed-woven boats as early as 3000 B.C.E.[12]

Until these suppositions, a somewhat less speculative origin myth, based on extant documentary records, had gained currency within surfing cultures. This narrative traced the origins of surfing to Eden-like Polynesian paradises, where people were at home in and at play with the forces and spirits of nature.[13] For a millennium the people of the South Pacific rode waves on small boards. The practice was highly ritualized, the story continues, and this extended to stand-up board surfing, which developed later, perhaps first in Hawai'i. Before trees were felled to construct boards, for example, the Kahuna placed a fish offering by the tree and prayers were said. Additional rites were performed at the board's dedication, all of which reflected an animistic spirituality.[14]

The arrival of Captain James Cook and other Europeans in 1778, however, with their guns, diseases, alcohol, and "strange new religion[,] led to the cultural implosion of the indigenous Hawaiian civilization," including the near extinction of surfing culture.[15] The surf-focused culture came under direct assault with the arrival of missionaries, beginning in 1820, who sought to destroy what they considered to be its pagan dimensions. This dark period of cultural genocide and deterioration almost ended the sport, according to surfing historians, and by the late nineteenth century surfing was rarely practiced.[16]

Duke Kahanamoku and the Resurrection of Surfing

After Jack London and other adventurers began to write about the practice in the late nineteenth century, however, and commercial interests saw its potential as a tourist attraction, a surfing renaissance began. This occurred first in Hawai'i and soon after in California, where surfers adopted much of surfing's Polynesian/Hawai'ian ethos. This revitalization was driven in part by George Freeth, the Irish Hawai'ian surfer lionized by Jack London in a 1907 magazine article. Freeth later moved to California, becoming a surfing icon as well as the state's first professional lifeguard.[17] But by most accounts, the most decisive figure in the revitalization and globalization of the sport was the charismatic full-blooded Hawai'ian swimmer and surfer, Duke Kahanamoku.

After swimming his way to an Olympic gold metal in 1912, Kahanamoku demonstrated surfing to enthusiastic crowds on both coasts of North America and then in Australia. Glenn Hening, who later in his activist career cofounded the Groundswell Society, commented, "The Duke promoted surfing around the world, and modern surfers see him as the embodiment of an ethical spirituality that may be just this side of a religious belief system."[18] Hening and many other soul surfers trace surfing's "aloha spirit" to Kahanamoku. Among soul surfers, discussion of surfing's aloha spirit is sometimes accompanied by understandings of the word *aloha* as originally having to do with one's frontal presence and breath, and with the exchange of breath or spirit, and even the breath of life.[19] For some surfers, and the native Hawai'ians they are inspired by and with whom they feel affinity, the expression of aloha is indeed as much a spiritual blessing as a salutation or goodbye. As Kekuhi Kealiikanakaole, a native Hawai'ian scholar explained, when I asked her about the meaning of Aloha:

> "Alo" means your frontal presence. So when we say, "he alo a he alo" we mean face to face. "Ha" means breath. The importance of this word . . . is that when each of us breathe those cavities that we use to have air enter and leave are the same cavities with which we share the breath of a friend, neighbor, relative or acquaintance. That is the meaning. And surfing, well for the local surfer guy, it's his/her daily spiritual experience, a sort of reconnection or meditation. On another level, the ocean for us is Kanaloa, or deep knowing and ancestral memories. This is why we need the salt water for cleansing, whether it's a sea bath or just a stroll.[20]

There are clear affinities between such ideas and dark green spiritualities of connection, including those that understand wind and waters as holy.

In the wake of Kahanamoku's travels, the mainstream of surfing evolved as a self-consciously "tribal" subculture in California and Australia, eventually expanding to other continents. As author Drew Kampion observed, as surf culture spread it maintained a Polynesian ethos in its rituals, language, symbols, lifestyle, and spirituality.[21] The ritualizing mentioned even included sacrifices (usually of real or model surfboards in bonfires) and prayers to Mother Ocean to call forth waves, and such rituals were loosely based on what was known or surmised about Polynesian and Hawai'ian rites.[22]

Tom Blake: Kahanamoku Apostle

Surfing historians credit Tom Blake (1902–1994) with the extension of Hawai'ian-flavored surfing spirituality to California. Born in northern Wisconsin, Blake saw a newsreel about surfing a decade later, met Duke Kahanamoku in a Michigan movie theater lobby as an eighteen-year-old, and soon afterward moved to Los Angeles to pursue the sport. He eventually revolutionized surfing by inventing lighter, hollow surfboards, thereby making surfing easier and more popular. Blake also became deeply involved in both lifeguarding and surfing subcultures in California, Hawai'i, and Florida before returning to Wisconsin in 1967. There he wrote the animistically titled "Voice of the Wave," which was published in *Surfing* magazine in 1969.[23] For its time the essay was remarkably innovative. Blake found a divine force in all of the waves in the universe, including ocean waves, concluding that "nature is synonymous with God."[24] In this essay and a subsequent one titled "The Voice of the Atom," Blake expressed reverence for the sea and a biocentric kinship ethics, which was also the ground of his vegetarianism and belief in the equality of all peoples.[25] He also articulated a metaphysics in which the atom was equated with the soul, and a belief that "even when we die, we are never lost, but revert back to the kingdom of the atom, nature, or God."[26] Blake here was articulating a kind of Gaian Naturalism akin to that found in many of those already discussed, wherein science and religion are reconciled in a pantheistic naturalism. He sometimes put his faith simply in this way: "Nature = God."[27]

Blake's spiritual message was not lost on soul surfers. For Kampion, Blake "enlivened the essential surfer's philosophy of respect—for others, for history, for the power of nature. . . . He believed that it was all God. The intrinsic sustaining balance of the natural world is self-evident [to] . . . each surfer. If you ride waves long enough and keep your eyes and heart open, you get it."[28] Kampion accurately read Blake's spiritual epistemology, one shared by many soul surfers, that the sacredness of nature will naturally occur to surfing's open-hearted practitioners. Through such interpretations, Blake became a patron saint to the devotees of the surfing cult, as did Kahanamoku.

A biography of Blake well illustrates perceptions of him as a surfing saint-guru.[29] In a review of it the author and surfboard shaper Dave Parmenter agreed, asserting that Blake was worthy of being at the right hand of Duke Kahanamoku in surfing's guru pantheon:

When all the waves had been ridden . . . what looms above it all is Blake's unique spirituality. He formulated a belief system that was predicated on the idea of "Nature = God," and he practiced this faith out-of-doors in what he called "The Blessed Church Of The Open Sky."

Some argue that surfing is a religion. If so, the great Hawaiian surfer and Olympic swimming champion Duke Kahanamoku would certainly have to be seen as surfing's messiah or prophet, and from the vantage point of the present day we can see that Tom Blake became his chief apostle. . . .

The resulting friendship, with Duke as the catalyst, helped to accelerate a modern rebirth of the Hawaiian sport of kings, which had been in a state of lethargy brought on by the decimation of the Hawaiian people and their culture by Western encroachment. . . . The missionaries brought their western God to Hawaii, but in the end it was surfing missionaries such as Duke Kahanamoku and Tom Blake who had the last word. Not only is surfing more widespread than many established religions; it has also proved to be a far more peaceful, benevolent, and inclusive "faith" than most. Aside from isolated pockets of territoriality, surfers of many races and languages co-exist with a degree of tolerance and harmony that should be envied by many world faiths.[30]

Parmenter also expressed a naturalistic metaphysics of interconnection and profound environmental concern reminiscent of other practitioners of dark green religion.[31]

Parmenter's perspective illustrates the ways in which many soul surfers had come to understand the narrative cosmogony of surfing by the early twenty-first century. Parmenter also noticed that surf culture had many of the things that usually constitute a religion (beliefs, saints, ethical ideals), and he had a sense that surfing had become a globalizing religious movement. Perhaps most remarkable, he expressed faith in the beneficence of this movement, that it could even play a role in promoting world peace and environmentalism, while still acknowledging that it had a shadow side.[32]

The emergence of such a perspective is difficult to imagine apart from the influence of other sources of dark green religion in American culture, as well as without the profound changes in religion that began largely in the 1960s and that decisively transformed the West's religious land- and seascape. Surfing had become a bricolage, incorporating ideas far and wide.

Surfing into the 1960s

During the 1960s cultural ferment, surfing's spiritual revival intensified as it fused with new religious and political currents, blending antiestablishment and antihierarchal attitudes with holistic metaphysics that were connected to psychedelics and to religions originating in Asia, found in indigenous societies, in contemporary Paganism, and in America's own metaphysical traditions. The impact was that surfing, for some, became a part of a wider American turn toward nature religion, and some of this assumed characteristics common in dark green religion.

The influence of the psychedelic age was then and can still be discerned in surfing cultures. Graphics from surf magazines, surf-film posters, surf-music album covers, and designs on surfboards and other elements of surfing's material culture—especially those dating to the 1960s and 1970s—illustrate the sport's psychedelic dimension.[33] Beginning in the late 1960s, surf movies revealed that the sport had "proudly and enthusiastically joined the counterculture," overtly promoting LSD and other drugs, including as spiritual aids.[34] The titles and advertising copy on film posters show the development of nature spirituality in the sport and how this was sometimes intertwined with the psychedelic era. The film *The Natural Art* (1969) was "an organic 90 minutes of positive vibrations." *Pacific Vibrations* (1970) resembled "Woodstock on a wave," and its famous poster was crafted by Rick Griffin, one of San Francisco's best-known psychedelic-era illustrators, who also produced cartoons in surfing magazines that depicted the sport as a mystical, nature-bonding experience.[35]

This is unsurprising because two of the most perennial themes in surf movies are surfing as an ecstatic and mystical experience and the pursuit of perfect waves. During the 1960s and 1970s, surf movies had not yet gone Hollywood; they were usually shown at civic auditoriums, fraternal clubs, and other small venues, where they were greeted with riotous enthusiasm, reminding those present of the experiences they all pursued. Having seen surf movies in such places, it is easy for me to retroactively apply scholarly lenses learned in part from the anthropologist Victor Turner, and to view these events as powerful ritual forms that produce and/or reinforce the perception that surfing induces liminal experiences. These events also fostered a collective identity, often expressed with references to the surfing "tribe." Turner can help us understand why some prominent soul surfers today suggest that surf film viewing is best when it is a collective experience, held in intimate, noncommercial venues.[36]

In addition to reinforcing the "stoked" feeling that surfing brings, surf films reprised the dream of Edenic return common within surfing cultures. The most famous surf film, Bruce Brown's *Endless Summer* (1963), depicted a global search for pristine paradises as well as "the perfect wave." According to Matt Warshaw, the film became "the sport's finest emotional and spiritual envoy," explaining even to those who had never surfed how surfing *feels*.[37] Similarly, *Morning of the Earth* (1972), which was produced by the Australian Albert Falzon, focused on surfing in Australian and Indonesian locales constructed as paradises. Its poster described the movie as "a fantasy of surfers living in three unspoiled lands and playing in nature's ocean." *Surfer* magazine's review explained that the film was "about the Garden of Eden, plus waves, minus serpent."[38]

Almost every issue of the hundreds of surfing magazines reprise the Edenic theme, showing artistic depictions and photographs of pristine beaches, beautiful waves, and ocean-loving communities. Articles often feature pilgrimages to such places and the pursuit of harmonious relationships with the people and habitats there. The two surfing magazines that best represent this genre are the beautifully produced *Surfer's Journal* (from 1992), which eschews (defiling) advertising, and *Surfer's Path* (from 1997). The latter magazine especially insists that the "surfer's path" must also involve the quest for environmental sustainability, announcing in 2004 that it would henceforth use only "100% post-consumer recycled paper [and] non-GMO soy-based inks." In 2005 it established Green Wave Awards to recognize environmental initiatives within the surf industry.[39] This magazine also explained its title by referring to spiritual pilgrimage: "Who knows what it means to be a surfer? Perhaps it's something in our exposure and connection to the passions of nature that makes our lives wildly different from those of the uninitiated. One thing we know for sure: we want those perfect waves. . . . Like the pilgrim or the holy man, we follow our own roads to our own perfection. Call it want you will, we call it *The Surfer's Path*."[40]

Such statements have much in common with the long-standing depiction of the sublime in nature in American and European landscape art, which is one of the major tributaries of dark green religion. Such art depicts natural habitats as sublime places and pilgrimages to them as a way to discover one's authentic self.[41]

Drew Kampion, twenty-four years old in 1968, began to make his own contributions to the construction of surfing as a nature religion when he became the editor of *Surfer* magazine.[42] According to Matt Warshaw, who also took a turn editing *Surfer*, Kampion "led the effort to transform the industry-leading magazine from a . . . sports publication into an innovative, mischievous, drug-influenced counterculture journal."[43] With the books he produced in subsequent years, and his contributions as an editor and writer for *Surfer's Path* a generation later, Kampion played an especially influential role in promoting surfing as a practice with religious value, also arguing the view common among soul surfers that surfing can put human follies and tragedies in perspective and can help people find peace of mind in a turbulent and troubled world. In diverse ways, including in their motion pictures, soul surfers articulate the peace and equanimity they find nowhere else than in the ocean.[44]

Like many in America and beyond during the 1960s and 1970s, some surfers were drawn to religions originating in Asia, which grew popular among those seeking alternatives to what they saw as a materialistic and violent mass culture. Most famous among such surfers was Gerry Lopez, who had what many considered the most elegant surfing style of all time and who was one of the first who learned to "rip" (surf awesomely) the Banzai Pipeline in Hawai'i. His image sitting in lotus position appeared repeatedly in surfing publications, beginning in 1968, as he became known for his Zen-like equanimity in monster surf.[45] Reflecting on this era and his surfer friends of the time, Lopez later recalled, "We became hippies and got into yoga and that whole self realization thing and started to realize that those moments when you were completely focused on riding a wave are actually kind of spiritual . . . religious moments."[46] Lopez led explorations of discovery to paradises he likened to heaven, in Indonesia and beyond. Indeed, surf travel to pristine, untrammeled surfing Shangri-las is a form of pilgrimage that has long been a centerpiece of surf culture.

Asian religion has continued to infuse surf culture and spirituality, as seen in art published in surfing magazines as well as in surfing-themed decor. Another example of surfing being linked to Asian religion is found in the views of Marilyn Edwards, the publisher of *Wahine,* a surfing magazine that caters to female surfers. She believes that surfing, as a Zen-like experience, is not only a male province. Blending surfing spirituality with an ecofeminist sensibility, she said, "When I see a female on a wave, I see the connectedness with the wave. Women's emotional energy is about unity. The masculine energy is more independent, more 'me' out front. And that is not true for all men, but sometimes men surf 'on' the wave, whereas women surf 'with' the wave."[47] Surfing is not about achievement, she continued, "It is about balance, blend and unity. . . . The Zen of surfing is about being mindful of the energy you are joining forces with, not conquering it." Among other things, Edwards was articulating the spirituality of connection and belonging shared by many soul surfers.[48]

Surfing Environmentalism

For some surfers this sense of belonging to nature represents an important dimension of the experience. When such feelings were incubated in the environmental age, they inspired kinship feelings with nonhuman organisms and environmentalist action.

Overt surfing environmentalism began as early as 1961 when Save Our Surf, the first surfing environmental organization, was founded in Hawai'i.[49] It was formed to stop a development that would have ruined a surfing break, but it soon developed an environmentalist agenda. In Southern California in 1984, surfer-activists formed the Surfrider Foundation, initially to prevent the destruction of prime surfing breaks and to promote the positive dimensions of surfing culture. Like Save Our Surf, however, Surfrider soon developed a clear environmentalist identity, even adding as a primary principle a concern for biodiversity.[50] This development was in large part due to Tom Pratte, one of Surfrider's cofounders, who had developed an affinity for Arne Naess, deep ecology, and radical environmentalism as an environmental studies student at California State University, Humboldt.[51] This was the campus where one of the early scholarly proponents of deep ecology taught, the sociology professor Bill Devall. Pratte hoped to shape Surfrider so that it would become effective at protecting marine ecosystems. By 2008 the foundation boasted fifty thousand members and more than eighty chapters and affiliated groups around the world.

Despite its avowed environmentalism, however, in 1994 a number of individuals split from Surfrider, complaining that it was insufficiently aggressive in defense of nature. They formed the Surfers' Environmental Alliance, borrowing its ecocentric mission statement directly from Aldo Leopold (demonstrating further the range of his influence), declaring that their goal was to "preserve the integrity, stability and beauty of the biotic community."[52] They nevertheless stressed that they still respected their comrades at Surfrider and considered themselves all part of the same tribe.[53]

In 2001, Glenn Hening led another start-up effort, cofounding the Groundswell Society with two surfer colleagues. The society celebrates indigenous cultures and their connection to the sea, evoking images of a past and hoped-for paradise in which people would live in harmony with nature. Hening sought to reprise the aloha spirit of the sport, which he felt had been marred by commercialism and violence. His passions extended to a desire to help the surfing community better appreciate and develop the best of its own culture, including its spirituality.[54]

There appear to be a number of affinities between surfing and dark green religion. The sport has a sacred story wherein an earlier, ecologically harmonious culture, which was spiritually attuned to nature, was nearly exterminated during the colonial mission period. Surfing was revived and spread globally by charismatic spiritual leaders during the twentieth century, leading many surfers to increasingly assume a religious and environmentalist identity. Some of them drew on the same sources that undergird other forms of dark green religion. One study even found a positive correlation between the length of time as a surfer and environmentalist concern.[55]

Surfing spirituality is, of course, grounded primarily in the experience of surfing and the often-ritualized behaviors associated with it. This includes the construction and aesthetic embellishment of the materials needed for the practice, which symbolize and express the surfer's identity.

Ritual and Religion

Surfing's most important ritual dimension is rising at dawn to greet the sun, waves, and sea creatures. The practice also has a collective if irregular service, involving attendance at surf films, which reminds surfers of the experience and reinforces tribal identity. Other identity-expressing and solidarity-promoting adornments, objects, and practices are prevalent: surfers read and scatter surf magazines about their homes, mark their automobiles with surfing symbols and slogans, decorate their houses with surf and nature-themed art, listen to surf music, and wear Hawai'ian shirts or dresses or clothing covered with ritual objects (like surfboards).

As we have seen, some surfers have come to see their practice as religious. Some arrive at this understanding by recognizing themselves and their subculture after reading or hearing such an analysis. After I posted online a draft article about surfing spirituality and invited surfers to comment, for example, I received numerous messages expressing approval.

I also received a request from *Drift* magazine editor Howard Swanwick to publish excerpts. When my article appeared, Swanwick explained his rationale for featuring it: "For most of my life it seemed that religious ideals are nothing more than conjecture, but then I started surfing. I have come to understand that my religion is nature, just as Blake discovered. . . . Bron Taylor's piece captured my imagination, and also summarized my own thoughts toward religion and secular beliefs."[56] Matt Walker, a senior editor of *Surfing*, read my piece and reacted in a way similar to Swanwick. He later called for an interview. In the article he subsequently wrote, he further buttressed my argument that surfing has a strong religious dimension:

> In the absence of all other forms of worship, surfing has become my religion. My rock. My go-to source for solace and celebration. A way to track time and form social bonds and—most importantly—a sanctuary where I feel a strong spiritual connection to something ultimately unknowable. Where, I find myself every once in a while—for no special reason—looking skyward and saying "thanks" to whatever strange cosmic forces wait behind it all. And, as weird as that sounds to some people, I know I'm not alone. In fact, I'm less alone than ever.[57]

This was both a personal confession and an observation from deep within the subculture to the effect that surfing was increasingly being understood as religious. Quoting widely from my article and our interview, Walker found "cool" the idea that surfing could be called "aquatic nature religion" and commented that after 150 years of "being told surfing was sinful," surfers had been "screaming for someone to recognize our favorite pagan ritual as a legitimate act of worship." Another illuminating passage reinforces that insiders increasingly recognize the religious dimensions of their practice: "Taylor's manifesto . . . is . . . the greatest validation of surfing's spiritual value by outside sources, a trend that's been on the rise for the past 10 to 15 years, as more new humans enter the water seeking another action sport thrill—and find themselves leaving somehow reborn."[58]

These two surfing-magazine editors, Swanwick and Walker, clearly want to promote an understanding of surfing as religion. Indeed, Walker confessed his own belief and worries about its possible shadow side—the territorial feelings and sense of superiority over nonsurfers and less practiced surfers that is common in surfing cultures. He then wrote, as have other soul surfers, that surfers should labor to teach the best of their spiritual traditions and to be more inclusive. He concluded by urging his readers to "invite everyone into our church." For, "if you—like me—believe surfing is a spiritual connection and whatever created this universe doesn't exclude one solitary soul, then you have a moral obligation to live out that belief."[59]

These sentiments expressed by Swanwick and Walker suggest that understanding surfing as religious is not something I have concocted. It is, rather, a phenomenon I have observed and with which some surfers identify. Moreover, at least some surfing spirituality is dark green and has inspired surfing environmentalism. In this light it is unsurprising that an increasing number of the nearly four hundred surfing magazines published globally aspire to publish in environmentally friendly ways.

The Experience of Surfing

It is the sensuous *experience* of surfing, however, that is the root of its religious ethos. For some surfers, such experience leads to feelings of humility, belonging, connection, and a reverence for life. Surfers also report that the practice can lead to personal ecstatic experience, healing, life purpose, and can even shed light on "the meaning of life."[60] Such is the rhetoric of surfing subcultures. Many surfers refer to the sea as Mother Ocean, just as the *wahine* did that day in a San Diego surf shop.[61] *Mother Ocean* as a trope goes back at least to *Surfer* magazine, with the beginning in 1970 of its environmentalist "For Our Mother Ocean" column.[62] Mother Ocean has become a metaphor for intimacy with the sea, functioning like *Mother Earth* does for terrestrial participants in dark green religion.

A segment from the movie *Five Summer Stories* (1972) illustrates the point. After footage of surfers both riding and wiping out on big waves that break over a reef at the famous Banzai Pipeline in Hawai'i, the film turned to more graceful surfing on smaller waves, as the background music changed from dramatic and energetic to melodic and gentle. These shifts seemed designed to evoke the sublime as the narrator's voice intoned, "On smaller days, Pipeline is the perfect place for intimate relationships with Mother Ocean." Here is the heart of surfing spirituality for many—its connection to Mother Ocean understood as a beneficent, personal presence. This is arguably a form of Gaian spirituality.

Other surfing neologisms, such as the exclamation "cowabunga!" and references to being "stoked," express the joy if not ecstasy that can accompany surfing. Such terminology testifies to the power of the practice. So does surf writing, which repeatedly returns to the experience of wave riding, understanding it as the sensual center of the sport. This practice does what many religions purport to do, namely, it transforms consciousness and facilitates the development of an authentic, awakened self. Some of the most dramatic examples of heightened consciousness are what happens perceptually in dangerous situations, especially when a surfer is riding "in the tube" of a large hollow wave. Such situations intensely focus one's attention, forcing one to truly "live in the moment." This kind of presence is a centerpiece of certain religions originating in Asia (especially Zen and some other forms of Buddhism). But it is also an idea that New Age subcultures have appropriated. Living in the moment is believed to bring peace, wisdom, and divine purpose.

Such notions are often equated with a Zen state of mind, as Gerry Lopez did in a *Surfer* magazine interview: "To be truly successful at riding a wave we're approaching a Zen state of mind . . . and you're in the pure moment. Other parts of your life might be in shambles, but because you're tapping into the source you're truly happy."[63] Lopez did not define what he meant by "the source." Neither did the surf shop youth who urged Agent Utah to find this source and "change his life" by getting in touch with it. Yet one can surmise that it has something to do with the source of life, however differently this can be understood, and that Lopez and the young surfer would both agree that connecting with this source is part of the surfing experience. Not incidentally, Agent Utah did discover the joy and peace of surfing and at the end of the film left his mundane existence as a law-enforcement officer to follow the surfer's path.

What is it about surfing that gives it a religious aura? Joseph Price, in an article analyzing the religious dimensions of outdoor recreational practices (including surfing), drew on a study by the research psychologist Mihaly Csikszentmihalyi, who concluded that there are characteristics of peak experiences that are commonly interpreted as religious and that are similar in diverse cultures. Csikszentmihalyi used the word *flow* to describe these experiences. He claimed that they "usually occur when a person's body or mind is stretched to its limits in a voluntary effort to accomplish something difficult and worthwhile."[64] For Csikszentmihalyi, and Price who drew upon his study, flow is "the state in which people are so involved in an activity that nothing else seems to matter; the experience itself is so enjoyable that people will do it even at great cost."[65]

Surfers who find their pastime addictive might well find this study interesting as they wonder why they are willing to assume its inherent risks. Jay Moriarity found part of the answer in the way surfing transforms consciousness. For this he offered a naturalistic explanation of fear, understanding it as an adaptive form of evolution: "A good dose of fear is soothing for the human psyche. When the brain detects danger, the human body sends out norepinephrine to every part of the body. Once this danger has passed, the body sends out dopamine to the brain, a pleasurable chemical, as a way to congratulate the brain for surviving. These chemicals are what make people want to surf big waves."[66]

Although Moriarity found this naturalistic explanation plausible, he nevertheless labeled surfing spiritual. Whatever brain chemistry may be involved in what surfers crave (which cognitive science will likely illuminate further in coming years), certain patterns are reflected in how surfers describe their experience.[67] This is certainly true when surfers recall dangerous surfing, as mentioned above, that can call into question one's ordinary sense of time: "Riding in the tube is by far the most frightening and exhilarating part of surfing. One top surfer in the 1970's, Shaun Thomson [sic], summed up its indescribable delights by saying that 'time slows down in the tube.'"[68] These words of South African surfing champion Shaun Tomson have been repeated often, as have similar formulations, whether in conversation, publications, or in online discussion groups. Asked how he could stay calm in the tube, for example, Gerry Lopez replied, "The faster I go out there the slower things seem to happen."[69] Glenn Hening concluded that even though surfing sometimes involves fear and pain, it is "from the unique and extraordinary vision while riding inside a perfect wave [that] the mystic kernel of the religious in surfing grows."[70]

From the many descriptions of surfers' experience, it is easy to see why they make such statements. It is also unsurprising that many surfers refer to surfing as going to church, or use other religious terminology, thus construing their experiences as spiritual or religious.

Connection, Communion, and Healing

As with most dark green religion, for soul surfers their practice evokes feelings of belonging and communion with other living beings, with the earth's environmental systems, and even with the universe itself. They also often believe that such connections are transformative and healing. Mandy Caruso, for example, wrote a story in which Mother Ocean washed away her fears and became an agent of healing by bringing her a sea turtle as an oracle of hope during a time when she was preparing for a mastectomy to treat breast cancer. In a *Surfer's Path* article, which was accompanied by paintings depicting her surfing with animal companions, Caruso related her story with words that demonstrated the importance of animistic Hawai'ian themes among surfers:

In the Hawaiian culture, all ohanas, all families, have guiding spirits that watch over them. These spirits, usually dead ancestors, take visible form in the shape of animals: sharks, owls, turtles. The belief is that . . . at crucial moments . . . your guiding spirit, your amakua, will appear to you, and you will know you're being given a message, a warning, or a blessing.

Now, being haole (white) and a malahini (not born Ka'maaina—in Hawaii), I liked the idea of the amakua, but I never expected to have one.

Yet, years before I learned to board surf, in the darkness before dawn, I would rise and drive to a little cove with the gentlest, most caressing bodysurfing waves in the world. . . . One morning, as I was . . . reveling in the luscious velvet caress of the waves, a head suddenly popped out of the foam beside me. My fast-beating heart caught in my throat as a large turtle floated to the surface of the water. His ancient gaze considered me for moments that seemed like eternities. It was as if the Earth herself had come to look at me.

Long, long the turtle looked at me, and I looked at the turtle. I heard a sound, knew a wave was coming, and glanced out at the entrance of the cove. I saw it would be a good, surfable wave, and glanced back at the turtle.

Still the turtle stayed right beside me, looking, watching, waiting.

The wave came, I leapt into it . . . and the turtle surfed right alongside me, in perfect position. Wave after wave we rode together that glittering, blue dawn, and the turtle stayed as close to me as my outstretched arm.[71]

The rest of Caruso's story described how she received strength and courage from her aquatic friend, and she concluded with gratitude to the ocean for her healing. Caruso thus found communion with another being through eye-to-eye contact and believed she received healing from nature, reprising the theme that the ocean and sea creatures can bring healing, serenity, and even ecstatic experience.

Many soul surfers believe that nature in general and Mother Ocean in particular can assist with physical and psychological healing.[72] Keith Glendon wrote similarly about a teenaged surfing star, Chad Compton, who was sent into a life-threatening coma after a skateboarding accident. Glendon described how the surfing tribe sent prayers and "healing vibes," while appealing "to the spirit of the sea," after which the teenager awoke and soon returned to the sea.[73] As Glendon put the credo-like moral of the story: "The sea holds a magic for those of us who know her. A magic so simple, pure and powerful it works as an unseen force in our souls. We're drawn to her. The spirit of the sea moves in us as we move within her. . . . The sea brings comfort, solace, release and escape. The sea brings healing. The spirit of the sea, for some of us, is the very essence of life."

Surfing-related healing may be more than physical or psychological, however, as Colleen McGloin argued in her study of surfing cultures in Australia. She described a documentary produced by aboriginal surfers that depicts an indigenous surfing contest, which was sponsored by the international surf company Billabong. According to McGloin, the film *Surfing the Healing Wave* (1999) revealed "a difference in philosophy and practice, both in conceptions of the beach and in the practice of surfing" between aboriginal and mainstream surfers.[74] In comparison to surf films produced by white surfers, there was less emphasis on competition, surfing shots, and beautiful women. Instead, there were pictures of families and children, earnest discussion of aboriginal struggles and land rights, and respectful depiction of rituals that took place. McGloin concluded that the event and the film contributed to personal and cultural healing, helping aboriginal "blackfellas" (a term used by aboriginals in Australia to refer to themselves) get back in touch with their cultures and turn away from destructive white ways.

McGloin also recorded how the aboriginal surfer Dhinawan G. contrasted his own surfing culture with that of "whitefellas": "When Aboriginal people are in the ocean, they know they are in their country. They belong to it. They don't own it. . . . Surf rage? What's that about, that's white man's culture. We know there is always another wave. Surfing's about being part of the wave. I have a shark tattoo on my body. This is . . . to remind me that the ocean is superior to me and that I shouldn't try to conquer it."[75] With these words, Dhinawan expressed both a spirituality of belonging and the kind of humility that corresponds to nonanthropocentric environmental ethics. His thoughts seemed to echo that of an earlier indigenous surfer, Duke Kahanamoku: "You know, there are waves coming in all the time, you don't have to worry about that. Just take your time—wave come. Let the other guys go; catch another wave."[76] Both Dhinawan and McGloin seemed unaware, however, that many nonindigenous surfers would applaud what she found in that aboriginal event and would wholeheartedly agree with the sentiments expressed by Dhinawan. Many nonindigenous surfers have drawn surfing-related ethics from Kahanamoku's aloha spirit—including surfing historian Matt Warshaw, who has promoted Kahanamoku's views; and Glenn Hening, whose Groundswell Society organizes events and programs that embody many of the virtues that McGloin found among aboriginal surfers.

Another long-term surfer who demonstrates such affinities is Pierce Flynn, who earned a doctorate in semiotics and served as executive director of the Surfrider Foundation from 1995 to 1999. Between 1996 and 1999 he also produced three *Music for Our Mother Ocean* CDs to raise funds for Surfrider. In 2001 Flynn was interviewed by Hening, who asked him about his best surfing experience. It had occurred only a short time before, Flynn said, and he elaborated:

> While surfing after time spent in the Sierra Nevada Mountains, I was mindful of how that snowmelt had fed the ocean nearby. I felt the Chumash Ancestors present somehow.[77] I felt appreciative to be alive. As I rode beautiful, rolling waves I noticed the moon starting to reflect in the wave faces and even on the droplets of my board. I felt stoned as a gopher, but it was a natural high, I joked pleasantly with the other surfers in the water and it felt like aloha ohana.
>
> My best surfing experiences are those ongoing moments, like this one, where I feel and intuit/think everything together and the eternal now emerges. I want everybody to somehow receive the benefits of this experience, it is so rare. That becomes my meditation and that enhances my surfing experience because it is now somehow shared with everything and everyone. I think this is the essential idea behind the Surfrider Foundation and what provides for its real greatness. Sharing the positive force that you have been given by the waves. Living aloha.[78]

Like many other soul surfers, Flynn feels affinity with indigenous, seafaring peoples, and this was woven into his own spirituality, including by means of his invocation of aloha.

Surfer intellectuals may be especially adept at expressing a spiritual belonging to nature, as Drew Kampion did in *The Book of Waves:* "Everything is waves. The universe of space and matter is charged with energy . . . waves of energy. Like echoes of the heartbeat of the absolute being, waves give expression to the divine will. They give form to the universe. . . . Waves are the imprint, the signature, not only of life, but of existence itself."[79] In *Stoked!,* Kampion wrote similarly: "Surfing is magic, riding liquid echoes of cosmic energy at the wild fringes of continents." These words were superimposed over the book's final photograph, a surfer sitting on his board facing a huge setting sun with hands raised in symbolic embrace of these cosmic energies.[80] Such writings and images show that for many surfers the heart of their spirituality lies in a deeply felt connection to Mother Ocean and the energies of the universe.

Equally critical for many soul surfers is the communion they feel with nonhuman creatures while engaged in their sport. As expressed by Chris Gallagher, "I think the soul [in soul surfing] comes into it more when a surfer appreciates nature and the true gift of surfing. Much of the satisfaction comes . . . from . . . the connection made with nature. Dolphins, whales, fish, birds, trees, reefs, sunsets—take these things away and you strip a perfect wave of its soul."[81] For many surfers, interspecies encounters are more important to surfing spirituality than experiences with fast and dangerous waves, even constituting the kind of Naturalistic Animism repeatedly found in dark green religion.

With my research into surfing spirituality well underway I had a conversation in December 2004 with Gordon LaBedz, an ardent surfer and physician from Southern California.[82] A tenacious Sierra Club activist, LaBedz helped the Surfrider Foundation during the 1990s to develop its chapter structure and thereby its economic viability.[83] LaBedz had also been a regular reader of the radical environmental journal *Earth First!*, and while critical of much in that movement, he shared its biocentrism. When I described how some surfers understood the practice as religious, he first expressed skepticism and said that he was an atheist. But he was nevertheless intrigued with the idea of a close relationship between religion and nature and asked, "What is spirituality?" I responded by asking him whether he had ever seen the Sierra Club poster with tree trunks and human legs intertwined, nearly indistinguishable, with prose stating that Sierra Club activists are motivated by a sense of belonging and connection to the earth (figure 1).

LaBedz had seen the poster and found it "powerful and moving." He especially appreciated "its powerful message about how we are all a part of nature." Bernard Zaleha, who was national vice president of the Sierra Club from 2004 to 2006, and was participating in the conversation, added that the poster was one of the favorites of the Carl Pope, then the club's executive director, who was also moved by the sentiments expressed in it.[84]

I returned to LaBedz's question about spirituality and answered that, for a growing number of scholars, there is no obvious boundary between spirituality and religion. I added that, while there is no consensus regarding the roots of the term *religion,* some trace its origins to words having to do with being bound to, tied, or connected, presumably in this context with something greater than oneself. I also suggested that religion confers meaning and provides transformative and healing power, and that for me this need not involve nonmaterial spiritual beings.

FIGURE 1. This Sierra Club poster includes statements that clearly reflect dark green religious sentiments, including:

This is not about getting back to nature. It is about understanding we've never left.

We were born here and we're part of it—like any ant, fish, rock, or blade of grass.

When you accept your connection to nature, suddenly you can't look at the world without seeing something very personal in it.

You are part of it, and you work for the planet because it gives you joy to do so.

You work for the planet because you belong to it.

As we continued the conversation we turned to the experience of surfing. LaBedz clearly understood and agreed with those who believe that surfing involves transformational systems of energy. I mentioned Sierra Club founder John Muir's dangerous and dramatic mountaineering experiences, which provoked instances of Zen-like satori where he felt time slowing down and the universe flowing through his body, enabling his escape, providing a kind of divine rescue. I mentioned similar experiences I have had, while surfing, for example, and also during my state park career when engaged in cliff or ocean rescues, when time seemed to stand still, allowing a remarkable clarity of vision, seeming to make possible a safe if unlikely outcome.

Like many surfers, LaBedz identified with such experiences. Then he mentioned that with rare exceptions he goes surfing every day at dawn. I commented on the sense of connection, communication, and even communion with nonhuman life that one can feel while offshore surfing. At this statement he became even more animated. He definitely felt deep kinship with the ocean creatures he encountered during his early mornings. Like many others for whom wildness is the centerpiece of spirituality, LaBedz spoke glowingly of how wild the ocean is and how wonderful it is to put the city behind him and have in front of him so much wildness.

LaBedz's thoughts and a short essay by Kampion are aquatic echoes of Thoreau's aphorism, "In wildness is the preservation of the world." In Kampion's words, "the wild restores the essential human spirit. The wild is where we come from. Every meeting with it brings us more fully into our eyes and ears and lungs and fingertips. Without the wild, we are asleep in our lives."[85] Kampion then described the ways that surfers encounter the wild and how it transforms their consciousness.

These are common perceptions among soul surfers.

Two days after my conversation with LaBedz, after he had returned home to California, he sent an e-mail to me and Zaleha: "5:30 AM, sitting next to the Seal Beach Pier by myself, looking out at Mother Ocean. I realized that you guys have convinced me that there is a religiosity to environmentalism. You guys won over a hardened atheist-materialist."

• • •

LaBedz's e-mail message, and the discussion throughout this chapter, underscore several impressions about surfing that apply to dark green religion more generally: whether nature-related practices and experiences can be considered religious depends on how religion-related terms are constructed and understood. Under the flexible definitions guiding this study, what might seem at first to be a mundane activity is revealed as sacred. This illustrates what the sociology of knowledge has long taught: what people perceive and believe is shaped by conversation. Therefore, as more surfers speak of their pastime as religious, more will come to see it in this way. As the surf magazine editors demonstrate, this is a process well underway. And the same sorts of dynamics are occurring with other outdoor sports and activities, although they seem not so far advanced: some fishers (especially fly-fishers), whitewater kayakers, skiers (especially backcountry), rock climbers and other mountaineers, for example, also have experiences they construe as religious.[86]

Observers of surfing enclaves certainly have noticed that the practice and its devotees engage in behaviors that resemble traditional religions. Surfers have myths, rituals, symbols, terminology, and technology; a sense that some places, animals, and plants are especially sacred; convictions regarding what constitutes proper relationships within the community of practitioners as well as with outsiders, human and not. As is the case with other forms of dark green religion, surfing spirituality is a bricolage. Some blend their surfing spirituality with religions (or aspects of them) that have Abrahamic or Asian roots. Others feel more affinity with indigenous traditions or Paganism. Still others are skeptical about conventional religious beliefs. This last kind of surfer finds sufficient resources in the surfing experience itself, and even in scientific ways of understanding it, to construct meaningful spiritual lives. For these surfers, it is enough to tap into the source of life, which from an evolutionary standpoint, whatever else it may be, is the sea itself.

For the current study it is most important to note that there are a significant number of surfers who, through the sport itself and the conversations and practices surrounding it, have developed a sense of connection and belonging to nature (to Mother Ocean in particular) and to the diverse life-forms they encounter during their practice. The resulting spirituality has both animistic and Gaian dimensions. Sometimes referring to themselves as soul surfers, they distinguish themselves from those who have not learned surfing's spiritual lessons, express humility about their place in the world and reverence toward it, and feel a deep sense of kinship and communion with nonhuman beings. They desire to help heal people and the planet. They also report that the practice itself can bring a wide range of benefits: physical, psychological, cultural, and spiritual.

And many soul surfers become ambassadors if not evangelists for the practice, introducing prospective devotees to their meaning-filled world.

As surfing continues to spread, there is every reason to expect that some engaged in it will continue to represent it as a contemporary religious alternative. Soul surfing does not appear to be extreme or dangerous, as do some forms of radical environmentalism. This is not to say that it would be surprising if some of its devotees were to take up militant tactics in the cause of environmental protection. While soul surfers may struggle with their own sense of spiritual superiority and territorial feelings, they are the ones who are the most aware and resistant to the shadow side of their sport. Soul surfers appear, therefore, to be a counterweight to the kind of territoriality and violence that sometimes accompanies the sport. Meanwhile, such surfers are helping the sport to gradually develop an environmentalist identity.

For many, this analytic surfing safari will be surprising. But there are other manifestations of dark green religion that are even more shocking, promising, and perilous.

CHAPTER 6

Globalization with Predators and Moving Pictures

Soul surfers generally understand they are part of the food chain, that they are not only predators but prey. Such recognition can dramatically alter perception.

For some people, being in habitats with predators capable of eating them evokes a sense of belonging and participation in the cycle of life. Indeed, realizing that sooner or later one is food, if only for microorganisms, can overturn anthropocentric hubris. Some follow mountain lion tracks, as did Edward Abbey. Others refuse to leave the water after shark sightings. Some, such as Doug Peacock, enjoy how alert and alive they feel when in *Ursus arctos* (brown bear) territory; Peacock is the bear researcher who inspired Abbey's Hayduke character in *The Monkey Wrench Gang*. Even being *attacked* by a large predator can evoke feelings of belonging and connection to nature, perceptions common in dark green religion.

In 1985 the Australian philosopher and ecofeminist Val Plumwood was canoeing in the Kakadu wetlands. One of the world's most dangerous animals, a saltwater crocodile, approached and then suddenly and repeatedly rammed her canoe. She later recalled that during the attack, for the first time, she understood that she was prey.[1] Plumwood steered to the slippery and muddy riverbank, thinking that she might escape by jumping from the canoe and pulling herself up into a tree by its lower branches. As she prepared to leap, she recalled, "the crocodile rushed up alongside the canoe, and its beautiful, flecked golden eyes looked straight into mine." If this was a vision of communion, it was unwelcome. The crocodile burst from the water as Plumwood leapt. It clamped down on her legs and spun, rolling her several times under water. The philosopher fought back and somehow managed to free herself and scramble out of the crocodile's range.

Plumwood survived severe injuries and despite a long, painful recuperation later reported feeling "a golden glow over my life" and deep gratitude. She did say, however, "[I am] unsure whom I should thank." The experience, she explained later, helped her to break past an assumed sense of human superiority and separateness from nature, a perspective she blamed on Western philosophy and religion. Put simply, the crocodile taught Plumwood a lesson. Or one might say it communicated with her. As she put it: "Large predators like lions and crocodiles present an important test for us. An ecosystem's ability to support large predators is a mark of its ecological integrity. Crocodiles and other creatures that can take human life also present a test of our acceptance of our ecological identity. When they're allowed to live freely, these creatures indicate our preparedness to coexist with the otherness of the earth, and to recognize ourselves in mutual, ecological terms, as part of the food chain, eaten as well as eater."

Through this experience Plumwood learned a lesson in belonging, "a humbling and cautionary tale about our relationship with the earth, about the need to acknowledge our own animality and ecological vulnerability." The experience also reinforced her compassion for nonhuman creatures. She urged authorities to refrain from killing the crocodile, noting that she was an intruder in its territory. This attitude is also commonly found among surfers attacked by sharks. While Plumwood gained a visceral understanding that we are all edible, she nevertheless concluded that all living things are more than just food; all organisms should therefore be treated with respect.

Plumwood was one of the world's leading environmental philosophers until her death from a stroke in 2008. "Becoming Prey" was widely read in environmental studies programs and by philosophers worldwide, providing evidence of the global nature of dark green religious perception.

Leopards in Trees

Late one night in 2000, I sat with five others around a fire, well outside the protective enclosure at the Mashatu Game Reserve in southern Botswana. It was a cloudless August night, my last one at the reserve. For nearly a week with a small group of ecotourists I had walked the savanna by day and after dark explored from the safety of a safari vehicle. We knew that leopards *(Panthera pardus)* inhabited trees just like the ones overhead, and that the largest males weigh nearly 200 pounds (91 kg) and can carry prey three times their size into those trees. On occasion that prey is human. Two nights before, we had spotted a leopard in a nearby tree feasting on an eland *(Taurotragus oryx)*, a large species of antelope.

Our guide was Chris van der Merwe, an ecotourism pioneer of Afrikaner heritage from Pretoria, South Africa. He invited those of us participating in his Deep Ecology Elephant Programme (DEEP) to sit outside the enclosure in what he called a vigil. He believed that by leaving the protected zone we might better understand ourselves as part of and not superior to nature. He hoped this would evoke or deepen a commitment to conserving biological diversity. What he did not fully realize was that by creating this program and nocturnal vigil he was participating in, creatively inventing, and globalizing dark green religion.

I had joined van der Merwe's program after a conference, drawn by the deep ecology theme when I was searching for a chance to see the continent's megafauna. I had been studying the deep ecology movement and wondered if van der Merwe's efforts were a manifestation of it, and if so, whether what I found would resemble deep ecology elsewhere. Van der Merwe was a freelance photojournalist who in 1992 covered the United Nations Conference on Environment and Development (popularly known as the Earth Summit) in Rio de Janeiro. Inspired by indigenous peoples and civil society pushing the nations toward environmental sustainability, he returned to South Africa and organized a symposium on sustainable tourism in 1996. Soon after he began developing the Deep Ecology Elephant Programme in southern Africa and Thailand.[2] Interestingly, he did not know much about deep ecology. He had come across the term online and could not recall where. He had not read anything by its leading proponents. But like many who have come to identify with deep ecology, he had in mind a basic, generic understanding of it, namely, that nature is sacred and all species have intrinsic value.

DEEP was premised on van der Merwe's rudimentary understanding of deep ecology and his belief in the intertwined destiny of humans and the rest of the living community. He intuitively gravitated toward the kinship ethics common in dark green religion. For van der Merwe, elephants were good teachers, at least indirectly through their humanlike behavior, so he arranged for scientists to teach us about the social and affective lives of elephants. In his literature and presentations, he discussed the case of Jann Weiss, a reputed psychic and expert in "interspecies communication," who seemed to have the uncanny, telepathic ability to communicate with elephants and other animals. Van der Merwe told us in a lecture that "whether humans and elephants can communicate is scientifically unproven," but he also said that a number of skeptical elephant experts reluctantly concluded that Weiss actually could. "Almost every researcher that has worked extensively with elephants (interestingly, they are mostly women)," van der Merwe wrote, "will say they believe elephants are capable of telepathy."[3]

Our chief instructor during DEEP, however, was no psychic. Jeanette Selier was a wildlife biologist with a doctorate who worked at an elephant research project in Tuli, Botswana. Despite her best efforts, Selier provided a very anthropomorphic view of elephants. She described their gender relationships, the macho posturing of juvenile males, and the role of female caretaking. After I noted that she both spoke anthropomorphically and then apologized for doing so, she responded that this was because of the professional taboo against describing nonhuman animals as having humanlike traits. But she explained this was very difficult to maintain because elephants *are* like humans in their emotional and social lives. In van der Merwe's program, focusing on the elephants was a strategy for evoking kinship with the animals as well as a conservation ethic. This was explicitly noted in a promotional flyer: "Through close observation of the elephants' strikingly anthropomorphic behavior and by other means [DEEP] facilitates an emotional and spiritual journey. The ultimate DEEP objective is that participants gain, or reaffirm, a sense of the vital importance of wilderness and biodiversity to human quality of life, humans own place in nature, and our role in conserving it."

The "other means" alluded to in this statement included walking and biking on the plains, rather than viewing the land exclusively from a safe perch atop a safari vehicle, which would have reinforced a sense of separateness from the surrounding countryside. Van der Merwe wanted us to imagine and feel what it was like to be a member of the species *Homo sapiens,* living off the land and part of the wider community of life in Africa, with all the vulnerabilities that come with that experience. He wanted us to feel what it meant to be an animal in Africa without distancing technology. One night during the program, I asked him how he understood ecotourism. He said it should tell us "how we fit in, how . . . we belong." By offering us the opportunity to be in some danger, either from elephants or large feline predators, whether by day or vigil at night, he turned his version of ecotourism into a ritual of belonging and connection.

The Messy Impulse to Connect with Nature

As innovative and creative as DEEP was, it was just one of many contemporary quests to reconnect with nature. This impulse exists around the world in sometimes unexpected ways and places. I have already discussed the global dimension of this pursuit, with individuals and groups from different times and regions influencing one another. In this and the following chapters, the story of dark green religion becomes all the more complicated, in part because global transportation and communication has become easier and environmental concern has intensified. The pace of transcontinental influence has increased, including within the environmentalist milieu. The more social sectors that are drawn into the milieu, the more difficult it becomes to trace influences, interests, and impacts.

Historians have shown that commercial interests have long influenced environment-related tourism—the national parks movement and the sport of surfing provide but two examples. The consequences are often ironic and sometimes tragic. Environmental protection movements have sometimes unintentionally created markets and enterprises that hinder or thwart environmental protection. Such dynamics have increased as individuals and groups engaged in cultural production have interacted with domestic and international governance organizations and with global media and other corporations. *All* this contestation is going on at the very same time that *all* of these actors are wrestling with a widely perceived environmental crisis. Much of the debate follows from competing ethical and spiritual claims regarding human responsibilities to nature.

I mention this complicated and contested cultural landscape to explain why some relevant and interesting questions are beyond the scope of the current volume. For example: Which came first, dark green spirituality or the business interests that might correspond with it? Are individuals and groups who have a commercial interest in environmental protection sincere or cynically using environmental concerns as leverage in marketing campaigns? The evidence and answers are usually unavailable because they depend on knowing the minds and motives of inaccessible actors. While I muster such evidence in several cases, my priority going forward is to portray the diversity, geographic range, and impact of dark green religion and the ways in which it is facilitating human connections to nature.

Connecting through Film and Performance

IN DISNEY'S WORLDS

The Walt Disney Company's motion pictures, theme parks, and television productions have had a significant global impact on popular culture. Many have criticized the company, arguing among other things that Disney erodes global cultural diversity, destroys wildlands to build its parks, promotes consumerism, and celebrates a version of the United States that justifies the deracination of American Indians. Such criticisms, however, look at only one side of the coin and provide a limited view of Disney's many social and environmental impacts. These critiques ignore how ideologies and spiritualities produced in Disney's worlds have been contested internally, and they fail to see that some of the company's productions promote progressive politics and have affinities with dark green religion.[4]

Since the 1930s, Disney movies and theme parks have presented an anthropomorphic and sentimental view of animals that has promoted human empathy for nonhuman organisms and, often, kinship feelings with them.[5] Disney movies have also had animistic, environmental, and even shamanic dimensions. In these films, humans commonly have animal or plant friends with whom they communicate, they cross boundaries into nonhuman societies, and they even shape-shift across species boundaries. In *The Jungle Book* (1967), after being rescued as a baby by a panther and raised by wolves (a knockoff of the story of Romulus and Remus), and despite many dangers, the feral child Mowgli resisted efforts to return him to human society, for his home and kin were in the forest. The concluding song, "The Bare Necessities," suggests a common environmental theme, that consuming nature is not the basis of happiness. But in the end, following his own instinct, Mowgli's attraction to a girl led him back to the human world in the "man-village"—but not before the boundary between humans and other animals eroded. This blurring of ordinary perceived divisions between humans and other animals also occurred in *The Little Mermaid* (1989) as Ariel temporarily became human, and even more so in *Tarzan* (1999), in which the boy who was raised by gorillas, as a man saved them from capture. An even more obvious example is *Bambi* (1942), which along with *Snow White and the Seven Dwarfs* (1937) presented a kind of animistic nature spirituality that emotionally connected the viewer to the film's nonhuman forest inhabitants. Few who saw *Bambi* were unmoved by the fawn's wrenching loss at the hands of a hunter or could easily forget how afraid the forest creatures were when faced with a human-caused forest fire. In this film, nature untrammeled by humans was depicted as miraculous and sublime. But also revered was the very life cycle that envelopes all creatures.

A half century later in *The Lion King* (1994), nature was again sublime but threatened. But most importantly for the current analysis, the film's dialogue and music presented as clear an expression of a metaphysics of interrelatedness, combined with a spirituality of connection and belonging to nature, as exists in film.[6] The movie began with animals gathering in an obviously healthy landscape and with the "Circle of Life" song:

From the day we arrive on the planet
And blinking, step into the sun . . .
It's the Circle of Life
And it moves us all
Through despair and hope
Through faith and love
Till we find our place
On the path unwinding
In the Circle
The Circle of Life

Shortly afterward, Mufasa (the current Lion King) and Simba (his young son), had a brief exchange about ruling over the beautiful kingdom and the respect for every aspect of the ecosystem that this requires:

Mufasa: Everything you see exists together, in a delicate balance. As king, you need to understand that balance, and respect all the creatures—from the crawling ant to the leaping antelope.

Simba: But, dad, don't we eat the antelope?

Mufasa: Yes, Simba, but let me explain. When we die, our bodies become the grass. And the antelope eat the grass. And so we are all connected in the great Circle of Life.

Shortly after this scene, Mufasa was murdered by Scar, his younger brother, and Simba was driven into exile. Scar took over the kingdom and it became desolate—a land plagued by famine because Scar was gluttonous and did not understand the natural balance. The rest of the story, despite many humorous moments, is a drama about whether Simba will accept his place in the Circle of Life—in other words, will he take responsibility for nature and assume his proper place in the natural order. After many adventures and dangers, and with help from Nala, his childhood lioness friend and eventual mate, Simba experienced the "magic" and love of nature: he heard his father speaking to him through a natural epiphany, in wind, clouds, and stars, reminding him of his obligations. Simba, by then grown up, accepted his responsibility, drove the uncaring usurper Scar from the land, and began a rule characterized by a love for all life. The movie ended with the natural order restored "to perfect harmony / with all its living things," according to the film's Academy Award–winning theme song.[7]

This exceptionally popular story has also been performed as a musical on Broadway and beyond, and in front of huge audiences at the Festival of the Lion King, a daily event at Disney's Animal Kingdom Park in Florida since its opening day in 1998.[8] When I saw this Lion King pageant at the park soon after it opened, I was struck by how the audience was pulled into the performance. Upon entering the theater, we were given cards with an animal on them and during the show we were asked to express specific animal sounds. As I watched the spectacle, it was difficult to discern the boundary between performance and ritual, between play and religion. The pageant reminded me of rituals of inclusion I have experienced elsewhere in the environmental milieu. It seemed to me, then and now, that the Lion King performance in this theme park setting could do something the film could not—get the audience personally and physically involved. As I often do in situations that involve at least *implicit* ritual, I wondered how the audience participants experienced and interpreted the event.

The film *Pocahontas* (1995), released the year after the Lion King restored harmony in Africa, represents an equally clear expression of dark green religiosity. It also has a ritualized presence at the Animal Kingdom. In Disney's version of this often-told story, the Indian "princess" and her people were able to hear and learn from nature's spirits. From Grandmother Willow they learned the most important lesson of their belonging to nature and of their sacred interconnections within the web of life. Meanwhile, although Europeans were primarily portrayed as agents of desecration, the good-hearted among them learned to respect indigenous peoples and Mother Earth. Like in the best-known versions of the inherited story, Disney's Pocahontas saved a European explorer. In this updated version, however, she did not die alienated from her sacred place in a foreign land. She stayed with her people to help them protect nature and learn to peacefully coexist with the newcomers. The animistic nature spirituality and environmental kinship ethic of the recast story was also on display in the movie and repeated at Pocahontas and Her Forest Friends, another Animal Kingdom Park attraction. This performance reiterated the Disney version of the story and thus the moral quest for kinship among all creatures. It even ended with an environmentalist entreaty, "Will you be a protector of the forest?"

According to many scholars and at least one band of contemporary Powhatan Indians, however, "the film distorts history beyond recognition."[9] It pleased many Native Americans, however, who found the portrayal of the Powhatan people respectful and authentic. The (non-Powhatan) American Indian Movement activist Russell Means, for example, who provided the voice of the animated Chief Powhatan character in the movie, exclaimed after filming, "I find it astounding that Americans and the Disney Studios are willing to tell the truth. It's never been done before . . . and I love it. The cooperation I got with every suggestion I made, even the smallest little things about our culture, have been incorporated into the script."[10]

This statement provides a window into how one Native American activist felt about the film. Just as I have wondered about how people experience these movies or their theme park versions, I have also been curious about the pedagogical and religious intentions of those who produce them. I found a clue in an interview with Stephen Schwartz, the lyricist for the film's signature song, "Colors of the Wind." Schwartz's lyrics directly challenged Euro-American understandings of landownership, asserting that one cannot "own" the creatures and spirit-filled entities that make up animate nature. In the words he had Pocahontas sing:

> You think you own whatever land you land on
> The earth is just a dead thing you can claim
> But I know ev'ry rock and tree and creature
> Has a life, has a spirit, has a name . . .
> The rainstorm and the river are my brothers
> The heron and the otter are my friends
> In a circle, in a hoop that never ends[11]

Toward the end of the song, Pocahontas sang a question: "How high does the sycamore grow?" And she answered: "If you cut it down, then you'll never know." Here the environmental message is inescapable, echoing the "circle of life" spirituality of belonging and connection in *The Lion King*.

About writing these lyrics Schwartz later commented: "It was just one of those magical things. . . . We knew what we wanted to say and we knew who the person was. We were able to find the parts of ourselves that beat in synchronicity with Pocahontas on those particular thoughts. The image of a sycamore echoes Chief Seattle's speech to Congress, in which he says, 'No one can own the sky' and 'What will you do when the rivers are gone?'" Ironically, historians have established that Chief Seattle never uttered these words.[12] They are thought to come from the pen of a Hollywood screenwriter, based only on a few historical fragments of a mid-nineteenth-century speech now lost to history. Nevertheless, many believe that these words accurately reflect the best of Native American spirituality.

Whether the speech was invented matters little when analyzing its role in popular culture and the environmental milieu. It was not only Schwartz who resonated with what he took to be the nature spirituality of Pocahontas and Chief Seattle's message. Both the song and the movie's musical score won Academy Awards, which is evidence of their affective resonance.[13] The film's directors, Mike Gabriel and Eric Goldberg, for their part, reported that they "tried to tap into [Pocahontas's] spirituality and the spirituality of the Native Americans, especially in the way they relate to nature." So in the case of this movie, there is strong evidence not only of dark green spirituality but also of an explicit intention to communicate it. Even a few minutes browsing Internet websites related to this film demonstrates that many who appreciate it (and some other Disney movies) do so because of the film's religious and environmental content—including, if not especially, the themes typical of dark green religion.

These themes are also represented in the educational displays, attractions, and gift shops at Disney's Animal Kingdom. At the Kilimanjaro Safari, where visitors ride a simulated Land Rover to view authentic African plant and animal life, poachers are identified as villains responsible for endangering species. This is, of course, a simplistic explanation for the near-extinction of many African species. It was chosen, little doubt, because it fit easily into the melodramatic genre typical in Disney's worlds. I was surprised, therefore, to find immediately upon leaving the ride museum-quality displays that explained the diverse interplay of social and ecological factors precipitating Africa's biodiversity crisis. It was clear that conservation professionals had prepared these exhibits. Although most visitors bypassed these panels to rush to the next adventure, I nevertheless wondered if there was any place in America where greater numbers of ordinary people would be exposed to such conservation education.

Other attractions also contributed to the intended green experience. The Affection Station provided a place where children could emotionally connect to animals, while at the Pangani Forest, according to the park's promotional brochure, one could have "an intimate up-close encounter with a magnificent troop of gorillas." Another venue offered a sublime nature experience—a "tropical oasis of Eden-like flora and fauna rich with cooling waterfalls and meandering streams." The Habitat Habit and Conservation Station promised to show visitors how to help their "animal friends" and touted Disney's conservation efforts.

None of these were more important than the Animal Kingdom's Tree of Life, which was planted right at the very center of the park. It was modeled on Africa's baobab tree, a good choice to symbolize life at an Africa-themed park. This tree is endemic to Africa and it is sometimes referred to as the African Tree of Life because it provides food, habitat, and even medicines for a wide array of organisms.[14] The theme park's tree was actually a massive, fourteen-story-high sculpture. Into its trunk and branches 325 animals were sculpted, including many of the world's threatened and endangered species. Jane Goodall had been an inspiration to some of those designing the park and she was invited to visit before it opened. While admiring the massive artwork she noted that there was no chimpanzee. Soon, David Greybeard, her favorite, was added. I found this story at a website that devoted considerable space to this tree, providing detailed pictures of many of the animals in it and links to conservationist websites advocating their protection. The website's owners had named their site Pansophists.com because they resonated with the dictionary definition of *pansophism:* "an ancient religion that worshipped everything that lives."[15]

This may be the kind of religion that inspires those who design and run Disney's Animal Kingdom Park. I cannot say what if any religion the park's director of animal programs professes, but in that position Jackie Ogden does express "respect and awe" for nature. Ogden earned her doctorate focusing on wildlife ecology because she wanted to help protect biological diversity and "save the world." Although she wishes it were easier to move people to protect nature, she believes that given the right opportunities, people can develop a love for animals. Conservationists must reach out "beyond the purist 5 to 10 percent" who already care, she told me in an interview, "and this is why zoos and the Animal Kingdom have an important and positive role to play in the conservation cause."[16] About her team at the park, she said in an online interview, "Our mission is to help inspire all of our guests to care more about wildlife."[17]

This (in addition to profit making) was apparently one of the motivations behind *Disney's True Life Adventures* television series and other nature documentaries the company produced between 1948 and 1960. Indeed, these productions inaugurated the very genre of nature documentary. Three of them earned Academy Awards and they were all widely seen both in theaters and on television. Nearly four decades after the *True Life Adventures* series ended, in April 2008, Disney president and CEO Robert Iger announced the formation of a new division devoted exclusively to nature documentaries. Dubbed "*Disney*nature," Iger stated its environmental mission: "We hope these films will contribute to a greater understanding and appreciation of the beauty and fragility of our natural world."[18] Even a brief perusal of the *Disney*nature website suggests that the films will be designed to evoke a sense of the sublime in nature and human kinship with nonhuman organisms, in part through the images and sounds on the website itself.[19]

This discussion has focused on the explicit and implicit spirituality and ethics present in a number of Disney productions that seem to express themes common in dark green religion. It seems that reverence for nature and feelings of kinship with the natural world can appear in unexpected ways and places, including in Disney's worlds.

THE ANIMATED BIOSPHERE BEYOND DISNEY'S ORBIT

In 2006 I spoke about the globalization of nature spirituality at Hamilton College in upstate New York. During the discussion a professor expressed skepticism about my finding of ecospirituality in some parts of the Disney empire. He did not think anything good could come from Disney and asserted that its productions only served the interests of its owners. After the discussion ended and the crowd dissipated, a young African American man approached and told me that, although he did not want to publicly contradict his professor, the television program *Captain Planet* (which I had also mentioned in my talk but is not produced by Disney) had inspired and precipitated his environmental activism and career choice. He believed that since he grew up in a heavily populated urban area, the borough of Queens in New York City, without that television show he would never have set out on this environmental path; moreover, he probably would never have visited wild natural places at all, which he had come to greatly value.

Captain Planet had its own inspirations and patrons. Ted Turner, the media mogul who created Cable News Network and Turner Network Television, came up with and funded the idea for this animated television show, which was produced between 1990 and 1996. The idea itself seemed drawn straight from James Lovelock's Gaia theory, as explained in the "series mythology" summarized at the program's website:

> Gaia, the spirit of Earth ["the archetypal mother [who] loves Earth's children unconditionally"], awakens from a century-long sleep to the pillaging of the planet by a largely oblivious humanity. Fearing for the future, she sends magic rings to five youngsters from around the globe—*Wheeler* (North America), *Linka* (Eastern Europe), *Gi* (Asia), *Kwame* (Africa) and *Ma-Ti* (South America)—Gaia's team in the battle against further destruction of the Earth. As the youngsters place the rings on their fingers, they are magically transported to Gaia's home, Hope Island, an uncharted, unpolluted tropical isle far from civilization. There, Gaia teaches them the secrets of nature. As they learn of their personal power, each identifies with one of the four ancient elements: Earth, Fire, Water, Wind and a very special new power, Heart, which symbolizes the compassion needed to save the Earth. Through the magic rings, the Planeteers learn to direct their powers in their mission to save Earth. Finally, they are ready to discover the greatest secret of all. When the Planeteers join their powers together, beams shoot from their rings, . . . and . . . a new hero literally bursts from the earth . . . *Captain Planet!* The environmental superhero [who] . . . demonstrates that the whole is, indeed, greater than the sum of its parts.[20]

In each episode, the précis concludes, Gaia's allies face down another threat, and then concrete guidance for solving environmental problems is provided. So the beneficent goddess of the earth, who loves life unconditionally, needs those who belong to her to unite to restore life on earth. Further clues into what sort of philosophy, or spirituality, are behind the program can be found by examining at the life and philanthropy of Ted Turner, whose foundation focuses on grantmaking related to population and the environment in order to "protect and restore the natural systems that make life possible."[21] Turner also famously gave a billion dollars to the United Nations Foundation (in part because of its work in health, education, and population stabilization). Turner has made biodiversity preservation a central personal priority, both through huge land purchases that have helped restore bison populations to viable numbers and by supporting nature documentaries.

He also established the Turner Tomorrow Award, a literature prize that Daniel Quinn won the first (and only) time it was awarded, specifically for the novel *Ishmael.*

It is difficult to predict, of course, which book, motion picture, or television program will spark or provide mythic reinforcement for environmental spirituality and action. As noted earlier, some environmentalists have been moved by J. R. R. Tolkien's *Lord of the Rings* trilogy, both the books and the motion pictures. Perhaps the most often-cited part of the trilogy is when Treebeard, the animate tree creature, became so riled by the destruction of his world that he led the other ents into battle against the forces that were destroying his sacred forest and threatening Middle Earth itself. First published in 1954 and 1955, the saga has been republished and translated repeatedly; and its global reach was enhanced with film versions produced between 2001 and 2003, which won a total of seventeen Academy Awards. Many other films express dark green themes. In *The Emerald Forest* (1985) a child of a dam builder in Amazonia is abducted and adopted by indigenous people; when he is finally found by his father, the child convinces him to help protect the forest and his tribe's ecospiritual culture. The animated film *Fern Gully: The Last Rainforest* (1992) depicts a sublime forest where nature spirits and native people live in harmony until loggers intrude; but a young fairy converts one of the logging crew to the ways of the forest and together they resist the forces of destruction. In *Happy Feet* (2006) an adorable emperor penguin, by dancing for researchers, convinces the wider human community that penguins wish to communicate their distress about overfishing, thereby precipitating a conservationist reversal of the practice. The heartwarming film, produced in Australia, won the Academy Award for Best Animated Feature in 2007.

Connecting through Documentaries and Science

Many other motion pictures and television programs, including nature documentaries, promote perceptions characteristic of dark green religion. Some of those involved in the production of these documentaries are obvious exemplars of dark green religion. Others leave insufficient tracks to be certain but enough evidence to speculate about their deepest motivations.

JACQUES-YVES COUSTEAU AND DAVID ATTENBOROUGH

The French marine explorer Jacques-Yves Cousteau and the (primarily) terrestrial naturalist Sir David Attenborough provide the most important early examples of filmmakers whose documentaries, much more than Disney's, resist anthropomorphism and the ideological subplots that critics have found in the Disney features.[22] Both men began their documentary careers in the mid-1950s, shortly after Walt Disney began producing his *True Life Adventures.*

Cousteau began with film documentaries and continued with television series and specials from the mid-1960s until his death in 1997. Cousteau mixed science with an affective appreciation of all he experienced, expressing delight, awe, and wonder before the mysteries in the world's oceans. As a preteen in the mid-1960s, I watched with wonder, as did many of my generation, the bizarre and adventurous scenes in *The Undersea World of Jacques Cousteau*. After he founded the conservationist Cousteau Society in 1974, a number of my lifeguard colleagues joined the group and proudly displayed its logo on their automobiles. It is not much of a stretch to suggest this was a way of symbolizing allegiance to our watery world. We were testimony to the global reach of this French naturalist and documentarian.

David Attenborough began his documentary career with a popular series of nature documentaries called *Zoo Quest,* which were broadcast on BBC television between 1954 and 1964.[23] This series involved capturing exotic animals and bringing them to zoos, a practice no longer considered ethical unless it is for science or to save endangered species. But since the early 1960s, he has also developed a series of documentaries unlikely to be matched for their scientific rigor and integration of multidisciplinary perspectives in analyzing the human/nature nexus. His most important work includes the *Life* trilogy, which consists of the three season-long BBC documentaries *Life on Earth* (1979), *The Living Planet* (1984), and *The Trials of Life* (1990) (*Trials* was also the first of several collaborations with media mogul Ted Turner). Intermixed with these have been nearly two dozen other documentaries he has produced or narrated, including *Planet Earth* (2006). The first nature film produced in high definition, *Planet Earth* may be the most powerful artistic depiction of nature as sublime that has been produced.

Although Attenborough has said in interviews that he is an agnostic who has never had a religious faith, he and his work are nevertheless worth scrutinizing for the themes and critiques common in dark green religion. If anything is clear about Attenborough, it is his delight and wonder in nature. Throughout his diverse and remarkable experiences exploring the world and its ecological interrelationships, he has done his best to enter into and understand the worlds and minds of animals on their own terms, suggesting his visceral affinity with dark green perceptions and beliefs. Moreover, he has a huge following globally, so it is reasonable to surmise that his work is striking a deep chord. That chord is the human need for meaning, which has not withered away with the assent of evolutionary cosmogony.

Attenborough's career is rooted in a childhood fascination with and connection to animals. When interviewed about *The Life of Birds* (1998), he confided that ever since he was a schoolboy he had had been "besotted" with birds. So the making of this documentary was a joyful experience that deepened his understanding of birds and his empathy for them:

> After this series I no longer watch, say, a pigeon drop from the sky into my garden in the same way as I used to. I know more about it; I have more empathy with it. I understand its problems and its abilities more than I ever did before. It's not enough for us to just put a name to a bird and look at because it's pretty. We see only a tiny fraction of a bird's existence. There is a huge amount of its life that we have no knowledge of. I hope this series will enable people to get inside the mind of a bird.[24]

This is an example of a certain kind of Naturalistic Animism, both in Attenborough's perception and his desire to help others to gain the fellow feeling that comes from it.

In *The Trials of Life,* which was also the first of several collaborations with media mogul Ted Turner, Attenborough conveys a similar message. The documentary tells the evolutionary story, detailing how human beings share the same struggle as all organisms to survive and pass their genes on to the next generation. The entire documentary is reminiscent of the empathetic passage by Darwin discussed in chapter 2 and is well summarized in Attenborough's concluding narration:

> If you watch animals objectively for any length of time, you're driven to the conclusion that their main aim in life is to pass on their genes to the next generation. Most do so directly, by breeding. In the few examples that don't do so by design, they do it indirectly, by helping a relative with whom they share a great number of their genes. And in as much as the legacy that human beings pass on to the next generation is not only genetic but to a unique degree cultural, we do the same. So animals and ourselves, to continue the line, will endure

> all kinds of hardship, overcome all kinds of difficulties, and eventually the next generation appears.[25]

Attenborough expresses a subtle kinship here of a kind common in dark green religion. It is highly significant that he chose to end his *Life* series, which was obviously a tremendous labor of love, with such a sentiment.

In that series and elsewhere, Attenborough affirmed biocentric ethics and underscored the idea of ecological interdependence. In *The Private Life of Plants* (1995; a six-part series also produced in cooperation with Ted Turner), *Life in the Undergrowth* (2005; about invertebrates), and *Life in Cold Blood* (2008; about reptiles and amphibians), Attenborough concluded with narrations expressing respect for plants' and animals' unique traits, our dependence on them, and exhortations to stop driving drive them to extinction. But it may be his first bird-focused documentary, *Attenborough in Paradise* (1996), in which he made his clearest biocentric confession. He began it by quoting and endorsing the words of the British naturalist and explorer Alfred Russel Wallace, who independently developed the theory that Darwin dubbed "natural selection."[26] "Wallace's emotions on discovering such marvels," said Attenborough, "must surely be echoed by all of us who follow him. This is what he wrote":

> I thought of the long ages of the past during which the successive generations of these things of beauty had run their course. Year by year being born and living and dying amid these dark gloomy woods with no intelligent eye to gaze upon their loveliness, to all appearances such a wanton waste of beauty. It seems sad that on the one hand such exquisite creatures should live out their lives and exhibit their charms only in these wild inhospitable regions. This consideration must surely tell us that all living things were not made for man, many of them have no relation to him, their happiness and enjoyments, their loves and hates, their struggles for existence, their vigorous life and early death, would seem to be immediately related to their own well-being and perpetuation alone.

Attenborough closed with a statement of simple agreement, "Indeed so."[27]

Careful scrutiny reveals that Attenborough had many moving and meaningful encounters with animals and was enthralled with how evolution leads to diverse and creative adaptations. His most famous animal encounter was in the twelfth episode of *Life on Earth,* when he was face-to-face with a female mountain gorilla in Rwanda, whispering unscripted into the camera:

> There is more meaning and mutual understanding in exchanging a glance with a gorilla than with any other animal I know. Their sight, their hearing, their sense of smell are so similar to ours that they see the world in much the same way as we do. We live in the same sort of social groups with largely permanent family relationships. They walk around on the ground as we do, though they are immensely more powerful than we are. So if there were ever a possibility of escaping the human condition and living imaginatively in another creature's world, it must be with the gorilla.

These words revealed Attenborough's perception of cross-species communication. This was accompanied by a feeling of communion with this gorilla; the next day she and two others played with and even groomed him, an experience he considered one of his most meaningful.[28]

It was not only the personal encounter with other animals that moved Attenborough; so did the beauty and diversity of nature itself. As one perceptive interviewer explained, although Attenborough had a long-standing interest in anthropology, he stopped making films with human subjects because "when he was confronted by the general human ignorance of the amazing beauty and diversity of the natural world, when he felt 'enthralled almost to the point of ecstasy' by his own observations, he knew that he could have no other mission in life than spreading news of that beauty and diversity to as many people as possible."[29] It is no great stretch to consider Attenborough one of the world's foremost missionaries of "ecstatic naturalism," to borrow a term coined by the philosopher Robert Corrington to describe nonsupernaturalistic Pantheism.[30]

Other Attenborough documentaries also convey ideas that are increasingly common in dark green religion and the global environmental milieu. This includes the history presented in *The First Eden* (1987), which argued that biological and cultural diversity have been retreating for nearly ten thousand years in the face of agriculture, which has displaced diverse ecosystems in favor of homogeneous agro-ecosystems while displacing and eradicating cultures with nature-based religions.[31] Attenborough has also produced documentaries about our own time of escalating biosimplification and environmental decline. In *State of the Planet* (2000), for example, he drew on interviews with many leading scientists, including Edward O. Wilson and Jared Diamond, to focus on the current anthropogenic extinction event, carefully analyzing the major factors driving it. Then in *The Life of Mammals* (2002–2003) he underscored that human overpopulation contributes overwhelmingly to such crises, and he strongly suggested that we should control our numbers.[32] Perhaps the most critical sentiment he articulated, one that goes hand in hand with biocentrism, is that human beings should and will be humble when we properly understand our place in nature and dependence upon it. In this, Attenborough echoes Leopold's aphorism that the land ethic enjoins people to become plain members and citizens of the planet. As Attenborough said in the final episode of *Life on Earth,* "there is no scientific evidence whatsoever" that humanity is "the ultimate triumph of evolution."[33]

The massive body of documentary work produced by Attenborough provides many examples of the naturalistic forms of dark green religion, even though Attenborough has been subtle when expressing opinions and reticent to talk about himself. The popularity of these films suggests a hunger for what he offers in them, namely, a way for humans, most of whom have little or no contact with wild nature, to enter imaginatively into communion with nature and its diverse creatures, and to do so in a way compatible with a scientific mind-set.

WILD KINGDOMS AND CROCODILE HUNTERS

There are other important documentaries and television programs beyond those produced by Disney, Cousteau, and Attenborough that also seem to express a dark green ethos. In the United States, *Mutual of Omaha's Wild Kingdom* began its television run in 1963 and continued until 1988. The Discovery Channel began broadcasting in 1985 and later became part of the global conglomerate Discovery Communications. That parent company has produced many nature documentaries and has even launched channels devoted exclusively to such programming. The second was called Planet Green and began broadcasting in 2008. Discovery Communications claimed it would be "the first 24-hour eco-lifestyle channel" devoted to environmental sustainability. Its board of strategic advisors includes a number of internationally known environmental figures, including Wangari Maathai, David Suzuki, and Terri Irwin, discussed presently.[34]

Discovery Communications' first nature-focused channel was Animal Planet, which became wildly popular after its launch in 1996. Among many other things, Animal Planet resurrected *Mutual of Omaha's Wild Kingdom* (in 2002) and promoted respect for and the conservation of sharks with its annual Shark Week (since 1987). It also broadcast the earth-venerating *Planet Earth* (2006), replacing Attenborough's narration with voice-over by the actress Sigourney Weaver for an American audience. *Planet Earth* broke records for sales of high-definition DVDs when it was released. Interestingly, as part of its DVD marketing effort, Discovery promoted the program's spiritual appeal by using the closing line from Tom Shales's review: "Rarely does television touch heart and soul as effectively as 'Planet Earth.'" Shales also asserted that viewers would "gain a new appreciation and feel a new respect for the planet." This was the deepest motivation for many of those involved in producing it.[35]

Discovery's Animal Planet also made a star out of Steve Irwin—as well as his wife Terri Irwin and their daughter Bindi—all of whom appeared in *Crocodile Hunter.* The series, which ran from 1997 to 2004, had spawned many additional film and conservationist projects by the time Irwin was killed by a stingray's barb in December 2006. After his death, his widow explained that David Attenborough was an inspiration to her husband. Attenborough returned the compliment, praising Irwin's abilities to communicate his love and appreciation of nature. Irwin's childlike love and wonder for nature and biocentric feeling was easy to see—no matter how ugly or dangerous a creature might appear, it was beautiful to him. Moreover, his desire for intimacy with nature and communion with her creatures was so intense that he repeatedly took risks in order to draw closer.

After her husband's death, Terri Irwin wrote a book explaining that he hunted crocodiles to save them because of his "reverence" and "love" for them.[36] She also said that he had an "uncanny connection" with other animals, likening it to telepathy or a sixth sense. She said he was able to communicate with animals and even knew where they would be before other people could see or hear them.[37] Some of this transspecies communication was with whales, a connection that led Irwin to contact Paul Watson of the Sea Shepherd Conservation Society because he wanted to build a boat to help stop whaling. Irwin's death prevented him from joining Watson's campaign, but he did so symbolically when Watson, with Terri Irwin's blessing, renamed one of his ships the MV *Steve Irwin.*

Terri Irwin explained the otherwise inexplicable aspects of her husband's life in this way: "Years in the wilderness lent him a deep understanding of the natural world [and] reinforced a unique connection with wildlife that would stay with him throughout his whole life."[38] Here she implicitly expressed a common premise of animistic spirituality: openhearted humans who immerse themselves in nature can learn to perceive its voices.

Like most public figures who promote dark green themes, Steve Irwin had critics. Some complained that he disturbed wildlife or that his showmanship distracted viewers from his intended subjects. Others complained that as an environmentalist he should not have lauded the Australian prime minister, who was indifferent to climate change. But to those who shared his passion for nature, he was a hero.

DISCOVERING RELIGIONS OF NATURE WITH DAVID SUZUKI

The dark green religion in the documentaries already discussed is subtle, requiring the right lenses to bring it into focus. The Canadian scientist and documentary producer David Suzuki, however, has been forthright in expressing his conviction that environmental concern is ultimately religious. He draws widely on a range of scholarship common in dark green religion, and his documentaries have been viewed around the world. Suzuki is the most prominent of the world's documentarians promoting such nature religion. Indeed, as early as 1985, in the documentary series *A Planet for the Taking*, he was calling for "a major 'perceptual shift' in our relationship with nature and the wild," a statement reminiscent of Thoreau that foreshadowed Suzuki's subsequent dark green missionary work. Suzuki won a United Nations Environmental Programme medal for the series in which he made this plea.[39]

Two documentary productions and two books show with special clarity Suzuki's consecration of nature and personal links to major figures within the dark green milieu.[40] As with Bill Rogers's compendiums discussed in chapter 4, looking closely at these works by Suzuki provides an excellent pathway into enclaves where people have affinity with and are engaged in dark green religion.

The first of these key sources was a book Suzuki coauthored with Peter Knudtson, *Wisdom of the Elders: Honoring Sacred Native Visions of Nature*.[41] Central to its argument and Suzuki's subsequent work was that scientists and indigenous peoples have similar insights regarding ecological interdependence, and that they often share common ethical and spiritual perceptions about the intrinsic value and sacredness of nature. Suzuki referred a number of times in this book to H. T. Odum, a pioneer of systems ecology who contributed to organicist understandings of the earth as a sacred, interrelated living system.[42] Perhaps most striking, however, was a quote Suzuki took from a 1990 public pronouncement written and signed by a group of prominent scientists (including Hans Bethe, Freeman Dyson, Stephen Jay Gould, James Hansen, Peter Raven, Carl Sagan, and Stephen Schneider). Although many of them disavowed belief in nonmaterial divine beings they nevertheless declared, "As Scientists, many of us have had profound personal experiences of awe and reverence before the universe. We understand that what is regarded as sacred is more likely to be treated with care and respect. Our planetary home should be so regarded. Efforts to safeguard and cherish the environment should be infused with a vision of the sacred."[43] In their expression of reverence, these words align with Gaian religiosity and biocentrism.

Five years later, in 1997, Suzuki produced a documentary for the Discovery Channel, *Yellowstone to Yukon: The Wildlands Project.* Based on conservation biology, the documentary provided a bioregional case study based on a project that Dave Foreman, the former Earth First! leader, cofounded with Michael Soulé in 1991. The project strives to protect large natural areas, with buffer zones around them and corridors between them, to preserve biological diversity. Another respected conservation biologist, Reed Noss, worked on the project with Foreman and Soulé, as did younger scientists recruited to the cause. Shortly thereafter the documentary aired, and the National Geographic Society published a book on the project. Douglas Chadwick, a wildlife biologist, wrote about the wealth of this northern Rockies ecosystem and argued that Indians had more insight into who its diverse species "really are" than did practitioners of "the dry mechanics of western behavioral science." When he lived on the "untamed core of the continent," Chadwick reported, "I belong to it," and he explained that such perception undergirded his belief that these wildlands should be protected. The accompanying photographs provide another example of art promoting the sublime: they included spectacular vistas as well as appreciation for the beauty of diverse nonhuman organisms.[44]

Another influential work by Suzuki was *The Sacred Balance,* a book that eventually became the basis for a four-part documentary first shown on Canadian public television in 2002 and then distributed globally.[45] Together the book and documentary provide a treasure trove of dark green themes and insights into the tributaries of such spiritualities. Significantly, the book began and ended with the words of Thomas Berry, who traced our environmental predicaments to the way we *think* about our place in nature.[46] Repeating Berry's view, Suzuki commented, "Through our loss of a worldview . . . we have lost our connection to the rest of the living planet. As Thomas Berry says, we must find a new story, a narrative that includes us in the continuum of Earth's time and space, reminding us of the destiny we share with all the planet's life, restoring purpose and meaning to human existence."[47] Suzuki underscored Berry's influence on his own thinking by ending his book with Berry's words: "The natural world is the maternal source of our being as earthlings and life-giving nourishment of our physical, emotional, aesthetic, moral and religious existence. The natural world is the larger sacred community to which we belong. To be alienated from this community is to become destitute in all that makes us human. To damage this community is to diminish our own existence."[48]

With the physicist Brian Swimme, Berry has influenced many to understand the scientific narrative of cosmological and biological evolution as a sacred story, and to recognize as well that many ancients and indigenous peoples have had compatible myths and ethical orientations to earthly life.[49] Berry thus provided the bookends for the narrative in Suzuki's book. By examining further themes in Suzuki's work one can see how he integrates and promotes dark green religion.

The central ideas in *The Sacred Balance,* both the book and documentary, were ecological interdependence (including Gaian organicism), spiritualities of belonging and connection, kinship ethics, and the sense that all life has intrinsic value. Suzuki also averred that a sense of awe, wonder, and humility can flow from the close observation of nature, and this comes easily to those who live in direct, daily contact with nature, especially indigenous people, those who procure food themselves, and scientists. Suzuki even made an explicit effort to instill in the reader reverence for air, water, earth, and fire. The second chapter of *The Sacred Balance,* for example, focused on air (breath, spirit, wind, atmosphere) and briefly explored how many religious traditions identify these as holy, or as divine breath. Then Suzuki reflected on the atmosphere, how it emerged, how fragile and thin it is, and how utterly dependent all life is upon it, concluding reverently, "Every breath is a sacrament, an essential ritual. As we imbibe this sacred element, we are physically linked to all of our present biological relatives, countless generations that have preceded us and those that will follow."[50]

Suzuki urged his readers to protect the atmosphere before turning to examine water, calling it "the tide of life itself, the sacred source." He then quoted Rachael Carson, whose own naturalistic nature spirituality began with her connection to the sea. Carson was a significant influence on Suzuki: she was one of the two most-quoted authors in *The Sacred Balance.*[51] In the 1930s and 1950s, Carson's ocean-inspired nature religion struck a chord, making her into a bestselling author well before she came to be known as the godmother of environmentalism.[52] I think this is partly because many people feel a special connection to the sea—even reverence for it as "the womb of life"—and Carson provides a literary archetype for such feelings.[53]

Carson's most forthcoming expression of spirituality may have occurred in 1954, when she spoke passionately to nearly a thousand women journalists of her love of nature and the mysteries of the cosmos. She also confided that she thought women have superior moral intuition to men (making her, arguably, the first ecofeminist), and urged the assembly to environmental activism.[54] Although her spirituality did not involve extra-worldly divine beings or hopes in an otherworldly afterlife—she appreciated the miracle and mystery of life on its own terms—she did at times express a subtle, naturalistic, animistic perception.[55] She is another important exemplar of dark green religion.

Suzuki drew on Carson's reverence for water as a springboard to express his own feeling of its sacredness: "We are water—the oceans flow through our veins, and our cells are inflated by water, our metabolic reactions mediated in aqueous solution. . . . As air is a sacred gas, so is water a sacred liquid that links us to all the oceans of the world and ties us back in time to the very birthplace of all life."[56]

Suzuki then moved from water to land in a chapter called "The Sacred Soil," drawing this time on Aldo Leopold to continue his narrative consecration of the main substances on which life depends. He quoted Leopold's straightforward declaration, "The land is one organism." So there would be no doubt, he ended the chapter with another Leopold passage that unambiguously connected earth to water and the atmosphere—fusing them all in his religious sensibility: "Land then, is not merely soil; it is a fountain of energy flowing through a circuit of soils, plants and animals. . . . We can be ethical only in relation to something we can see, feel, understand, love, or otherwise have faith in."[57] In the documentary Suzuki put it this way: "Soil is where the planet's energy cycle comes full circle, and death turns into life."[58] Given that religion is often about overcoming death, it should not be surprising that those informed by ecology, including soil science, would understand as sacred the life-resurrecting power of soil.

"The Divine Fire" was the next chapter, and it was foremost an expression of a scientific creation myth, a cosmogony, that celebrated the sun and other forms of heat for their essential, creative, life-giving characteristics. Suzuki briefly discussed the big bang, the science of metabolism, and other ways in which heat and energy flows precipitate and facilitate life. But his reverence for the sun and the unfolding universe was even clearer through his engagements with Brian Swimme during the documentary—so much so that when I saw it, I mused that the presentation resembled a new form of solar religion. Here is part of how the online summary of the third episode explained it:

> The Fire of Creation begins with the sun filling the sky, bursting into the star-pricked blackness of space with a pyrotechnic spectacle of shifting, scorching images. This [according to] Brian Swimme . . . is the way the cosmos began: in a single Big Bang. . . .
>
> . . . Swimme considers each day's dawn as a cosmic act of generosity—a vast giveaway of energy. We are all children of the sun, accumulating cosmic energies, transforming them into matter. Throughout the ages human beings have revered this sacred flame [and] the findings of science amplify that reverence.[59]

Cosmology shows, according to Swimme, that the sun's energy surges into "all beings [through] photosynthetic organisms. We are the sun in a new form." In Swimme's nature religion, the central feeling is "belonging to the universe"—Thomas Berry's key idea that initially drove Swimme to collaborate with and promote the Universe Story.[60]

Through the above framework and presentations, Suzuki made the case that "we *are* the air, we *are* the water, we *are* the earth, we *are* the sun" and that "there is no environment 'out there' that is separate from us."[61] It is unsurprising that Suzuki would feature ecopsychologists (including Paul Shepard) in *The Sacred Balance,* applauding their efforts to breach the divide between humans and nature that most involved in dark green religion consider typical of Western societies.[62] And he urged people to engage in a practice that can be understood as a simple ritual: "Go out into nature. . . . Feel the rain and wind on your face, smell the fragrance of soil and ocean, gaze at the spectacle of the myriad stars in clear air or countless animals making their annual migration. Doing so will rekindle that sense of wonder and excitement we all had as children discovering the world and will engender a feeling of peace and harmony at being in balance with the natural world that is our home." The lesson that comes from such direct sensory experience, Suzuki said, is that "nature is not our enemy, it is our home; in fact, it sustains us and is in every one of us. All living things are our relatives and belong with us in the biosphere."[63]

This lesson of kinship, so central to dark green religion, Suzuki repeated in the usual ways, noting that the similarity in our DNA and participation in the same evolutionary process links us intimately to all otherkind, quoting prominent scientists who derive just such a lesson from this knowledge as well as indigenous voices expressing similar perceptions and sentiments.[64] These perceptions included animistic beliefs, as expressed by an Inuit hunter who said that all creatures have "souls that do not perish with the body, and which must therefore be propitiated lest they should revenge themselves on us for taking away their bodies."[65] Suzuki also seemed to endorse a kind of Naturalistic Animism by quoting and endorsing statements by the ecologist Joseph Meeker. About this Meeker statement—"The conversation of mankind is an open and continuing dialogue that connects our bodies and minds intimately with the processes of nature that permeate all life forms"—Suzuki commented, "Like any other dialogue, it requires attention." Thus did Suzuki generally endorse the epistemology of Naturalistic Animism as well as dark green religion. Suzuki quoted Meeker a second time to underscore that such perceptual alertness can lead to interspecies communication: "Learning to converse well with the world can begin by listening carefully to the messages sent ceaselessly by our bodies and by the other forms of life that share this planet. The best conversations are still those that play variations on the great and ancient theme, 'I'm here; Where are you?' "[66] Suzuki then made his own naturalistic materialism clear: "We long to escape death, so we reject the mortal body and its communication with the world around it and search for abstract, eternal knowledge. But science—as well as our myths—tells us where immortality lies: it lies in the world we belong to, in the matter we are made from." And he quoted Thomas Hardy's poem, "Transformations," which is about a naturalistic life after death, commenting afterward about how the body enters and reanimates "the being of Earth."[67]

Suzuki also promoted the idea of the natural connections between humans and nature and, thus, the possibility of rekindling such bonds when they erode. He cited the work of Edward O. Wilson, the famous Harvard University biologist and biodiversity expert. Wilson initially on his own, and later with his protégé and collaborator Stephen Kellert (at Yale University), propounded the biophilia theory. This theory posits that our affective, aesthetic, and moral appreciation of nature, and our sense of kinship with other organisms, can be understood as evolutionary outcomes that generally promote environmentally adaptive behaviors.[68] To drive home the point, in his documentary Suzuki accompanied Wilson to Walden Pond, symbolically linking them both to Thoreau, their spiritual elder. At this place, which is sacred to many environmentalists, Wilson explained why human beings deeply value and appreciate nature—and need to do so.[69]

Suzuki buttressed and embellished this and the other perspectives common in dark green religion throughout the rest of his book, often by appealing to well-known if not famous scientists and environmental activists, and always buttressing these views with statements by indigenous thinkers. In the book he explained at some length Lovelock's Gaia theory, for example, signaling that he found it more than plausible. In the corresponding documentary he was more effusive, likening it to the ancient Hindu understanding that "the Earth is alive," thereby strongly embracing Lovelock's organicist worldview.[70]

Suzuki's book demonstrates, again, the influence of many leading architects of dark green religion. But he also introduced figures and schools of analysis heretofore not discussed, which have also contributed to the bricolage of dark green religion.

ETHNOBIOLOGY AND TRADITIONAL ECOLOGICAL KNOWLEDGE

One of the reasons Suzuki refers frequently to the world's indigenous peoples is that he has been profoundly influenced by ethnobiology (the study of the ways different human groups relate to and use the environment) and the closely related idea of "traditional ecological knowledge" (TEK).[71] TEK inheres in cultural groups (usually indigenous people and rural peasants) who have lived long enough in a given region to acquire intimate knowledge about the ecosystems they depend on and how to derive their sustenance without degrading those environments. I surmise such influence because Suzuki spotlighted the work of two anthropologists who advanced the TEK perspective: Gerardo Reichel-Dolmatoff, who studied the Desana in the Amazon and how their cosmology promoted reciprocal moral obligations between humans and other organisms; and Steven Lansing, who found that in culturally Hindu Bali (Indonesia), traditional and environmentally sustainable agricultural was intertwined with ritual obligations at water temples.[72]

An excellent way to explore TEK further is with some passages from the Canadian environmental scientist and anthropologist Fikret Berkes, whose words demonstrate the affinity that many devoted to this area of study have with dark green religiosity. For Berkes, TEK is "a cumulative body of knowledge, practice, and belief, evolving by adaptive processes and handed down through generations by cultural transmission, about the relationship of living beings (including humans) with one another and with their environment." It inspires "an ethic of nondominant, respectful human-nature relationship, a sacred ecology." It shapes "environmental perception and [gives] meaning to observations of the environment." Finally, "A fundamental lesson of traditional ecological knowledge is that worldviews do matter."[73]

Like other participants in dark green religion, Berkes roots contemporary environmental problems in human "alienation from nature," but he believes that indigenous, relational epistemologies can teach a way back.[74] By learning from indigenous peoples, those who are not alienated in this way, it is possible to develop "an alternative view of ecosystems [as] pulsating with life and spirit, incorporating people who *belong* to that land and who have a relationship of peaceful coexistence with other beings."[75]

Many other ecologists and anthropologists would agree. Indeed, many of those pioneering the disciplines of ethnobiology and ecological anthropology, and disciplines with similar interests, have come to appreciate if not express personal affinity with the nature-based religions of the indigenous people with whom they are often well acquainted. Moreover, they often become engaged in efforts to protect these peoples from the encroaching forces of market society, taking this as moral obligation. This is an important aspect of such dark green religion—to protect and defend those peoples considered the best remaining stewards of this critically important spiritual and ecological knowledge. Certainly, this is Suzuki's view as well.

CHAPTER 7

Globalization in Arts, Sciences, and Letters

Parareligion and Dark Green Naturalism

In this chapter I borrow the term *parareligion* from the anthropologist Jonathan Benthall as shorthand for what some call implicit religion or quasi religion. Some use such terms to refer to religion-resembling phenomena that they do not consider to actually *be* religious. I am using the term *parareligion*, however, without assuming it needs some currently missing trait to be "real" religion. Instead, I use it in a way that reflects this study's flexible definitional strategy, which does not seek to resolve religion's boundaries.[1]

Gaian Naturalism and Naturalistic Animism, and thus much of the phenomena already examined, are examples of the kind of naturalistic dark green religion that could be considered parareligion. The scientists quoted by David Suzuki, discussed in the previous chapter, who express "awe and reverence before the universe," who urge people to consider the earth as sacred and environmental protection a religious duty, provide one example; so do many of the others Suzuki drew upon, including Leopold, Carson, Odum, Soulé, Wilson, Kellert, and Lovelock. To further reinforce affective connections with nonhuman organisms, Suzuki also included in his *Sacred Balance* the final passage from Darwin's *Origin of Species* regarding the grandeur of an evolutionary worldview. Then Suzuki added this passage from Albert Einstein (1879–1955): "A human being is part of the whole, called by us the universe. . . . He experiences himself . . . as something separate from the rest, [which is] a kind of optical delusion of his consciousness. This delusion is a kind of prison for us, restricting us to our personal desires and to affection for a few persons nearest to us. Our task must be to free ourselves from this prison by widening our circle of compassion to embrace all living creatures."[2]

Passages like these echo themes typical of dark green religion. They represent the impulse to use poetic if not religious terminology to express perceptions and feelings most meaningful to their authors.[3] Of special note is a 1986 statement by the well-known biologist Paul Ehrlich, again quoted by Suzuki: "I am convinced that a quasi-religious movement, one concerned with the need to change the values that now govern much of human activity, is essential to the persistence of our civilization."[4]

Many are surprised to hear scientists promoting naturalistic nature religion or using religious terminology to express their respect for nature. This is less surprising when one knows something about Ernst Haeckel (1834–1919), who coined the word *ecology*.

Haeckel was a German zoologist and philosopher who, in 1866, developed a phylogenetic tree of life to illustrate his explicit assertion that "man has evolved from apes just as these have evolved from lower animals." This was, as Richard Noll put it, "an explosive admission that Darwin deliberately avoided in *On the Origin of Species*." Haeckel also fused a Darwinian worldview with a pantheistic philosophy, which helps account for why he became a very popular scientific author, "rivaled, perhaps, only by recent scientists such as Carl Sagan and E. O. Wilson." Haeckel hoped for nothing less, Noll wrote, than the spread of "an explicitly pantheistic and atheistic 'Monistic Religion' based on 'the good, the true, and the beautiful' in Nature [that] would replace Christianity [and in which] Nature itself would be worshipped through a new aesthetic vision in science . . . as reflected through the prismatic truth of evolution."[5]

Haeckel's nature spirituality would be taken in both naturalistic and overtly spiritual ways: Einstein was reportedly an admirer, as was Rudolf Steiner (1865–1925). Einstein had affinity with the naturalistic pole of dark green religion. Steiner, the German theosophist, had more affinity with the spiritual pole. Steiner sought esoteric truths in nature and encouraged others to do so as well. Through the philosophy he developed called anthroposophy, the invention of biodynamic farming, and the Waldorf schools he inspired, he contributed substantially to sustainability movements and green politics in Europe and beyond.[6] Steiner significantly influenced the Australian Bill Mollison (b. 1928), who pioneered permaculture, a self-sustaining form of organic farming that has been spreading for decades, especially within the countercultural branches of the global environmentalist milieu.[7] These countercultural streams, while scientific in *some* ways, have also involved beliefs that nonmaterial energies or spirits animate life-forms, which need to be worked with respectfully, including through rituals, when gaining sustenance from the earth. This stream is a form of Gaian and/or animistic spirituality, and it has influenced some in bioregional and sustainability movements.[8]

The naturalistic pole of dark green religion has more affinity with conservation biology. According to Stephen Humphrey, one of the founders of the Society for Conservation Biology (in 1986), the discipline is animated by biophilia and a mission to apply ecological knowledge to conserve biodiversity.[9] Three of the discipline's architects—David Ehrenfeld, Michael Soulé, and Reed Noss—have been staunch critics of anthropocentric and humanistic philosophies.[10] Ehrenfeld, for example, who was appointed the first editor of *Conservation Biology* (in 1987), published *The Arrogance of Humanism* in 1978, which remains a landmark in nonanthropocentric environmentalism. Drawing on religion-tinged language to make his point, he elegantly expressed melancholy over the extinction crisis: "We must live in our century and wait, enduring somehow the unavoidable sadness . . . nothing is free of the taint of our arrogance. We have defiled everything, much of it forever, even the farthest jungles of the Amazon and the air above the mountains, even the everlasting sea which gave us birth."[11]

For his part, Soulé, a Buddhist who took a multiyear sabbatical from academia to study and meditate, organized a 1981 conference in Los Angeles to explore the relationships between religion and ecology. He invited Arne Naess to speak, which spurred a long and close friendship in which Naess became "a major influence" in his life, Soulé recalled later. He subsequently invited Naess to give the keynote address at the second conservation biology conference, "because he provided a better philosophical foundation for conservation and biodiversity than anybody since Leopold."[12] Noss, who became the second editor of *Conservation Biology,* had also been attracted to radical environmentalism in the early 1980s, while a graduate student, but left the movement by the end of the decade, frustrated by the hostility to science that he found among many involved. Yet as he rose to prominence in the scientific world, he continued to promote deep ecology and biodiversity protection.[13]

Rejecting (and Defending) Dark Green (Para)religion

Science-grounded parareligious phenomena are not always welcomed, and they can be confusing. They can be confusing because it is unclear what terms like *quasi religion* and *sacred* mean. Neither Ehrlich nor the scientists quoted by Suzuki defined these terms. Most people do understand that the word *sacred,* as vague as it is, has something to do with what people consider holy or of ultimate value. But Richard Dawkins, who in the early twenty-first century became one of the world's leading scientific atheists, would like those who do not believe in nonmaterial divine beings to stop using religious terminology, even for worthy environmental goals.

In *The God Delusion,* Dawkins sought to debunk the possibility explored throughout *Dark Green Religion* that nature-inspired wonder, delight, and awe might be considered religious. Such religion-tinged respect for nature has become so common, however, that Dawkins was compelled to address it before launching his assault on religion. He began his book, therefore, with an epigraph from Einstein: "I don't try to imagine a personal God; it suffices to stand in awe at the structure of the world, in so far as it allows our inadequate senses to appreciate it."[14] Dawkins then acknowledged "a quasi-mystical response to nature and the universe is common among scientists and rationalists." He continued, however, that such a response "has no connection with supernatural belief."[15] Instead, he offered Darwin's comforting conclusion that there is "grandeur in this [evolutionary] view of life," and followed this with a parallel thought expressed in *Pale Blue Dot,* by the astronomer Carl Sagan: "How is it that hardly any major religion has looked at science and concluded, 'This is better than we thought! The universe is much bigger than our prophets said, grander, more subtle, more elegant.' . . . Instead they say, 'no, no, no! My god is a little god, and I want him to stay that way.' A religion, old or new, that stressed that magnificence of the Universe as revealed by modern science might be able to draw forth reserves of reverence and awe hardly tapped by the conventional faiths."[16] Dawkins did not quote Sagan's next sentence, "Sooner or later, such a religion will emerge," presumably because he found the idea distasteful. But he did accurately note that "all Sagan's books touch the nerve-endings of transcendent wonder that religion monopolized in past centuries." Then, Dawkins revealed, "My own books have the same aspiration."[17]

Despite this aspiration, Dawkins strongly objected to such wonder being referred to in religious terms and to, what he called, the "failure to distinguish what can be called Einsteinian religion from supernatural religion." He then criticized the cell biologist Ursula Goodenough, who had called herself a "religious naturalist" and wrote a book titled *The Sacred Depths of Nature,* for hiding her atheism behind religious language. Dawkins contended that it is "destructively misleading" when scientists label as religious their aesthetic and affective experiences when contemplating nature because "for the vast majority of people, 'religion' implies 'supernatural.'" Dawkins even declared that it is "intellectual high treason" when atheists and others who do not really believe in the "interventionist, miracle wreaking . . . prayer-answering God" confuse people with pantheistic or other religious language.[18]

This critique was likely disheartening to those in the World Pantheist Movement, nontheistic naturalists who are an excellent example of Gaian Naturalism. Originally named the Society for Scientific Pantheism (in 2006), the group's website quoted a famous statement attributed to Einstein: "A knowledge of the existence of something we cannot penetrate, of the manifestations of the profoundest reason and the most radiant beauty—it is this knowledge and this emotion that constitute the truly religious attitude; in this sense, and this alone, I am a deeply religious man." Then the site asked its visitors:

> Is Nature your spiritual home? Do you feel a deep sense of peace and belonging and wonder in the midst of nature, in a forest, by the ocean, or on a mountaintop? Are you speechless with awe when you look up at the sky on a clear moonless night and see the Milky Way strewn with stars as thick as sand on a beach? . . . Do you find it impossible to believe in supernatural beings, and difficult to conceive of anything more worthy of reverence than the beauty of nature or the power of the universe? If you answered yes to these questions, then you will feel thoroughly at home in the World Pantheist Movement. Our caring and celebratory approach focuses on nature rather than the supernatural, on what we can see and do and live out rather than on invisible entities that we can only imagine.

The next section argued that the group's "naturalistic reverence for nature" satisfies the human need for meaning "without sacrificing logic or respect for evidence and science." The site also listed as "honorary members" a number of individuals who are good exemplars of Gaian Naturalism, including Lovelock, Suzuki, Sagan, and Goodenough.[19]

There are many difficulties in Dawkins's hard line against mixing religious terminology with nontheistic nature appreciation. Foremost may be that he must labor to show that those he otherwise appreciates—but who blur the boundaries between science and religion through symbolic and metaphorical writing—are not *really* religious (as he understands religion, of course). He did this with Einstein by quoting additional passages from him:

> I am a deeply religious nonbeliever. This is somewhat a new kind of religion. . . .
>
> I do not believe in a personal God. . . . If something is in me which can be called religious then it is the unbounded admiration for the structure of the world so far as our science can reveal it. . . .
>
> I have never imputed to Nature a purpose or a goal, or anything that could be understood as anthropomorphic. What I see in Nature is a magnificent structure that we can comprehend only very imperfectly, and that must fill a thinking person with a feeling of humility. This is a genuinely religious feeling that has nothing to do with mysticism.[20]

What Dawkins does not adequately explain is why nontheists draw on religious terminology to express their most heartfelt perceptions and feelings about the world and why they care for it. Part of the answer is that humans are social beings, and religious communities can create and powerfully reinforce social mores. Suzuki hinted at this in *The Sacred Balance* when he spoke of the joys of working in communities to protect and restore nature, and he described such activities as religious.[21]

The World Pantheists provided another example of dark green religion promoting collective ethical action as they urged website visitors to unite, endorse the Earth Charter, and campaign against social injustice and global warming. These sorts of expressions reveal the impulse to institutionalize dark green religious feeling and to influence public policies and social structures. The Earth Charter is one example of several institutional initiatives inspired, in part, by participants in dark green religion. Before discussing the charter and other international developments, which illuminate further the influence of dark green religion, additional means by which dark green religion is expressed and promoted deserve attention.

Connecting through Nature Writing and Art

Long before motion pictures and documentaries, dark green religion was expressed and promoted through writings in science, philosophy, fiction, and poetry. Nature writing is more familiar than most of the phenomena I examine under the dark green religion microscope. I have found no better summary of the perceptions and feelings at the root of most nature writing than an essay by Joseph Wood Krutch, first published in 1950 in the *Saturday Review,* and then as an introduction to his collection, *Great American Nature Writing.*[22]

JOSEPH WOOD KRUTCH AND NATURE WRITING

Krutch began by observing that "the legend of a golden age when man lived in harmony with nature seems to be almost as old as civilization itself" and that there is "a vast body of scholarly writings devoted to the analysis of what is loosely called 'the appreciation of nature' as a literary phenomenon." Then, after acknowledging that Darwin and Thoreau were both influenced by many others before them, he noted:

> If it is true not only that Thoreau was the most original of the modern nature writers, but also that nearly everyone who has come after has learned something from him, then it ought to be possible to put one's finger upon some aspect of his uniqueness. Perhaps no man before him had ever taken quite so literally the term 'fellow creatures' and perhaps that is one of the most significant things about him. When he spoke of having 'a little fishy friend in the pond,' when he held interviews with a woodchuck or hoped that one of his games had taught the fox something, he was expressing in his own special humorous way a sense of intimacy and of fellowship to some degree novel. . . . Thoreau could feel as he did, not so much because he was tender toward inferior creatures as because he did not think of them as inferior: because he had none of that sense of superiority or even separateness which is the inevitable result of any philosophy or any religion which attributes to a man a qualitative uniqueness and therefore, inevitably, suggests that all other living things exist for him.[23]

In this, Krutch not only recognized Thoreau's unique perspective, he saw the animistic dimension to Thoreau's own and much subsequent nature writing.[24] Like Leopold, who died shortly before Krutch wrote this essay, and like historian Lynn White's critique seventeen years after this essay, Krutch blamed Christianity for the prevailing anthropocentric attitude that "refuses to admit" that humankind was descended from apes and "continuous with the rest of nature." After discussing figures, including Darwin's own grandfather, Erasmus Darwin, who cleared the way for Darwin's revolutionary theory, Krutch concluded that Thoreau's basic feeling of oneness with nature and kinship with her creatures had affinity with the ancient idea of "the world soul or, if one prefers . . . the Great God Pan." Moreover:

Much 'nature writing' today reflects more or less definitely this sense of identity, material as well as spiritual, with the fellow creatures which it studies and describes. *It implies if it does not state a kind of pantheism in which the symbol of the unity of all living things is not an elusive spirit but a definable material thing.* Yet this definable material thing is also a symbol and being such does not necessarily imply any thoroughgoing materialistic philosophy. It implies merely that Life itself rather than something still more mysterious called the 'cause of life' is the bond between fellow creatures.[25]

Thus, as one of the earliest "ecocritics," Krutch perceived the heart of the nature-writing genre: animistic and Gaian connections with nature. He saw this clearly, I think, because of his affinity for such spiritualities, which he expressed a few years later in *The Voice of the Desert.* There he wrote of listening to the earth's many landscapes but especially the desert, describing how it evokes a deep sense of belonging, humility, and awe. He concluded by referencing the eighteenth-century distinction between the beautiful and the sublime: "The sublime . . . inspires awe . . . and [is] powerful; it carries with it the suggestion that it might overwhelm us if it would. By these definitions there is no doubt which [sublime rather than merely beautiful] is the right word for the desert." For Krutch, nature and especially the desert were sacred, a theme Edward Abbey would embellish in *Desert Solitaire.*[26]

Krutch, like many contemporary scholars *of* nature writing, and most of the nature writers past and present, was engaged in the production of what I am calling dark green religion. Dark green themes also increasingly appear in nature-focused magazines, including *Orion,* and in widely distributed publications such as *National Geographic* and *Outside.* These are some of the surprising sources of dark green spirituality. Other tributaries appear in the borderlands between New Age, pagan, and environmentalist enclaves.

ECOTOPIAN, PAGAN, AND NEW AGE WRITING

There is an "ecotopian" genre, for example, that imagines paths to and the elements of human societies that find their ways back to harmony with a sacred Mother Earth. Ernest Callenbach inaugurated this genre when he published *Ecotopia* in 1975.[27] The writings of the pagan-witch Starhawk provide another example. Born of Jewish heritage and named Miriam Simos in 1951, she later changed her name to fit her new religious identity. As Starhawk she became well known in religious and political countercultures for her effort to revive Paganism in general and

Wicca (sometimes called Witchcraft or the Craft) in particular. Starhawk believed these traditions originated in the pre-Abrahamic nature religions of Europe, making her argument in her widely read *Spiral Dance* in 1979.[28] In 1980 "she and her coven-sisters founded *Reclaiming,* a center for feminist spirituality and a school of Witchcraft," and she eventually also became an important activist in the antiglobalization movement.[29] She also wrote popular novels in Callenbach's ecotopian tradition, but even more so than Callenbach expressed in them dark green, even radical environmental themes.[30]

The very same day in 1979 that Starhawk published *The Spiral Dance,* Margot Adler, a National Public Radio reporter in the United States, published another influential book about the growth and types of earth-revering Paganism.[31] Both Adler and Starhawk managed to turn contemporary Paganism in an environmentalist direction. This was no small accomplishment, for there are aspects to Paganism, including its hedonistic ethos and the tendency to emphasize ritualizing as a means to ecstatic experience, that hinder political activism.

Pagan themes, however, are increasingly found in popular culture, even if they are not recognized as such. The African American writer Alice Walker, for example, won the Pulitzer Prize for her 1982 book, *The Color Purple,* which Steven Spielberg turned into a motion picture in 1985 that was nominated for eleven Academy awards.[32] The setting was the rural southern United States in the early twentieth century, and although most of the attention was focused on the violence toward its black women characters or on its lesbian themes, a key part of the book and film was about how the oppressed women found healing. They did so by rejecting patriarchal Abrahamic religion, embracing each other, and coming to an understanding that they belong to a sacred and beneficent Mother Earth.

In her book *Anything We Love Can Be Saved: A Writer's Activism,* Walker later reflected on this work and her religious sentiments. She explained how one character learned from the other that "God is everything that is, ever was or will be." She then confided, "In day-to-day life, I worship the Earth as God—representing everything—and Nature as its spirit."[33]

Walker was influenced by early ecofeminist scholarship and by views that understand Native Americans as having deep reverence for Mother Earth: "If our awareness is beginning to change, it is thanks in part to feminism and feminist scholarship, and to a resurgent belief in the sacredness of the feminine, which was deliberately erased, demonized, and disparaged in all major religions. But thanks also to indigenous peoples who . . . have risen up to speak in defense of the ancient Goddess/God of all pagans and heathens, Mother Earth." Speaking especially to those of African descent, Walker urged a return to pagan, ancestral traditions: "It is fatal to love a God who does not love you. A God specifically created to . . . enlarge the tribal borders of someone else. We have been beggars at the table of a religion that sanctioned our destruction. Our own religions denied, forgotten; our own ancestral connections to All Creation something of which we are ashamed. I maintain that we are empty, lonely, without our pagan-heathen ancestors; that we must lively them up within ourselves, and begin to see them as whole and necessary and correct."[34]

Walker also has written of animistic experiences, such as communion with a horse (including through eye-to-eye contact), learning lessons from animals, and having dialogues with trees and the earth itself in which they describe what it feels like be so oppressed by humans (in a way reminiscent of the Council of All Beings).[35] Elsewhere, Walker has described her trust in the universe, which reflects a common understanding of religion: that it has to do with trusting powers greater than oneself.[36] Within a spiritual framing she calls pagan, Walker thus provides another example of dark green religion—but more on the naturalistic than the spiritual side of the continuum. Some Pagans are entirely naturalistic in their worldviews and do not believe literally in goddesses or nature spirits but rather consider these to be symbolic expressions of human connections to nature. Despite her regular use of goddess imagery and other religious terminology, in 1989 Walker told Oprah Winfrey (who played one of the main characters in the film version of *The Color Purple*): "There is no heaven. This is it. We're already in heaven, you know, and so . . . for the earth to survive, we have to acknowledge each other as part of the . . . same family."[37]

Starhawk, Adler, and Walker show that Paganism, by emphasizing Mother Earth as sacred and sometimes equating her with the body of the goddess, is fertile ground for environmentalism. Both Walker and Starhawk, who live in Northern California, have supported campaigns against logging in the redwood biome. Given the earthly ground of contemporary Paganism, it is unsurprising that when Paganism does lead to political action it would have a strong ecofeminist dimension. But many would be surprised to find environmental action promoted in New Age enclaves. There has been, however, at least a modest greening of New Age spirituality, and some of this is dark green and politically engaged.

DARK GREEN THEMES IN THE NEW AGE

New Age religion deserves its reputation for otherworldliness and political indifference. This is in part because it views consciousness change as the prerequisite to the desired harmony between the earthly and heavenly dimensions of the universe. Yet some New Age thinkers view environmental protection and restoration as critically important to the emerging age of peace and harmony.[38]

The bestselling novels by James Redfield, which center around an ancient, recently discovered Mayan document said to contain the Celestine Prophecy, provide a striking example.[39] The prophecy provides the keys to uniting earth and heaven and explains the path to a prosperous and peaceful future. This path includes, on the one hand, human lovemaking, which "opens up a portal from the afterlife to the Earthly dimension [and] is a holy moment in which a part of Heaven flows into the Earth." But equally important is the protection of cultural and biological diversity: cultural diversity because the prophesy comes from indigenous peoples whose teachings show the way to the New Age; biological diversity because intact, biologically diverse wilderness areas are the "sacred portals" between the afterlife and earthly experience. To create harmony in the universe, therefore, between earthly and otherworldly dimensions, humans must protect and restore the world's "majestic, cathedral forests."[40] As in most dark green religion, Christianity is also seen as an obstacle to the envisioned harmony, and in Redfield's stories the prophesy must be protected from Catholic and governmental agents who do not want its secrets revealed.

Some who resonate with dark green religion would charge that in Redfield's novels nature is not intrinsically valuable but is rather a means to human spiritual ends. Redfield would likely view such complaints as typical of the dualistic, polarizing thinking that, if the planet is to be healed, must be overcome with positive, conscious energy. He might well also quote one of his characters to the effect that a spiritual approach, producing human consciousness change, is *the* way to save the planet's biota: "Once we reach the critical mass . . . and the insights begin to come in on a global scale . . . we'll grasp how beautiful and spiritual the natural world really is. We'll see trees and rivers and mountains as temples of great power to be held in reverence and awe. We'll demand an end to any economic activity that threatens this treasure."[41] Then we'll understand, Redfield explains through the character,

> the natural areas of the Earth have to be nurtured and protected for the sources of the incredible power that they are. . . . As the human race evolves spiritually, we will voluntarily decrease the population to a point sustainable by the Earth. We will be committed to living within the natural energy systems of the planet. Farming will be automated . . . and . . . the trees necessary for construction will be grown in special, designated areas. This will free the remainder of the Earth's trees to grow and age and finally mature into powerful forests. Eventually, theses forests will be the rule rather than the exception, and all human beings will live in close proximity to this kind of power.

Here Redfield's Gaian and animistic spirituality is in plain view, and it exemplifies a New Age form of dark green religion. As ecological alarm grows, many in New Age subcultures continue to be preoccupied with unseen dimensions of the universe, but others, including Marianne Williamson, are grafting environmentalism onto their worldviews.[42] As environmental concern intensifies, this new trend likely will as well. Moreover, as participants in New Age subcultures are drawn into the environmentalist milieu, the bricolage will continue. Significant numbers of those engaged in New Age enclaves already express dark green spirituality and these individuals, in turn, are influencing some environmentalists.[43]

PHOTOGRAPHY AND OTHER ARTS

I have already described the critical the role art has played in fostering perceptions of nature as sublime and intrinsically valuable, discussing literature, motion pictures and documentaries, and to a lesser extent poetry and photography, while pragmatically ignoring music.[44] The importance of all of these arts in dark green religion cannot be underestimated. Like the literary examples just discussed, some of this can be surprising, for example, discovering the permanent exhibit of animistic and earth-revering Zimbabwean art located underground at the Atlanta airport, which included interviews with the artists who connected their love of nature with respect for their ancestors.[45]

The archetypal exemplar of photographic nature religion may be Ansel Adams (1902–1984), who became famous for his black-and-white landscapes (and many books reproducing them) focused especially on California's Sierra Nevada.[46] For Adams (like Muir), these mountains were his most sacred places. He expressed great affinity for Thoreau and the pantheistic poetry of Walt Whitman, and he became good friends with Robinson Jeffers, another important dark green poet.

Adams considered himself a Pantheist and sought to evoke a perception of the sacred in nature. He viewed his art as the most important part of his environmental activism, which he engaged in largely through the Sierra Club after joining in 1919. He later served as a board member for many years, beginning in 1936.[47] The leadership of the National Park Service, as well as millions of park visitors, have been moved by his photography.[48] The U.S. Congress even named a wilderness (and mountain) in his honor, which is also where his ashes were scattered after his death.[49]

The creation of national parks was itself inspired in part by a longing to return to an Edenic paradise, and visual art (including photography) played a critical role in presenting the parks as sites of transcendent meaning.[50] Indeed, many of the architects and interpreters in the Park Service have sought to evoke in visitors precisely such a sense of the sublime in nature. Focusing on Yosemite National Park, for example, Kerry Mitchell has scrutinized how the Park Service orchestrates the entire visitor experience: managing "viewscapes" to focus attention on the grandeur of the most spectacular cliffs and waterfalls: subtly suggesting what visitors should feel, presumably the sublime, through *The Spirit of Yosemite,* a documentary shown regularly at the park's visitor center.[51] The Park Service also permits the Ansel Adams Gallery in the park itself, on the floor of Yosemite Valley. The gallery features Adams's photographs and photographic books and thus enables visitors to purchase objects that will remind them of their favorite sacred places upon their return to civilization.[52]

The strategic link between photography and other arts, and the protection of nature in national parks, is long-standing. This connection has been extended as national parks and other protected areas, such as biosphere reserves, have spread globally. Indeed, the connection between conservation, nature spirituality, and ethics is increasingly considered important when deciding how nature reserves are established, managed, and interpreted.[53]

Perhaps the most important general in the strategic deployment of photography as a conservation strategy was David Brower (1912–2000), a mountain climber credited with thirty-three first ascents in the Sierra Nevada, who was elected to the Sierra Club board in the early 1940s and became the club's executive director in 1952.[54] Brower is considered by many to be the most important environmental leader of the twentieth century, apart from John Muir himself. Many Sierra Club members, moreover, believe he was also the most authentic representative of Muir's spirit among all of the club's subsequent directors—in part because of his tenacity and also because of statements like, "To me, God and nature are synonymous."[55]

Brower was also a long-time friend of Ansel Adams (they first met in 1933) who recognized the evocative and political power of the arts.[56] Brower once remarked that he first heard the mountains speak through poets and only later, in a more direct way, through mountain music (the diverse sounds one hears in the wilderness as well as all of one's sensory experiences of nature).[57] Perhaps this is one reason why he could easily see the potential of a conservation strategy in Adams's photography and in art in general. In the 1950s, therefore, Brower funded large exhibit-format photography books, usually spiced with poetry and prose, which together portray nature as pristine and sublime. Perhaps the two most famous of these were *This Is the American Earth* (1960) and *The Place No One Knew* (1963).[58] The latter was a beautifully photographed lament over the construction of Glen Canyon Dam on the Colorado River, which drowned vast canyons behind it. Filled with prose that hit all of the major themes found in dark green religion, it included expressions of belonging to nature, kinship with other than human organisms, and (a naturalistic) Gaian religiosity well before James Lovelock resurrected Gaia.[59] It was also a successful rallying cry against all large-scale dam projects, and the 2000 edition transformed the book from a eulogy for a lost canyon to a quest to restore it to its pre-dam grandeur.[60] In 1965, with Adams as his coeditor, Brower and the Sierra Club also published *Not Man Apart,* which included photographs by Adams and many others and took its title from lines in "The Answer," a Robinson Jeffers poem.[61] This poem resonated with many who have affinity with dark green spirituality; indeed, it is one of the greatest examples of biocentric poetry in American letters. It reads in part:

> Integrity is wholeness
>   the greatest beauty is
> Organic wholeness, the wholeness of life and things, the divine beauty
>   of the universe. Love that, not man
> Apart from that, or else you will share man's pitiful confusions
>   or drown in despair when his days darken.[62]

Beyond such fusing of poetry and photography into a new form of sacred text, Brower also pioneered green political advertising. Most famously, he and his comrades depicted a proposal for two dams on the Grand Canyon as a desecration akin to flooding the Sistine Chapel to get closer to its spectacular ceiling.[63] The advertisement fell on fertile cultural soil and led to dramatic increases in Sierra Club memberships and political power.

A generation after these innovations, deep ecology activists gave this sort of mission strategy a new spin by preparing huge books juxtaposing photographs of intact forests with those devastated by clear-cut logging. The pictures were, as before, supplemented by words from scientists, activists, and poets who decried "industrial forestry," argued that forests have intrinsic value, and urged a halt to such defiling acts. In what is probably the grandest example of such books as a conservation (if not also a religious) tool, copies of one such title were distributed to members of the U.S. Congress in the hope that they would see the light and halt logging on public lands.[64]

Such large-format photography books are now found in millions of homes worldwide—and their message is clear: the places least touched by humans and the most diverse biologically are the most sacred. Many of these books are also explicitly designed to evoke human sympathies for animals. An especially stunning one is Frans Lanting's *Eye to Eye: Intimate Encounters with the Animal World,* with its photographs of animal eyes.[65] In his introduction, Lanting explained how, as a youth in Holland, he read a novel by the Nobel Prize–winning Swedish author Selma Lagerlöf titled *The Wonderful Adventures of Nils* (1907).[66] Lagerlöf told the story, Lanting explained, of "a boy who shrinks to the size of an elf" and then spent a year living with a family of geese "to see the world through their eyes"; but the child was saddened when he returned to his human size and his companions suddenly were afraid of him. Eventually, the geese asked the boy to become an advocate for them, and this inspired Lanting's career as a naturalist and conservationist. Lanting continued, expressing a kind of Naturalistic Animism, "The conditions under which I work are often a far cry from Nils's intimacy with his wild geese. [But there] were times when I shrank in size and learned to see the world through other eyes." His book was designed, he said, "to celebrate the kinship of all life."[67]

If one were to interview a host of wildlife photographers, the desire to connect with nonhuman organisms and the hope to promote felt kinship with them would be commonly expressed. With the right lenses, when observing many works of nature-focused art, dark green religion comes into focus.

Connecting through Interpretation at Museums, Zoos, Aquariums, and Protected Areas

In addition to the already discussed Disney Animal Kingdom Park and various national parks, interpretive displays with conservationist messages are found at many other venues—museums, aquariums, zoos, biosphere reserves, and the like. Some such exhibits have dark green themes. The National Museum of Anthropology in Mexico City, where I spent a full day in January 2008, provides an excellent example of how dark green religious themes are being presented powerfully to the public.

At the museum, the first permanent exhibit introduced the discipline of anthropology. Its most important panels were in both Spanish and English. These were among the most often read panels in the museum, their prominent placement and bilingual display signaling that the curators considered the information in them to be especially important. The first panel explained the age of the earth, the second described evolution and characterized it as a fact. The third panel included these words: "thus, anthropology, through the study of fossil remains and modern primates, can trace the evolutionary relationships, presenting a mirror that reminds us that we are part of the history of the world and the animal kingdom, and not as we had believed, that we were created to have nature at our service." Note the dark green themes: belonging to nature, we are animals, and a rejection of Western religious cosmogony.

A large adjacent panel described the genus *Australopithecus* (an early bipedal hominid that scientists believe is a human ancestor). Together these panels expressed clear biocentric and kinship ethics; they also sought to overturn anthropocentric arrogance. The perceptive reader would recognize that (colonial) Abrahamic religions were being criticized for promoting precisely such destructive misperceptions, especially what the panels said was the false earlier view that nature was created only for humans. I was surprised to see all of this stated so forthrightly. Throughout the rest of the museum, other themes typical of dark green religion were expressed, including links between the domestication of plant and animal species, human overpopulation, deforestation, declining ecosystem diversity, declining resilience and agricultural productivity, famine, warfare, and environmental/social collapse. Moreover, although the museum displays forthrightly examined the close links between pre-Christian religions and violence (including human sacrifice), on the whole the connections between religion and nature in pre-Christian Mesoamerica were described in a positive way. Traditional ecological knowledge was explained and its interrelatedness with pagan, nature-related spirituality that yet survives in Mesoamerican indigenous communities was acknowledged and portrayed sympathetically. Also praised was the Paganism still present, in more fragmented form, within the now dominant forms of Christian religion. I concluded that this museum blended professional and up-to-date biocultural understandings, a measure of national pride, and a subtle anticolonial and antitheist attitude. The outcome was a celebration of the spiritual connections human beings once had with nature in Mesoamerica, still have in some measure, and could have again in a more robust way. It might not be going too far to suggest that the museum was a globalized and localized bricolage of dark green religion, in other words, it reflected ideas being developed by people around the world while illustrating them with examples from the region.

A few months after my day at the anthropology museum, I traveled to Puerto Williams, Chile, which is the world's southernmost town and the capital of the country's Antarctic province, an area that extends from the Darwin Cordillera at the Beagle Channel to the South Pole. The Beagle Channel was named for the ship Darwin sailed on his most famous voyage (he explored the area in 1832). I imagined that this remote town, in this stunningly beautiful and ecologically pristine place, resembled small coastal towns in Alaska or Norway a century earlier.

I was there in part because in 2005 UNESCO (the United Nations Educational, Scientific and Cultural Organization) approved a proposal to establish a Cape Horn Biosphere Reserve. I had an opportunity to discuss the reserve with scientists, philosophers, and others involved with the Omora Foundation and several universities, all of whom had been involved in the effort to establish the reserve or were there to consider the next steps for it.[68] Several of them had long been involved in the research and interpretation at the Omora Ethnobotanical Park, a few kilometers from Puerto Williams, and they were led by the Chilean ecologist, conservation biologist, musical composer, philosopher, and professor (from the University of North Texas), Ricardo Rozzi.

After earning an master's in ecology in his native Chile, Rozzi went on to earn a second master's in environmental philosophy before adding a doctorate in ecology. This interdisciplinary background provided him with the intellectual range needed to integrate many dark green themes into his research, writing, and conservation efforts. He regularly speaks positively, for example, of the seminal thinkers and scientists that this volume explores, including Aldo Leopold and his leading interpreter, J. Baird Callicott; Rachel Carson; and Reed Noss. Rozzi explains the importance of traditional ecological knowledge and a corresponding concern for the conservation of both biological and cultural diversity; and he stresses both ecological interdependence and an evolutionary kinship ethics. The Rozzi-orchestrated *Multi-ethnic Bird Guide* illustrates these themes. It blends scientific and indigenous perspectives on the ecological systems and aviary life in South America, including human stories and bird sounds on two accompanying audio CDs. Rozzi took as examples the Yahgan and Mapuche, two distinct groups of indigenous people inhabiting the region:

> The traditional ecological knowledge contained in the Yahgan and Mapuche ornithological narratives permits us to expand our ways of knowing about, and inhabiting, nature, and of living together with the birds and their ecosystems. . . . The indigenous narratives share two central notions with the contemporary, ecological-evolutionary perspective: 1) the sense of kinship between human beings and birds, derived from common genealogies or evolutionary histories, and 2) the sense of biotic communities or ecological networks, of which humans and birds form part.[69]

The next section, "Our Relatives, the Birds," described how the eyes of birds and humans, and other evidence from modern biology, demonstrate that we share a common ancestor. It continued that this insight about birds and humans being relatives is reflected in long-standing Mapuche and Yahgan narratives, which often begin with the idea that "in ancestral times . . . birds were humans." Rozzi then provided a picture of Ernst Haeckel's tree of life in order to extend even more widely the kinship ethic. The caption said that the tree "illustrates the scientific-evolutionary theory of Charles Darwin, which proposes that human beings possess a common evolutionary origin shared with all living beings." Rozzi subsequently concluded: "From the point of view of contemporary environmental ethics, the three cultural perspectives—Mapuche, Yahgan and scientific—emphasize the *intrinsic value* of avifauna because *the birds are our distant evolutionary relatives.* This implies that, to some degree, the existence of birds can be subject to moral considerations based on ontological and ethical judgments on par with those we use to judge the value of human life." Rozzi also believes it is important to acknowledge that "human beings are not separate from nature"—and that the intrinsic value of all life and practical considerations regarding the prerequisites for human well-being lead to an ethics that respects and protects both cultural and biological diversity.[70] The programs he and his collaborators are establishing at Omora Ethnobotanical Park and that are envisioned for the Cape Horn Biosphere Reserve are developing ways to express and teach such ethics and life practices.

During the dedication of the Omora Ethnobotanical Park, as a member of the Chilean and international socioecological research network, I saw officials involved with biosphere reserve programs from around the world, as well as Chilean politicians, military officers, scientists, philosophers, and community members, visit the park's miniature forest-within-a-forest. The forest in this case consisted of scores of lichens, mosses, and liverworts endemic to the region, nestled *within* a lush forest ecosystem.[71] These organisms were featured at stations with symbolic, large magnifying glasses (without glass), which directed attention to specific species and the adjacent names for them. The visitors also used real magnifying glasses to see these beautiful and bizarre life-forms. As I examined the lichens and the people examining them, I thought of the way the park's interpreters had set up the viewing stations and mused about how ritual focuses attention on that which is considered sacred. These stations did precisely that. Guides and visitors expressed delight at what they were seeing, and the overall tone of the gathering was reverence for these diminutive life-forms.

After this ceremonial walk I spoke with Ximena Arango, an ecologist from Colombia and a member of the Omora Foundation's research and educational team. For a number of years she had been studying, among other things, the region's most charismatic woodpecker, while also developing interpretive programs for park visitors and local school children. When I asked her why she was living in this remote part of the world working on these projects, she said simply, "I just love the life." Later, she communicated her own feelings of connection and belonging to nature, that this was something she had always felt, even as a youngster growing up in the large urban center of Bogota.[72]

Connecting through the United Nations

Like many involved in efforts to preserve biological and cultural diversity, Rozzi and his colleagues were motivated by and engaged in what I have been calling dark green religion. As such they are participating in a long and rich spiritual tradition while also extending its reach. That reach is global, as evidenced by the substantial support for these sorts of efforts from international institutions, including the United Nations, as well as by Chilean governmental and educational institutions.

Probably the best known United Nations report addressing environmental sustainability (even famously defining the term *sustainable development*) was *Our Common Future,* which was issued by the World Commission on Environment and Development in 1987. Commonly known as the Brundtland Report—for the chairwoman of the commission, Gro Harlem Brundtland, then prime minister of Norway—the report was written in very measured tones. It nevertheless reflected some dark green themes, including an apocalyptic vision of environmental and social decline and the importance of protecting indigenous peoples and their spiritual traditions and ecological knowledge. Despite its dominant anthropocentric tone, it also made one of the earliest biocentric statements in an official UN document, recognizing a "moral obligation to other living beings."[73]

The United Nations Educational, Scientific and Cultural Organization was founded in 1945 to help the international community develop standards and guidelines "to forge universal agreements on emerging ethical issues," especially those having to do with the construction of environmentally sustainable, equitable, and peaceful societies.[74] It has also been involved in promoting dark green religion. A year after the Brundtland Report, for example, UNESCO's Man and the Biosphere Program—established in 1971 to administer a global network of biosphere reserves—published an oversized book that was described as a follow-up for a popular audience. *Man Belongs to the Earth* established its dark green tone not only with its title but by lauding Rachel Carson and Ernst Haeckel for their insights. Haeckel was praised as the man who "stressed the importance of the relation of the animal both to its organic as well as to its inorganic environment." With *Silent Spring,* the foreword declared, Carson brought sudden "new awareness of the intricate relationships that link living organisms and their environment, of man's oneness with nature and the extent of his influence over it."[75] Elsewhere in the book, the spirituality of belonging to nature was clear, as was the sense that without such perception it would be impossible to protect and restore the vitality of the earth's ecosystems. The book declared that for man to restore the natural balance of the earth, "he must recognize his true position in the order of things and come to terms with the environment of which he is part."[76] Sprinkled through the book were passages from poets and philosophers, sages from various religious traditions, as well as scientists such as Carl

Sagan, which reinforced the book's promotion of perceptions of ecological interdependence and kinship toward nonhuman organisms, and of understandings of the preciousness (and precarious state) of the biosphere.[77]

Although the title of the book was said to be drawn from Chief Seattle (erroneously, as explained previously), the important thing for the current analysis is that these words expressed what the authors wished to say. The words also appeared inside the book, reinforcing the spirituality of belonging and the kinship ethics that have become increasingly common in the global environmentalist milieu.[78] These words still resonate with people around the world. In 2005 I found excerpts from Chief Seattle's famous speech on napkins in an Amsterdam bagel shop: "We know the sap which courses through the trees as we know the blood that courses through our veins. We are part of the earth and it is part of us. The perfumed flowers are our sisters. The bear, the deer, the great eagle, these are our brothers. The rocky crests, the dew in the meadow, the body heat of the pony, and man all belong to the same family."

Four years after *Man Belongs to the Earth* was published, the United Nations Conference on Environment and Development was held in Rio de Janeiro in 1992. Pressure had built on the UN such that it created a venue for a wide spectrum of civil society and began to create better lines of communication with nongovernmental actors. This summit provided many opportunities for dark green spirituality to be expressed, often in solidarity with the world's indigenous peoples—who were, despite the organizers' overtures to civil society, given almost no access themselves to the official meeting. Within the environmentalist milieu, however, indigenous peoples were recognized as critically important to the long-term health of the biosphere and its biodiversity, and they were acknowledged to be imperiled themselves. Representatives from the world's largest religious traditions were also present, advocating strong reforms to protect the environment and the world's most marginal people.

It was in the midst of the summit's ferment that Maurice Strong, a Canadian who served as its general secretary, proposed the creation of an Earth Charter. The idea was to mimic the strategy behind the United Nations Universal Declaration of Human Rights so that, after ratification, individuals, institutions, and nation-states would voluntarily improve their environmental performance or capitulate to pressure to do so. A prominent group of international figures, as well as representatives of civil society, were enlisted to draft and promote the charter.

These figures included the former leader of the Soviet Union, Mikhail Gorbachev, who like Strong had affinity with dark green religion. Strong's speeches, for example, have been laced with Gaia theory–inspired earthen spirituality and Gorbachev confessed in 1997 his own naturalistic form of earthen spirituality: "I believe in the cosmos . . . *nature is my god.* To me, *nature is sacred.* Trees are my temples and forests are my cathedrals."[79] Moreover, many of those involved in the charter's drafting process had been profoundly influenced by Thomas Berry and his call to consecrate the scientific, evolutionary cosmogony and consider all of its diverse fruit sacred. It should not be surprising, therefore, that the initial draft of the Earth Charter, as well as the final version presented at the 2002 World Summit on Sustainable Development in Johannesburg, South Africa, was the most impressive international example yet of dark green religion.[80]

On the Globalization and Dangers of Dark Green Religion

Several things should by now be clear: dark green religion is an important part of environmentalist milieu; it is a global phenomenon with diverse manifestations in different cultures and social sectors; its participants wish to change the way we feel, think, and relate to the natural world; and they spread their faith in ways that sometimes involve ritual and religion-resembling practices. The activist impulse that flows from dark green religion is engaged at the local and regional levels, but as the movement spreads its ambitions have grown to include transformation of the multilateral and national institutions that shape human societies and determine their environmental impacts.

Beauty is in the eye of the beholder, as the truism says. So is whether one finds promise or peril in dark green religion. The dangers seem to fit into six broad categories.

Those so infused with a sense of kinship for nonhuman organisms and intense feelings of belonging to nature might venture too close to the wrong animal, or too deeply into an ecosystem about which they know too little, to prevent what would be a premature union with that animal or that ecosystem. I do not mean to be flippant, for there are examples: the philosopher who was nearly devoured by a crocodile; the crocodile hunter who succumbed to a stingray's barb; and Timothy Treadwell, who loved and filmed grizzly bears, one of whom eventually killed and ate him and his girlfriend.[81]

The second danger encountered is rather different and grounded in the provocative accusation by Richard Dawkins that atheists who use religious terminology to describe their sense of natural awe and wonder are guilty of "high treason." When I first read this charge, I realized that given my own definitional flexibility I might even stand so accused. So I was thankful I did not live in a country with an established atheist church . . . and a death penalty. Here, of course, I have intended to be flippant.

But in all seriousness, Dawkins would likely argue that I should not call "religious" or even analyze as "parareligion" the affective connections to nature that many people have. I hope my profession in chapter 1—that I am disinterested in patrolling the boundary between what some people count as religion and others do not—will be sufficient for most readers. Perhaps it would even satisfy Dawkins should he encounter this work. It is, of course, fine with me if Dawkins prefers to clearly state his own operational definition (which he does) and make his own arguments based on it. I am doing much the same. My definition of religion is more flexible for the simple strategic reason that it serves my interpretive purposes.

I do find Dawkins's definitional fundamentalism ironic, however. As a social scientist, it strikes me as odd to deny people their own ways of describing themselves, or to say they should not use a term like *sacred*—when they try to express verbally what is most precious to them—*unless* they believe in nonmaterial divine beings. It seems to me that such rigidity hinders Dawkins from fully appreciating the extent to which "religion" might well be changing dramatically and decisively, and for the long term, in the wake of the cognitive revolution that Darwin precipitated. These changes, which have barely been under way for 150 years, in the main are those about which Dawkins would approve. Belief in a personal miracle-making God has been decisively on the wane in most advanced industrial countries, even in the United States, one of the most religious of the highly developed countries. Meanwhile, belief in God as an impersonal force, even a force of nature, is increasing.[82] Such understandings Dawkins would not accept as constituting belief in God or religion. But by constraining his definition of religion in this way, real and significant worldview changes that *are* underway are opaque to him.

It is also ironic that Dawkins wishes to enforce his own orthodox atheism on other naturalists. In this, Dawkins's own polemics resemble a trait all too common in religious traditions: sectarianism and strong mechanisms for worldview maintenance, including the shaming of wayward adherents. It seems much more reasonable, if rationality is the axial value, to expect Dawkins to wrestle more seriously with why colleagues who share his atheism nevertheless agree, in various ways, that humans should resacralize their perception of the universe and biosphere. Moreover, it is reasonable to expect Dawkins to explain why those he criticizes feel they can say such things, and use religious terminology, without sacrificing either their rationality or integrity. It is not clear, on Dawkins's premises, that these people are as dangerous as the accusation of treason suggests.

The third of the perceived dangers is that dark green religion is spiritually dangerous, drawing people away from God and threatening their eternal fate. This danger is nearly the opposite of the second. A version of it would identify each type of dark green religion I have discussed as a form of Paganism whose devotees worship the creation rather than the creator. This is certainly a strong current in Abrahamic cultures that is well documented elsewhere.[83] The negative reaction to dark green spirituality by those with such worldviews is understandable, given their beliefs. Conversely, participants in dark green religion are, with few exceptions, critical of if not hostile to the sorts of religions, and religious people, who would express these concerns. For the most part, despite occasional efforts to hybridize religious traditions, most of the world's major religions have worldviews that are antithetical to and compete with the worldviews and ethics found in dark green religion.[84]

The fourth alleged danger, which is often rooted deeply in the perceived spiritual danger, is that dark green religion is fascistic and/or is part of a conspiracy to establish a totalitarian global government. We saw such criticism leveled previously at radical environmentalists. In this chapter, the most common target for such criticisms and fears would be the United Nations. Efforts to create an Earth Charter as a means to promote and enforce strong international environmental treaties feed directly into such fears—especially among those who highly value national sovereignty and worry about religious freedom.[85] An Internet search on the United Nations or Earth Charter quickly reveals the depth of such fears as well as alarm about environmentalism in general.

The fifth perceived danger underlies a common attack on environmentalists in general: that they exaggerate environmental problems and thereby skew social priorities in ways that hurt human economies and the people who depend upon them. Critics may add that such alarmism leads to extremist and illegal tactics that exacerbate the already significant negative impacts that follow from the alarmism alone. It is easy to find examples of such charges, including against David Suzuki, Ted Turner, and many others described in this volume as participants in dark green religion.[86]

The third, fourth, and fifth dangers are thus spiritual, political, and economic, respectively. They are generally voiced from the political right. The sixth danger is perceived by those who lean both politically right and left, both religiously conservative and liberal, as well as by some atheistic humanists. This fear is that those who promote kinship ethics or the intrinsic value of nature devalue human beings and ignore what should properly be accorded greater moral priority, namely, human life.[87] Like the disconnect between those from the mainstream world religions and those involved in dark green religion, the differences here may be intractable. Those with anthropocentric values tend to fear that biocentric values produce indifference to human suffering, and those with biocentric values tend to believe that anthropocentric values lead to indifference to the well-being of the rest of the community of life. The evidence points both ways.

The best way to evaluate these fears may not be through philosophical debate, as important as that may be. The best way may well be to study those producing and expressing these competing value systems and to assess their *near-term influence* and project their *long-term impacts.* This approach may be the most judicious way to evaluate whether dark green religion should be embraced or feared.

CHAPTER 8

Terrapolitan Earth Religion

Nature and religion have long been intertwined. We have seen that a significant part of human religiosity has affinity with what I have been calling dark green religion. Nature-based spirituality has both deep roots and new expressions. As environmental alarm has intensified, this sort of religion has been rekindled, revitalized, invented, ecologized, localized, and globalized. What remains mysterious is the extent of its *near-term influence* and *long-term impacts,* as well as whether we are witnessing the emergence of a global, civic, earth religion.

Back to Africa

In 2002 I traveled back to Africa to look for clues regarding the influence and prospects of dark green religion. My objective was to observe the United Nations World Summit on Sustainable Development (the WSSD), which was to be held near Johannesburg, South Africa. The WSSD drew over thirteen thousand accredited delegates representing approximately two hundred nations, as well as representatives of corporations and nongovernmental organizations (NGOs). It was envisioned as a meeting to make progress toward the implementation of Agenda 21, a detailed vision for sustainable development articulated at the Rio Earth Summit a decade earlier. Progress was also envisioned for other environmental agreements made at Rio, such as the Convention on Biological Diversity.

As I listened to the rhetoric leading up to the WSSD, it occurred to me that the ambitious stated goal was to make sustainability the axial social organizing principle of human civilization. The prolegomena to the meeting, indeed, seemed to echo Al Gore's 1992 challenge to humanity in *Earth in the Balance,* "We must make the rescue of the environment the central organizing principle of civilization."[1] This book was written a year before the Earth Summit, before Gore became vice president of the United States (in 1993), and more than eight years before Gore failed in his bid to become president when the U.S. Supreme Court ruled controversially that there would be no recount in the disputed voting in Florida. When I read Gore's book I was stunned to see a mainstream U.S. politician articulating so many themes commonly found in the dark green religious milieu: Gore contended that Western civilization had become dysfunctional and destructive and that the roots of the environmental crisis were "spiritual." When making such statements, Gore knew he was going out on a limb: "As a politician, I know full well the special hazards of using 'spiritual' to describe a problem like this one. . . . But what other word describes the collection of values and assumptions that determine our basic understanding of how we fit into the universe?"[2]

Gore also knew that in American politics it was dangerous to say anything that might appear to deviate from mainstream Christian understandings. He carefully acknowledged that the notion of dominion in the Abrahamic traditions *could* promote environmental stewardship, saying this depended on one's interpretation of the tradition. But despite such statements and his life-long identity as a Christian, he expressed *greater* affinity with themes common in dark green religion: "If we could find a way to understand our own connection to the earth—all the earth—we might recognize the danger of destroying so many living species and disrupting the climate balance." After citing with approval James Lovelock's Gaia theory, he added, "The simple fact of the living world and our place on it evokes awe, wonder, a sense of mystery—a spiritual response—when one reflects on its deeper meaning." People experience God, Gore added, "in every corner of creation."[3]

In pluralistic political contexts, the more diverse the constituency, the more cautious a politician must be when it comes to speaking about religion, for fear of giving offense to one or another group. This makes it difficult to know precisely the nature of Gore's religious views. Even if he were post-Christian in his deepest beliefs, he could not afford to say so publicly and, moreover, to be effective in pursuing his political objectives, there would be little to gain and much to lose by coming out in such a way. Yet Gore took real risks in writing the way he did. In the United States and many Western countries, a politician would be very unwise to criticize Western civilization or its religious underpinnings. I wondered when reading this book if it represented dramatic new evidence of the escape of dark green religion from its largely countercultural breeding grounds and its penetration of societal mainstreams.

As my airplane landed in Johannesburg and I reflected on how some of the rhetoric surrounding the WSSD cohered with Gore's earlier writing, I wondered if more politicians would articulate dark green environmental convictions at the event and aggressively promote environmental rescue. I also wondered how, where, and in what ways the activists assembling from around the world, who had for some time been the public face of dark green religion, would engage these powerful political actors.

The stage for this environmental morality play had several venues. The main event was held at the Sandton Convention Centre, where the governmental delegates huddled and lobbyists from diverse nongovernmental sectors (business, environmental, religious, human rights, indigenous, and more) gathered in an effort to influence them. Nearby the IUCN (the United Nations–sponsored International Union for Conservation of Nature) held a forum with natural and social scientists from around the world. There were two other official venues: Ubuntu Village was the more privileged one, where nation-states and selected civil society actors, including the lobbyists for industries and NGOs with strong connections to the UN, hosted their displays and seminars. The Nasrec Exposition Grounds was farther away, both geographically and in terms of political power. It was the main site where religious groups and representatives of diverse grassroots organizations gathered, including indigenous peoples, fishers, farmers, environmentalists, peace activists, and social-justice campaigners.

The Peoples' Earth Summit

Another important site related to the WSSD was an Anglican boarding school near the convention center. This was where the Peoples' Earth Summit (the PES) was held. The events there were neither organized nor accredited by the United Nations. Instead, the PES was hosted by well-known international environmental organizations, including Greenpeace, Friends of the Earth, and the Earth Island Institute, as well as by foundations and educational institutes such as the Gaia Foundation, Schumacher UK, and the magazines *Resurgence* and *The Ecologist*.

The Gaia Foundation's website shows the interlocking relationships among those inspiring and attending the PES, all of whom are involved in dark green religion: "The idea of creating a 'Gaia' Foundation emerged in the early 1980s, from Liz Hosken, Edward Posey and a group of ecological pioneers from the South, including Prof. Wangari Maathai (Kenya) and the late José Lutzenberger (Brazil). Their common vision was to demonstrate how human development and wellbeing are derived from the health and understanding of the living planet (Gaia), and indeed the Universe itself, of which we are an inextricable part." The website also noted that (the late) Sir Laurens van der Post, a South African author, documentary producer, and conservationist, was the foundation's first patron, and Thomas Berry its current one. Both are good representatives of dark green religion.[4] *Resurgence* (which is affiliated with Schumacher UK and inspired by the writings of E. F. Schumacher, who wrote *Small Is Beautiful* in 1973, a classic text in dark green religion) and *The Ecologist* (and its publisher Edward Goldsmith) have also been influential promoters of dark green religion.[5]

The main event at the PES was a five-day World Sustainability Hearing, which featured an array of speakers, including grassroots activists battling for sustainability and environmental justice in a wide variety of ways and places, prominent activist-intellectuals, and also natural scientists and social scientists describing how certain technologies and policies harm people and the environment. The speakers generally agreed that the global extension of market society, which governments and corporations nearly everywhere promote, erodes or thwarts democracy while devastating the environment and the poor. Sixteen of the presenters were also Goldman Environmental Prize winners, an award that often goes to those engaged in dark green religion.[6]

The critical mythos of the hearing reflected dark green themes, including the conviction that most people used to lived sustainably but that a fall from an earthly paradise occurred, resulting (variously, depending on the speaker) from agriculture, hierarchy, patriarchy, monotheism, technology, and capitalism, all of which disconnect us from nature and produce greed, indifference, and injustice. The globalization process itself was said to destroy traditional and sustainable agro-ecosystems. This involved, in essence, an increasing and sacrilegious commodification of life, according to these critics, which in turn depended on the theft of intellectual property from indigenous people and the destruction (if not theft) of their lands. According to this declensionist narrative, globalization—fueled by corporate greed and power and a corresponding erosion of democracy—thus destroyed both biological and cultural diversity.

Although much of the analysis at the hearing and during other PES events was scientific and political, nature spirituality was also prevalent. Much of what occurred there reminded me of radical environmental wilderness gatherings, where the boundary is always thin between activism, entertainment, and nature-venerating ritual. Evenings were filled with strategy sessions and planning for protests as well poetry, music, and drumming. Indigenous people were accorded a special role, once again reflecting the dark green religious belief that, at their best and least assimilated, indigenous cultures offer practical and spiritual wisdom about how to live close to nature.

One evening there was a sunset ritual orchestrated by sangomas, traditional healers in southern Africa. Sangomas typically use medicines derived from plants or animals (sometimes ritually sacrificed), and through ritual processes calling on ancestors for support, they seek to prevent misfortune and to promote health and happiness. As seen previously, some scientists have lauded indigenous traditions as repositories of valuable ecological and pharmaceutical knowledge—this perspective was prevalent at the PES and accounts in part for the respect accorded practitioners of traditional African religions. During one sunset ceremony I attended, for example, the sangomas took turns beseeching the ancestors for help in reharmonizing life on earth. Since African traditional religion has a reputation for being more anthropocentric and less inclined to nature reverence than indigenous religions in many other regions, I was intrigued. After the ritual, I asked Bertram Fredericks, one of the sangomas from South Africa, how African traditional religion intersects with the kind of environmental concerns that had drawn people there from around the world. "The ancestors live in a corporeal world alongside and near to our own," he told me. This surprised me because my previous impression was that ancestors are believed to be spiritual beings living in a nonmaterial domain. To allay my confusion he explained that the line between the earthly world and that of the ancestors is thin and that rituals bridge these worlds: "Since both realms are corporeal and connected, so is their well-being." He added, "We must take good care of the earth so that when we are ancestors we will also inhabit a healthy world." This understanding of the relationship between the well-being of humans currently alive, their ancestors, and the earthly environment may be a new, religious-ecological hybrid. It is certainly one of many forms of nature-related religion being constructed and promoted as awareness grows regarding the severity of anthropogenic environmental decline.

Jane Goodall was in heavy demand at official WSSD venues, but she also gave a presentation at the World Sustainability Hearing, expressing Gaian and animistic spirituality and respect for indigenous peoples. Explaining that the stuffed chimpanzee she carried with her symbolizes their voices, she said, "I like to take the voice of animals into places where I speak." As she does regularly in her talks, she also asserted that "the chimp has done more than any other animal to show us how we are part of it all." She added, "Hopefully in the West we are moving toward the wisdom of indigenous people" and, striking a Gaian note, "Mother Earth is crying out for help today."

With this as her prologue Goodall began a detailed talk about forest conservation in Africa and South America, explained her institute's collaborations with indigenous peoples and how much she had learned from them, particularly the Mbuti (Pygmies), whom she knew particularly well.[7] Along the way she expressed her deep love for the forest: "For me, the forest symbolizes all the things we need. For me, being in the forest is like being in heaven on earth." Goodall suggested that we all need to be connected to nature for "without a connection something in us is starved"—and people who are malnourished in this way become selfish. She concluded by praising the broad movement she was a part of for spreading knowledge, love, and compassion for all species.[8]

• • •

One evening, the Gaia Foundation sponsored a panel called "A Decade of Commitment." It featured activists and intellectuals reflecting on how to persevere despite the daunting obstacles faced by environmental and social-justice activists. The repeated refrain was that the required compassion and commitment depends on a deep sense of belonging and connection to the biosphere. Vandana Shiva, a physicist and ecofeminist from India who is famous worldwide among environmentalists, after reviewing many fronts in the environmental struggle, argued that "to be human we have to reconnect to animals, to other species, for we are connected in the earth family. We need to reembed ourselves in the earth community as a way of connecting to human society."[9] Subsequent speakers made similar comments. Jacqueline McGlade, an oceanographer, professor, and advisor to the Gaia Foundation in the United Kingdom stated, "We need to dig deep inside and reconnect with nature if we are to even begin to understand our influence on nature." She also claimed that telekinesis was happening all over the planet, implying (in concert with New Age thought) that what we envision in our minds has the power to change the realities that we see.[10]

Responding in part to these such comments, Rory Spowers, the author of a book about the environmental revolution who had affinity with deep ecology, stated, "Consciousness is not secondary to the changes we seek." Therefore, strengthening the "perennial philosophy" is needed. Here Spowers referenced an idea first articulated by Leibniz and popularized by Aldous Huxley that the mystical branches of all religions, and especially indigenous religions, are grounded in oceanic experiences in which the individual ego erodes and one perceives the self as just a small part of an enormous, sacred cosmos. "The most important thing is connecting," Spowers stressed. Moreover, "we must emphasize what we are *for,* earth community, more than what we are *against,*" which in that evening's context was understood to be the escalating destruction of nature under the diverse forces of globalization.[11]

Next to speak was Herbert Girardet, chairman of Schumacher UK. An author and documentary filmmaker, Girardet had long been involved in efforts to defend the rights of indigenous peoples and what he understands as their nature-beneficent spiritualities. As part of this effort, he raised alarm about Amazonian deforestation in a 1989 documentary, *Halting the Fires* (produced with the Brazilian Octavio Bezerra and broadcast widely on public television in the United Kingdom and United States). With this film and a book released shortly before the Rio Earth Summit, Girardet promoted biocentric spirituality and argued that a dramatic change in consciousness was imperative if we are to save the planet. After discussing what he called the "planetary emergency" and arguing that we need a new alliance among all international NGOs to battle it, he turned to the importance of recognizing our belonging to nature: "Disconnectedness is a major problem. . . . The one thing we are really sure of is our interconnectedness."[12]

After Girardet's reflections, a Euro-African sangoma from Zimbabwe named Colin Campbell, who had apprenticed with sangomas of the Balete tribe in or near Botswana, asserted that indigenous people in Africa "understand that the universe is alive. Everything has consciousness, knowingness." Moreover, he continued, "The universe constantly speaks. It may not be in the way that we do, but there are different ways of communicating." Campbell concluded that "we need to seek nature's guidance" and cultivate our abilities to hear from her diverse entities. To this Helena Norberg-Hodge, an editor at *The Ecologist* magazine and a board member of the International Forum on Globalization (IFG), after first discussing how the antiglobalization movement is creating new alliances, added, "We need to rebuild communities at the local level and reconnect to nature, and one way to do this is by promoting local food systems." The IFG was funded in large part by Douglas Tompkins, an entrepreneur and mountaineer who founded the corporations North Face and Esprit; he had an epiphany in the late 1980s when reading Arne Naess and other deep ecologists, after which he left the business world and became one of the major funders of deep ecology and radical environmental projects, while also purchasing large natural areas in Chile and seeking to convert them to nationally managed biological reserves. He would later say that he found great inspiration in the activism of David Brower and the poetry of Robinson Jeffers.[13]

It is significant that this theme of connection emerged so strongly on an evening dedicated to finding ways to remain committed to the Earth during a time when environmental decline was so obvious and depressing to those gathered. To remain spiritually faithful, the presenters suggested, one must be connected to the source of life, the earth itself. Cormac Cullinan, an attorney and the author of *Wild Law,* continued the discussion with a Thoreau-like statement that "this connection we share is in nature," and "it is this wildness that drives evolution."[14] He said repeatedly that we must stress these common values and perceptions if we are to be effective. Ricardo Navarro, a Goldman award winner from El Salvador and then chairman of Friends of the Earth International (which not incidentally, was founded by David Brower after he was replaced as executive director of the Sierra Club), agreed: "Disconnectedness is a major problem. One thing we are really sure about is our interconnectedness." Cullinan responded, "We're trying to imagine what it might look like, this new world. The ideology we share is the Earth ideology—we all owe allegiance to the earth." Vandana Shiva wrapped up the evening: "We need Earth-centered thinking if we are ever going to take the power back" from corporate elites and politicians.

These interrelated ideas, that we need "earth-centered" values and loyalty, hints at the possibility that what is emerging here is a kind of earth nationalism or civic earth religion. It seems clear that such an ideology, where it exists and is emerging, is grounded in a spirituality of belonging and connection to an earth and universe considered sacred.

• • •

The themes present during this "Decade of Commitment" panel were promoted in a variety of ways elsewhere. Immediately outside the panel's location, for example, there was an experiential exhibit called "A Walk through Time: From Stardust to Us." This involved a series of visually stunning photographs and artistic renderings on large panels, with a few words on each depicting different moments in the unfolding of the universe from the big bang onward. Though there was not enough space to do so at the Johannesburg meeting, the panels ideally are placed at a distance proportional to the distance in time they represent—the walk itself is then a kind of ritual pilgrimage from deep time to the present. Indeed, the display was designed to evoke a feeling of humility and reverence for this beautiful and mysterious universe, including the diversity of life on earth. This message was most clear toward the end of the panels, where viewers realize what latecomers they are in this cosmic odyssey: "The deep-past lives in each of us, in all of us—each cell, each thought. Walking through the grand pageant of life on Earth can be humbling, sometimes overwhelming. It is also exhilarating. *Where do we come from? What are we? Where are we going?*" A panel titled "The Future" quoted Thoreau's nature-reverencing aphorism "in wildness is the preservation of the world." It then urged "infinite gratitude for the past . . . joy in the present . . . commitment to the future." A final panel presented excerpts from the Earth Charter, which represents another new form of earth-related religious production that consecrates a scientific narrative of cosmological and biological evolution and urges protection and reverence for the entire community of life.

Interestingly, the "Walk through Time" was created by employees of Hewlett-Packard as part of the company's sponsorship of the Earth Day celebration in 1997, showing again that it is not only environmental activists who are engaged in activities that have affinity with dark green religion. The "Walk" was later entrusted to the Foundation for Global Community for further dissemination. The foundation's mission statement reflects the kind of biocentric spirituality of belonging and connection commonly found in dark green religion.[15]

• • •

Toward the end of my time in Johannesburg, I arranged an interview with two of the leaders of the African tree-planting Greenbelt Movement, founded by Wangari Maathai, who became internationally famous in 2004 when she was awarded the Nobel Peace Prize. Nanga Tiango, an attorney for the movement, expounded on the philosophy of connection and the ethics of kinship animating it. Although he had not been present at the "Decade of Commitment" session, he spoke in concert with it, stating that we must "reconnect" to nature and recognize that "we are all part of the universe, that man is not superior to the other animals. . . . We are all part of the earth and we should preserve it, both for use by other species, and for future generations." He also demonstrated another form of nature-related religious bricolage by explaining how he and other Africans are blending traditional African religion, Christianity, and environmentalism. "Christians are for the protection of the universe," he told me. "Christians want to be linked with the ancestors [and to] preserve nature for future generations."[16]

Equally interesting for understanding the ways in which dark green religion is hybridized within the global environmentalist milieu was his musing about how colonizers who once suppressed African traditional religions were now proclaiming that they are valuable. Tiango added that Africa's native religions have traditional ecological knowledge and values concerning how to protect the commons. These traditional religions even teach "how to communicate with the mountains," he told me. Tiango was surprised at this shift in attitudes by people of European heritage but delighted that it was becoming acceptable to fuse his traditional African religious feelings with science and ecological concern, as well as with his Christianity. His views in this regard were shared both by his partner at the WSSD, Gathuru Mburu, and by his mentor, Wangari Maathai.[17] This is another example of how religion is dramatically changing in the ecological age through a host of often mutually reinforcing influences.

The Official World Summit on Sustainable Development

At the WSSD's official venues, religion was also engaged as diverse groups tried to influence international policies related to nature. And it was not only at the antiglobalization side meetings that dark green religion was in play.

At the Nasrec Exposition Grounds, for example, environmental organizations and representatives of a host of religions were present, as were aid, development, and social-justice groups affiliated with them. To name a few: World Vision (an evangelical Christian relief organization), the Conference of Catholic Bishops, the Network of African Earthkeeping Christian Communities of South Africa, the Jesuits, the Arab Network for Environment and Development, the Green Front of Iran, the Khoi-San Indigenous Peoples Cultural Village, the World Wildlife Fund (with displays urging devotion to "Mother Earth"), United Global Citizens (from Korea), Soka Gakkai (an international organization founded in Japan and based on Buddhist principles), the World Council of Churches, and the Baha'is. The Earth Charter was presented in an educational seminar. Meanwhile, Tibetan Buddhist monks labored over a sand mandala, a symbol of interconnectedness and change.

Despite the official recognition of civil society that the Nasrec venue represented, its distance from the main conference center symbolized how environmental and religious NGOs were at the periphery of the WSSD in terms of power and influence. Yet there was evidence that religious environmentalism and dark green religion were more influential at the WSSD than Nasrec's peripheral location might suggest.

Such evidence could easily be found at Ubuntu Village, the official WSSD exposition site, where a "Sacred Space" had been constructed. According to the sign at its entrance, this space was "to enable groups to manifest the vital contribution of the spiritual dimension to . . . Sustainable Development through rituals, ceremonies, prayer, meditations and other sacred activities." A variety of activities occurred throughout the week, including a "Spirituality and Sustainability" ceremony on the final day of the conference. During this ceremony there were prayers, chants, and rituals from spiritual leaders from many traditions—Buddhist, Baha'i, Sufi, Christian, Hindu, and indigenous (including African sangomas and Maasai elders). After a number of them offered prayers and comments, Linley Black, an attorney from New Zealand, announced that the Earth Charter had been positively mentioned in the just-released draft of the political declaration being prepared by the national delegates. She said that she hoped this language would survive the last-minute negotiations, adding resolutely, "We are not going to let Mother Earth cry alone without our support." She then read the most overtly religious passages from the Earth Charter and asserted that the fourth pillar of sustainability was spirituality.[18] (In the environmental milieu, the ecological, economic, and social dimensions of life are commonly considered the three pillars of sustainability).

Robert Ohero, chair of the Tiano Indian Committee from the Caribbean Islands, then took up Black's theme of respect for Mother Earth, offering a song in the spirit of unity and solidarity and in thanks to Mother Earth. A Maasai elder spoke afterward, saying that "in the Maasai tradition too, we're all relatives." After offering a traditional prayer for rain and healing, he added that prosperity, love, and relatedness all go together. While a variety of beliefs were expressed during the ceremony, common themes included the mutual dependence of humankind and nature.

Ubuntu Village was also the location for an impressive exhibit featuring the Earth Charter, sponsored by Soka Gakkai, the Japanese lay Buddhist organization founded in 1930. The group had made environmental sustainability and support for the Earth Charter as a key part of its international identity and mission.[19] Thabo Mbeki, president of South Africa, visited the exhibit with his wife; this was *after* he had, during his official opening address at the WSSD, cited the Earth Charter as part of "the solid base from which the Johannesburg World Summit must proceed."[20] Interestingly, at a forum devoted to the Earth Charter at the Ubuntu venue, András Szöllösi-Nagy, deputy assistant director general of UNESCO, invoked religious imagery referring to the charter's principles as "new commandments." He was neither the first nor the last to liken it to earlier divine commandments.

Another Earth Charter event, this one sponsored by the Earth Council, was featured in the IUCN Exhibition Hall. Keynote speakers at this "Celebration of the Earth Charter" included Jan Pronk (special envoy to the summit representing UN General Secretary Kofi Annan), Carlos Rodriguez (minister of the environment in Costa Rica), Parvez Hassan (former chair of the IUCN Commission on Environmental Law), and Steven C. Rockefeller (cochair of the Earth Charter's international steering committee).

Toward the end of the session, an artist from the United States, Sally Linder, described the Ark of Hope that she and craftsmen had created to help promote the Earth Charter. The ark was made from a sustainably harvested tree in Germany and the words of the charter were printed on papyrus and placed inside the ark's lid, so they were readable when the lid was opened. On four sides of the ark, artists had painted scenes representing earth, water, fire, and air, and on the top, spirit; also included were symbols from indigenous cultures and the world's largest religions traditions. Anyone familiar with the Ark of the Covenant in Abrahamic religions, in which, according to the biblical tradition, the Ten Commandments and other holy relics were placed, would recognize the religious and ethical implications that this new ark—and of its implied environmental covenant between nature and humankind.[21]

THE "WELCOME CEREMONY" AND CRADLE OF HUMANITY

The WSSD was not a religious event, of course. Yet a religious dimension was apparent at some of the side events. There were even times when an event had a religious dimension that closely resembled religious ritual. Speeches and a theatrical performances during the WSSD's "Welcome Ceremony," as well as the events where similar spiritual and ethical themes were expressed later in the week, can be read as earth-venerating rituals. They seemed designed to evoke certain feelings and to pose ethical challenges. In the case of the "Welcome Ceremony," the spiritual and moral challenge posed was directly if subtly to the governmental delegates who would soon be in the midst of high-stakes negotiations.

The ceremony began with a welcoming speech by Thabo Mbeki. He introduced the ceremony, and thus the summit, with a cosmogony that identified evolution as the process by which the biosphere came to be. He also explicitly mentioned a nearby archeological site, Sterkfontein, where fossils of the prehuman *Australopithecus,* dating back four million years, had been found in long-forgotten caves. Designated a World Heritage Site by the United Nations two years previously, this Cradle of Humanity was invoked in many of the summit's speeches and ceremonies, including in Mbeki's inaugural address to the convention and these words during the "Welcome Ceremony": "We welcome the peoples of the world to the place that is recognized as the cradle of humanity. The Johannesburg World Summit for Sustainable Development is therefore, for all of us, a homecoming, a return to the base from where all humanity evolved to cover the globe."[22] Here the evolutionary cosmogony, grounded in the scientific consensus that humanity emerged from Africa, was used to convey kinship among all human beings.

Many other speakers made reference to the Sterkfontein fossils during the WSSD, and pilgrimages were made to the caves themselves. Jane Goodall accompanied Mbeki and UN General Secretary Kofi Annan on a visit. After viewing the *Australopithecus,* in his speech at the caves, Mbeki again stressed how this site connects us to our evolutionary history and thus to each other. In this, his comments paralleled those in his "Welcome Ceremony" talk. But then he elaborated, suggesting that the evolutionary story implies a broader kinship, for the site not only demonstrates that Africa is everyone's home and that we all have "common ancestors," it also "traces the evolution of the significant part of our Earth as well as the interdependence of peoples, plants and animals, thus, in many ways [it is] teaching all of us how we can co-exist and ensure enduring prosperity for all species."[23]

In the pageant that followed the "Welcome Ceremony," the affinity for dark green religious themes continued, clearly expressing a nonsectarian reverence for "Mother Earth." It began with a young boy recalling his grandmother's stories about earlier times when the gods were everywhere and "animals could speak and do unbelievable things." His grandfather then spoke to him and his sister, invoking the Cradle of Humanity as he showed them a fossil stone from Sterkfontein. After explaining its significance, he exclaimed that it showed that "Africa is the mother of all human beings!" His granddaughter, squealing with delight at this idea, implored her grandfather to say more. He responded dramatically: "In the beginning there was the wind!"—immediately, the lights faded and stormy music began.

As the music grew louder, as if out of nowhere, Africa's famous and distinctive baobab tree slowly arose. Its limbs, represented by human actors covered with smaller branches and leaves sprouting from them, waved in the wind. The baobab was a fitting symbol for the emergence of life because it is woven into some indigenous origin myths and provides habitat for a wide array of organisms. As the tree towered higher and higher, a mysteriously voiced narrator slowly and solemnly extolled the wonder of this great tree.

The second act depicted Eden and seemed designed to evoke a sense of the sublime in nature. Dressed in elaborate and beautiful animal costumes, the performers danced joyously and harmoniously to African-inspired rhythms and music around a beautiful water hole. Few watching this scene would be unmoved by it. But then the mood suddenly changed as the music became ominous, the lighting changed again, and the plants and animals vanished. The family returned and looked around pensively. Finally the boy asked, "What happened, Grandfather, to this beautiful earth? Where are the forests, the animals, the beautiful birds and colorful flowers?" The Grandfather responded, "Life began with the earth, then came the plants, the animals, and finally the human beings. Yes! We are all children of Mother Earth. That is why we must take care of her and be her custodians. She is the hand that feeds us and the heart that heals us. But . . . greed and foolishness are eating deep into the fabric of humankind. We are failing to love and care for Mother Earth."

At this point the family turned around and watched, with the audience, as the music became more dissonant and a huge iconic earth descended. Upon this orb apocalyptic scenes were then projected, depicting people and animals suffering and dying as a result of environmental degradation caused by logging, industrial pollution, and war. After this bleak imagery the boy plaintively asked, "Mommy, is there anything we can do?" She answered positively, "Yes my child, there is much that you can do, for as I speak, the leaders of the nations are gathering. But their task is not an easy one, for the life and health of Mother Earth depends on their decisions." The mood and music then shifted once again, this time back from dystopian to utopian as a score of beaming children marched in, carrying dozens of large banners celebrating the earth and its beauty, human goodness, and the hope represented by the summit itself.

DENOUEMENT

The hopefulness with which the WSSD began on the 26 August had disappeared by its conclusion on 4 September. By all accounts, very little was accomplished, and those hoping the nations would move toward adopting the Earth Charter were disappointed when, during the final negotiations, specific reference to it was stripped from the summit's political declaration. This may have been, at least in part, because some religious groups were unwilling to support the charter and because others opposed it directly. Apparently the Roman Catholic Church was opposed, despite a personal appeal from Mikhail Gorbachev to Pope John Paul II to support it. The two main reasons for the discomfort, according to Steven C. Rockefeller, was its language about women's reproductive health, which some took as code for abortion rights, and the capitalization of the word *Earth,* which some considered to symbolize Pantheism.[24]

After it became clear that the WSSD would not lead to dramatic international environmental cooperation, a large contingent of civil society staged a walkout, mocking the nations with the chant, "You won't, we will!," putting a brave face on devastating defeat. Even Kofi Annan, who normally would be responsible for touting the accomplishments of this UN-sponsored meeting, could only claim afterward that they had prevented retrenchment on many issues, forestalling a return to the state of affairs before the Earth Summit a decade earlier.

Despite the abject political failure, and disappointment that the Earth Charter had gained little political traction, there were signs at the WSSD that dark green religion and many of the themes typical of it were extending their global reach. Although the Earth Charter cannot be said to be the new sacred text for dark green religion, it does express many dark green themes and it did gain a higher profile and some support at the WSSD. Moreover, some of its language about human responsibilities to "the greater community of life" remained in the official Johannesburg Declaration, and during the summit strong statements of support for the charter were articulated by a number of world leaders and civil society groups.[25] From the "Welcome Ceremony" to the Johannesburg Declaration, the WSSD suggested that dark green religion had escaped its countercultural breeding grounds and was contending for the hearts and minds of the international community.

Terrapolitan Earth Religion

By now this much should be clear: dark green religion is no phantom. By combining a flexible definition of religion with a framework for understanding its main forms, and adding a wide range of examples, the apparition has materialized.

Instead of being represented by a single charismatic leader and sacred text, it has many. Without an established religious hierarchy, its devotees nevertheless recognize their gurus and saints, ritual innovators and practitioners, opponents and enemies. Without *official* institutions registering as religious bodies, it nevertheless has institutions devoted to promoting its beliefs and practices. It not only has precipitated its own organizations and institutions, it has been infiltrating a wide variety of existing institutions in its quest to overturn the dominant order and create a sustainable world based upon a reverence for life. It seeks to end the world now unfolding, in order to prevent the end of the world as we have known it.

Are we witnessing the emergence of a global, civic, environmentalist, earth religion? Decades ago, Paul Ehrlich suggested that such a quasi religion was needed, and so did the political theorist William Ophuls, who argued that such a religion was a necessary basis for a sustainable society. Another political theorist, Daniel Deudney, aptly labeled the notion terrapolitan earth religion.[26]

Grasping the meaning of terrapolitan earth religion begins with understanding "civil" or "civic" religion. These synonyms denote a kind of nationalism in which a nation is invested with transcendent meaning and sacred purpose, and group identity and loyalty are forged through such shared perceptions.[27] The overall message is that God (diversely understood) is responsible for establishing the nation and securing its future. The nation is consecrated in a variety of ways, for example, through myths about its sacred dimensions and calling, sermons and texts (speeches and political documents), and rituals (festivals, parades, pageants, inaugurations). The nation is also sacralized by the way it modifies environments: through architecture, including the construction of monuments, memorials, governmental buildings; and through zoning and landscape design, such as with the designation and shaping of parks and other public spaces. An important aspect of civic religion, especially in religiously diverse nations, consists of references to the divine that are generic—not specific to just one tradition. In this way religious references do not hinder the kind of "we feeling" needed to create a sense of a shared identity and sacred calling, a prerequisite to patriotism. Civil religion may also include ethical obligations that can have a prophetic dimension: if the people do not fulfill their duties, divine blessing and protection might be withdrawn, likely with devastating consequences. Deudney noted as well that nationalism also involves "an identity and loyalty based upon the experiences and feelings of connectedness to a particular place or area."[28] This point about connection suggests why civil religion might be easily fused with dark green religion.

By whatever name, civic religion has many critics. The political left, following Feuerbach and Marx, has long considered religion a force that obfuscates the ways elites oppress others and that justifies political domination, and the left views civil religion as no different. Postmodern critics, meanwhile, are always alert for hegemonic narratives that erase cultural differences and promote totalitarianism. They would no doubt be suspicious of any narrative that positively construes the globalization of dark green religion. Some religious critics find civic religion idolatrous because it involves trusting and relying on the nation rather than God. But Deudney believes that "Gaian Earth Religion," "Terrapolitan Earth Religion," and "Earth Nationalism" are significantly different and far less dangerous than other forms of civic religion; given its basis in environmental science and its recognition of ecological interdependence, he believes that such religion erodes nationalism by replacing it with loyalty to the planet.[29] "One reason for believing that the emergence of 'green culture' will replace or moderate state and ethnic nationalism rather than make it more truculent," he contended, "is that environmental awareness brings with it awareness of the interconnected and interdependent character of the earth's diverse inhabitants."[30] This is a compelling argument I would summarize this way: The traits typical of dark green religion—such as a stress on ecological interdependence, an affective connection to the earth as home and to nonhuman organisms as kin, and the overturning of anthropocentric hubris—are unlikely to promote either the suppression of others or lead to cultural homogenization, let alone virulent strains of nationalism. This is in no small measure because both biological and cultural diversity are highly valued as the fruits of evolution.[31]

Deudney also argued that earth religion is needed because secular understandings simply cannot inspire the "here feelings," the feelings of belonging to place, that are needed to undergird the widespread transformations upon which the planetary future depends.[32] When I spoke with Ximena Arango, the Colombian ecologist introduced previously, and explained the fears that some express toward nature-based spiritualities, she responded simply, in a way that paralleled Deudney's argument. Oppressive behaviors, she said, do not follow an understanding that "everyone is a part of the earth."[33]

Deudney's attempts to ameliorate fears of earth-based religiosities and identities is part of an ambitious effort toward the comprehensive "green" transformation of all aspects of human life that is essential to prevent catastrophe.[34] Deudney avers that existing political systems are, however, religiously, ideologically, and structurally constrained and incompatible with the form of political sovereignty, one "situated in an intergenerational public," that is needed. Legitimate authority must, in contrast, be both international and include future generations, and provide the basis for a new "federal-republican Earth constitution." Moreover, this constitution must be "terrapolitan," reflecting loyalties and identities rooted in the earth.[35] This in turn depends, Deudney contends, on the globalization of Gaian Earth Religion as the basis for earth nationalism. Deudney signaled his sympathy for Lovelock's Gaia hypothesis by adding that "Gaia is the most salient metaphorical structure spanning the divide between ecological science and Earth identity narratives."[36]

Ardent nationalists, devotees of many of the world's religions who maintain they have unique spiritual insights, and those on the alert for hegemonic globalism in any form, will be hostile to Deudney's terrapolitan vision. Deudney anticipated their objections. To those who fear Gaian earth religion and that a federal-republican earth constitution would become another repressive fundamentalism, Deudney argued that this would be unlikely because "Earth religion is a relative rarity—a moderate worldview with a scientifically credible cosmology." Moreover, "Unlike restraint based on hierarchical domination, republican political orders are complexes of mutual power restraint." Nor, he continued, would an international system based on a federal-republican earth constitution involve world government or overturning existing environmental laws and treaties. Indeed, "Such an Earth constitution would . . . not be consistent with a centralized and hierarchical world state or government" because it would not vest power in one group of living people but rather in all living and future ones. Nor would such a constitution overturn existing environmental laws and treaties; rather, it would "establish a system for voiding measures and acts inconsistent with its principles."[37]

Deudney personally disavows belief in nonmaterial spiritual beings, including views that in this book I have called Gaian Spirituality. Given his affinity with Lovelock, he is another good example of Gaian Naturalism. As a practical political matter, however, he thinks both naturalistic and spiritual forms of Gaian earth religion would suffice, concluding that Gaian religion is "well suited to serve as the 'civic religion' for a federal-republican Earth constitution. It potentially could underpin the social norms and behaviors of restraint that are necessary to achieve a sustainable society . . . providing a system of meaning that can span generations and foster a sense of transgenerational communal identity." Deudney thus sees great potential in Gaian religion, even suggesting that "the multiple existing processes of environmental governance formation now underway can be viewed as subcommittee meetings of an Earth Constitutional Convention."[38] Included in these processes would be the various United Nations meetings called to address the world's interconnected environmental problems.

How likely are such transformations? In many ways, Deudney's vision is radical. But he assumes that existing international political and economic systems are the fulcrums for the needed changes, which is a moderate stance compared to those who hope for the collapse of industrial civilization or who are pursuing a bottom-up bioregional revolution. While appreciative of the bioregional impulse, Deudney insists it is no panacea, because any reorganization along bioregional lines would be unlikely to occur "without widespread violence and dislocation."[39] This is a key reason he focuses on reforming the international system.

Is a decentralist Gaian revolution a real possibility? Given the global nature of so many environmental problems and the mobility of capital, as inspirational and valuable as decentralist environmentalism might be, it is clear that it cannot constrain the abuses often perpetrated by those who control great concentrations of wealth and power. Decentralized authority cannot constrain international powers, which is why something like Deudney's strengthened international governance is essential to halt and reverse destructive environmental trends.[40]

To summarize the question: How likely is it that dark green religion, including a possible terrapolitan form, might ameliorate the worst tendencies of the current international system, or provide a basis for a sustainable planetary future? The diverse examples in this book, which document the emergence and globalization of dark green religion, provide substantial evidence of its near-term and growing international influence. But to consider its prospects and likely long-term impacts, we must carefully examine both the expansion of such religion as well as the obstacles to it and enemies of it.

CHAPTER 9

Conclusion

Dark Green Religion and the Planetary Future

Background: On Trends and Prediction

Before examining obstacles that will hinder dark green religion from becoming a powerful social force, as well as some trends and factors likely to spur it on, it is worth noting several things:

First, *evolutionary theory has precipitated profound changes.* Most forms of what I am calling dark green religion will have been unfolding for only 150 years by the time this book is published, the years since the publication of *On the Origin of Species* in 1859. There were individuals and groups with dark green perceptions, and important antecedents and tributaries to dark green religion before that momentous publishing event, but nearly everything in the world of religion began to change afterward, at least where awareness of evolutionary theory spread.

Second, *the diversity and creativity in dark green religious production during this century and a half has been stunning. Moreover, the spread of such nature spirituality has been breathtakingly rapid.* Advances in travel and communication technologies have dramatically accelerated the pace of change.

This is not to say that dark green religion is on its way to prevalence. Prediction about its prospects would be foolish. Hostility in Western cultures to forms of spirituality that venerate the earth is unlikely to disappear. There is, moreover, widespread resistance to the profound worldview alteration the Darwinian revolution involves; this also means resistance to dark green religion, because it generally and strongly embraces evolutionary understandings. There are even plausible theories, based in evolutionary biology and cognitive science, that traditional religious perception and beliefs regarding nonmaterial spirits or divine beings are an evolutionary outcome. Some of these theories suggest that religion evolved because it promotes human survival (fostering ecologically adaptive behaviors by individuals or groups). Other such theories contend that religion is a by-product of behaviors that promote survival (usually because when humans are hyperalert to danger they are more likely to survive, which makes them more likely to perceive beings that are not present, because negative results from such misperception are less than the positive/adaptive function of hyperalertness). These sorts of theories suggest that religion, as conventionally defined, is unlikely to wither away.[1]

Even where it seems there has been little change, as is the case with much conservative religion, however, important changes are unfolding. Intensified fundamentalist rebellion against the modern world and its secularizing power, for example, reflects in part the threat posed by evolutionary understandings. This competing scientific view must be ignored or explained away. Yet this is difficult because so much of the world's globalizing infrastructure depends on science, and therefore on universities, where it is difficult to isolate and ignore the biological sciences.

Third, *social change does not usually come rapidly—but it can.* Dark green religion has, in terms of human cultural evolution, exploded on the scene and has rapidly gone global. As already shown, a significant amount of this influence has occurred within the world's educated intelligentsia. Yet dark green religion has a long way to go to affect the world's teeming billions. This majority, however, does not set international and national environmental policies. So when it comes to the possible influence of dark green religion, its impact on the global intelligentsia may be decidedly more important. It is also true, as adaptive-management theorists have noted, that "good ideas acquired in one generation can spread rapidly and be passed to the next generation directly"—a process "that cannot occur in organic evolution."[2] Thomas Kuhn's *Structure of Scientific Revolutions* provided a famous analysis of how the Copernican Revolution and other worldview-altering changes have occurred—sometimes rapidly—when the time was ripe.[3] So, rapid social change might occur and do so across diverse societal sectors.

Fourth, *when rapid social change occurs it is often precipitated by a perceived grave threat or emergency.*[4] This is another point emphasized by adaptive-management theorists and one to keep in mind when considering the future of dark green religion and how it might influence cultural and ecological systems. Indeed, and for example, to underscore the urgency of the situation, people increasingly speak of climate "crisis" rather than "change," or of the "sustainability emergency" rather than of "sustainable development."

To summarize this background: There are times when a decisive change in ideas and practices occurs. This can develop over many generations or rapidly, pressed forward by some perceived crisis or by fantastic new information, emerging from the ground up or the top down or from synergies between popular and elite sectors. So when considering influences, impacts, and trends, it is good to have in mind both near-, medium-, and long-term possibilities. It is especially critical to recognize that social and ecological systems are made up of so many variables that confident prediction would be hubristic. But looking for clues about the trends and possibilities is not a futile exercise. As much or more than prediction, this has to do with envisioning possibilities, an act that itself may contribute to positive outcomes.

With this backdrop in place and the previous case studies in mind, we are ready to consider whether dark green religion will play an important role in the future of religion and the biosphere.

Earth Charter Revelation?

Does the Earth Charter initiative reveal anything about the prospects for a dark green, terrapolitan earth religion? Here is some of what one would expect as positive evidence: First, there would be generic statements of the sacredness of the earth with which most people would feel comfortable, whether they are self-consciously secular, nominally religious or parareligious, or religious in a more conventional sense. Second, there would be clearly stated ethical principles that convey a sense of moral responsibility toward nonhuman organisms and a conviction that they deserve respect and reverent care. Third, there would be a steady increase in behaviors that reflected such dark green perceptions and values.

With the Earth Charter, all three of these elements are present. As shown previously, the charter has significant support, including from world leaders, while conversely some believe it is spiritually and politically dangerous. By digging more deeply into the drafting process that led to the document presented in Johannesburg, however, it is possible to gain a clearer sense of this manifestation of civic earth religion as well as about the obstacles it faces.[5] Indeed, I believe the initial "Benchmark Draft" of the charter, which was offered for further discussion and refinement in 1997, provides the clearest collective statement of dark green religion yet produced; it could even be considered an attempted draft of a new sacred text for a proffered terrapolitan earth religion.

It began thus: "Earth is our home and home to all living beings. Earth itself is alive. We are a part of an evolving universe. Human beings are members of an interdependent community of life with a magnificent diversity of life forms and cultures. We are humbled before the beauty of Earth and share a reverence for life and the sources of our being." It continued: to avoid "the destruction of ourselves and the diversity of life" a "fundamental change of course is needed," including to "industrial-technological civilization." A long list of ethical principles and commitments followed, for example, (1) "Respect Earth and all life. Earth, each life form, and all living beings possess intrinsic value and warrant respect independently of their utilitarian value to humanity"; (2) "Care for Earth, protecting and restoring the diversity, integrity, and beauty of the planet's ecosystems." The draft also pledged that its signatories would "reaffirm that Indigenous and Tribal Peoples have a vital role in the care and protection of Mother Earth" and declared that "they have the right to retain their spirituality, knowledge, lands, territories and resources." Its coda added, "We must preserve a . . . deep sense of belonging to the universe."[6]

This Earth Charter draft included most of the themes prevalent in dark green religion. It was informed by environmental apocalypticism; it viewed industrial societies as inherently destructive and indigenous ones as superior; and it expressed understandings of ecological interdependence, biocentric values, and an organicist Gaian Spirituality. This Gaian Spirituality was indebted in part to James Lovelock and in part to beliefs about the spiritual perceptions of indigenous peoples. There were also echoes of Aldo Leopold's land ethic (in the draft's words about ecosystem diversity, integrity, and beauty) as well as of Thomas Berry's universe story (in the concluding language about belonging to the universe).[7]

But this was only the initial public draft. The charter soon underwent significant changes leading to the release of "Benchmark Draft II" in April 1999.[8] Thomas Derr, an astute Christian critic of the initiative, noted that this version muted the biocentrism and "quasi-religious" nature mysticism present in the first draft. Writing for a group that focuses on questions of religious liberty and that is suspicious of international institutions, especially the United Nations, Derr pointed out that the reference to "Mother Earth" had been deleted in the second draft and the statement about the earth being alive was replaced with "Earth, our home, is alive with a unique community of life" (a phrase retained in the final version).[9] This revision was, Derr did not need to explain, less offensive to monotheists and others wary of Paganism. Derr also accurately noted that the overall tone had become more anthropocentric, in keeping with the United Nations priorities regarding sustainable development and human rights.[10] He concluded, accurately, that despite these changes the second as well as the final draft—the one that was eventually pitched to the United Nations at the Johannesburg World Summit on Sustainable Development—was still clearly biocentric and subtly pantheistic, citing the charter's kinship ethics and its expressed intent to awaken a "new reverence for life."[11]

Derr's careful analysis shows that those critical of dark green themes are very good at spotting them. He also demonstrated that most such themes in the original draft remained in the final version. He did not, however, spotlight all of them, including the charter's evolutionary cosmogony, expressed as, "Humanity is part of a vast evolving universe"; and the overtly religious assertion that "the protection of Earth's vitality, diversity, and beauty is a sacred trust." He did notice the concessions made by those he called "the Charter's originators." Perceptively, he asserted that the leaders of the initiative had retained some things in the charter they regarded as "indispensable"—I think these were all dark green themes. Derr's critique provides an example of those who think that the Earth Charter is inconsistent with their own religious beliefs and ethical values. This is most obvious in one of Derr's final comments, which drew more on what he knew or supposed about the charter's proponents than it did on the document itself:

> There is also, undoubtedly, a kind of neo-paganism among many Charter supporters, whose antipathy to modern society in all its aspects, from industrial to religious, has led them back to a radical pre-modernism, a pan-religiousness that appears to be some (partly imagined) basic form of religious life before the destructive divisiveness of the historic religions appeared. Many supporters ascribe sentience, psychic and spiritual reality, to all things, not only to living creatures but also to natural entities like rivers, forests, ecosystems, even stars—a kind of mystic ecocentrism, one might say. All supporters, apparently without exception, attribute intrinsic value, even rights, to non-human entities.[12]

Clearly, even though Derr noticed what he considered to be improvements through the various drafts, the Earth Charter was not something he could support. He also concluded that its language about the intrinsic value of nature would prevent adoption by the United Nations.

I draw the following conclusions from the Earth Charter initiative, the revisions it has gone through, and the reception it has received: The Earth Charter is one of many manifestations of dark green religion, and the positive reception it has received is a sign of the growing importance of such religion. Despite refinement of the document in ways designed to make it acceptable to a wider range of the human community, the charter is viewed as spiritually dangerous to many, and some fear that such religion could be repressively imposed on them. Given such views and fears, the Earth Charter is an unlikely "sacred text" for the kind of terrapolitan earth religion envisioned by Daniel Deudney.

A comparative reference point that buttresses this conclusion: Conservative Christians, both Catholic and Protestant, have been some of the most ardent supporters of religious nationalism. This is because such civic religion generally assumes that it is *their* God (the God of Abraham) who established the nation and its earthly mission. It would be difficult for proponents of Gaian earth religion to draw such people into viewing the protection of the earth as a sacred trust if these religious people think that by doing do they might countenance an idolatrous worship of nature. Such concern explains much of the uneasiness among conservative monotheists toward environmentalists. Ever on the alert for Paganism, they certainly can see such spirituality in environmentalists. As the present study has amply demonstrated and as Jonathan Benthall put it, "Almost all strands of the environmentalist movement affirm a sense of the sacred, the spiritual or the aesthetic—however it is defined—in the cosmos." Benthall concluded that "from a global scale, such as Greenpeace or Friends of the Earth, down to regional, national and local organizations, these have a parareligious aspect."[13] This conclusion and my own fieldwork support James Proctor's finding that large numbers of people in Europe and the United States express "deep trust in nature as inherently spiritual or sacred."[14] For many with religious understandings grounded in the Abrahamic traditions, these are disturbing developments.[15]

In an autobiographical epilogue to his most famous book, published in 1995, James Lovelock made a similar observation. He began by describing his father's "kinship with all living things" and distress even "to see a tree cut down," then subtly implied that his father shared the kind of natural Paganism that he thinks is common among country people. "I owe much of my own feeling for natural things to walks with him down country lanes and along ancient drives which had . . . a sweet seemliness and tranquility," he continued. Then, he conjectured that our sense of beauty, wonder, and excitement in perceiving "the true nature of things" is consistent with a Darwinian view that such pleasures reward us for pursuing "a balanced relationship between ourselves and other forms of life."[16] This prologue led to an especially revealing paragraph:

> My father never told me why he believed that everything in this world was there for a purpose, but his thoughts and feelings about the countryside must have been based on a mixture of instinct, observation, and tribal wisdom. These persist in diluted form in many of us today and are still strong enough to power environmental movements which have come to be accepted as forces to be reckoned with by other powerful pressure groups in our society. As a result, the churches of the monotheistic religions, and the recent heresies of humanism and Marxism, are faced with the unwelcome truth that some part of their old enemy, Wordsworth's Pagan, "suckled in a creed outworn", is still alive within us.[17]

This statement revealed Lovelock's affinity with a kind of naturalistic Paganism—a feeling Joseph Wood Krutch spoke of similarly when describing the "kind of pantheism" commonly expressed by American nature writers. Lovelock's statement was also noteworthy for its recognition of the enduring conflict between such religion and monotheistic religions, as well as of what Lovelock and others engaged with dark green religion consider to be the hubristic, anthropocentric ideologies of humanism and Marxism.

In short, both sides of the divide—those who see the sacred above and beyond the world and those who view the world as sacred—understand that these worldviews are incompatible. This accounts for the ambivalence and sometimes hostility toward environmentalism that is often found among those involved in Abrahamic religions as well as similar feelings toward them by those engaged in dark green religion. Yet as Lovelock also suggested, "The idea of Mother Earth or, as the Greeks called her, Gaia, has been widely held throughout history and has been the basis of a belief that coexists with the great religions."[18]

It might just be that the mutual dependence of all people on the earth's ecosystems will yet unite them in common cause to reverse the headlong rush toward biocultural simplification. There is, after all, only one thing that all humans share, namely, dependence on the earth. Presumably, nothing is more likely to unite people than ensuring the health of these ecosystems upon which they all depend. There are, indeed, important efforts underway to encourage environmental stewardship within the world's major religions, and these include ways to speak about the value and even sacredness of the earth without contradicting traditional religious doctrines.[19] On the other hand, for dark green religion in general, or terrapolitan earth religion in particular, to gain the critical mass necessary to decisively influence national and international environmental politics, it may be that the religious forms that fear and resist them must lose adherents and social power. This is a process that is well underway in many advanced industrial countries, but it appears that in many countries such a development will take a long time, if it happens at all.

Dark Green Social Epidemic?

If earth-revering dark green religion were to become a social epidemic, on the other hand, it could precipitate wide-scale political, economic, and ecological changes, even in the face of ambivalence and hostility. I borrow the idea from Malcolm Gladwell's *Tipping Point,* which argued that ideas, tastes, or practices can and do spread rapidly like viruses, coming as if from nowhere and with unstoppable momentum. Social epidemics can be both positive and negative, he explained, as he provided examples from criminology, social psychology, fashion, and social mores. Gladwell's choice of the word *epidemic* is pertinent to this study because some fear the spread of dark green religion. If understood as a social possibility, however, those engaged in dark green religion would find hopeful the possibility that their spiritual and moral sentiments, and earth-revering practices, might spread like a virus.

Gladwell argued that there are three keys to understanding social epidemics. The first is "the law of the few," by which he meant that individuals make a huge difference to whether things "tip" (positively or negatively). Three types of individuals are essential: "connectors" are those who build networks among people, "mavens" are teachers who share the essential knowledge within these emerging networks, and "salespeople/persuaders" are those who convince others to think and behave in new ways. Critical virtues found variously among these types are positive energy, charm, and optimism, all of which help to overcome resistance to innovation.[20]

The second key to social epidemics Gladwell labeled "the lesson of stickiness." By this he meant ways of communicating ideas that people easily remember and even have difficulty forgetting. To risk a painful pun, a social epidemic of nature religion could be called a pandemic. If the pun is bad enough, the idea may be memorable.[21]

The third key, according to Gladwell, is "the critical importance and power of Context/Environment." Gladwell believes that when it comes to promoting positive epidemics or stopping bad ones, establishing an optimistic and positive atmosphere, often through small changes that may initially seem unimportant, is critical. Gladwell concluded his book by suggesting that knowing these principles can make it easier for individuals to facilitate positive social change: "Tipping Points are a reaffirmation of the potential for change and the power of intelligent action. Look at the world around you. It may seem an immovable, implacable place. It is not. With the slightest push—in just the right place—it can be tipped."[22]

The idea of a tipping point is not new; it has long been an important notion in the American counterculture.[23] An explicitly spiritual version common in New Age and environmentalist subcultures is the fable "The Hundredth Monkey." In this story, when enough monkeys on one island learned a new behavior, potato washing, as if by magic the practice began on nearby islands. The implication was that this occurred by a telepathic transmission of consciousness from one group of monkeys to the other. This transmission could not occur until enough monkeys on the first island joined in thinking "potato washing." The lesson was that everyone must optimistically and continually do their part to promote the needed spiritual, ecological, and political changes, because one never knows who the decisive monkey will be.[24]

Many would view Gladwell's clever book as an oversimplification of how social change happens. Yet it provides useful lenses for an observer looking for signs that dark green religion (or environmentalism in general) might be on the cusp of becoming a decisive social force.

Dark Green Religion has drawn attention to the diversity and regional breadth of those who have been promoting such perception. There are many interlocking networks of activists, intellectuals, scientists, politicians, and cultural creatives (in the terminology of Paul Ray and Sherry Anderson) who are engaged in and promoting dark green spirituality and ethics.[25] As I near the end of this book, however, I am aware that I have left unexplored many important examples.

Educators as Mavens

Teachers are "mavens," a group that Gladwell spotlights and that merits greater attention. I have already discussed teacher-scholars who have promoted dark green religion, including natural scientists, ecological anthropologists, and ethnobiologists. While reviewing historical watersheds in the development of such religiosity, I have also pointed out how some environmental philosophers, historians, literary critics, and religion scholars are both observers of these trends and sometimes also enthusiasts for them. Here I wish to underscore the critical role that environmental studies scholars (broadly understood as an interdisciplinary field that explores all aspects of nature-human relationships) play in dark green spirituality by providing three especially interesting examples.[26]

The first spotlighted scholar is the environmental historian Donald Worster, who excavated from Darwin's notebooks the remarkable statement of felt kinship with nonhuman organisms cited earlier. Many points in Worster's writings demonstrate his affinity with such sentiments and with other dark green themes. In one revealing passage in the concluding pages of the first edition of *Nature's Economy* (1977), Worster discussed the conversion of Joseph Wood Krutch from "melancholic humanist" to "a kind of pantheist or ethical mystic, caught up in the joy of belonging to 'something greater than one's self.'" Worster attributed this change to a repeated reading of Thoreau and to "an education in ecological principles [that] . . . confirmed him in an organismic sensibility" and that led "directly to a moral awakening: a new sense of biological relatedness and communalism." Signaling his affinity with Krutch, Worster continued:

> Krutch was clear-eyed enough to perceive that ecology, "without reverence or love," could become naught but "a shrewder exploitation of what it would be better to admire, to enjoy, and to share in," but his own approach to the science helped turn him from the pursuit of self toward a "sense of the community of living things."
>
> From its impact on Krutch and others, it is clear that ecological biology could still lead to natural piety, no matter how many of its leading scientists had purged themselves of such tendencies.[27]

In *Dark Green Religion* I have suggested the possibility that most scientists have natural piety and that those who do are increasingly willing to express it. For his part, after making the above point, Worster subtly applauded how Aldo Leopold and many others drew on understandings of ecological interdependence as a basis for values. Worster then suggested that scientists and moralists should work together to break down the barrier between "Is" and "Ought" in the quest for ethical truth, which he suggested might well be found in just such an "ecological ethic of interdependence." He contended, moreover, that when it comes to ethics, "there is really no place to go but nature." He concluded this seminal book with these words:

> Perhaps, too, a quasi-religious conversion, similar to Krutch's, will be needed to open men's eyes to the "oneness" in or beyond nature. Whether this development is likely to come out in our culture the historian is not ready to predict. More to the point here is whether the experience of the past indicates that such an amalgamation of science and moral values is at all feasible. The answer to that question is a cautious yes. Ecological biology, while in general reinforcing certain values more than others, has been and remains intertwined with many of man's ethical principles, social aims, and transcendental ambitions. There is no reason for believing that this science cannot find an appropriate theoretical framework for the ethic of interdependence. If the bioeconomics of the New Ecologists cannot serve, then there are other, more useful, models of nature's economy that await discovery.[28]

Thus, in one of the most widely read texts in environmental history and environmental studies, it is apparent that Worster was a keen observer of what I am calling dark green religion. He insightfully showed how, for many, ethics and religion have become intertwined with science—specifically, the science of ecological interdependence. The paragraph above and other passages not cited suggest that he also has sympathy for these trends and hopes they will be increasingly successful. As a cautious historian, however, he refrained from prediction.[29]

The second scholar I highlight is the philosopher J. Baird Callicott. In 1971, as a young professor at a University of Wisconsin campus, Callicott taught the first university course in environmental ethics. In the following years, Callicott became a leading interpreter and promoter of Leopold's land ethic, arguing that Leopold saw earlier and clearer than anyone else how to ground environmental ethics in an evolutionary-ecological worldview. Callicott argued as well that religions originating in Asia, and those typical in indigenous traditions, were more compatible with Leopold's land ethic than Abrahamic ones. Then in 1994, he published *Earth's Insights*, which is arguably an exercise in constructive, terrapolitan earth religion. In it he considered both the resources and obstacles to a Leopold-compatible environmental ethics within a wide variety of the earth's traditions and regions. While he found some of these religions more amenable to a land ethic than others, he concluded that they could all move in such a direction while retaining their core beliefs. But he also insisted that when religious beliefs do not cohere with what can be known scientifically, they should give way or be modified. In essence, he was arguing that people around the world, whatever their particular beliefs and in their own ways, could come to understand the ecological community as having intrinsic, even sacred value.[30]

A decade after *Earth's Insights,* Callicott wrote an essay titled "Natural History as Natural Religion." This autobiographical reflection included a humorous admission that there was some hubris in the endeavor he and other scholars had set out for themselves, trying to infuse philosophy and religion with an evolutionary-ecological worldview and a corresponding environmental ethic. He traced this mission to Lynn White, who had convinced them that better religious ideas were the key to arresting environmental decline. But Callicott also noted that there was evidence in the "greening of religion" phenomenon that their effort was having some modest success. After reiterating the main thesis in *Earth's Insights*—that most traditional religions *could* become green—Callicott candidly concluded his essay promoting (what I would call) naturalistic dark green religion:

> If it weren't for ecology we would not be aware that we have an "ecologic crisis." If it weren't for the theory of evolution we would be both blind and indifferent to the reduction in global biodiversity. The world's newly green religions thus tacitly orbit around the evolutionary-ecological worldview. I myself consider most religions . . . to be grounded in primitive superstition and ignorance. . . . I am, however, immensely grateful for the greening-of-religions . . . *The religious potential of natural history that Leopold so beautifully tapped but only scarcely explored is perhaps centuries away from its full actualization. But while a true—that is, an epistemically sound and scientifically compatible—religion gestates, people now have to be reached where they are with some kind of environmental ethic.* . . . If the popular traditional religions can be marshaled to achieve a better fit between global human civilization and the natural environment in which it is embedded, I shall not worry their green apologists . . . with logical and philosophical quibbles.[31]

Callicott was no doubt sincere in his appreciation of the greening of mainstream religions. Yet he does seem to envision the eventual emergence of a religion of natural history that would supplant the forms he considers out of synch with a scientific worldview. In the meantime, he implies, this religion of natural history gestates. That religion could be called dark green religion.

The final point to note about Callicott is that he saw the role of philosopher-teachers in a way similar to Gladwell—as contributing significantly to radical change. He cited an article by Earth First! cofounder Dave Foreman to buttress his belief that "academic philosophy" had been a critical spur to radical environmental activism. Foreman had said such philosophy had a tremendous positive impact because it was now widely taught and urged conservationists, with dramatic results, to consider the ethical challenge represented by the idea that nature has intrinsic value.[32] My own experience teaching environmental ethics and environmental studies courses within academic settings affirms these observations—there are always students who are moved by and drawn to Leopold and others who articulate ecocentric values and spiritualities. Moreover, notions like "deep ecology" and "intrinsic value" are "sticky" in Gladwell's sense. They are easy to remember and difficult to forget. Like a virus, they are hard to kill.

The third scholar I wish to discuss is William Cronon, perhaps the most prominent environmental historian in the generation after Donald Worster and Roderick Nash. I bring him into focus not so much to analyze his writings for evidence of their sympathy for dark green religion but because of Cronon's reaction to a manifestation *of* such religion. First, I must provide background.

In 1992, Neil Evernden published *The Social Creation of Nature.*[33] Soon afterward, debates spread as to whether, given the widespread impact of human activities, any "nature" remains available to function as a basis for environmental conservation or restoration. The controversy intensified when Cronon published the essay "The Trouble with Wilderness."[34] Cronon argued that the idea of a wilderness, defined as a place "untrammeled" by humans in America's 1964 Wilderness Act, is untenable and ethically problematic—untenable because there is no such place and *ethically* problematic because it distracts people from caring for the environment nearly every place else. Cronon was harshly criticized. Many felt he was attacking something sacred: biologically diverse wilderness reserves.[35]

Assailed by some in the environmental community who he considered compatriots and allies, Cronon offered an apology that was as much religious recantation as an explanation of his argument:

> One problem with "The Trouble with Wilderness," then, is that in reminding those who worship at the altar of wilderness that their God (like all deities) has a complicated and problematic past, I have perhaps not been as respectful of this religious tradition as I ought to have been. I mean this quite genuinely: to the extent that I have given offense by treading too carelessly on hallowed ground, I sincerely apologize. Had I been writing about Judaism or Christianity or Islam or Buddhism, or about the spiritual universes of native peoples in North America and elsewhere, I certainly would have been more careful to show my respect before entering the temple to investigate and comment on its architecture and origins. The reason I did not do so in this case is that the religion I was critiquing is my own, and I presumed a familiarity which readers who do not know me can be forgiven for doubting.
>
> . . . I criticize wilderness because I recognize in this, my own religion, contradictions that threaten to undermine and defeat some of its own most cherished truths and moral imperatives. I have not argued that we should abandon the wild as a way of naming the sacred in nature; I have merely argued that we should not celebrate wilderness in such a way that we prevent ourselves from recognizing and taking responsibility for the sacred in our everyday lives and landscapes.[36]

One mark of the power of a religion is its sanctioning power. Cronon's pledge of allegiance to the wilderness church was, in my estimation, a sign of the social force of dark green religion, its ability to enforce conformity within the community of believers. But the other side of that coin is that participants in religion in general find meaning and a sense of belonging through their common participation in their tradition. This kind of belonging is also a part of dark green religion, part of why it *is* a social force to be reckoned with, as well as evidence *of* it. As with most religions, the deeper the participant enters the dark green religious milieu, the easier it is to recognize one's brethren and to notice when they stray from the path. For his part, Cronon's reply shows that he knows the elders of the tradition he shares with his critics. He implicitly expressed his fidelity to Thoreau by insisting that he had no intention of abandoning an understanding of the wild as sacred. In this, he showed that he belonged by affirming his own faith that "in wildness is the preservation of the world."

In their own ways and with their own words, Worster, Callicott, and Cronon noticed, described, and expressed what I am calling dark green religion. Like them, I will not predict how this phenomenon will spread. I would be surprised to see it break out like some new ecotopian contagion, however, in part because I think there are countertrends that may well prevent such a development.

Corporations as Sustainability Persuaders

There are nevertheless signs that dark green religion is gathering strength and breaking out in new places and ways. It is arguably at the heart of what can be called the sustainability revolution, and corporations are increasingly the persuaders/salespeople. This may seem surprising, but there is greater receptivity among business people to the global sustainability movement than ever before. There is growing cross-fertilization between environmentalists and business people, and green themes are increasingly expressed in corporate mission statements and advertising. That corporations feel a need to articulate environmental commitments is evidence that a green cultural transformation is well underway. When corporations do express green commitments, they set the bar higher for their own environmental performance, influence corporate culture itself, and also provide leverage to environmentalists who can then urge a company to live up to its creed.

Two Japanese examples illustrate this phenomenon. The first takes us back to Johannesburg during the WSSD, when a consortium of Japanese power companies inserted a four-page advertisement into the *International Herald Tribune* declaring their commitment to both nuclear power and renewable energy. On the front page was a photograph of an origami crane, symbolizing gratitude, with the words, "Let's be Grateful to Mother Earth." Of course, most environmentalists do not support nuclear power and viewed this advertisement cynically. That these companies chose to promote their business by appealing to tropes usually associated with Native Americans, is nevertheless noteworthy. It is worth pondering what role such images, increasingly used in corporate advertising, have and will play in promoting dark green religion. Is it possible that corporate advertising will provide the tipping point toward terrapolitan earth religion?

Some readers may think I have taken leave of my senses at this point. But as remote as such a corporate contribution to dark green religion may seem, I keep running into tantalizing possibilities. Some seem of little import, like Gaia Traffic, a regional bus system in Bergen, Norway, that when I was last there touted its fleet of low-emission buses. Or the biocentric essays and activist exhortations that regularly appear in the catalogs of the outdoor apparel and equipment company Patagonia. These would seem unlikely to influence large numbers of people. But on an April 2008 visit to Freiburg, Germany, which is known as a leading green city, I encountered an advertisement that surprised me perhaps more than any other experience reported in this book. I picked up an issue of *Time* titled "How to Win the War on Global Warming." In the middle of it was an advertisement by a Japanese electronics company for rechargeable batteries.

The advertisement began with large words proclaiming that "Sanyo is at the forefront of making clean energy an everyday reality." It then declared, "Rare is the corporation that devotes its resources to making the world—and the future—a better place. But, with its Think Gaia corporate philosophy, Sanyo leads the way, delivering on its unique vision of dealing with energy and environmental issues." This Gaia philosophy appeared in a banner across the bottom of the ad, and it drew its central proposition directly from Lovelock's Gaia hypothesis: "Sanyo sees the earth as a single living organism and, for the state of future generations, is striving to create the products needed to help us live in harmony with the planet."

On the corporate website (with text in fifteen languages), the company went into more depth, even expressing an animistic sensibility:

> "GAIA" is a term that encompasses the Blue Planet, "Earth," and the infinite varieties of "life" that live and breathe on it. It describes the world as a single living organism, where all life and nature co-exist interdependently. SANYO is committed to listening to GAIA's voice and engaging in activities that are beneficial to life and the Earth.
>
> As a testament to this, SANYO pledges to respond by developing only products that are absolutely essential to life and the Earth. We aim to bequeath a beautiful Earth to future generations. This is SANYO's Brand Vision—Think GAIA . . . All for the Earth. All for life. All for GAIA."[37]

In a further description, the site sounded as though it were making the argument in this book, that dark green religion is a globalizing social force: " 'Gaia' is a word rapidly taking hold in the 21st century, which describes the world as a single living organism, where all life and nature co-exist interdependently. The Earth has traditionally been viewed as 'the Earth' or 'Globe.' However, from now on, SANYO will view the Earth as an independent organic body and refer to it as Gaia." I have never seen a clearer confession of Gaian Earth Religion. A note hyperlinked to the word *Gaia* traced the idea directly to Lovelock, explaining that he "proposed the idea of earth as a living, green organism where mankind and all living things live in harmony. He used 'Gaia,' the name of the goddess Earth Mother in Greek mythology, to describe this living organism (Earth)." The final section of the website's text decried materialism and advanced the idea that people must symbiotically coevolve with all life, pursing sustainable solutions to ensure "positive co-existence with Gaia."

This remarkable promotional campaign raises many questions. Is Sanyo the first corporation to officially sign on to Gaian Spirituality? Is this a reflection of Japanese religious heritage, especially Shinto, which involves animistic perceptions and a reverence for nature? What influence, if any, will this campaign have on Sanyo's own business practices, their competitors, or consumers? Is this a sign that dark green religion is poised to go mainstream, that the movement toward earth-revering nature religion is becoming a green pandemic?

That a green pandemic is unfolding is essentially the argument of sustainability pioneer Paul Hawken. Hawken may be prone to ecotopian visions; his first book lauded the intentional community in Scotland known as Findhorn, which was founded upon animistic perception.[38] But in the 1990s he focused on promoting environmentally friendly capitalism.[39] A decade later, after a study of diverse social movements, he concluded that "environmental activism, social justice initiatives, and indigenous culture's resistance to globalization, all have become intertwined" and are precipitating "the largest social movement in all of human history."[40] He found that undergirding these trends were many of the elders of dark green religion, including Darwin, Emerson, Thoreau, Muir, Leopold, Gandhi, Carson, and Brower—and he expressed affinity with them. These individuals and the movements they inspired were united in their perception of "the sacredness of all life." Hawken concluded passionately: "It has been said that we cannot save our planet unless humankind undergoes a widespread spiritual and religious awakening. . . . Would we recognize a worldwide spiritual awakening if we saw one? . . . What if there is already in place a large-scale spiritual awakening and we are simply not recognizing it?"[41]

Here Hawken sounded like Jane Goodall, who has repeatedly stressed that she is hopeful because humans are ingenious, resilient, and capable of compassion. To paraphrase Hawken's conclusion: it is not too late to save both human and natural communities; but to do so, both social-justice and environmental advocates must unite and recognize that their causes are mutually dependent.

By spotlighting individuals, movements, and trends that share his values, Hawken was hoping to encourage and strengthen them. Perhaps he even thinks that his writings might provide the tipping point to a green future. At the very least, he represents another example of, and passageway into, the global bricolage of dark green religion.

The Peril and Promise of Dark Green Religion

Dark green religion is no phantom. Although unrecognized by the Parliament of World Religions, it is as widespread as most religions, more significant than some, and growing more rapidly than many others.[42] It has neither a priesthood nor institutions officially devoted to its promotion. Nor does it have an officially adopted sacred text. It does have, however, revered elders, creative leadership, and texts its adherents consider sacred. It does generate significant resources and it has institutional manifestations. Most critically, it has a coherent set of beliefs that its adherents find compelling. Rather than rescue from this world, it offers an enveloping sense of belonging to the biosphere, which is considered sacred.

Dark green religion is not easily fused with the world's longstanding religious traditions. Yet dark green religiosity is influencing the world's religions and producing novel hybrids. The influence of dark green religion thus extends beyond the environmentalist milieu and secular cultures in advanced industrial societies. It can be widely seen, including in the Earth Charter movement, and is influencing theological reflection in a variety of traditions.[43] It is also increasingly influential within the Parliament of World Religions itself, which has increasingly taken "Healing the Earth" as a central religious mission.[44] Such greening of religion would not have occurred to the extent it has in the absence of dark green forms. The increasing environmental concern of the world's predominant religions is further evidence of the possibility, however remote, of terrapolitan earth religion.

There is little doubt that dark green religion is perilous, including a terrapolitan form of it. So, for that matter, is every religious worldview in which the pure, pristine, and sublime are contrasted with that which is impure, polluted, or desecrating. The *dark* in dark green religion is to remind those engaged in such spiritualities to be alert to their shadow side.[45] Some engaged in dark green religion have been indifferent to the suffering of marginalized peoples, whether African slaves, indigenous people, or the urban poor, who have little chance to share the experience of wild nature. This shadow side can also include self-righteousness and a tendency to demonize adversaries. In general, however, the main themes of dark green religion—which include the idea that all living things have intrinsic value—do not easily lend themselves to indifference toward human suffering, let alone to virulent streams of religious, ethnic, or territory-based hatred.

Another way to address the danger of dark green religion is through risk analysis, so here is a brief argument based on one. When it comes to religion, reasonable people argue that negative consequences outweigh the positive.[46] With regard to dark green religion, I would argue, the dangers are miniscule compared to the risks of an anemic response to what are potentially catastrophic environmental dangers. Dark green religion could help prevent an anemic response; it might already be doing so.

To elaborate, here are four propositions, each of which depends on verifiable claims:

1. Those involved in the extreme branches of dark green religion (radical environmentalism) are unlikely to precipitate significant social or environmental harms through the tactics they deploy; this is because, generally speaking, they recognize the mutual dependence of human beings, nonhuman organisms, and the entire environment.[47]
2. Future scenarios by natural and social scientists since the early 1990s have grown steadily more apocalyptic with regard to the health and resilience of environmental and social systems. Strategies involving modest risks that might contribute significantly to reducing possible or likely catastrophic outcomes should be aggressively pursued.
3. Dark green religion has been mobilizing a wide variety of individuals to engage in efforts to arrest environmental decline. This kind of religion is likely to spread because the social and environmental factors that gave rise to it are unlikely to change in the foreseeable future.
4. Since dark green religion involves only modest risks, but could help human beings alter their potentially catastrophic course, it ought to be welcomed instead of feared. Dark green religion represents a potentially valuable contribution to the social mobilization necessary for the creation of environmentally sustainable and socially just lifeways.

It is always legitimate to fear and be on the alert for religions that might repress individual liberties or erode democratic institutions and hopes. Such concerns ought not to be minimized. When what is known about the history and forms of dark green religion is examined judiciously, however, such fears should ebb. Far more dangerous is the present course, with increasing numbers of human beings ingeniously managing to increase per capita consumption of the world's ecosystems, directly causing a concomitant decline in available ecosystem services, which threatens widespread environmental and social collapse sometime in the twenty-first century.[48] If these trends are not reversed, suffering will intensify. These are nature's laws, from which human beings are not exempt.[49]

It might seem that dark green religion, with its stress on ecological interdependence and kinship, and its deep sense of the value of biological and cultural diversity, could provide a counterweight to the current ominous trends. It is difficult to be optimistic, however, even if one believes such religion is salutary and has the potential to foster positive trends toward sustainability. The weight of evidence seems to be that the decline of ecosystems and the global competition for resources is intensifying, precipitating new conflicts and exacerbating others. It seems clear that these destructive trends have *much* more momentum than the movements around the world that have arisen to resist them.

Yet, the resistance that is dark green religion is young and powerful in its own way. At its best it is attractive—even "sexy" to use contemporary parlance—mostly due to its love and reverence for life. It has compelling stories, expressed in writing, film, ritual, music, and spoken word. All of these are capable of moving and motivating. It offers an enriching and meaningful understanding of how the world came to be and of the human place in that world. Although dark green religion has no officially recognized institutional forms, those engaged in it learn to recognize each other and find community.

I sometimes muse over what I have found through my long immersion in the environmental milieu. I think that like an anthropologist from an entirely different planet I have somehow stumbled across a new global earth tribe, one largely unnoticed by other scholarly observers. The tribe is unnamed and little noticed because the scholarly fashion is to stress national, regional, ethnic, and gender differences rather than commonalities, connections, and bridges. But everywhere I find the same thing: people with wildly different backgrounds sharing "dark green" perceptions and values. They may be a minority. They sometimes feel isolated and alone. But as best they can, in their own ways, and against long odds, they stand up for life.

A Personal Coda

It does not matter what I think about dark green religion. Nor does it matter what it is called or whether one concludes that the term *religion* is aptly applied to the phenomena I have described. What matters is whether people are moved and inspired when they encounter such spirituality. What matters is whether they find meaning and value in its beliefs and practices, whether they identify with it and are drawn to others engaged in it, whether it will spread and influence the way people relate to, live from, and change the biosphere.

I will nevertheless offer a few personal reflections. I do so not to satisfy curiosities about what I believe or to impart spiritual wisdom. I have no spiritual wisdom, and I really do not think what I *believe* matters. Rather, it simply seems proper to join the conversation in a more personal way, as a form of reciprocity and to express respect to those whose views I have taken the liberty to analyze. Perhaps doing so will establish a better basis for future conversations about the value and consequences of dark green religion. I consider this part of a dialogue about what it might take to grapple toward environmentally sustainable modes of existence.

I begin with a profession. With Loren Eiseley, I am convinced that the theory of evolution is the best explanation for the beauty, diversity, and fecundity of the biosphere. I also agree with him that nothing in the world fully explains the world. As he put it, "I am an evolutionist . . . [but] in the world there is nothing to explain the world. Nothing to explain the necessity of life, nothing to explain the hunger of the elements to become life, nothing to explain why the stolid realm of rock and soil and mineral should diversify itself into beauty, terror, and uncertainty."[50] This humble admission captures, I think, the idea that the universe is a Great Mystery. Understanding it is, in the final analysis, beyond our meager if still considerable abilities. The Great Mystery is an apt expression for this kind of acknowledgment, which accurately or not Charles Eastman attributed to Native Americans cultures.[51] Aldo Leopold liked and also used the expression. Rachael Carson expressed affinity with such sentiments, stating, "every mystery solved brings us closer to the threshold of a greater one."[52] She then noted that many questions will remain unanswered. For Carson and Leopold, such humility involves acknowledging that it is impossible to see *behind* those forces we can see, taste, hear, smell, and touch. I concur. The mystery is beyond our ken, at least from this vantage point in what we call time.[53]

This does not mean we should dispense with religion—at least if we start with a malleable definition. When I consider how much misery religion has brought, however, and how much human and natural capital is consumed in producing and maintaining it, I am not easily convinced that its positives outweigh its negatives. So, I often think we need an entirely new religion. At least, I think this until I remember that the kind of affective connections to the earth and its living systems, the feelings of wonder and awe at the beauty and bizarre surprises in our universe, the kinship some people feel toward their fellow living travelers in this earthly odyssey—all have long been part of the human experience.

It seems to me, however, that it would be much easier to develop sustainable societies if religions were firmly grounded in an evolutionary-ecological worldview. Religious thinkers since Darwin have gone through excruciating contortions in their efforts to graft such a worldview onto their faith traditions, which generally consider essential some sort of nonmaterial spiritual dimension and one or more divine beings inhabiting it. The result simply fails the laugh test for many if not most scientifically literate people.

How much better it would be if we would simply let go of ancient dreams ("whistling in the dark," as Leopold once put it) for which there is no evidence and many reasons to doubt. Far better to ground our future philosophies, whether or not we call them religious, in what we can confidently say is the real world. This is the world we can understand through our senses (including when aided by our ingenious gadgets). The diverse examples in this book show that worldviews based on the senses can be just as evocative, inspiring, and meaningful as those purportedly based on divine (and nonreplicable) revelations.

Even though I am a naturalist, in the absence of any compelling explanation for the universe as a whole or the life that is in and around me on this little blue planet, I can think of no better term than "miracle" to describe all I perceive. Even the bizarre fact that I am here to perceive it, reflect on it, and share my musings strikes me as nothing less than miraculous. In this, I fully understand the impulse of scientists and others who fall back on religious terms to express their deepest feelings of delight and wonder at all they sense and know.[54]

What I have been long looking for is a sensible religion, one that is rationally defensible as well as socially powerful enough to save us from our least-sensible selves. If there is a *sensible* post-Darwinian religion, then, there must be a *sensory* post-Darwinian religion. For this, dark green religion is a reasonable candidate.

Afterword on Terminology

I began this study by suggesting that explanatory power can be achieved by deploying a flexible definition of *religion* as an analytic strategy. I also indicated that it does not matter to me whether anyone concludes that *religion* is a good term for the types of experiences, perceptions, values, and practices that I have described and called dark green religion.

I chose the trope *dark green religion* for several reasons. An important one is that it has not been used before, so it has no baggage, positive or negative, and hopefully no obvious meaning that would preclude my ability to give it a useful, operational definition. A second reason is that by adding the modifier *dark* I could through wordplay present a useful double meaning—*dark* as in a deep shade of green, involving a belief in the intrinsic value of nature, and *dark* as in perilous, evoking some people's fear of places without light. I hope this terminology has served its function.

This explanation made, I wish to say I feel no ownership nor do I have an expectation the phrase will be useful beyond this study. This is in part because I think there may be, thinking long term, more useful tropes for the phenomena I have tried to explain and characterize in this book. It seems to me that there are several candidates. One is Pantheism, but I do not think this would be apt. Its etymological roots are too intimately connected to the belief in or study of god. Even though some dark green religions might consider the earth as, literally, divine, not all of them do. Better candidates are deep ecology, Paganism, and nature religion.

I did not want to use *deep ecology* because it has been so closely associated with the philosophy of Arne Naess and the politics of radical environmentalism, and because some proponents of deep ecology reject the idea that it has anything to do with religion. I felt these facts would constrain the broader field of view I wanted to provide.

I did not want to use *Paganism* because of the ongoing negative baggage the term has in many cultures and because many involved in contemporary Paganism are polytheistic and believe in nonmaterial divine beings, which is not essential to the phenomena I sought to illuminate. I thought, therefore, that using the term *Paganism* could be confusing. Nevertheless, all four types of dark green religion are found among those who consider themselves Pagan. In these pages I have shown how James Lovelock and Henry David Thoreau expressed affinity for Paganism, an understanding that has something to do with reveling in the wonders of nature and having reverence for them. So it might just be that Paganism is best suited, in the long term, to represent the phenomena described in this book—precisely *because* of the associations it provokes (and here I mean those associations that, like Thoreau and Lovelock assumed, are not pejorative).

I did not want to use the term *nature religion* in part because Catherine Albanese used it in her important book *Nature Religion in America*, defining it more broadly than what I had in mind. In this volume, I wanted to limit my focus to those who consider nature to be sacred in some way. She used *nature religion* to refer more broadly to religions in which nature was an important reference point and symbolic center. Since her book is well known to scholars, I thought it might introduce confusion to use her term. I think, however, that it may be a good candidate for referring to what I have distinguished as nature-as-sacred religions. This is an understanding commonly evoked in people's minds when they hear the term *nature religion*, and so on that score it is amenable. *Nature religion* has the added advantage of lacking the pejorative associations that Paganism calls up in some minds. If scholars use *nature religion* to refer to religions that consider nature sacred, however, they will need clarify their own, governing definition.

Scholarly tropes are not magic and nobody owns them. Neither are definitions. The key is to be as clear as possible in the hopes that the language chosen will illuminate the world.

Acknowledgments

This book would not exist were it not for the willingness of many to speak to me about their deepest values and perceptions. I feel privileged to be entrusted with these views and am grateful to all who shared them with me.

I have benefited from a number of scholars for their perceptive readings of the entire manuscript: Jonathan Benthall, Michael York, Graham Harvey, Max Oelschlaeger, Michael E. Zimmerman, Edward T. Linenthal, and Yamini Narayanan. All provided helpful substantive comments as well as much appreciated encouragement. York added a close copy editor's eye after the manuscript was completed and continues to be one of my favorite conversation partners. Benthall's response and his own scholarship enhanced my confidence that this work would appeal to a wide audience, including anthropologists. Zimmerman filled in some important historical details. Narayanan commented as the final chapters emerged, and her enthusiasm was a blast of positive energy that helped me through many months of long hours' writing. Kocku von Stuckrad, Sarah Pike, Robin Wright, and Ricardo Rozzi also read chapters and made comments that led to significant improvements. I am also grateful to Daniel Deudney, with whom I periodically discuss politics and nature religion, for his blessing in borrowing one of his apt neologisms, and to Penny Bernard for facilitating valuable experiences in Africa and for many valuable conversations.

I am deeply in debt to a number of graduate students in the religion and nature program at the University of Florida. Bridgette O'Brien performed numerous, critical time-saving tasks as well as fabulously helpful research assistance down the home stretch. Bernard Zaleha and Luke Johnston, with their knowledge of American environmental history and international sustainability movements, respectively, provided a number of valuable leads during my research. Such leads are acknowledged, to the best of my memory, in additional notes available at www.brontaylor.com. A number of other young scholars, through their professionalism and hard work on the *Journal for the Study of Religion, Nature, and Culture,* helped preserve the time needed to write this book: Gavin Van Horn, Joseph Witt, Luke Johnston, Robin Globus, and Todd Levasseur. Along with Michael Lemons, they provided feedback on some manuscript chapters, Globus serving ably as the first reader on the initial chapters, while Van Horn and Witt contributed significantly to the research that went into chapter 3, in part through our collaboration on two previously co-authored articles. While many have provided moral support during recent years, I am especially grateful to O'Brien and Zaleha in this regard. Danielle Keeter, an undergraduate student who took to the religion and nature field like a fish discovering water, not only ran down sources, but through meticulous reading caught many errors and significantly improved every chapter she read. I have also appreciated feedback from and conversations with Margot Adler and Judy Harrow.

This book would not have been completed when it was without the efficiency and competence of the executive leadership of the Society for the Study of Religion, Nature, and Culture, especially Luke Johnston, Laura Hobgood-Oster, Terry Terhaar, Kristina Tiedje, and Kocku von Stuckrad. I am also grateful for the remarkable Website assistance from Daniel Whittaker, Ipsita Chatterjea, and Sean Connors and able office assistance from Anne Newman.

My deepest debts are to my immediate family, Beth Corey-Taylor, Anders, Kaarin, and Kelsey. Without their forbearance, brilliance, independence, support, and diversions—even insights and occasional proofreading—this project would have been much more difficult to complete.

To one and all: thank you!

APPENDIX

Excerpts with Commentary on the Writings of Henry David Thoreau

The following excerpts parallel the paragraphs in chapter 3 that summarized the major themes in Thoreau's work and that are especially pertinent to this study. I have generally quoted Thoreau's earlier writings, such as *Walden* (1854), his most famous and best-known work, toward the beginning of each section. "Walking," which was published in 1862 in the *Atlantic Monthly* and includes his most famous aphorism, "in Wildness is the preservation of the World," is available online and in many anthologies.[1] "Walking," "Wild Apples," and "Huckleberries" are excerpted from *Henry David Thoreau: Collected Essays and Poems*, edited by Elizabeth Hall Witherell.[2] The latter two essays were prepared for publication in the *Atlantic Monthly* during the last few months of Thoreau's life in 1862 (and published posthumously). They were extracted and reworked from a longer manuscript, "Wild Fruits," which became available in *Faith in a Seed* and *Wild Fruits*, both edited by Bradley Dean.[3] Because Thoreau found the time shortly before his death to revise these essays, there are fewer errors and confusing parts in them than elsewhere in the "Wild Fruits" manuscript. *The Maine Woods* (1864) was written during eleven summers and earlier than "Wild Fruits," which was unfinished when he died. Some of *The Maine Woods* was published while Thoreau was alive; I took excerpts from it from a book collecting many of Thoreau's major works, *Henry David Thoreau: A Week on the Concord and Merrimack Rivers; Walden, or Life in the Woods; the Maine Woods; Cape Cod*.[4] The "Notes on the Texts" and the chronologies in the two Library of America editions helpfully locate the times of writing, publication, and editorial challenges that resulted from Thoreau's untimely death. Also very helpful is *The Annotated Walden,* edited by Philip Van Doren Stern.[5]

The excerpts below are divided into themed sections that parallel the discussion in chapter 3. Thoreau's words appear as regular text, without quotation marks, with spellings and punctuation as in the original. Italics indicate passages I believe are especially pertinent to this volume's themes, and my own comments are in brackets. Thoreau's original emphasis or italics appear in small caps.

The Simple, Natural, and Undomesticated (Free) Life

Most of the luxuries, and many of the so-called comforts of life, are not only not indispensable, but positive hindrances to the elevation of mankind. With respect to luxuries and comforts, the wisest have ever lived a more simple and meagre life than the poor. . . . There are nowadays professors of philosophy, but not philosophers. . . . To be a philosopher is not merely to have subtle thoughts . . . , but so to love wisdom as to live according to its dictates, a life of simplicity, independence, magnanimity, and trust. It is to solve some of the problems of life, not only theoretically, but practically.[6]

Men labor under a mistake. The better part of the man is soon plowed into the soil for compost. By a seeming fate, commonly called necessity, they are employed, as it says in an old book, laying up treasures which moth and rust will corrupt and thieves break through and steal. It is a fool's life, as they will find when they get to the end of it, if not before. (155) [Calling the New Testament an "old book," Thoreau attacks hubris by valuing humans as compost.]

The mass of men lead lives of quiet desperation. What is called resignation is confirmed desperation. From the desperate city you go into the desperate country, and have to console yourself with the bravery of minks and muskrats. A stereotyped but unconscious despair is concealed even under what are called the games and amusements of mankind. (150)

I went to the woods because I wished to live deliberately, to front only the essential facts of life, and see if I could not learn what it had to teach, and not, when I came to die, discover that I had not lived. . . . I wanted to live deep and suck out all the marrow of life, to live so sturdily and Spartan-like as to put to rout all that was not life, to cut a broad swath and shave close, to drive life into a corner, and reduce it to its lowest terms, and, if it proved to be mean, why then to get the whole and genuine meanness of it, and publish its meanness to the world; or if it were sublime, to know it by experience, and be able to give a true account of it in my next excursion. . . . Still we live meanly, like ants. . . . Our life is frittered away by detail. . . . Simplicity, simplicity, simplicity! I say, let your affairs be as two or three, and not a hundred or a thousand. . . . Simplify, simplify. (222)

The customs of some savage nations might, perchance, be profitably imitated by us, for they at least go through the semblance of casting their slough annually; they have the idea of the thing, whether they have the reality or not. (202–3; 193 for other examples)

How near to good is what is WILD!

Life consists with wildness. The most alive is the wildest. Not yet subdued to man, its presence refreshes him. One who pressed forward incessantly and never rested from his labors, who grew fast and made infinite demands on life, would always find himself in a new country or wilderness, and surrounded by the raw material of life. He would be climbing over the prostrate stems of primitive forest trees.[7]

Hope and the future for me are not in lawns and cultivated fields, not in towns and cities, but in the impervious and quaking swamps. When, formerly, I have analyzed my partiality for some farm which I had contemplated purchasing, I have frequently found that I was attracted solely by a few square rods of impermeable and unfathomable bog—a natural sink in one corner of it. That was the jewel which dazzled me. I derive more of my subsistence from the swamps which surround my native town than from the cultivated gardens in the village. . . . How vain, then, have been all your labors, citizens, for me! (241–42) [In other words, how vain have been the efforts of the townfolk to civilize him.]

My spirits infallibly rise in proportion to the outward dreariness. Give me the ocean, the desert, or the wilderness! In the desert, pure air and solitude compensate for want of moisture and fertility. The traveler Burton says of it—"Your MORALE improves; you become frank and cordial, hospitable and single-minded. . . . In the desert, spirituous liquors excite only disgust. *There is a keen enjoyment in a mere animal existence.*" (242)

In literature it is only the wild that attracts us. Dullness is but another name for tameness. . . . English literature, from the days of the minstrels to the Lake Poets,—Chaucer and Spenser and Milton, and even Shakespeare, included,—breathes no quite fresh and, in this sense, wild strain. It is an essentially tame and civilized literature, reflecting Greece and Rome. Her wilderness is a green wood,—her wild man a

Robin Hood. There is plenty of genial love of Nature, but not so much of Nature herself. Her chronicles inform us when her wild animals, but not when the wild man in her, became extinct. (244)

In short, all good things are wild and free. There is something in a strain of music, whether produced by an instrument or by the human voice—take the sound of a bugle in a summer night, for instance—which by its wildness, to speak without satire, reminds me of the cries emitted by wild beasts in their native forests. It is so much of their wildness as I can understand. *Give me for my friends and neighbors wild men, not tame ones. The wildness of the savage is but a faint symbol of the awful ferity with which good men and lovers meet.* (246) [This remarkable passage laments the disappearance of the wild human being and suggests that commentators who think Thoreau never escaped prudish Victorian sexual mores might have missed something.]

I love even to see the domestic animals reassert their native rights,—any evidence that they have not wholly lost their original wild habits and vigor. (246)

I rejoice that horses and steers have to be broken before they can be made the slaves of men, and that men themselves have some wild oats still left to sow before they become submissive members of society. (247)

We have a wild savage in us, and a savage name is perchance somewhere recorded as ours. (248)

I would not have every man nor every part of a man cultivated, any more than I would have every acre of earth cultivated. (249)

While almost all men feel an attraction drawing them to society, few [today] are attracted strongly to Nature. In their reaction to Nature men appear to me for the most part, notwithstanding their arts, lower than the animals. . . . How little appreciation of the beauty of the landscape there is among us! (251)

As I came home through the woods with my string of fish, trailing my pole, it being now quite dark, I caught a glimpse of a woodchuck stealing across my path, and felt a strange thrill of savage delight, and was strongly tempted to seize and devour him raw; not that I was hungry then, except for that wildness which he represented. *Once or twice, however, while I lived at the pond, I found myself ranging the woods, like a half-starved hound, with a strange abandonment, seeking some kind of venison which I might devour, and no morsel could have been too savage for me. The wildest scenes had become unaccountably familiar. I found in myself, and still find, an instinct toward a higher, or, as it is named, spiritual life, as do most men, and another toward a primitive rank and savage one, and I reverence them both. I love the wild not less than the good.*[8]

The West of which I speak is but another name for the Wild; and what I have been preparing to say is, that *in Wildness is the preservation of the World.* Every tree sends its fibers forth in search of the Wild. The cities import it at any price. Men plow and sail for it. From the forest and wilderness come the tonics and barks which brace mankind. Our ancestors were savages. The story of Romulus and Remus being suckled by a wolf is not a meaningless fable. The founders of every State which has risen to eminence have drawn their nourishment and vigor from a similar wild source. It was because the children of the Empire were not suckled by the wolf that they were conquered and displaced by the children of the Northern forests who were.[9] [In this passage from "Walking," Thoreau intimated that his fundamental loyalty was to the wild earth and that the well-being of human beings and their societies was completely dependent on it.]

The Wisdom of Nature

But since I left those shores the woodchoppers have still further laid them waste, and now for many a year there will be no more rambling through the aisles of the wood, with occasional vistas through which you see the water. My Muse may be excused if she is silent henceforth. How can you expect the birds to sing when their groves are cut down?[10] [Here in *Walden,* Thoreau averred that nature was needed for poetry and spirituality—as a muse—and conservation was needed to protect the muse; at this time conservation was more indirectly valued than in later writings.]

I served my apprenticeship and have since done considerable journeywork in the huckleberry field. Though I never paid for my schooling and clothing in that way, it was some of the best schooling that I got and paid for itself. . . . THERE was the university itself where you could learn the everlasting Laws, and Medicine and Theology, not under Story, and Warren, and Ware, but far wiser professors than they. Why such haste to go from the huckleberry field to the College yard?

As in old times they who dwelt on the heath, remote from towns, being backward to adopt the doctrines which prevailed in towns, were called heathen in a bad sense, so I trust that we dwellers in the huckleberry pastures, which are our heathlands, shall be slow to adopt the notions of large towns and cities, though perchance we may be nicknamed huckleberry people. But the worst of it is that the emissaries of the towns come more for our berries than they do for our salvation.[11]

A Religion of Nature

There is nothing inorganic. These foliaceous heaps lie along the bank like the slag of a furnace, showing that Nature is "in full blast" within. *The earth is not a mere fragment of dead history,* stratum upon stratum like the leaves of a book, to be studied by geologists and antiquaries chiefly, *but living poetry like the leaves of a tree, which precede flowers and fruit—not a fossil earth, but a living earth;* compared with whose great central life all animal and vegetable life is merely parasitic.[12] [It is hard to imagine a clearer statement of organicism, unless it is the next excerpt.]

I experienced sometimes that the most sweet and tender, the most innocent and encouraging society may be found in any natural object, even for the poor misanthrope and most melancholy man. There can be no very black melancholy to him who lives in the midst of Nature and has his senses still. (263)

But I was at the same time conscious of a slight insanity in my mood, and seemed to foresee my recovery. In the midst of a gentle rain while these thoughts prevailed, I was suddenly sensible of such sweet and beneficent society in Nature, in the very pattering of the drops, and in every sound and sight around my house, an infinite and unaccountable friendliness all at once like an atmosphere sustaining me, as made the fancied advantages of human neighborhood insignificant, and I have never thought of them since. Every little pine needle expanded and swelled with sympathy and befriended me. *I was so distinctly made aware of the presence of something kindred to me, even in scenes which we are accustomed to call wild and dreary, and also that the nearest of blood to me and humanest was not a person nor a villager, that I thought no place could ever be strange to me again.* (264) [This is one of Thoreau's most personal expressions of kinship and friendship with all life-forms, along with his felt sense of the personhood and beneficence of nature; more such passages follow.]

"How vast and profound is the influence of the subtile powers of Heaven and of Earth!"

"*We seek to perceive them, and we do not see them; we seek to hear them, and we do not hear them;* identified with the substance of things, they cannot be separated from them."

"They cause that in all the universe men purify and sanctify their hearts, and clothe themselves in their holiday garments to offer sacrifices and oblations to their ancestors. It is an ocean of subtile intelligences. They are everywhere, above us, on our left, on our right; they environ us on all sides." (266) [In an adjacent note, Philip Van Doren Stern (borrowing from Lyman Cady) indicated that Thoreau took these three quotes from *The Doctrine of the Mean,* which is attributed to Tzu See, Confucius's grandson. This is an early example of how often those engaged in dark green religion are influenced by religious philosophies originating in Asia or find in such traditions words that resonate with their own perceptions and feelings; in this case, the quotes capture an animistic perception. See also the notation on "intelligences" after the next excerpt.]

The indescribable innocence and beneficence of Nature—of sun and wind and rain, of summer and winter—such health, such cheer, they afford forever! and such sympathy have they ever with our race, that all Nature would be affected, and the sun's brightness fade, and the winds would sigh humanely, and the clouds rain tears, and the woods shed their leaves and put on mourning in midsummer, *if any man should ever for a just cause grieve. Shall I not have intelligence with the earth? Am I not partly leaves and vegetable mould myself?* (269) [In an adjacent note, Stern equated "intelligence" with "communication"; in context, then, this passage has both pantheistic (earthly) and animistic (floral) intimations. Stern also noted a comment in an early draft of the manuscript that did not end up published, "God is my father and my good friend—men are my brothers—but nature is my mother and sister." It may be that this was left out because Thoreau increasingly eschewed theistic language.]

Man at length stands in such a relation to Nature as the animals which pluck and eat as they go. The fields and hills are a table constantly spread. Diet-drinks, cordials, wines of all kinds and qualities, are bottled up in the skins of countless berries for their refreshment, and they quaff them at every turn. *They seem offered to us not so much for food as for sociality, inviting us to a pic-nic with Nature. We pluck and eat in remembrance of her. It is a sort of sacrament—a communion—the* NOT *forbidden fruits, which no serpent tempts us to eat. Slight and innocent savors which relate us to Nature, make us her guests entitle us to her regard and protection.*[13]

[The next excerpts from *The Maine Woods* are among Thoreau's most animistic.]

Strange that so few ever come to the woods to see how the pine lives and grows and spires, lifting its evergreen arms to the light,—to see its perfect success; but most are content to behold it in the shape of many broad boards brought to market, and deem *THAT* its true success! But the pine is no more lumber than man is, and to be made into boards and houses is no more its true and highest use than the truest use of a man is to be cut down and made into manure. There is a higher law affecting our relation to pines as well as to men. A pine cut down, a dead pine, is no more a pine than a dead human carcass is a man. Can he who has discovered only some of the values of whalebone and whale oil be said to have discovered the true use of the whale? Can he who slays the elephant for his ivory be said to have "seen the elephant"? These are petty and accidental uses; just as if a stronger race were to kill us in order to make buttons and flageolets of our bones; for everything may serve a lower as well as a higher use. Every creature is better alive than dead, men and moose and pine-trees, and he who understands it aright will rather preserve its life than destroy it.

Is it the lumberman, then, who is the friend and lover of the pine, stands nearest to it, and understands its nature best? Is it the tanner who has barked it, or he who has boxed it for turpentine, whom posterity will fable to have been changed into a pine at last? *No! no! it is the poet . . . —who knows whether its heart is false without cutting into it . . . —No, it is the poet, who loves them as his own shadow in the air, and lets them stand.* I have been into the lumber-yard, and the carpenter's shop, and the tannery, and the lampblack-factory, and the turpentine clearing; but when at length I saw the tops of the pines waving and reflecting the light at a distance high over all the rest of the forest, I realized that the former were not the highest use of the pine. It is not their bones or hide or tallow that I love most. *It is the living spirit of the tree, not its spirit of turpentine, with which I sympathize, and which heals my cuts. It is as immortal as I am, and perchance will go to as high a heaven, there to tower above me still.*[14] [This is from the section titled "Chesuncook." The last sentence of this passage is one of Thoreau's most animistic (and counter-homocentric). It was removed when the essay was initially published in the *Atlantic Monthly,* probably because it was considered pagan and blasphemous. Thoreau took offense at the deletion and asked that the sentence be published in the next issue, but the editor refused (1050).]

[The next excerpt is from "The Allegash and East Branch," the third and final part of *The Maine Woods.* It begins with Thoreau's delight and amazement over phosphorescent wood, which he saw for the first time during this forest journey with his American Indian guide, Joe Polis.]

The next day the Indian told me their name for this light,—ARTOOSOQU',—and on my inquiring concerning the will-o'-the-wisp, and the like phenomena, he said that his "folks" sometimes saw fires passing along at various heights, even as high as the trees, and making a noise. I was prepared after this to hear of the most startling and unimagined phenomena witnessed by "his folks," they are abroad at all hours and seasons in scenes so unfrequented by white men. *Nature must have made a thousand revelations to them which are still secrets to us.* (731) [This demonstrates respect for the intimate knowledge of nature among indigenous Americans, but Thoreau was also dismissive of much of this knowledge; in this he was like many contemporary ethnobiologists.]

I did not regret my not having seen this before, since I now saw it under circumstances so favorable. *I was in just the frame of mind to see something wonderful, and this was a phenomenon adequate to my circumstances and expectation, and it put me on the alert to see more like it.* [This is a remarkable acknowledgment of the importance of a preexisting disposition to perceive—a modern understanding of the social construction of reality.] *I exulted like "a pagan suckled in a creed"* that had never been worn at all, but was bran new, and adequate to the occasion. *I let science slide, and rejoiced in that light as if it had been a fellow-creature. I saw that it was excellent, and was very glad to know that it was so cheap. A scientific* EXPLANATION, *as it is called, would have been altogether out of place there.* That is for pale daylight. Science with its retorts would have put me to sleep; it was the opportunity to be ignorant that I improved. *It suggested to me that there was something to be seen if one had eyes. It made a believer of me more than before. I believed that the woods were not tenantless, but choke-full of honest spirits as good as myself any day,—not an empty chamber, in which chemistry was left to work alone, but an inhabited house,—and for a few moments I enjoyed fellowship with them.* Your so-called wise man goes trying to persuade himself that there is no entity there but himself and his traps, but it is a great deal easier to believe the truth. *It suggested, too, that the same experience always gives birth to the same sort of belief or religion. One revelation has been made to the Indian, another to the white man. I have much to learn of the Indian, nothing of the missionary. I am not sure but all that would tempt me to teach the Indian my religion would be his promise to teach me* HIS. Long enough I had heard of irrelevant things; now at length I was glad to make acquaintance with the light that dwells in rotten wood. Where is all your knowledge gone to? It evaporates completely, for it has no depth. (731–32) [I think this passage makes clear that Thoreau had his doubts, as would nearly any modern person with a scientific background, about animistic perception. He indicates that, on the one hand, his animistic fellowship with woodland spirits was "for a few moments" only. But he also considers those experiences, although momentary, authentic glimpses into an entirely real world not usually perceived by civilized humans but available to those who are receptive to them.]

I believe that there is a subtile magnetism in Nature, which, if we unconsciously yield to it, will direct us aright.[15] [This excerpt from "Walking" suggests a pantheistic, panentheistic, or organicist worldview. It is one of Thoreau's most pantheistic-sounding passages, in which nature itself is perceived to be a divine guide to those who are open to such guidance.]

When I would recreate myself, I seek the darkest wood, the thickest and most interminable and, to the citizen, most dismal, swamp. I enter a swamp as a sacred place,—a SANCTUM SANCTORUM. *There is the strength, the marrow, of Nature.* (242)

I believe in the forest, and in the meadow, and in the night in which the corn grows. (239)

I am no worshipper of Hygeia, who was the daughter of that old herb-doctor Æsculapius, and who is represented on monuments holding a serpent in one hand, and in the other a cup out of which the serpent sometimes drinks; but rather of Hebe, cup-bearer to Jupiter, who was the daughter of Juno and wild lettuce, and who had the power of restoring gods and men to the vigor of youth. She was probably the only thoroughly sound-conditioned, healthy, and robust young lady that ever walked the globe, and wherever she came it was spring.[16] [Thoreau essentially stated that he worshiped the renewing power of spring.]

Every morning was a cheerful invitation to make my life of equal simplicity, and I may say innocence, with Nature herself. I have been as sincere a worshipper of Aurora as the Greeks. I got up early and bathed in the pond; that was a religious exercise, and one of the best things which I did. . . . That man who does not believe that each day contains an earlier, more sacred, and auroral hour than he has yet profaned, has despaired of life, and is pursuing a descending and darkening way. . . . The Vedas say, "All intelligences awake with the morning." [This is yet another reference to that which can only be considered an animistic perception, one of the many passages that also shows the influence of the Vedic scriptures on Thoreau's religious imagination.] Poetry and art, and the fairest and most memorable of the actions of men, date from such an hour. All poets and heroes, like Memnon, are the children of Aurora, and emit their music at sunrise. To him whose elastic and vigorous thought keeps pace with the sun, the day is a perpetual morning. (220, 221) [Religion is about more than belief—it is about practice—and here Thoreau made an astute observation about the religious dimensions of some of his daily nature-related rites.]

Laws of Nature and Justice

The greater part of what my neighbors call good I believe in my soul to be bad, and if I repent of anything, it is very likely to be my good behavior. What demon possessed me that I behaved so well?[17]

A simple and independent mind does not toil at the bidding of any prince. (193)

There is something servile in the habit of seeking after a law which we may obey. We may study the laws of matter at and for our convenience, but a successful life knows no law. It is an unfortunate discovery certainly, that of a law which binds us where we did not know before that we were bound. Live free, child of the mist—and with respect to knowledge we are all children of the mist.[18]

Nowadays almost all man's improvements, so called, as the building of houses, and the cutting down of the forest and of all large trees, simply deform the landscape, and make it more and more tame and cheap. . . . I looked again, and saw him standing in the middle of a boggy stygian fen, surrounded by devils, and he had found his bounds without a doubt, three little stones, where a stake had been driven, and looking nearer, I saw that the Prince of Darkness was his surveyor. (230) [John Muir would soon also liken those who defiled nature to Satan.]

But all this is very selfish, I have heard some of my townsmen say. I confess that I have hitherto indulged very little in philanthropic enterprises. . . . While my townsmen and women are devoted in so many ways to the good of their fellows, I trust that one at least may be spared to other and less humane pursuits. You must have a genius for charity as well as for anything else. As for Doing-good, that is one of the professions which are full. Moreover, I have tried it fairly, and, strange as it may seem, am satisfied that it does not agree with my constitution. Probably I should not consciously and deliberately forsake my particular calling to do the good which society demands of me, to save the universe from annihilation; and I believe that a like but infinitely greater steadfastness elsewhere is all that now preserves it. But I would not stand between any man and his genius; and to him who does this work, which I decline, with his whole heart and soul and life, I would say, Persevere, even if the world call it doing evil, as it is most likely they will.[19]

If I knew for a certainty that a man was coming to my house with the conscious design of doing me good, I should run for my life. . . . Philanthropy is almost the only virtue which is sufficiently appreciated by mankind. Nay, it is greatly overrated; and it is our selfishness which overrates it. A robust poor man, one sunny day here in Concord, praised a fellow-townsman to me, because, as he said, he was kind to the poor; meaning himself . . . I would not subtract anything from the praise that is due to philanthropy, but merely demand justice for all who by their lives and works are a blessing to mankind. (207–9)

Our manners have been corrupted by communication with the Saints. . . . If, then, we would indeed restore mankind by truly Indian, botanic, magnetic, or natural means, let us first be as simple and well as Nature ourselves, dispel the clouds which hang over our own brows, and take up a little life into our pores. Do not stay to be an overseer of the poor, but endeavor to become one of the worthies of the world. (211)

To preserve wild animals implies generally the creation of a forest for them to dwell in or resort to. So it is with man.[20]

The civilized nations—Greece, Rome, England—have been sustained by the primitive forests which anciently rotted where they stand. They survive as long as the soil is not exhausted. Alas for human culture! (243)

An Ecocentric Moral Philosophy

[The next several excerpts from "Huckleberries" represent some of Thoreau's most mature thinking. They show his double critique of centralized economic power and of unbridled human numbers, and the concomitant decline in biological diversity (before the concept was developed) and thus his ecocentric moral sentiments. Some environmentalists would also find in such passages support for their anticapitalist and/or Malthusian convictions.]

I suspect that *the inhabitants of England and the continent of England have thus lost in a measure their natural rights, with the increase of population and monopolies. The wild fruits of the earth disappear before civilization,* or only the husks of them are to be found in large markets. *The whole country becomes, as it were, a town or beaten common,* and almost the only fruits left are a few hips and haws.

What sort of a country is that where the huckleberry fields are private property? When I pass such fields on the highway, my heart sinks within me. I see a blight on the land. Nature is under a veil there. I make haste away from the accursed spot. Nothing could deform her fair face more. I cannot think of it after but as the place where fair and palatable berries, are converted into money, where the huckleberry is desecrated.

It is true, we have as good a right to make berries private property, as to make wild grass and trees such—it is not worse than a thousand other practices which custom has sanctioned—but that is the worst of it, for it suggests how bad the rest are, and to what result our civilization and division of labor naturally tend, to make all things venal.[21]

All our improvements, so called, tend to convert the country into the town. But I do not see clearly that these successive losses are ever quite made up to us. . . . It is my own way of living that I complain of as well as yours. . . .

Thus we behave like oxen in a flower garden. The true fruit of Nature can only be plucked with a fluttering heart and a delicate hand, not bribed by any earthly reward.

Among the Indians, the earth and its productions generally were common and free to all the tribe, like the air and water—but among us who have supplanted the Indians, the public retain only a small yard or common in the middle of the village . . . I doubt if you can ride out five miles in any direction without coming to where some individual is tolling in the road—and he expects the time when it will all revert to him or his heirs. *This is the way we civilized men have arranged it.* (495)

I am not overflowing with respect and gratitude to the fathers who thus laid out our New England villages. . . . If they were in earnest seeking thus far away "freedom to worship God," as some assure us—why did they not secure a little more of it, when it was so cheap and they were about it? At the same time that they built meeting-houses *why did they not preserve from desecration and destruction far grander temples not made with hands?* (495–96)

["Huckleberries" then turns to some remarkably prescient, practical suggestions about landscape design in the construction of townships, suggesting that rivers/riparian areas be kept "a common possession forever" (496)—and that the hills and mountains should be protected as sacred places/temples (497).]

I think that each town should have a park, or rather a primitive forest of five hundred or a thousand acres . . . , a common possession forever, for instruction and recreation. (500) [The effort to protect and restore the commons (community-owned or controlled land managed for the well-being of all) is a common denominator of much radical environmentalism globally. Such passages are another reason that environmental activists generally view Thoreau as an elder in their movement.]

I know it is a mere figure of speech to talk about temples nowadays, when men recognize none, and associate the word with heathenism. Most men, it appears to me, do not care for Nature, and would sell their share in all her beauty, for as long as they may live, for a stated and not very large sum. Thank God they cannot fly and lay waste the sky as well as the earth. We are safe on that side for the present. It is for the very reason that some do not care for these things that we need to combine to protect all from the vandalism of a few. (497–98) [This passage sounds prophetic when read in our own time of intensifying alarm about the destruction of the atmospheric commons.]

Loyalty to and the Interconnectedness of Nature

I wish to speak a word for Nature, for absolute freedom and wildness, as contrasted with a freedom and culture merely civil—to regard man as an inhabitant, or a part and parcel of Nature, rather than a member of society. I wish to make an extreme statement, if so I may make an emphatic one, for there are enough champions of civilization: the minister and the school-committee, and every one of you will take care of that.[22]

Fishermen, hunters, woodchoppers, and others, spending their lives in the fields and woods, in a peculiar sense a part of Nature themselves, are often in a more favorable mood for observing her, in the intervals of their pursuits, than philosophers or poets even, who approach her with expectation. *She is not afraid to exhibit herself to them.*[23] [Here in *Walden* and in the previous excerpt, the famous introduction to "Walking," are strong expressions of belonging and loyalty to nature, as well as the idea that those who live off the land are more likely to have a spiritual understanding than "civilized" people.]

Thus it appears that the sweltering inhabitants of Charleston and New Orleans, of Madras and Bombay and Calcutta, drink at my well. In the morning I bathe my intellect in the stupendous and cosmogonal philosophy of the Bhagvat-Geeta, since whose composition years of the gods have elapsed, and in comparison with which our modern world and its literature seem puny and trivial; and I doubt if that philosophy is not to be referred to a previous state of existence, so remote is its sublimity from our conceptions. (418)

I lay down the book and go to my well for water, and lo! there I meet the servant of the Bramin, priest of Brahma and Vishnu and Indra, who still sits in his temple on the Ganges reading the Vedas, or dwells at the root of a tree with his crust and water jug. I meet his servant come to draw water for his master, and our buckets as it were grate together in the same well. The pure Walden water is mingled with the sacred water of the Ganges. With favoring winds it is wafted past the site of the fabulous islands of Atlantis and the Hesperides, makes the periplus of Hanno, and, floating by Ternate and Tidore and the mouth of the Persian Gulf, melts in the tropic gales of the Indian seas, and is landed in ports of which Alexander only heard the names. (418) [The deep and global interrelationships in nature, captured in these reflections, are reinforced by Thoreau's understanding of the positive role death plays in natural cycles. Like many ecologists, he viewed death as a prerequisite for nature's vitality and not something to be feared or unduly mourned, as in the next excerpts.]

Our village life would stagnate if it were not for the unexplored forests and meadows which surround it. We need the tonic of wildness—to wade sometimes in marshes where the bittern and the meadow-hen lurk, and hear the booming of the snipe; to smell the whispering sedge where only some wilder and more solitary fowl builds her nest, and the mink crawls with its belly close to the ground. (433–34)

At the same time that we are earnest to explore and learn all things, we require that all things be mysterious and unexplorable, that land and sea be infinitely wild, unsurveyed and unfathomed by us because unfathomable. We can never have enough of nature. We must be refreshed by the sight of inexhaustible vigor, vast and titanic features, the sea-coast with its wrecks, the wilderness with its living and its decaying trees, the thunder-cloud, and the rain which lasts three weeks and produces freshets. We need to witness our own limits transgressed, and some life pasturing freely where we never wander. We are cheered when we observe the vulture feeding on the carrion which disgusts and disheartens us, and deriving health and strength from the repast. There was a dead horse in the hollow by the path to my house, which compelled me sometimes to go out of my way, especially in the night when the air was heavy, but the assurance it gave me of the strong appetite and inviolable health of Nature was my compensation for this. *I love to see that Nature is so rife with life that myriads can be afforded to be sacrificed and suffered to prey on one another; that tender organizations can be so serenely squashed out of existence like pulp—tadpoles which herons gobble up, and tortoises and toads run over in the road; and that sometimes it has rained flesh and blood! With the liability to accident, we must see how little account is to be made of it. The impression made on a wise man is that of universal innocence. Poison is not poisonous after all, nor are any wounds fatal. Compassion is a very untenable ground.* It must be expeditious. Its pleadings will not bear to be stereotyped. (434) [This acceptance and even reveling in the circle of life is common among ecologists, in my experience; there is a certain matter-of-factness about it or, alternatively, an expression of delight in the very process of eating and being eaten. This is a common way of thinking among participants in dark green religions, especially the most ecologically literate among them.]

. . . Such is the home of the moose, the bear, the caribou, the wolf, the beaver, and the Indian. Who shall describe the inexpressible tenderness and immortal life of the grim forest, where Nature, though it be mid-winter, is ever in her spring, where the moss-grown and decaying trees are not old, but seem to enjoy a perpetual youth; and blissful, innocent Nature, like a serene infant, is too happy to make a noise, except by a few tinkling, lisping birds and trickling rills?

What a place to live, what a place to die and be buried in! There certainly men would live forever, and laugh at death and the grave. There they could have no such thoughts as are associated with the village graveyard,—that make a grave out of one of those moist evergreen hummocks![24] [In this passage from "Ktaadn" in *The Maine Woods,* Thoreau conveyed an important idea in all religion, namely, what comprised an authentic death; he also seemed to express a post-theistic naturalism.]

Moral Evolution

One farmer says to me, "You cannot live on vegetable food solely, for it furnishes nothing to make bones with"; and so he religiously devotes a part of his day to supplying his system with the raw material of bones; walking all the while he talks behind his oxen, which, with vegetable-made bones, jerk him and his lumbering plow along in spite of every obstacle.[25] [This is a great example of how Thoreau made a point with ironic humor.]

There is a period in the history of the individual, as of the race, when the hunters are the "best men," as the Algonquins called them. We cannot but pity the boy who has never fired a gun; he is no more humane, while his education has been sadly neglected. This was my answer with respect to those youths who were bent on this pursuit, trusting that they would soon outgrow it. No humane being, past the thoughtless age of boyhood, will wantonly murder any creature, which holds its life by the same tenure that he does. The hare in its extremity cries like a child. I warn you, mothers, that my sympathies do not always make the usual philanthropic distinctions. (341)

Such is oftenest the young man's introduction to the forest, and the most original part of himself. He goes thither at first as a hunter and fisher, until at last, if he has the seeds of a better life in him, he distinguishes his proper objects, as a poet or naturalist it may be, and leaves the gun and fish-pole behind. The mass of men are still and always young [immature, morally and spiritually] in this respect. (341; also see 342)

Is it not a reproach that man is a carnivorous animal? True, he can and does live, in a great measure, by preying on other animals; but this is a miserable way—as any one who will go to snaring rabbits, or slaughtering lambs, may learn—and he will be regarded as a benefactor of his race who shall teach man to confine himself to a more innocent and wholesome diet. Whatever my own practice may be, *I have no doubt that it is a part of the destiny of the human race, in its gradual improvement, to leave off eating animals, as surely as the savage tribes have left off eating each other when they came in contact with the more civilized.* (344) [It is interesting to consider whether the many contemporary greens who eschew eating animals or even using animal products in some ways echo Thoreau's sentiments in *Walden*.]

. . . Yet, for my part, I was never unusually squeamish; I could sometimes eat a fried rat with a good relish, if it were necessary. I am glad to have drunk water so long, for the same reason that I prefer the natural sky to an opium-eater's heaven. (345)

I carry less religion to the table, ask no blessing; not because I am wiser than I was, but, I am obliged to confess, because, however much it is to be regretted, with years I have grown more coarse and indifferent. Perhaps these questions are entertained only in youth, as most believe of poetry. My practice is "nowhere," my opinion is here. Nevertheless I am far from regarding myself as one of those privileged ones to whom the Ved [Vedas] refers when it says, that "he who has true faith in the Omnipresent Supreme Being may eat all that exists," that is, is not bound to inquire what is his food, or who prepares it; and even in their case it is to be observed, as a Hindoo commentator has remarked, that the Vedant limits this privilege [of animal eating] to "the time of distress." (345) [In such sections from *Walden,* one can see a drift away from anthropocentrism and a hope that human beings as a whole will leave behind hunting and fishing as they mature spiritually and become more intimate with nature. In the next excerpt, Thoreau indicated that the natural life leads to health, including the idea now prevalent in green circles that people should eat locally the natural produce of the season.]

Live in each season as it passes; breathe the air, drink the drink, taste the fruit, and resign yourself to the influences of each. . . . Be blown on by all the winds. Open all your pores and bathe the tides of nature, in all her streams and oceans, at all seasons. Miasma and infection are from within. . . . For all nature is doing her best each moment to make us well. She exists for no other end. Do not resist her. With the least inclination to be well we should not be sick. . . . Nature is but another name for health.[26]

In short, as a snow-drift is formed to where there is a lull in the wind, so, one would say, where there is a lull of truth, an institution springs up. But the truth of blows right on the over it, nevertheless, and at length blows it down. What is called politics is comparatively something so superficial and inhuman, that, practically, I have never fairly recognized that it concerns me at all.[27] [This excerpt from "Life without Principle" follows harsh criticism of imperial adventurism by agents of the United States in the Amazon. Here Thoreau's anarchistic feelings fused with his trust in nature: eventually, he seems to have believed, bad institutions will crumble because they do not cohere with truth, a sentiment not uncommon among latter-day participants in dark green religion. Such dark green religionists would today make more clear that the truth to which they refer is the dependence of society on nature and that unsustainable societies will not last.]

Ambivalence and Enigma

[The next excerpt is an enigmatic passage from "Ktaadn," the first section of *The Maine Woods,* published posthumously in 1864 but based on travels in 1857. It is noteworthy for many things, including an apparent, remnant, dualism between humans and nature, an ambivalence toward wild nature (as both savage and beautiful), and what seem to be contradictory views about animistic perception and those most likely to have it, namely, nature-dwelling Indians. In this excerpt Thoreau labeled such perception "superstitious"—but it is also clear that he found value in such perceptiveness and the way it brings one close to nature; indeed, the end of the passage expresses a belief in the profound mystery of life, a conviction that this includes the mysterious spirit that animates living things, as well as a deep and profound longing for deeper contact and communion with nature.]

Perhaps I most fully realized that this was primeval, untamed, and forever untameable *Nature,* or whatever else men call it, while coming down this part of the mountain. . . . It is difficult to conceive of a region uninhabited by man. We habitually presume his presence and influence everywhere. And yet we have not seen pure Nature, unless we have seen her thus vast and drear and inhuman, though in the midst of cities. *Nature was here something savage and awful, though beautiful. I looked with awe at the ground I trod on, to see what the Powers had made there, the form and fashion and material of their work. This was that Earth of which we have heard, made out of Chaos and Old Night. Here was no man's garden, but the unhandselled globe. It was not lawn, nor pasture, nor mead, nor woodland, nor lea, nor arable, nor waste-land. It was the fresh and natural surface of the planet Earth, as it was made for ever and ever,—to be the dwelling of man, we say,—so Nature made it, and man may use it if he can. Man was not to be associated with it.* [Here, perhaps, remains a man/nature dualism.] *It was Matter, vast, terrific,—not his Mother Earth that we have heard of, not for him to tread on, or be buried in,—no, it were being too familiar even to let his bones lie there,—the home, this, of Necessity and Fate. There was there felt the presence of a force not bound to be kind to man. It was a place for heathenism and superstitious rites,—to be inhabited by men nearer of kin to the rocks and to wild animals than we. We walked over it with a certain awe,* stopping, from time to time, to pick the blueberries which grew there, and had a smart and spicy taste. Perchance where *OUR* wild pines stand, and leaves lie on their forest floor, in Concord, there were once reapers, and husbandmen planted grain; but here not even the surface had been scarred by man, but it was a specimen of what God saw fit to make this world. What is it to be admitted to a museum, to see a myriad of particular things, compared with being shown some star's surface, some hard matter in its home! *I stand in awe of my body, this matter to which I am bound has become so strange to me. I fear not spirits, ghosts, of which I am one,—*THAT *my body might,—but I fear bodies, I tremble to meet them. What is this Titan that has possession of me? Talk of mysteries!—Think of our life in nature,—daily to be shown matter, to come in contact with it,—rocks, trees, wind on our cheeks! the* SOLID *earth! the* ACTUAL *world! the* COMMON SENSE! CONTACT! CONTACT! WHO *are we?* WHERE *are we?*[28] [In summary, this passage expresses ambivalence and a struggle for meaning but does not provide compelling evidence that Thoreau had moved profoundly beyond dualistic, anthropocentric beliefs toward considering nature and her creatures sacred and communion with them possible.]

This afternoon's experience [of hunting moose] suggested to me how base or coarse are the motives which commonly carry men into the wilderness. *The explorers and lumberers generally are all hirelings, paid so much a day for their labor, and as such they have no more love for wild nature than wood-sawyers have for forests. Other white men and Indians who come here are for the most part hunters, whose object is to slay as many moose and other wild animals as possible. But, pray, could not one spend some weeks or years in the solitude of this vast wilderness with other employments than these,—employments perfectly sweet and innocent and ennobling? For one that comes with a pencil to sketch or sing, a thousand come with an axe or rifle. What a coarse and imperfect use Indians and hunters make of Nature! No wonder that their race is so soon exterminated.* I already, and for weeks afterward, felt my nature the coarser for this part of my woodland experience, and was reminded that our life should be lived as tenderly and daintily as one would pluck a flower. (683–84) [Thoreau was ambivalent about Indians: he thought them knowledgeable and wise because of their first-hand contact with nature but did not think they always exhibited a proper love for wild nature. In this passage, he expressed a superior attitude and a callous, or at least a matter-of-fact view about the demise of Indian cultures. Perhaps ironically, a paragraph later he wrote two of his most animistic passages (see 684–85, and esp. 731, 732). Later in *The Maine Woods,* reflecting on his Indian guide's singing a missionary-taught song in his native language, Thoreau again betrayed his ambivalence, grounded in a clear sense of superiority. Of course, he considered himself superior to most people, of whatever background.]

His singing carried me back to the period of the discovery of America, to San Salvador and the Incas, when Europeans first encountered the simple faith of the Indian. There was, indeed, a beautiful simplicity about it; nothing of the dark and savage, only the mild and infantile. The sentiments of humility and reverence chiefly were expressed. (730)

Notes

Chapter 1

1. For an exhaustive study, see Ernst Feil, *On the Concept of Religion* (Binghamton, U.K.: Global Publications, 2000).

2. David Chidester, *Authentic Fakes: Religion and Popular American Culture* (Berkeley: University of California Press, 2005), 75; Jonathan Z. Smith, "Religion, Religions, Religious," in *Critical Terms for Religious Studies*, ed. Mark C. Taylor (Chicago: University of Chicago Press, 1998), 281–82; Benson Saler, *Conceptualizing Religion: Immanent Anthropologists, Transcendent Natives, and Unbounded Categories* (Leiden, the Netherlands: Brill, 1993), 68.

3. Saler, *Conceptualizing Religion*, 74.

4. Saler borrowed the "family resemblance" phrase from Ludwig Wittgenstein, *Philosophical Investigations* (Malden, MA: Blackwell, 2001 [1953]). Others exploring this approach include Kocku von Stuckrad, who traced what he called the "polyfocal approach" to Friedrich Nietzsche; see Stuckrad's "Discursive Study of Religion: From States of the Mind to Communication and Action," *Method & Theory in the Study of Religion* 15 (2003): 260–62. Also see William P. Alston, "Religion," in *Encyclopedia of Philosophy*, ed. Paul Edwards (New York: Macmillan and the Free Press, 1967), 141–42; Martin Southwold, "Buddhism and the Definition of Religion," *Man* 13 (1978): 362–79, esp. 370–71; Jonathan Benthall, Return to Religion: Why a Secular Age Is Haunted by Faith (London: I. B. Tauris, 2008); Melford Spiro, "Religion: Problems of Definition and Explanation," in *Anthropological Approaches to the Study of Religion*, ed. Michael Banton (London: Tavistock, 1966), 85–126. See the additional notes at www.brontaylor.com for my own list of characteristics that deserve analysis, or Bron Taylor, "Exploring Religion, Nature, and Culture," *Journal for the Study of Religion, Nature, and Culture* 1, no. 1 (2007): 5–24.

5. Saler, *Conceptualizing Religion*, 226. I agree.

6. Wade Clark Roof, *A Generation of Seekers* (San Francisco: Harper, 1993), 76–77, see also 30, 76–79, 129–30; Brian J. Zinnbauer, Kenneth I. Pargament, and others, "Religion and Spirituality: Unfuzzying the Fuzzy," *Journal for the Scientific Study of Religion* 36, no. 4 (1997), 549–64; Paul Heelas et al., *The Spiritual Revolution: Why Religion Is Giving Way to Spirituality* (Malden, MA: Blackwell, 2005); Robert C. Fuller, *Spiritual but Not Religious: Understanding Unchurched America* (Oxford: Oxford University Press, 2001), esp. 87–100.

7. Peter Higbie Van Ness, *Spirituality, Diversion, and Decadence: The Contemporary Predicament* (Albany: State University of New York Press, 1992), 13–14; Anna S. King, "Spirituality: Transformation and Metamorphosis," *Religion* 26 (1996), 345. See also Fuller, *Spiritual but Not Religious,* 85–98.

8. King, "Spirituality," 346, 347 (next quote).

9. James D. Proctor, "Religion as Trust in Authority: Theocracy and Ecology in the United States," *Annals of the Association of American Geographers* 96, no. 1 (2006): 193, 195 (respectively). Proctor also wrote, "theocracy thus seems stronger in the United States than many European countries, ecology appears to be of equivalent or greater strength elsewhere" (194).

10. Bron Taylor, "Earth and Nature-Based Spirituality (Part I): From Deep Ecology to Radical Environmentalism," *Religion* 31, no. 2 (2001): 175–93; Bron Taylor, "Earth and Nature-Based Spirituality (Part II): From Deep Ecology and Bioregionalism to Scientific Paganism and the New Age," *Religion* 31, no. 3 (2001): 225–45. For another study that found feeling part of nature to be linked to environmentalism, see P. Wesley Schultz et al., "Implicit Connections with Nature," *Journal of Environmental Psychology* 24 (2004): 31.

11. Bron Taylor, "Ecology and Nature Religions," in *Encyclopedia of Religion,* ed. Lindsay Jones (New York: Macmillan, 2005); Lawrence Sullivan, "Worship of Nature," in *Encyclopedia of Religion,* ed. Mircea Eliade (New York: Macmillan, 1987).

12. Charles Darwin, *On the Origin of Species* [1859] *and the Voyage of the Beagle* [1839], with an introduction by Richard Dawkins (New York: Knopf, 2003).

13. John Lubbock, *The Origin of Civilization and the Primitive Condition of Man* (London: Longmans, Green, 1889).

14. David Chidester, "Animism," in *Encyclopedia of Religion and Nature,* ed. Taylor; Edward Burnett Tylor, *Primitive Culture: Researches into the Development of Mythology, Philosophy, Religion, Art and Custom* (London: J. Murray, 1871).

15. Friedrich Max Müller, *Natural Religion* (Whitefish, MT: Kessinger, 2004 [1889]).

16. Frazer approvingly quoted Müller's statement, "The worship of the spirits of the departed is perhaps the most widely spread form of natural superstition all over the world," in Sir James George Frazer, *Worship of Nature* (Whitefish, MT: Kessinger, 1975), 18, 17 (block quote that follows), 9 ("slow and gradual," "despiritualization" in subsequent paragraph).

17. Catherine L. Albanese, *Nature Religion in America: From the Algonkian Indians to the New Age* (Chicago: University of Chicago Press, 1990), 200, 13.

18. Anna Bramwell, *Blood and Soil: Walter Darré and Hitler's Green Party* (Buckinghamshire, U.K.: Kensal, 1985). These are movements, she asserted, in which "a pantheistic religious feeling is the norm." Anna Bramwell, *Ecology in the 20th Century: A History* (New Haven, CT: Yale University Press, 1989), 17, see also 13.

19. *Organicism* as I will use the term means, not only the belief that the biosphere and universe are analogous to a biological organism, but also that this organism is somehow sacred and is due reverence. For seminal studies, see Clarence Glacken, *Traces on the Rhodian Shore: Nature and Culture in Western Thought from Ancient Times to the End of the Eighteenth Century* (Berkeley: University of California Press, 1967); and Donald Worster, *Nature's Economy: A History of Ecological Ideas,* second ed. (Cambridge: Cambridge University Press, 1994 [1977]), esp. 13, 15.

20. It may be that Spinoza was influenced by a contemporary, James Hutton, a Scottish scholar known as the father of geology. James Lovelock noted that Hutton asserted in 1785, "I consider the earth to be a superorganism, and its proper study is by physiology.'" Lovelock then commented, "The notion of Gaia, of a living Earth, has not in the past been acceptable in the mainstream and consequently seeds sown in earlier times did not flourish but instead remained buried in the deep mulch of scientific papers." James Lovelock, *Gaia: A New Look at Life on Earth,* rev. ed. (Oxford: Oxford University Press, 1995 [1979]), xvii–xviii.

21. In Pantheism, the divine is immanent—the world as a whole is divine, holy, or sacred in some way. Panentheism adds that there is also some superordinate, creative intelligence that is a part of this divine whole, with whom it is possible to be in relation. Naess (1912–2008) was the Norwegian philosopher who coined the term *deep ecology* in 1972 to express the idea that nature has intrinsic value, namely, value apart from its usefulness to human beings, and that all lifeforms should be allowed to flourish and fulfill their evolutionary destinies. See Arne Naess, "The Shallow and the Deep, Long-Range Ecology Movement: A Summary," *Inquiry* 16 (1973): 95–100; and George Sessions, "Spinoza and Jeffers on Man in Nature," *Inquiry* 20, no. 4 (1977): 481–528.

22. Roderick Frazier Nash, *The Rights of Nature: A History of Environmental Ethics* (Madison: University of Wisconsin Press, 1989), 20. Nash also noted here that Spinoza was writing at a time where new sciences, such as astronomy, aided by increasingly powerful telescopes, were also challenging anthropocentric (and geocentric) beliefs.

23. For Jean-Jacques Rousseau's main texts, see *Discourse on the Arts and Sciences [and Polemics]* (Dartmouth College Press, 1992 [1750]); *The Social Contract* (New York: Penguin, 2006 [1762]); and *A Discourse upon the Original Foundation of the Inequality among Mankind* (London: R. and J. Dodsley, 1761 [1755]).

24. Jean-Jacques Rousseau, *Reveries of a Solitary Walker* (London: Penguin, 2004 [1782]; reprint, New York: Penguin, 1980), 108 (this and following quotes), and also see p. 107.

25. Jean-Jacques Rousseau, *Julie, or the New Heloise* (Lebanon, NH: Dartmouth College Press, 1997 [1761]).

26. Perhaps most clear in Rousseau, *Reveries,* esp. 137–38.

27. Most notably in Rousseau, *Original Foundation of the Inequality.*

28. For his expansive embrace of all beings and the universe, see Rousseau, *Reveries,* 100, 112.

29. For analysis and examples, see R. F. Nash, *Rights of Nature,* 94–119; Roger S. Gottlieb, ed., *This Sacred Earth: Religion, Nature, Environment* (New York: Routledge, 1996); Roger S. Gottlieb, *A Greener Faith: Religious Environmentalism and Our Planet's Future* (Oxford: Oxford University Press, 2006); Martin Palmer with Victoria Finlay, *Faith in Conservation: New Approaches to Religions and the Environment* (Washington, DC: World Bank, 2003); Mary Evelyn Tucker, *Worldly Wonder: Religions Enter Their Ecological Phase* (LaSalle, IL: Open Court, 2003); Gary T. Gardner, *Inspiring Progress: Religion's Contributions to Sustainable Development* (New York: Norton, 2006).

30. Lynn White, "The Historical Roots of Our Ecologic Crisis," *Science* 155 (1967), all quotes from 1205–6. White thought that all Abrahamic religions carried an antinature bias.

31. The term *biocentrism* literally means "life-centered" ethics, where all lifeforms are valued. The term is apt even though White did not use it and it became popular only after he published his article. *Ecocentrism,* literally "ecosystem-centered" ethics, considers ecosystems, not individual lifeforms or even species, to be the proper and primary locus of moral concern.

32. White, "Historical Roots," 1206.

33. See Dieter T. Hessel and Rosemary Radford Ruether, *Christianity and Ecology: Seeking the Well-Being of Earth and Humans,* Religions of the World and Ecology, ed. Mary Evelyn Tucker and John Grim (Cambridge, MA: Harvard University Press, 2000); and James Nash, "Christianity(9)—Christianity's Ecological Reformation," in *Encyclopedia of Religion and Nature,* ed. Taylor.

34. Yi-Fu Tuan, "Discrepancies between Environmental Attitude and Behaviour: Examples from Europe and China," *Canadian Geographer* 12 (1968): 176–91. See also Ole Bruun and Arne Kalland, *Asian Perceptions of Nature: A Critical Approach* (London: Curzon, 1995).

Chapter 2

1. By *ecologized* I mean developed ecological understandings and concern.

2. See Colin Campbell, "The Cult, the Cultic Milieu and Secularization," *A Sociological Yearbook of Religion in Britain* 5 (1972): 119–36, reprinted in *The Cultic Milieu: Oppositional Subcultures in an Age of Globalization,* ed. Jeffrey Kaplan and Heléne Lööw (Walnut Creek, CA: AltaMira, 2002), 12–25.

3. Some scholars eschew the word *Animism* because embedded in its origins, they say, is the demarcation of putatively superior monotheistic religions from those considered inferior, primitive, indigenous. On such views see David

Chidester, "Animism," in *Encyclopedia of Religion and Nature,* ed. Taylor, 78–81. Other scholars advance an understanding of Animism that focuses on the personhood of nonhuman entities, with no pejorative implication. See Graham Harvey, *Animism* (New York: Columbia University Press, 2006); Nurit Bird-David, "'Animism' Revisited: Personhood, Environment, and Relational Epistemology," *Current Anthropology* 40 (1999): 567–91; and Alf Hornborg, "Knowledge of Persons, Knowledge of Things: Animism, Fetishism, and Objectivism as Strategies of Knowing (or Not Knowing) the World," *Ethnos* 71, no. 1 (2006): 1–12. My understanding of Animism has affinity with such approaches.

4. Jack Kerouac, *Dharma Bums* (Cutchogue, NY: Buccaneer, 1958).

5. Gary Snyder, *Turtle Island* (New York: New Directions, 1969).

6. Gary Snyder, *The Old Ways* (San Francisco: City Lights, 1977), 15.

7. Author interview with Gary Snyder, Davis, CA, June 1993. All direct quotes attributed to Snyder but not otherwise cited are from this interview.

8. Gary Snyder, *The Real Work: Interviews and Talks 1964–1976* (New York: New Directions, 1980), 94.

9. In a 1993 letter, Snyder told me that, given Western antipathy to Paganism, *deep ecology* was a better term to use when discussing nature spirituality. For more discussion, see Bron Taylor, "Resacralizing Earth: Pagan Environmentalism and the Restoration of Turtle Island," in *American Sacred Space,* ed. David Chidester and Edward T. Linenthal (Bloomington: Indiana University Press, 1995).

10. The "Buddhist-shamanist" quotation is from Snyder, *Real Work,* 33.

11. Christopher D. Stone, *Should Trees Have Standing?* (Los Altos, CA: William Kaufmann, 1974); Christopher D. Stone, "Should Trees Have Standing? Toward Legal Rights for Natural Objects," *So. California Law Review* 45 (Spring 1972): 450–501.

12. Snyder, *Real Work,* 74.

13. Gary Snyder, *The Practice of the Wild* (San Francisco: North Point, 1990), 184, 19. For more on this sacrament, see Snyder *Real Work,* 85–91, and also 82.

14. From a 1979 interview published in Snyder, *Real Work,* 159.

15. Snyder, *Old Ways,* 13–14.

16. John Seed et al., *Thinking Like a Mountain: Towards a Council of All Beings* (Philadelphia: New Society, 1988), 11. See also Joanna Macy, "Council of All Beings," 425–29, and John Seed, "Re-Earthing," 1354–58, in *Encyclopedia of Religion and Nature,* ed. Taylor; and Bron Taylor, "Earth First!'s Religious Radicalism," in *Ecological Prospects: Scientific, Religious, and Aesthetic Perspectives,* ed. Christopher Key Chapple (Albany: State University of New York Press, 1994), 185–209.

17. Seed et al., *Thinking Like a Mountain,* 7.

18. Darwin's "Notebooks on Transmutation," quoted in Donald Worster, *Nature's Economy: A History of Ecological Ideas,* 2nd ed. (Cambridge: Cambridge University Press, 1994 [1977]), 180.

19. Charles Darwin, *On the Origin of Species* [1859] *and the Voyage of the Beagle* [1839], with an introduction by Richard Dawkins (New York: Knopf, 2003), 913.

20. Darwin delayed publishing his evolutionary theory for fear of the powerful religious forces that he knew would arise in opposition. After publication of *Origin of Species* and clergy protests, Darwin allowed the phrase "by the creator" to be inserted in subsequent editions: "There is a grandeur in this view of life, with its several powers, having been originally breathed *by the Creator* into a few forms or into one." Charles F. Urbanowicz, "On Darwin: Countdown to 2008/2009," www.csuchico.edu/~curbanowicz/DarwinSacFeb2002.html (my emphasis). According to Urbanowicz, Darwin later regretted the decision.

21. Katy Payne, *Silent Thunder: In the Presence of Elephants* (New York: Penguin, 1999).

22. Jeffrey Moussaieff Masson and Susan McCarthy, *When Elephants Weep: The Emotional Lives of Animals* (New York: Delta/Random House, 1996); Donald R. Griffin, *Animal Minds: Beyond Cognition to Consciousness*, new ed. (Chicago: University of Chicago Press, 2001 [1992]).

23. See, for example, Marc Bekoff, *Minding Animals: Awareness, Emotions, and Heart* (Oxford: Oxford University Press, 2002); Marc Bekoff, *The Emotional Lives of Animals* (Novato, CA: New World Library, 2007); and Marc Bekoff, Colin Allen, and Gordon Burghardt, eds., *The Cognitive Animal: Empirical and Theoretical Perspectives on Animal Cognition* (Cambridge, MA: MIT Press, 2002).

24. Bekoff, *Emotional Lives of Animals*, 49, 50.

25. Ibid., 51 (quotes this paragraph); Marc Bekoff, ed., *The Smile of a Dolphin: Remarkable Accounts of Animal Emotions* (New York: Random House/Discovery, 2000).

26. Jane Goodall, *Reason for Hope: A Spiritual Journey* (New York: Time Warner, 1999), 80; 81 and 79 (next two quotes).

27. Jane Goodall and Marc Bekoff, *The Ten Trusts: What We Must Do to Care for the Animals We Love* (San Francisco: Harper San Francisco, 2003), 171, 169–71 for the full story. Goodall and Bekoff also tell the story in Goodall, *Reason for Hope*, 215–17, 250; and Bekoff, *Emotional Lives of Animals*, 50.

28. Bekoff, *Emotional Lives of Animals*, 50.

29. Goodall and Bekoff, *Ten Trusts*, 49–50.

30. Jane Goodall, *40 Years at Gombe* (New York: Stewart, Tabori & Chang, 2000), 11.

31. Goodall, *Reason for Hope*, 81.

32. All Goodall interview quotations are from this 11 April 2003 interview in Black Mountain, North Carolina.

33. Goodall, *Reason for Hope*, 3, 11 (respectively).

34. On out-of-body experiences and the spirit continuing after death, see ibid., 151–67; on reincarnation, 264; for Goodall's affinity with indigenous peoples and "Mother Earth" spirituality, 223 and 251.

35. Ibid., 72; 72 and 73 (block quote that follows).

36. Dana Lyons, *The Tree* (Bellevue, WA: Illumination Arts Publishing, 2002). See also www.danalyons.com.

37. Dana Lyons, "Tree Music," in *Encyclopedia of Religion and Nature*, ed. Taylor, 1656.

38. See Rupert Sheldrake and Aimée Morgana, "Testing a Language—Using Parrot for Telepathy," *Journal of Scientific Exploration* 17, no. 4 (2003): 601–15. Many of the citations in this article are themselves to examples of Naturalistic Animism, including Roger Fouts, *Next of Kin: My Conversations with Chimpanzees* (New York: Avon, 1997); and Irene M. Pepperberg, *The Alex Studies: Cognitive and Communicative Abilities of Grey Parrots* (Cambridge, MA: Harvard University Press, 1999).

39. Goodall, *Reason for Hope,* 161, 172.

40. Ibid., 173 (my emphasis). This experience was in May 1981, six years after the death of Goodall's husband from cancer.

41. Ibid., 267.

42. Goodall, "Primate Spirituality," in *Encyclopedia of Religion and Nature,* ed. Taylor, 1306.

43. Ibid., 1304. Goodall expressed similar ideas about experiences in nature leading to animistic and pagan nature worship in her *Reason for Hope,* 189, and during my interview with her.

44. Aldo Leopold, *A Sand County Almanac: With Essays on Conservation from Round River* (New York: Sierra Club and Ballantine Books, 1986 [1949]), the five passages respectively are from pp. 239, 240, 261, 262, and 263. The "land" is Leopold's terminology for all that makes up an ecosystem, so the land ethic is equivalent to an ecosystem ethic. Leopold was pragmatic, but his deepest ethical convictions were ecocentric, contrary to the argument in Bryan G. Norton, *Sustainability: A Philosophy of Adaptive Ecosystem Management* (Chicago: University of Chicago Press, 2005).

45. Leopold, *Sand County with Round River,* 261, 246, xvii–xix (respectively).

46. Ibid., 116–17.

47. The science writer Connie Barlow believes the first use of this expression appeared in Edmund Osborne Wilson, *On Human Nature* (Cambridge, MA: Harvard University Press, 2004 [1978]). See Connie Barlow, "The Epic of Evolution: Religious and Cultural Interpretations of Modern Scientific Cosmology," *Science and Spirit,* February 1998.

48. Rick McIntyre, ed., *War against the Wolf: America's Campaign to Exterminate the Wolf* (Osceola, WI: Voyageur Press, 1995); Curt Meine, *Aldo Leopold: His Life and Work* (Madison: University of Wisconsin Press, 1988), 187–191, cf. 321–27; Marybeth Lorbiecki, *Aldo Leopold: A Fierce Green Fire* (Oxford: Oxford University Press, 1996), esp. 65–73.

49. Leopold, *Sand County with Round River,* 138–39.

50. Lorbiecki, *Aldo Leopold,* 161–65.

51. Leopold, *Sand County with Round River,* 130, see also 137.

52. Ibid., 141. Thoreau's aphorism was originally published in "Walking," June 1862, in *Atlantic Monthly,* which maintains an online version at www.theatlantic.com/doc/186206/thoreau-walking. The passage also appears in Henry David Thoreau, "Walking," in *Walden and Other Writings* (New York: Random House, 1981 [1862]), 613.

53. Lawrence Holt, *Wild by Law: The Rise of Environmentalism and the Creation of the Wilderness Act,* DVD, directed by Lawrence Holt and Diane Garey, originally aired on PBS's *American Experience* series, 1992.

54. Curt Meine, "Leopold, Aldo," *Encyclopedia of Religion and Nature,* ed. Taylor, 1007. See also David Pecotic, "Ouspensky, Pyotr Demianovich," 1225–27, in the same volume.

55. Leopold, *Sand County with Round River,* 190.

56. In Aldo Leopold, Susan L. Flader, and J. Baird Callicott, *The River of the Mother of God and Other Essays by Aldo Leopold* (Madison: University of Wisconsin Press, 1991), 95. Also in Meine, "Leopold, Aldo," 1007.

57. Meine, *Aldo Leopold,* 506. For another essay subtly revealing Leopold's nature spirituality, see "Goose Music," in Leopold, *Sand County with Round River,* 226–33.

58. Meine, *Aldo Leopold,* 506–7.

59. James Lovelock, *Gaia: A New Look at Life on Earth,* rev. ed. (Oxford: Oxford University Press, 1995 [1979]). His most compete articulation of the theory appears in James Lovelock, *The Ages of Gaia: A Biography of Our Living Earth* (New York: Norton, 1988).

60. James Lovelock, *The Revenge of Gaia: Earth's Climate Crisis and the Fate of Humanity* (New York: Basic Books, 2006), xiii, 16. The first quote appears only in this edition's "Preface to the U.S. edition." The quote in the next paragraph is from 148.

61. Ibid., xvii.

62. Ibid., 137.

63. Ibid., 2–3, 137, 3, 134, 122, viv (respectively).

64. Ibid., 111–12.

65. Ibid., 142, 8.

66. Lovelock cited Edward Goldsmith, *The Way: An Ecological World-View,* rev. and enlarged ed. (Athens: University of Georgia Press, 1998 [1992]).

67. Lovelock, *Revenge of Gaia,* 136, 148, 139 (respectively).

68. James Lovelock, "Gaian Pilgrimage," in *Encyclopedia of Religion and Nature,* ed. Taylor, 685, see also 683–95.

69. Leopold, *Sand County with Round River,* 240.

70. Lovelock, *Revenge of Gaia,* 148.

71. Ibid., 140, 141.

72. Ibid., 141, 153. These arguments resemble those of Garrett Hardin in *Living within Limits* (New York: Oxford University Press, 1993).

73. Lovelock, *Revenge of Gaia,* 143.

74. Lovelock, "Gaian Pilgrimage," 685.

Chapter 3

This chapter draws on Bron Taylor, "Religion and Environmentalism in America and Beyond," in *The Oxford Handbook of Religion and Ecology,* ed. Roger S.

Gottlieb (Oxford: Oxford University Press, 2006), 588–612; Bron Taylor and Gavin Van Horn, "Nature Religion and Environmentalism in North America," in *Faith in America,* vol. 3, *Personal Spirituality Today,* ed. Charles H. Lippy (Westport, CT: Praeger, 2006); and Bron Taylor and Joseph Dylan Witt, "Nature in New and Alternative Religions in America in America: Cases from Radical Environmentalism to Adventure Sports," in *New and Alternative Religions in the United States,* ed. W. Michael Ashcraft and Eugene V. Gallagher (Westport, CT: Greenwood, 2006).

1. Quoted in Catherine L. Albanese, *Nature Religion in America: From the Algonkian Indians to the New Age* (Chicago: University of Chicago Press, 1990), 34.

2. Eduardo Mendieta, "Casas, Bartolomé de las," in *Encyclopedia of Religion and Nature,* ed. Taylor, 271–72.

3. Albanese, *Nature Religion,* 19–28. Commenting on this manuscript, indigenous religions specialist Robin Wright said that Albanese's list applies pretty well outside of North America.

4. John Gatta, *Making Nature Sacred: Literature, Religion, and Environment in America from the Puritans to the Present* (Oxford: Oxford University Press, 2004), 70.

5. This broad history draws especially on Albanese's *Nature Religion;* Perry Miller, *Errand into the Wilderness* (Cambridge, MA: Harvard University Press, 1986 [1956]); Carolyn Merchant, *Ecological Revolutions: Nature, Gender, and Science in New England* (Chapel Hill: University of North Carolina Press, 1989); Peter N. Carroll, *Puritanism and the Wilderness: The Intellectual Significance of the New England Frontier, 1620–1700* (New York: Columbia University Press, 1969); and Roderick Frazier Nash, *Wilderness and the American Mind,* 4th ed. (New Haven: Yale University Press, 2001 [1967]).

6. Edmund Burke, *Philosophical Enquiry into the Origin of Our Ideas of the Sublime and Beautiful,* ed. Adam Phillips (Oxford: Oxford World Classics, 1990 [1757]), 53.

7. Burke does not use the term *holy,* but his use of *sublime* is akin to Rudolf Otto's use of *holy* in the mid-twentieth century. See Rudolf Otto, *The Idea of the Holy,* 2nd ed. (Oxford: Oxford University Press, 1950 [1923]).

8. Burke, *Philosophical Enquiry,* 53, 54.

9. Ibid., 77, 145.

10. Nash, *Wilderness,* 49.

11. See Phillips's "Introduction" in Burke, *Philosophical Enquiry,* xi.

12. For his distinction between the sublime and beauty, see Immanuel Kant, *Observations on the Feeling of the Beautiful and Sublime,* Second Paperback Edition 2003 ed. (Berkeley: University of California Press, 2003 [1764]), 46–50. I have said less about Kant because his discussion says less about nature than do Burke's writings.

13. Tilar J. Mazzeo, "Romanticism—American," in *Encyclopedia of Religion and Nature,* ed. Taylor, 1424–26; Leo Marx, *The Machine in the Garden: Technology and the Pastoral Ideal in America* (New York: Oxford University Press, 1964).

14. Gatta, *Making Nature Sacred,* 27 (on Jefferson), 35–70 (on the nature-related spirituality of Quakers and Calvinists).

15. Walt Whitman, *Leaves of Grass,* 150th Anniversary ed. (Oxford: Oxford University Press, 2005 [1855]), vi. See Gatta, *Making Nature Sacred,* 71–99 (on Cole, Bryant, and Cooper), 110–16 (Whitman), 116–25 (Melville); and Nash, *Wilderness,* 100–101, 67–83 (on the other figures mentioned in this paragraph).

16. Lawrence Buell, *The Environmental Imagination: Thoreau, Nature Writing, and the Formation of American Culture* (Cambridge, MA: Belknap Press of Harvard University Press, 1996), 406, cf. 405–8.

17. Susan Fenimore Cooper, *Rural Hours* (New York: Putnam, 1850). More conventionally religious than Thoreau, Susan Cooper nevertheless included animistic-sounding paeans to "the spirit of the forest," according to Buell, *Environmental Imagination,* 265.

18. "Nature" [1836] in Ralph Waldo Emerson, *Ralph Waldo Emerson: Essays and Lectures* (New York: Library of America/Penguin, 1983), 9 (first passage), 10 (second passage), 11 (final passage).

19. Gatta, *Making Nature Sacred,* 89; Nash, *Wilderness,* 126. For contrast, see Buell, *Environmental Imagination,* 119–20.

20. "A snowstorm was more to him than Christ," according to Walter Harding, *The Days of Henry Thoreau: A Biography* (New York: Knopf, 1965), 464, quoted in Rebecca Kneale Gould, "Thoreau, Henry David," in *Encyclopedia of Religion and Nature,* ed. Taylor, 1635.

21. For the initial publication of "The Dispersal of Seeds," in which this faith is expressed, see Henry David Thoreau, *Faith in a Seed: The Dispersion of Seeds and Other Late Natural History Writings,* ed. Bradley P. Dean (Washington, DC: Island Press, 1993). See pp. 3–17 for the valuable introduction by Robert Richardson, which explains Darwin's influence on Thoreau's late scientific work.

22. As Max Oelschlaeger concluded, "It is no exaggeration to say that today all thought of the wilderness flows from *Walden*'s wake." Max Oelschlaeger, *The Idea of Wilderness: From Prehistory to the Age of Ecology* (New Haven, CT: Yale University Press, 1991), 171. For a review of those who have asserted Thoreau's seminal nature, see Buell, *Environmental Imagination,* 362–69, esp. 365–66.

23. Albanese, *Nature Religion,* 82, 92–93 (respectively).

24. Donald Worster, *Nature's Economy: A History of Ecological Ideas,* second ed. (Cambridge, MA: Cambridge University Press, 1994 [1977]), 107, quoted in Albanese, *Nature Religion,* 92.

25. Worster, *Nature's Economy,* 99, 109, 100 (respectively).

26. Buell, *Environmental Imagination,* 209 (both quotes).

27. Ibid., 363. Buell noted this as evidence that the image of Thoreau as an ecocentric prophet "did not originate in 1950" (363).

28. According to Buell, *Environmental Imagination,* 365. Although neither Thoreau nor Krutch used the term *Animism,* according to Buell, Krutch thought Thoreau promoted a "genuine sense of intimate 'fellowship' with the natural world, a more reciprocal ethos than that of Saint Francis" (363) .

29. Oelschlaeger, *Wilderness Idea,* 169–70.

30. Roderick Frazier Nash, *The Rights of Nature: A History of Environmental Ethics* (Madison: University of Wisconsin Press, 1989), 37.

31. This is especially obvious in the "Ktaadn" section of *The Maine Woods,* according to David M. Robinson, *Natural Life: Thoreau's Worldly Transcendentalism* (Ithaca, NY: Cornell University Press, 2004), 215n18.

32. Nash, *Wilderness,* 85; Edward Abbey, *Down the River* (New York: Plume, 1991 [1982]), 20.

33. Buell noted "the strong (although not unanimous) perception of Thoreau as a patron of radical environmental activism" in *Environmental Imagination,* 543–44.

34. On pilgrimage and canonization, see ibid., 311–69. For an introduction to the "lived religion" school of scholarly analysis with which this discussion has affinity, see David Hall, ed., *Lived Religion in America: Toward a History of Practice* (Princeton, NJ: Princeton University Press, 1997).

35. Thoreau, *Faith in a Seed,* 17. See also Richardson's entire introduction to that book, 1–17.

36. See quotations from Burroughs in Rebecca Kneale Gould, *At Home in Nature: Modern Homesteading and Spiritual Practice in America* (Berkeley: University of California Press, 2005), 277n60, see also 123–24.

37. Ibid., 129. See also Rebecca Kneal Gould, "Back to the Land Movements," in *Encyclopedia of Religion and Nature,* ed. Taylor 150.

38. John Burroughs, *Time and Change* (Amsterdam: Fredonia, 2001 [1912]), 246–47.

39. Quoted in Gould, *At Home in Nature,* 128.

40. John Burroughs, *In the Light of Day: Religious Discussions and Criticisms from a Naturalist's Point of View* (Boston: Houghton Mifflin, Riverside Press, 1900), 169, quoted in Gould, *At Home in Nature,* 127.

41. Burroughs, *Time and Change,* 246, 259.

42. Ibid., vi, 3 (respectively).

43. Gould, *At Home in Nature,* 124, 126. All further quotes this paragraph are from p. 7.

44. The Nearings' *Maple Sugar Book* (1950) and *Living the Good Life* (1954) made the couple well-known advocates for rural living. See Gould, "Back to Land," 150.

45. Gould, "Back to Land," 150–51, 151 (respectively).

46. Gould, *At Home in Nature,* 24, and see esp. chapter 1, "Conversion," 11–37.

47. For more evidence, see Bron Taylor, "Bioregionalism: An Ethics of Loyalty to Place," *Landscape Journal* 19, nos. 1–2 (2000): 50–72, and the primary sources cited; Michael Vincent McGinnis, ed., *Bioregionalism* (New York: Routledge, 1999); and Robert L. Thayer, *Lifeplace: Bioregional Thought and Practice* (Berkeley: University of California Press, 2003).

48. In *At Home in Nature,* Gould convincingly argued that "Burroughs borrowed heavily from Thoreau, whether consciously or otherwise" (274n23).

49. Richard Austin Cartwright, *Baptized into Wilderness: A Christian Perspective on John Muir* (Louisville, KY: John Knox Press, 1987).

50. Stephen Fox, *The American Conservation Movement: John Muir and His Legacy* (Madison: University of Wisconsin Press, 1981); Michael P. Cohen, *The Pathless Way: John Muir and American Wilderness* (Madison: University of Wisconsin Press, 1984).

51. John Muir, *My First Summer in the Sierra* [1911], in *Muir: Nature Writings,* ed. Cronon, 231, cf. 283 (on plants), 224, 232 (on insects).

52. Quoted in Cohen, *Pathless Way,* 134.

53. Muir, *My First Summer,* in *Muir: Nature Writings,* ed. Cronon, 245.

54. Muir, *Muir: Nature Writings,* ed. Cronon, 839. This passage was also quoted by Fox, *American Conservation,* 43, citing *The Boston Recorder,* 21 December 1866.

55. Fox, *American Conservation,* 43. See also p. 45 on Muir's biocentrism.

56. John Muir, *A Thousand Mile Walk to the Gulf,* ed. William Bade (New York: Houghton Mifflin, 1916); John Muir, *My First Summer in the Sierra* (New York: Houghton Mifflin, 1911).

57. John Muir, "Cedar Keys" [1916], in *Muir: Nature Writings,* ed. Cronon, 825. "Cedar Keys" was chapter 6 in Muir's *Thousand Mile Walk to the Gulf;* all citations here are from the essay in Cronon's Library of America volume. For a similar opinion, see "Wild Wool" [1875] in Muir, *Muir: Nature Writings,* ed. Cronon, 602–3. "Wild Wool" was first published in April 1875 in the *Overland Monthly.*

58. Muir, "Cedar Keys," 826, 825, 827 (respectively).

59. For Thomas Berry's main writings, see *The Dream of the Earth* (San Francisco: Sierra Club Books, 1988); *The Great Work* (New York: Bell Tower, 1999); *Evening Thoughts* (San Francisco: Sierra Club Books, 2006); and Brian Swimme and Thomas Berry, *The Universe Story: From the Primordial Flaring Forth to the Ecozoic Era; A Celebration of the Unfolding of the Cosmos* (San Francisco: HarperCollins, 1992). Berry inspired many other works, including Loyal Rue, *Everybody's Story: Wising up to the Epic of Evolution* (Albany: State University of New York Press, 2000); and Michael Dowd, *Thank God for Evolution* (New York: Plume, 2009). In a letter to one of his closest friends, Muir wrote effusively of his mystical feelings of having become a part of the Sierra woods: "I'm in the woods woods woods, and they are in *me-ee-ee!*" Quoted in Steven J. Holmes, *The Young John Muir: An Environmental Biography* (Madison: University of Wisconsin Press, 1999), 220; and also in Cohen, *Pathless Way,* 124.

60. Muir, "Cedar Keys," 826.

61. Quoted in Cohen, *Pathless Way,* 23.

62. Muir, "Cedar Keys," 827.

63. This is also Cohen's conclusion in *Pathless Way,* 25.

64. See, for example, his effusive writing about Yosemite's Cathedral Peak, in Muir, *My First Summer,* in *Muir: Nature Writings,* ed. Cronon, 180 (as a holy place), 183 (about sublime trees), 269, 238, 301 (on stone sermons and cathedral-like altars).

65. Ibid., 301, 275 (previous quote), see also 289. Many outdoor enthusiasts refer to natural areas as their church.

66. John Muir, *The Mountains of California* [1894], in *Muir: Nature Writings,* ed. Cronon, 350, 351 (the next quote about *Calypso borealis*), 355 (the block quote after that).

67. Kocku von Stuckrad, "Mountaineering," 1119–20, and Greg Johnson, "Rock Climbing," 1398–400, in *Encyclopedia of Religion and Nature,* ed. Taylor.

68. Muir, *Mountains of California,* 363–64. Muir also spoke of nature's love from animals (367) and waterfalls (370), the latter of which also provide sacramental baptism; see Holmes, *Young John Muir,* 213.

69. Muir, *My First Summer,* in *Muir: Nature Writings,* ed. Cronon, 296–97. Perhaps here is an echo of Thoreau's aphorism about wildness being the salvation of the world.

70. Ibid., 296, see also 288.

71. Muir, "Wild Wool," 602–3. It seems likely that Muir's views in this essay were influenced by Thoreau's writings, including his "wildness" aphorism: after suggesting that these superior wild sheep be bred with the domestic ones to improve them, Muir concluded, "A little pure wildness is the one great present want, both of men and sheep" (606).

72. Muir, *My First Summer,* in *Muir: Nature Writings,* ed. Cronon, 264.

73. "No one of the rocks seems to call to me now nor any of the distant mountains," Muir wrote in 1874 to Jeanne Carr after a brief visit to Yosemite, according to William Cronon's "Chronology" in his *Muir: Nature Writings,* 843.

74. Muir, *Mountains of California,* 373.

75. Fox, *American Conservation,* 112.

76. Muir's attitudes toward American Indians were ambivalent. He sometimes expressed dislike (and fear) of the "dirty" Indians he encountered in the Sierra Nevada. Nevertheless, he wondered if he would like them better if he knew them better; see Muir, *My First Summer,* in *Muir: Nature Writings,* ed. Cronon, 194–95, 281–85. But like Thoreau, Muir also felt spiritual affinity with American Indians, a long-standing feeling among the conservationists who Muir and Thoreau inspired; see Fox, *American Conservation,* 350. About Muir's alleged insensitivity to human suffering, his biographer concluded, "Muir's wilderness ideals must be understood and critiqued as products of their cultural context at the same time as they may be valued as . . . an attempt to forge a larger and better vision of humanity in harmony with nature." Steven J. Holmes, "Muir, John," in *Encyclopedia of Religion and Nature,* ed. Taylor, 1127.

77. Philip Burnham, *Indian Country, God's Country: Native Americans and the National Parks* (Washington, DC: Island Press, 2000); Robert H. Keller and Michael F. Turek, *American Indians and National Parks* (Tucson: University of Arizona Press, 1998); Mark David Spence, *Dispossessing the Wilderness: Indian Removal and the Making of the National Parks* (Oxford: Oxford University Press, 1999).

Chapter 4

1. The Earth Liberation Front (ELF), along with *elves* as a term that refers to its activists, are tropes invented in 1992 by radical environmental activists involved in the Earth First! movement. Even though many radical environmental activists have insisted that Earth First! is separate from the ELF and the Animal Liberation Front, the boundaries between these groups are permeable.

2. Of those implicated with Rogers, fourteen had been convicted of one or more charges by the middle of 2008—noncooperating defendants received long prison sentences—and four were still fugitives. Nevertheless, radical environmental arson attacks have continued.

3. William C. [Avalon] Rogers, ed., *Mountains and Rivers Compel Me: A Deep Ecology Reader for Forest Activists* (William C. Rogers, ca. 1995). Because the two anthologies produced by Avalon are not available to readers, I have only provided pagination for quotes in the additional notes online at www.brontaylor.com.

4. The graphic appeared earlier in E. F. Washington, "The Council Fire" [graphic], *Entmoot!: The Washington Earth First! Newsletter* (Spring 1994): 3. The title of this tabloid, *Entmoot,* referred to the ent gatherings in the Tolkien novels. See chapter 2 in this book for Jane Goodall's appreciation for the Tolkien novels.

5. William Anderson, *Green Man: The Archetype of Our Oneness with the Earth* (San Francisco: HarperCollins, 1990).

6. Marion Zimmer Bradley, *The Mists of Avalon* (New York: Knopf, 1983).

7. For details, including an analysis of the ecological importance of the region, see Bron Taylor, "Earth First! Fights Back," *Terra Nova* 2, no. 2 (Spring 1997): 29–43.

8. Rogers drew a number of articles and graphics for his anthologies from green anarchist tabloids, including *Live Wild or Die,* which was first published in 1989. One such article was "Pacifism as Pathology," written by Ward Churchill, then a controversial professor who claimed Native American ancestry and argued that pacifists were deluded and failed to recognize that violence is sometimes the only means of self-defense and social change. Ward Churchill, "Pacifism as Pathology" [article and graphic], *Live Wild or Die,* no. 5 (1994): 15. The additional notes at www.brontaylor.com address accusations that Churchill was not a Native American that he engaged in research misconduct, the latter of which led to his dismissal from a professorship at the University of Colorado.

9. One such reproduced article was first published in a small-distribution tabloid produced by Earth First! activists in the northern Rockies. See Pajama, "Bombthrowing: A Brief Treatise," *Wild Rockies Review* 6, no. 1 (1993): 9. Another was first published by Tom Stoddard as "How Far Should We Go?," *Earth First!* 9, no. 2 (1988): 27.

10. Edward Abbey, *Desert Solitaire* (Tucson: University of Arizona Press, 1988 [1968]), 205.

11. Edward Abbey, *The Monkey Wrench Gang* (New York: Avon, 1975).

12. Dave Foreman and Bill Haywood, eds., *Ecodefense: A Field Guide to Monkeywrenching,* 2nd ed. (Tucson: Ned Ludd, 1987 [1985]).

13. Ron Arnold, *Ecoterror: The Violent Agenda to Save Nature—the World of the Unabomber* (Bellevue, WA: Free Enterprise, 1997); Doug Bandow, *Ecoterrorism: The Dangerous Fringe of the Environmental Movement,* Backgrounder No. 764 (Washington, DC: Heritage Foundation, 1990).

14. For a detailed analysis of such bricolage, see Bron Taylor, "Diggers, Wolves, Ents, Elves and Expanding Universes: Bricolage, Religion, and Violence from Earth First! and the Earth Liberation Front to the Antiglobalization Resistance," in *The Cultic Milieu: Oppositional Subcultures in an Age of Globalization,* ed. Jeffrey Kaplan and Heléne Lööw (Walnut Creek, CA: AltaMira, 2002).

15. The additional notes at www.brontaylor.com provide extensive references for the people and groups mentioned here in this overview of the sources of radical environmentalism's worldview; see also Bron Taylor, "The Tributaries of Radical Environmentalism," *Journal of Radicalism* 2, no. 1 (2008): 27–61. Many of these individuals and organizations have not endorsed radical environmentalism, which further illustrates hybridity.

16. Dave Foreman, *Confessions of an Eco-Warrior* (New York: Harmony Books, 1991).

17. For the best single source of his views, see Paul Shepard, *Coming Home to the Pleistocene* (Washington, DC: Island Press, 1998).

18. Foreman's negative views toward the world's major religions did not appear in the chapter excerpted by Rogers but he made them known regularly, including in the later chapters of his *Confessions.*

19. From an article Foreman published under a pseudonym: Chim Blea, "The Heritage of Western Civilization," *Earth First! Newsletter* 2, no. 5 (1982): 6.

20. Daniel Quinn, *Ishmael: A Novel* (New York: Turner/Bantam, 1992); Daniel Quinn, *The Story of B* (New York: Bantam, 1996). See also Daniel Quinn, "Animism—Humanity's Original Religious Worldview," in *Encyclopedia of Religion and Nature,* ed. Taylor, 83–91. The additional notes at www.brontaylor.com provide the sources Quinn says he drew upon.

21. Edward Abbey, *Abbey's Road* (New York: Plume, 1991).

22. Foreman, *Confessions,* 3, 9, 10 (respectively). The rhetoric of these quotations has been common in Foreman's speeches, which are inspirational to many environmentalists.

23. Further evidence of the idea's influence is that Rogers included it in his compilation by reprinting an essay in which Seed urged biocentric spirituality. The quoted article first appeared as John Seed, "Anthropocentrism," *Earth First!* 3, no. 6 (1983): 15, and was reprinted in John Seed et al., *Thinking Like a Mountain: Towards a Council of All Beings* (Philadelphia: New Society, 1988).

24. For these views, see Seed et al., *Thinking Like a Mountain,* 36; and Pierre Teilhard de Chardin, *The Phenomenon of Man* (New York: Harper, 1976 [1959]).

25. Author interview with Dave Foreman, Tucson, AZ, 23 February 1993.

26. The essay Rogers printed, titled "Shadows from the Big Woods," began with these words, "The idea of wilderness needs no defense. It only needs more defenders" (223); and later stated, "The earth is not a mechanism but an organism, a being with its own life and own reasons" (225). Abbey, *The Journey Home: Some Words in Defense of the American West* (New York: Dutton, 1977), 223–26.

27. Abbey, *Desert Solitaire,* 163 ("earthist"), 208 ("pagan Gentile"), 50 ("increasingly pagan" and "learning finally").

28. Ibid., 176. With other mystics, Abbey considered such experience largely beyond words; see ibid., 212.

29. Ibid., 155 (this and the previous block quote).

30. Ibid., xii (block quote), 147.

31. Ibid., 210.

32. Abbey, *Journey Home,* 237, 238.

33. Abbey, *Desert Solitaire,* x–xi.

34. Ibid., 14, 15.

35. Ibid., 33, see also 22. Abbey's experience of killing the rabbit resembles Thoreau's reflection on wanting to devour a woodchuck or deer; see Henry David Thoreau, ed., *The Annotated Walden: Walden; or Life in the Woods, together with Civil Disobedience,* ed. Philip Van Doren Stern (New York: Barnes and Noble, 1970 [1854]), 339; or the excerpts in the appendix A section titled "The Simple, Natural, and Undomesticated (Free) Life."

36. Abbey, *Desert Solitaire,* 74–75, 186, 189–90. For the poet Robinson Jeffers's similar views, see Bron Taylor, "Death and Afterlife in Jeffers and Abbey," in *Encyclopedia of Religion and Nature,* ed. Taylor, 455–56.

37. I first wrote about this in Bron Taylor, "The Religion and Politics of Earth First!," *The Ecologist* 21, no. 6 (November/December 1991): 258–66; and in more detail in Bron Taylor, "Green Apocalypticism: Understanding Disaster in the Radical Environmental Worldview," *Society and Natural Resources* 12, no. 4 (1999): 377–86. See also Robin Globus and Bron Taylor, "Environmental Millennialism," in *Oxford Handbook on Millennialism,* ed. Catherine Wessinger (Oxford: Oxford University Press, forthcoming).

38. James Barnes, "Dieback: A Vision of Darkness," *Earth First!* 17, no. 8 (1997): 13. For key texts on population dynamics and carrying capacity that profoundly influenced radical and other environmentalists, see William Catton, *Overshoot: The Ecological Basis of Revolutionary Change* (Urbana: University of Illinois Press, 1980); Jared Diamond, *Collapse: How Societies Choose to Fail or Succeed* (New York: Viking, 2005); and Garrett Hardin, *Living within Limits* (New York: Oxford University Press, 1993).

39. Edward Abbey, "A Response to Schmookler on Anarchy," *Earth First!* 6, no. 7 (1986): 22.

40. Hardin, *Living within Limits.*

41. Rogers attributed this prophesy to a Cree Indian woman, but its origin is unclear; elsewhere it is attributed to the Hopi. For an early source on the rainbow warrior prophesy, see William Willoya and Vinson Brown, *Warriors of*

the Rainbow: Strange and Prophetic Indian Dreams (Healdsburg, CA: Naturegraph, 1962); and for the myth's adoption by Greenpeace, see Robert Hunter, *Warriors of the Rainbow: A Chronicle of the Greenpeace Movement* (New York: Holt, Rinehart & Winston, 1979).

42. On rituals of exclusion and inclusion, see David Chidester, "Rituals of Exclusion and the Jonestown Dead," *Journal of the American Academy of Religion* 56, no. 4 (1988): 681–702. For detailed descriptions of the ritual dimensions of radical environmentalism, see Bron Taylor, "Earth First!'s Religious Radicalism," in *Ecological Prospects: Scientific, Religious, and Aesthetic Perspectives,* ed. Christopher Key Chapple (Albany: State University of New York Press, 1994), 185–209.

43. Letter to the author from Mark Davis, summer 1992.

44. On bioregionalism, see Bron Taylor, "Bioregionalism: An Ethics of Loyalty to Place," *Landscape Journal* 19, nos. 1–2 (2000): 50–72; and Bron Taylor, "Bioregionalism and the North American Bioregional Congress," in *Encyclopedia of Religion and Nature,* ed. Taylor, 190–2.

45. The article appeared in Rogers's first compendium and was widely republished elsewhere. For the original article, see David Abram, "The Perceptual Implications of Gaia," *The Ecologist* 15, no. 3 (1985): 96–103. Rogers took his excerpts from a reprint in *ReVision* 9, no. 2 (1987): 9–15.

46. Abram's reprint in *ReVision,* 10.

47. Ibid., 10 ("surrounding physical world"), 11 (remaining quotes this paragraph). Abram cited James J. Gibson, *The Perception of the Visual World* (Boston: Houghton Mifflin, 1950); James J. Gibson, *The Senses Considered as Perceptual Systems* (Boston: Houghton Mifflin, 1966); and Maurice Merleau-Ponty, *The Phenomenology of Perception,* trans. Colin Smith (London: Routledge & Kegan Paul, 1962). See also David Abram, "Merleau-Ponty and the Voice of the Earth," *Environmental Ethics* 10 (1988): 101–20.

48. Abram's reprint in *ReVision,* 14. The inconsistent capitalization is Abram's.

49. David Abram, "The Ecology of Magic," *Orion* 10, no. 3 (Summer 1991): 4.

50. Ibid., 5, 7–8 (block quote that follows).

51. For the website and the quotes from it, see Alliance for Wild Ethics, www.wildethics.com. For the full passage in which this quotation appears, see David Abram, *Spell of the Sensuous: Perception and Language in a More-Than-Human World* (New York: Pantheon, 1996), 22.

52. For his river conversation, see "Norway Confluence: Launching the International Alliance for Wild Ethics," www.wildethics.com/projects/norway_06.html. For the interview, conducted in summer 2000, see "D. Abram Interviewed by Derrick Jensen," www.wildethics.com/essays/interview_derrick_jensen.html.

53. Derrick Jensen, *A Language Older Than Words* (New York: Context, 2000), 24, 26, 27 (respectively). See also Derrick Jensen, *Listening to the Land: Conversations about Nature, Culture, and Eros* (New York: Sierra Club Books, 1995); Theodore Roszak, *The Voice of the Earth: An Exploration of Ecopsychology*

(New York: Touchstone, 1992); and Bill Willers, ed., *Learning to Listen to the Land* (Washington, DC: Island Press, 1991).

54. See John Zerzan's *Elements of Refusal* (Seattle: Left Bank Books, 1988); *Future Primitive* (Columbia, MO: C.A.L. Press, 1994); the volume he edited, *Against Civilization: Readings and Reflections* (Eugene, OR: Uncivilized Books, 1999; 2nd ed., Los Angeles: Feral House, 2005); and also the journal *Green Anarchy,* online at www.greenanarchy.org, and www.primitivism.com.

55. Derrick Jensen, *Endgame,* vol. 1, *The Problem of Civilization,* and vol. 2, *Resistance* (New York: Seven Stories Press, 2006). For the Churchill quotation, see *Endgame,* 2:839, and also note 8, this chapter.

56. Jensen, *Endgame,* 2:887. For documentation of the themes summarized, above, see *Endgame,* vol. 1, esp. "premises" 7 and 9 on pp. x, xi. See also *Endgame* 1:87, 99, 365, 397–401, 427–43; and 2:517–18. On animism, see *Endgame* 2:533, 534, 545, 557, 575, 601, 639; for "by any means necessary" rhetoric, see 2:841; on societal collapse, see 2:518, 755, 889–91.

57. This is a central contention in Abram's *Spell of the Sensuous;* see "Animism and the Alphabet," 93–135.

58. See "D. Abram Interviewed by Derrick Jensen," www.wildethics.com/essays/interview_derrick_jensen.htm.

59. See Forum on Religion and Ecology, www.religionandecology.org.

60. Barry Lopez, "The Language of Animals," in *Wild Earth,* ed. Tom Butler (Minneapolis, MN: Milkweed, 2002); Barry Lopez, "The Language of Animals," *Wild Earth* 8, no. 2 (1998): inside front cover, 2–6. *Wild Earth* is the journal created by Dave Foreman after he left Earth First!

61. Gary Paul Nabhan, "Cultural Parallax in Viewing North American Habitats," in *Reinventing Nature? Responses to Postmodern Deconstruction,* ed. Michael Soulé and Gary Lease (Washington, DC: Island Press, 1995); and Gary Paul Nabhan, *Enduring Seeds: Native American Agriculture and Wild Plant Conservation* (San Francisco: North Point, 1989).

62. See "About the Myrin Institute," www.myrin.org/about.html.

63. "About the Orion Society," www.orionsociety.org/pages/os/about.cfm (accessed April 2008; no longer available).

64. Quoted in Charlie Custer, "Speaking for the Trees," *Independent (Southern Humboldt News),* 1998, 8.

65. An article by Eric Brazil in the *San Francisco Chronicle,* 12 February 1998, A1.

66. See Julie Butterfly Hill's blog at www.juliabutterflyhill.wordpress.com; and Julia Butterfly Hill, *The Legacy of Luna* (San Francisco: Harper, 2000).

67. Author interview with Alisha Little Tree, Sinkyone Wilderness, Northern California, 6 June 1993.

68. Quoted in Seed et al., *Thinking Like a Mountain,* 91–92; for Innes's entire "testimony," see 91–95.

69. This and subsequent quotations are from an author conversation with "Reverend Fly" (Chris Bennett), "Goat" (John Sellers), and others at the national Earth First! Rendezvous, Nicolet National Forest, Wisconsin, 5 July

1997. The term *grock* comes from the novel by Robert A. Heinlein, *Stranger in a Strange Land* (New York: G. P. Putnam, 1961). Providing another example of bricolage, the novel became the basis for the Church of All Worlds, a pagan group invented in Northern California that has many radical environmental members.

70. Paul Watson, *Seal Wars: Twenty-Five Years on the Front Lines with the Harp Seals* (Buffalo, NY: Firefly Books, 2002), 49. See also Paul Watson, *Ocean Warrior: My Battle to End the Illegal Slaughter on the High Seas* (Toronto: Key Porter, 1994).

71. Paul Watson, "An Open Letter to Norwegians," *Sea Shepherd Log* (1st Quarter 1993): 5. For more on the animistic subject of interspecies communication between humans and whales, see Dick Russell, *Eye of the Whale* (Washington, DC: Island Press, 2004).

72. *Whale Wars*, www.animal.discovery.com/tv/whale-wars.

73. My request resulted from discussions we had 12 and 13 February 2003, during the Revolutionary Ecology conference at California State University, Fresno. Watson's published response appeared as "Biocentric Religion, A Call for," in *Encyclopedia of Religion and Nature*, ed. Taylor, 176–79. All quotations are from this essay, which has many affinities with and was likely influenced by the work of David Suzuki, described in chapter 7 of this book.

74. For an introduction to and analysis of such claims, see Michael E. Zimmerman, "Ecofascism," in *Encyclopedia of Religion and Nature*, ed. Taylor, 531–32.

75. For detailed analysis of the competing views about what tactics are permissible, which of these are considered violent, and the overall likelihood that radical environmentalists will turn from a record that has not as yet involved campaigns to kill or maim their adversaries, see B. Taylor, "Diggers, Wolfs, Ents, Elves and Expanding Universes"; Bron Taylor, "Religion, Violence, and Radical Environmentalism: From Earth First! to the Unabomber to the Earth Liberation Front," *Terrorism and Political Violence* 10, no. 4 (1998): 10–42; Bron Taylor, "Revisiting Ecoterrorism," in *Religionen im Konflikt*, ed. Vasilios N. Makrides and Jörg Rüpke (Münster, Germany: Aschendorff, 2004), 237–48; and Bron Taylor, "Threat Assessments and Radical Environmentalism," *Terrorism and Political Violence* 15, no. 4 (2004): 172–83.

Chapter 5

Most of the material in this chapter has appeared in one or more of these publications: Bron Taylor, "Aquatic Nature Religion," *Journal of the American Academy of Religion* 75, no. 4 (2007): 863–74; Bron Taylor, "Surfing into Spirituality, and a New, Aquatic Nature Religion," *Journal of the American Academy of Religion* 75, no. 4 (2007): 923–51; Bron Taylor, "Sea Spirituality, Surfing, and Aquatic Nature Religion," in *Deep Blue: Critical Reflections on Nature, Religion and Water*, ed. Sylvie Shaw and Andrew Francis (London: Equinox, 2008), 213–33.

1. Matt Warshaw, *Above the Roar: 50 Surfer Interviews* (Santa Cruz, CA: Waterhouse, 1997), inside cover.

2. Jay Moriarity and Chris Gallagher, *The Ultimate Guide to Surfing* (Lyons: London, 2001), 10 (capitalization in original).

3. Brad Melekian, "Is God a Goofyfoot: If So, Surfing May Be the Next World Religion," *Surfer* 46, no. 3 (March 2005), www.surfermag.com/magazine/archivedissues/godgoofy/index.html.

4. Steffen Mackert, *Surf: A Visual Exploration of Surfing*, ed. Robert Klantan (Berlin: Die Gestalen Verlag, 2005), 3.

5. See Colleen McGloin, "Surfing Nation(S)—Surfing County(S)" (PhD diss., University of Wollongong, Australia, 2005), www.library.uow.edu.au/adt-NWU/public/adt-NWU20060206.143742/index.html, 70–75.

6. Estimates of surfer numbers range from five to twenty-three million globally; see Matt Warshaw, *The Encyclopedia of Surfing* (New York: Harcourt, 2003), 605.

7. Moriarity and Gallagher, *Ultimate Guide*, 73, 75.

8. Ibid., 77.

9. Post by TinCanFury, 23 August 2003, http://everything2.com/index.pl?node_id=717980.

10. McGloin, "Surfing Nation(S)," for example, 217.

11. Glenn Hening and Bron Taylor, "Surfing," in *Encyclopedia of Religion and Nature*, ed. Taylor, 1610–11.

12. Ben R. Finney and James D. Houston, *Surfing: A History of the Ancient Hawaiian Sport*, rev. ed. (Rohnert: Pomegranate Art Books, 1996 [1966]). For more discussion of Peruvian wave riding, see Bolton Colburn et al., *Surf Culture: The Art History of Surfing* (Corte Madera, CA: Ginko, 2002), 32–81, 82–103, 228–29.

13. For a typical example, see Drew Kampion, *Stoked!: A History of Surf Culture* (Salt Lake City, UT: Gibbs Smith, 2003).

14. Ibid., 34. The website of the Hawaiian Boarding Company demonstrates that surfboard making as a spiritual practice endured into the twenty-first century; see www.hawaiibc.com/surf.htm.

15. Mackert, *Surf*, 8.

16. Kampion, *Stoked!*, 30–36; Finney and Houston, *Surfing History;* Nat Young, *A History of Surfing* (Sidney, Australia: Palm Beach Press, 1983); Colburn et al., *Surf Culture*, esp. 82–100.

17. Matt Warshaw, ed., *Zero Break: An Illustrated Collection of Surf Writing, 1777–2004* (Orlando, FL: Harcourt Books, 2004), ix.

18. Hening and Taylor, "Surfing," 1610.

19. Kampion, *Stoked!*, 38; Mackert, *Surf*, 17.

20. E-mail to author from Kekuhi Kealiikanakaole, 6 October 2005.

21. Kampion, *Stoked!*, 46.

22. See Ben Finney in Colburn et al., *Surf Culture*, 87–88. See also Abraham Fournlander, comp., *Fournlander's Collection of Hawaiian Antiquities and Folklore*, Memoirs of the Bernice P. Bishop Museum 4–6, ed. Thomas G. Thrum

(Honolulu: Bishop Museum Press, 1916–17). The practice of surfboard sacrifice to bring larger surf is depicted in a number of surfing films, including *Point Break* (1991) and *Big Wednesday* (1978). A proper rite, including solemn prayers to the god of the sea, is described at the Hawaiian Boarding Company, www.hawaiibc.com/surf.htm.

23. Warshaw, *Encyclopedia of Surfing*, 67.

24. Gary Lynch and Malcolm Gault-Williams, *Tom Blake: The Uncommon Journey of a Pioneer Waterman* (Corona Del Mar, CA: Croul Family Foundation, 2001), 205–6.

25. Ibid., 216, 219, 222.

26. Ibid., 217.

27. Kampion, *Stoked!*, 46; Warshaw, *Encyclopedia of Surfing*, 67; Lynch and Gault-Williams, *Tom Blake*, 217, see also 181–82.

28. Drew Kampion, *The Way of the Surfer* (New York: Harry N. Abrams, 2003), 187.

29. Lynch and Gault-Williams, *Tom Blake*.

30. David Parmenter, www.tomblakebiography.com (accessed June 2006; no longer available). Although Parmenter overstated the tolerance and harmony found in surfing cultures, others have exaggerated surfing-related violence, as noted in Warshaw, *Zero Break*, xix. On such violence see Nat Young, ed., *Surf Rage* (Angorie, NSW, Australia: Palm Beach Press/Nymboida Press, 2000); and Anonymous, "Haole Go Home," in *Zero Break: An Illustrated Collection of Surf Writing, 1777–2004*, ed. Matt Warshaw (Orlando, FL: Harcourt Books, 2004).

31. See Warshaw, *Above the Roar*, 93.

32. Moriarity and Gallagher's *Ultimate Guide to Surfing* depicts surfing as uniting all nationalities and races (88). Tom Blake earlier asserted that surfing's spiritual teachings promote respect for all living things as well as world peace. Lynch and Gault-Williams, *Tom Blake*, 214.

33. See Kampion, *Stoked!*; and Kampion, *Surfer Way*. For the famous "Tales from the Tube" cartoons, created by Rick Griffin, in which the surfer experiences mystical experiences and even "satori" through surfing, see Warshaw, *Above the Roar*, 72; and Colburn et al., *Surf Culture*, 136–39. For psychedelic designs on surfboards in 1975, see Colburn et al., *Surf Culture*, 209.

34. Matt Warshaw, *Surf Movie Tonight!: Surf Movie Poster Art, 1957–2004* (San Francisco: Chronicle Books, 2005), 11.

35. Ibid., 67 ("an organic 90 minutes"), 71 ("Woodstock on a wave"), see also 67–76.

36. For Turner, rituals promote "liminal" religious perception and offer "decisive keys to the understanding of how people think and feel about relationships and about the natural and social environments in which they operate." Victor Turner, *The Ritual Process* (London: Routledge, 1969), 6. His thesis about how rituals also sometimes create new social possibilities is equally apropos to the present analysis.

37. Warshaw, *Surf Movie*, 11.

38. Ibid., 80–81.

39. See *Surfer's Path,* no. 50 (August/September 2005), which according to Drew Kampion (in an e-mail to the author, 25 June 2006) began its green publishing process with issue 42 (May/June 2004).

40. "About Us," *Surfer's Path,* www.surferspath.com/49/aboutus.html (accessed August 2005; no longer available).

41. John Sears, *Sacred Places: American Tourist Attractions in the Nineteenth Century* (New York: Oxford University Press, 1989).

42. Four years later he became the editor of the even more widely distributed *Surfing.*

43. Warshaw, *Encyclopedia of Surfing,* 311–12.

44. Not only surfers trace such feelings to the sea. See Peter Bentley and Philip J. Hughes, *Australian Life and the Christian Faith: Facts and Figures* (Melbourne, Australia: Christian Research Association, 1998); and Nancy M. Victorin-Vangerud, "The Sacred Edge: Women, Sea and Spirit," *Sea Changes: The Journal of Women Scholars of Religion and Theology* 1 (2001), www.wsrt.net.au/seachanges/volume1/index.shtml.

45. See the 1968 photograph of board-shaping guru Richard Allan Brewer, meditating with Gerry Lopez and Reno Abellira, an image that "defined an era." Kampion, *Surfer Way,* 52 (text), 53 (photograph). See also Kampion, *Stoked!,* 105; and Warshaw, *Above the Roar,* 80.

46. Undated *Surfer* magazine interview, www.surfermag.com/magazine/archivedissues/intrvu_gerrlopez/index4.html. For an extended interview with Lopez, see Kampion, *Surfer Way,* 109–21.

47. Glen Hening and contributors, "Interview with Marilyn Edwards, Publisher, *Wahine* Magazine," in *Groundswell Society Annual Publication,* 3rd ed. (Oxnard, CA: Groundswell Society, 2001), 24 (this quote), 25 (the next quote), www.groundswellsociety.org/publications/ThirdEdition/index.cfm.

48. For another example, see James Meacham, "The Tao of Surfing," http://facs.scripps.edu/surf/tao.html (accessed June 2006; no longer available at this URL).

49. Kampion, *Stoked!,* 161.

50. See Surfrider Foundation, www.surfrider.org.

51. Kampion, *Stoked!,* 161.

52. The organization's website is www.seasurfer.org. They quoted Aldo Leopold, *A Sand County Almanac: With Essays on Conservation from Round River* (New York: Sierra Club and Ballantine Books, 1986 [1949]), 262.

53. See the Surfers' Environmental Alliance mission statement at Surfline, www.surfline.com/mag/coastwatch/greencards/sea_usa.cfm.

54. Author conversations with Glenn Hening. See also Hening and Taylor, "Surfing."

55. J. Williams, "A Study of the Influence of Surfing and Surf Culture on the Identity of Its Participants, inside the Case Study of Surf Tourism in Newquay" (bachelor's thesis in geography, University of Exeter, 2002), 31, cited in Nick Ford and David Brown, *Surfing and Social Theory: Experience, Embodiment, and Narrative of the Dream Glide* (London Routledge, 2006), 73.

56. Howard Swanwick, "Afterthought," *Drift* 1, no. 3 (2007): 148, www.driftmagazine.co.uk. The draft article I submitted was eventually published; see B. Taylor, "Surfing into Spirituality."

57. Matt Walker, "Keeping the Faith: Surfing Is Officially a Religion. So, What Now?," *Surfing*, July 2008, 128.

58. Ibid., 128 (all quotes this paragraph). Walker acknowledged that not all surfers accept surfing as a religion, but he quoted Steven Kotler as an example of one who, reluctantly, has; see Steven Kotler, *West of Jesus: Surfing, Science, and the Origins of Belief* (New York: Bloomsbury, 2006), esp. 129.

59. Ibid., 133 (both quotes).

60. Ben Marcus, *Surfing and the Meaning of Life* (St. Paul, MN: Voyageur Press, 2006).

61. *Wahine* is borrowed from the Hawai'an word for "woman."

62. Kampion, *Stoked!*, 161.

63. Undated *Surfer* magazine interview, www.surfermag.com/magazine/archivedissues/intrvu_gerrlopez/index4.html.

64. Mihaly Csikszentmihalyi, *Flow: The Psychology of Optimal Experience* (San Francisco: Harper & Row, 1990), 3. See also Ford and Brown, *Surfing and Social Theory*, 157–61.

65. Csikszentmihalyi, *Flow*, 4, also quoted in Joseph L. Price, "Naturalistic Recreations," in *Spirituality and the Secular Quest*, ed. Peter Higbie Van Ness (New York: Crossroad, 1996), 425.

66. Moriarity and Gallagher, *Ultimate Guide*, 10.

67. For a discussion, see Kotler, *West of Jesus*.

68. Moriarity and Gallagher, *Ultimate Guide*, 52.

69. Matt Warshaw, "Religion and Surfing," in *The Encyclopedia of Surfing*, ed. Matt Warshaw (New York: Harcourt, 2003), 345. Further examples are Hening and Taylor, "Surfing," 1610–11; Foodoggy, "The Seed of Stoke," 22 February 1997, www.altsurfing.org/alt/foondoggy/foon011.htm#stoke (accessed June 2006; no longer available); and GrouchyOldMan, "Time stands still in the tube," written 1976, http://everything2.com/e2node/Time%2520stands%2520still%2520when%2520you%2527re%2520in%2520the%2520tube.

70. Hening and Taylor, "Surfing," 1610.

71. Mandy Caruso, "Healing Waters," *Surfer's Path*, no. 50 (2005), 126.

72. Kotler, *West of Jesus*.

73. Keith Glendon, "Chad Compton: The Comeback Kid," *Carbon* 2, no. 1 (2005), 74, 70 (the next quote).

74. McGloin, "Surfing Nation(S)," 252, see also 263–83, esp. 274.

75. Ibid., 252.

76. Quoted in Warshaw, *Above the Roar*, 2.

77. The Chumash are the indigenous people who, upon European contact, had scores of settlements from the Santa Monica Mountains to central California (around San Luis Obispo), inland to the Central Valley, and including the Channel Islands.

78. Glen Hening, "Mati Waiya: A Chumash Way of Thinking" in *Groundswell Society Annual Publication,* 3rd ed., by Glen Hening and contributors (Oxnard, CA: Groundswell Society, 2001), 186, www.groundswellsociety.org/publications/ThirdEdition/index.cfm.

79. Drew Kampion, *The Book of Waves: Form and Beauty on the Ocean* (Santa Barbara: Arpel Graphics/Surfer Publications, 1989), taken from www.drewkampion.com/books.htm (accessed May 2005; no longer available).

80. Kampion, *Stoked!,* 214–15.

81. Moriarity and Gallagher, *Ultimate Guide,* 77.

82. LaBedz was in Gainesville, FL, for a Sierra Club meeting.

83. For LaBedz's role with Surfrider, see the organization's description at Surfline, www.surfline.com/mag/coastwatch/greencards/surfrider_usa.cfm.

84. Zaleha is another good example of a person espousing dark green religion. His master's thesis focused on naturalistic pantheism, nature religions that I label Gaian Naturalism. See Daniel Bernard Zaleha, "The Only Paradise We Ever Need: An Investigation into Pantheism's Sacred Geography in the Writings of Edward Abbey, Thomas Berry, and Matthew Fox, and a Preliminary Survey of Signs of Emerging Pantheism in American Culture" (Master's thesis, University of Florida, 2008).

85. Kampion, *Surfer Way,* 128.

86. See Samuel S. Snyder, "New Streams of Religion: Fly Fishing as a Lived Religion of Nature," *Journal of the American Academy of Religion* 75, no. 4 (2007): 896–922; Whitney Sanford, "Pinned on Karma Rock: Whitewater Kayaking as Religious Experience," *Journal of the American Academy of Religion* 75, no. 4 (2007): 875–95; and Greg Johnson, "Rock Climbing," 1398–400, and Kocku Von Stuckrad, "Mountaineering," 1119–20, in *Encyclopedia of Religion and Nature,* ed. Taylor.

Chapter 6

1. For her account, see Val Plumwood, "Being Prey," *Terra Nova* 1, no. 3 (1996), 33–44. Quotations are from the online version at http://valplumwood.com/2008/03/08/being-prey.

2. Unless otherwise noted, van der Merwe's views were conveyed to me in conversations during or shortly after I participated in the program in late 2000.

3. See Chris van der Merwe, *Deep Ecology Elephant Programme (the Deep Guide)* (Pretoria, South Africa: First Light Adventure, 1999), 26. A New Age teacher, Weiss seeks especially to communicate with animals that she considers highly evolved, like dolphins, as well as with nonplanetary beings, including angels; see Weiss Transformation Processes, www.weissprocesses.com/index.htm.

4. I first made this argument in Bron Taylor, "Disney Worlds at War," in *Encyclopedia of Religion and Nature,* ed. Taylor, 489–93. Two books I read after drafting the analysis in this chapter provide further evidence that dark green

religion is gaining traction worldwide through motion pictures. David Whitley noted, for example, that seven of fourteen animated films Disney produced between 1990 and 2004 were "structured so that young viewers will align themselves with a point of view of animals or even . . . with whole cosmologies that center on sustaining the qualities of the environment as a whole." David Whitley, *The Idea of Nature in Disney Animation* (Aldershot, Hampshire, U.K.: Ashgate, 2008), 119. See also David Ingram, *Green Screen: Environmentalism and Hollywood Cinema, Representing American Culture* (Exeter: University of Exeter Press, 2000). In revising this chapter, I credited Whitley where I drew from his information or insights; otherwise, where observations he made are similar to my own but are uncredited, we arrived at them independently.

5. B. Taylor, "Disney Worlds at War." I found novel insights about all of the films Whitley examined in his *Nature in Disney Animation,* but for those films most relevant to dark green religion, see his discussions of *Snow White and the Seven Dwarfs* (1937), *Cinderella* (1950), *The Jungle Book* (1967), and *The Little Mermaid* (1989).

6. For the script and lyrics, see *The Lion King*'s unofficial website, www.lionking.org.

7. See Academy Awards Database, http://awardsdatabase.oscars.org/ampas_awards/BasicSearchInput.jsp.

8. According to the *Wikipedia* entry about Disney's Animal Kingdom Park, nearly ten million people visited it in 2007. Many scholars look askance at *Wikipedia* entries but I use them, especially in this chapter, for two reasons: they provide quick access to basic facts (which I double-source whenever possible), and *Wikipedia* is, itself, a good example of popular culture.

9. "The Pocahontas Myth," Powhatan Renape Nation, www.powhatan.org/pocc.html. See also Christian F. Feest, "Pride and Prejudice: The Pocahontas Myth and Pamunkeyin," in *The Invented Indian,* ed. James A. Clifton (New Brunswick, NJ: Transaction, 1990), 49–70.

10. The Russell Means quotation and the ones that follow from Stephen Schwartz, Mike Gabriel, and Eric Goldberg are from an anonymous online review at www.movieweb.com/movie/pocahontas/pocprod1.txt (accessed May 2003; no longer available May 2008).

11. These lyrics are widely available online, including at www.lyricstime.com/pocahontas-soundtrack-colors-of-the-wind-lyrics.html.

12. Albert Furtwangler, *Answering Chief Seattle* (Seattle: University of Washington Press, 1997).

13. See the Academy Awards Database, http://awardsdatabase.oscars.org/ampas_awards/BasicSearchInput.jsp.

14. Baobab is the common name for eight tree species in the genus *Adansonia* that are native only to Africa, Australia, and Madagascar. See Thomas Pakenham, *The Remarkable Baobab* (London: Weidenfeld & Nicolson, 2004); or the "Tree of Life" website, www.treeoflifegallery.org/our_story/the_baobab_tree.htm (accessed June 2008; site discontinued).

15. See "Tree of Life," Pansophists website, www.pansophist.com/TOL.htm.

16. Author telephone interview with Jackie Ogden, 21 October 2004. Her comment about purists had to do with those who oppose all animal captivity.

17. From the interview in the magazine *gradPSYCH*, http://gradpsych.apags.org/sep05/cover-ogden.html.

18. For the online announcement, see the Disney blog at http://disneyandmore.blogspot.com/2008/04/disney-launches-new-film-label-disney.html, 21 April 2008.

19. The first build of *Disney*nature's website (accessed May 2008) was stunning and reminded me of David Abram's site. It is no longer available in this version, but its replacement (http://disney.go.com/disneynature) has some of the original's beautiful motion pictures, which reflect the idea of nature as sublime.

20. "Series Mythology," *Captain Planet* website, www.turner.com/planet/seriesmyth.html. For the description of Gaia in brackets, see www.turner.com/planet/gaia.html.

21. See www.turnerfoundation.org.

22. Steven Watts, *The Magic Kingdom: Walt Disney and the American Way of Life* (Columbia: University of Missouri Press, 2001).

23. The *Wikipedia* entry on Sir David Attenborough is unusually comprehensive; see http://en.wikipedia.org/wiki/David_Attenborough. Unless otherwise indicated, my discussion draws from it or from Attenborough's own website, www.davidattenborough.co.uk.

24. Gareth Huw Davies, "Meet Sir David," PBS, ca. 1998, www.pbs.org/lifeofbirds/sirdavid/index.html.

25. This quotation is from *The Trials of Life Wikipedia* entry, http://en.wikipedia.org/wiki/The_Trials_of_Life.

26. For the background, see David Quammen, *Song of the Dodo: Island Biogeography in an Age of Extinctions* (New York: Scribner, 1996), esp. 97–114, an account to which Bernard Zaleha drew my attention.

27. According to the *Wikipedia* entry at http://en.wikipedia.org/wiki/Attenborough_in_Paradise, which did not provide pagination, Attenborough was quoting from Alfred Russel Wallace, *The Malay Archipelago, the Land of the Orang-Utan and the Bird of Paradise: A Narrative of Travel, with Studies of Man and Nature* (London: Macmillan, 1869).

28. See the "Gorilla Encounter" section in the *Wikipedia* entry for *Life on Earth*, http://en.wikipedia.org/wiki/Life_on_Earth_%28TV_series%29#12._.22Life_in_the_Trees.22.

29. Laurie Taylor, "Interview: Watching David Attenborough," *New Humanist* 123, no. 1 (2008), http://newhumanist.org.uk/1673.

30. Robert S. Corrington, *Nature and Spirit: An Essay in Ecstatic Naturalism* (New York: Fordham University Press, 1992); Robert S. Corrington, *Nature's Religion* (Lanham, MD: Rowman & Littlefield, 1997).

31. The second and fourth episodes of *The First Eden* presented a cosmogony reminiscent of that articulated by Paul Shepard and common among

radical environmentalists. It also echoed much of the history found in the writings of Jared Diamond, especially his *Guns, Germs, and Steel: The Fates of Human Societies* (New York: Norton, 1997).

32. *The Life of Mammals* was developed with Discovery Communications and it was shown as part of the *Animal Planet* series, extending its reach. See also David Attenborough, *The Life of Mammals* (Princeton, NJ: Princeton University Press, 2002).

33. For the full text, see "The Compulsive Communicators" in the *Wikipedia* entry for *Life on Earth,* http://en.wikipedia.org/wiki/Life_on_Earth_%28TV_series%29.

34. See "Planet Green Announces World Class Board of Advisors," Discovery Communications, 26 February 2008, http://corporate.discovery.com/news/press/08q1/PlanetGreenBOA-2-26-08.html.

35. See Tom Shales, "Wonders Never Cease on 'Planet Earth,'" *Washington Post,* 24 March 2007, C01, www.washingtonpost.com/wp-dyn/content/article/2007/03/23/AR2007032301868.html.

36. Terri Irwin, *Steve and Me* (New York: Simon Spotlight Entertainment, 2007), 64, see also 80, 257, 260.

37. Ibid., 160 ("uncanny connection"), 63–64, 58–69, 126–27, 130–31, 150, 159–60, 277 (for diverse examples). The most interesting cases of "uncanny connection" concern Irwin's supposed communication with "Darwin's Turtle" (68–69, 227).

38. Ibid., 147. For Irwin's communication with whales and his hope to defend them, see ibid., 130–32, 225, 228.

39. For further details, see the David Suzuki *Wikipedia* entry, http://en.wikipedia.org/wiki/David_Suzuki; and his biography at the David Suzuki Foundation website, www.davidsuzuki.org/About_us/Dr_David_Suzuki.

40. With his "mapping theory" in Martin Marty, *A Nation of Behavers* (Chicago: University of Chicago Press, 1976), Marty got me thinking about identity clusters the way I do in this book, as, for example, when I note the connection between individuals and groups engaged in dark green religious production. The collaboration between Ted Turner and David Attenborough, and their respective institutions, is but one example.

41. David Suzuki and Peter Knudtson, *Wisdom of the Elders: Honoring Sacred Native Visions of Nature* (New York: Bantam, 1992).

42. Ibid., 41, 70, 125, 226, 229. For Odum's organicism and sense of the sacred in nature, see Howard T. Odum and Elisabeth C. Odum, *A Prosperous Way Down: Principles and Policies* (Boulder: University of Colorado Press, 2001), esp. 75, 286.

43. Suzuki and Knudtson, *Wisdom of the Elders,* 227, and see 168 for other excerpts. For further evidence that such views are common among conservation scientists see David Takacs, *The Idea of Biodiversity: Philosophies of Paradise* (Baltimore, Maryland: John Hopkins University Press, 1996); and Bron Taylor, "Conservation Biology," in *Encyclopedia of Religion and Nature,* ed. Taylor, 415–18.

44. Douglas Chadwick, *Yellowstone to Yukon,* National Geographic Destinations (Washington, DC: National Geographic Society, 2000), 190, 193; Florian Schulz, *Yellowstone to Yukon: Freedom to Roam: A Photographic Journey* (Seattle: Mountaineers Books, 2005).

45. David Suzuki, *The Sacred Balance: Rediscovering Our Place in Nature* (Vancouver, BC: Greystone; Seattle: Mountaineers Books, 1999 [1997]). The website for the four-part series includes a précis for each episode, www.sacredbalance.com/web/series.html.

46. Thomas Berry, *The Dream of the Earth* (San Francisco: Sierra Club Books, 1988), cited in Suzuki, *Sacred Balance,* 9, 25, 207, 240. None of the Berry references in Suzuki's book were paginated.

47. Suzuki, *Sacred Balance,* 25. Note the similarity between Suzuki's idea of "the continuum" and Paul Watson's discussed in chapter 4.

48. Quoted in ibid., 240.

49. Thomas Berry, *The Great Work* (New York: Bell Tower, 1999); Brian Swimme and Thomas Berry, *The Universe Story: From the Primordial Flaring Forth to the Ecozoic Era: A Celebration of the Unfolding of the Cosmos* (San Francisco: HarperCollins, 1992).

50. Suzuki, *Sacred Balance,* 51. Here again are understandings that Paul Watson echoes in his reflections on biocentric religion, discussed in chapter 4.

51. Ibid., 75, see also 154. The only author Suzuki quoted more often was E. O. Wilson.

52. Rachel Carson's books in this genre were *The Sense of Wonder* (New York: Harper & Row, 1965 [first published as an essay with a different title, 1956]); *The Edge of the Sea* (Boston: Houghton Mifflin, 1955); *The Sea around Us* (New York: Oxford University Press, 1950); and *Under the Sea Wind* (New York: Dutton, 1941).

53. The apt "womb of life" description is from Jonathan Benthall, *Returning to Religion: Why a Secular Age Is Haunted by Faith* (London: I. B. Tauris, 2008), 124.

54. Rachel Carson, *Lost Woods: The Discovered Writings of Rachel Carson,* ed. Linda Lear (Boston: Beacon, 1998), 148–63, esp. 159.

55. A 1942 memo from Carson to a person in the marketing department of the publisher of her first book, *Under the Sea Wind,* provides a revealing window into Carson's biocentric motive and, I think, reveals an animistic imagination; see Carson, *Lost Woods,* 54–62.

56. Suzuki, *Sacred Balance,* 75, and see 154 for another of his Carson quotations.

57. Suzuki, *Sacred Balance,* 104, 78 (respectively).

58. From "About This Episode," the précis of "The Fire of Creation" at the series website, www.sacredbalance.com/web/series.html.

59. See ibid. for this quote; for the next quote, see "Cosmologist Brian Swimme on Watching the Sunrise," www.sacredbalance.com/web/drilldown.html?sku=79.

60. Swimme and Berry, *Universe Story.*

61. Suzuki, *Sacred Balance,* 7.

62. For his discussion of ecopsychology, see Suzuki, ibid., 179–82.

63. Ibid., 217 (both quotes).

64. Ibid., 131.

65. Ibid., 176.

66. Meeker's quotations and Suzuki's comments are from ibid., 197, as is the next quote.

67. Ibid., 198. These quotes and reflections are reminiscent of what others engaged in dark green religion have said.

68. Edward Osborne Wilson, *Biophilia: The Human Bond with Other Species* (Cambridge, MA: Harvard University Press, 1984); Stephen R. Kellert and Edward O. Wilson, eds., *The Biophilia Hypothesis* (Washington, DC: Island Press, 1993); Stephen R. Kellert, *Kinship to Mastery: Biophilia in Human Evolution and Development* (Washington, DC: Island Press, 1997).

69. For a study that makes an argument similar to the biophilia theory but about the human affinity for certain colors of plants, see David Webster Lee, *Nature's Palette: The Science of Plant Color* (Chicago: University of Chicago Press, 2007).

70. Suzuki, *Sacred Balance,* 140–45. The quotation about the living earth is from "About This Episode," the précis of episode two, "The Matrix of Life," at www.sacredbalance.com/web/series.html.

71. See the additional notes online at www.brontaylor.com for an extended discussion of anthropology as a tributary to dark green religion. Figures discussed include Richard Schultes, the founder of ethnobotany, and the ecological anthropologist Roy Rappaport and his intellectual progeny, as well as Darrell A. Posey, William Balée, and Leslie Sponsel. Had more space been available, an entire chapter could easily have been devoted to the role of anthropology in general and these people in particular.

72. For his discussion of the Desana, see Suzuki, *Sacred Balance,* 11, referring to Gerardo Reichel-Dolmatoff, *Amazonian Cosmos* (Chicago, Illinois: University of Chicago Press, 1971). See also Gerardo Reichel-Dolmatoff's "Cosmology as Ecological Analysis: A View from the Rainforest," *Man* 2, no. 3 (1976): 307–18; and *The Forest Within: The Worldview of the Tukano Amazonian Indians* (Totnes, U.K.: Themis-Green Books, 1996). Suzuki described Lansing's work in the documentary, which essentially repeated the argument in J. Stephen Lansing, *Priests and Programmers: Technologies of Power in the Engineered Landscape of Bali* (Princeton, NJ: Princeton University Press, 1991).

73. Fikret Berkes, *Sacred Ecology: Traditional Ecological Knowledge and Resource Management* (Philadelphia: Taylor and Francis, 1999), 8, 163, 14, 182 (respectively).

74. Ibid., 3. The idea that the heart of indigenous perception, which is sometimes labeled Animism, is in communication and relationship, including reciprocal moral obligation among humans and other organisms, is increasingly in vogue. See, for example, Nurit Bird-David, "'Animism' Revisited: Personhood, Environment, and Relational Epistemology," *Current Anthropology* 40 (1999): 567–91; Graham Harvey, *Animism* (New York: Columbia University Press, 2006); Graham Harvey, "Animism—a Contemporary Perspective," in *Encyclopedia of*

Religion and Nature, ed. Taylor, 81–83; and the discussion of David Abram's views in chapter 4.

75. Berkes, *Sacred Ecology,* 182. Also evident in the book's concluding paragraphs (182–83) are Berkes's affinities with other individuals and movements who are influential within the dark green religious milieu, including C. S. Holling (and others involved in "adaptive management" science and practice), Gregory Bateson, Fritjof Capra, Aldo Leopold, Yi-Fu Tuan (and other topophilia enthusiasts), E. O. Wilson (and biophilia devotees), Arne Naess (and deep ecology supporters), and James Lovelock (and Gaia theory enthusiasts).

Chapter 7

1. Edward I. Bailey, *Implicit Religion in Contemporary Society* (Leuven, Belgium: Peeters, 1997); Jonathan Benthall, *Returning to Religion: Why a Secular Age Is Haunted by Faith* (London: I. B. Tauris, 2008). Benthall's preference for *parareligion* over *implicit* or *quasi religion* is for stylistic reasons (personal communication, June 2008), as it is for me as well. Benthall first encountered the term in William Bainbridge, "After the New Age," *Journal for the Scientific Study of Religion* 43 (2004): 381–94.

2. For the full Darwin quotation, see David Suzuki, *The Sacred Balance: Rediscovering Our Place in Nature* (Vancouver, BC: Greystone; Seattle: Mountaineers Books, 1999 [1997]), 123. Suzuki found his Einstein quotation in Penney Kome and Patrick Crean, *Peace, a Dream Unfolding* (San Francisco: Sierra Club Books, 1986).

3. For more statements by scientists expressing dark green religious themes, including ecological interdependence, Gaian organicism, and kinship ethics, see Suzuki, *Sacred Balance,* 57, 102, 124–26, 130.

4. Paul R. Ehrlich, *The Machinery of Nature* (New York: Simon and Schuster, 1986), no page given, quoted in Suzuki, *Sacred Balance,* 27.

5. All quotes are from Richard Noll, "Haeckel, Ernst," in *Encyclopedia of Religion and Nature,* ed. Taylor, 735. And see Ernst Heinrich Philipp August Haeckel, *Generelle morphologie der organismen: Allgemeine grundzüge der organischen formen-wissenschaft, mechanisch begründet durch die von Charles Darwin reformirte descendenztheorie,* 2 vols. (Berlin: De Gruyter, 1988 [1866]). Haeckel's most important nature religion–promoting works were *The Riddle of the Universe at the Close of the Nineteenth Century,* trans. Joseph McCabe and Philip Lamantia (New York: Harper & Brothers, 1900); *The Wonders of Life: A Popular Study of Biological Philosophy,* trans. Joseph McCabe (New York: Harper, 1905); and *Monism as Connecting Religion and Science: The Confession of Faith of a Man of Science,* trans. J. Gilchrist (London: A. and C. Black, 1894).

6. Nick C. Thomas, "Steiner, Rudolf—and Anthroposophy," in *Encyclopedia of Religion and Nature,* ed. Taylor, 1596–97. On a number of occasions I have encountered environmentalists in Europe who were influenced by Steiner

or the Waldorf schools. Steiner also influenced the architect of contemporary paganism, Gerald Gardner, according to Ronald Hutton, *The Triumph of the Moon: A History of Modern Pagan Witchcraft* (Oxford: Oxford University Press, 2000), 223.

7. Bill Mollison, *Introduction to Permaculture* (Tyalgum, Australia: Tagari, 1991). Many pagans are involved in permaculture, according to Lynne Hume, "Paganism in Australia," in *Encyclopedia of Religion and Nature,* ed. Taylor, 1243–44.

8. The Scottish Findhorn community exemplifies the spiritual pole of dark green religion in the bioregional movement; see Katherine Langton, "Findhorn Foundation/Community (Scotland)," in *Encyclopedia of Religion and Nature,* ed. Taylor, 658–60. A popular sustainability author even wrote his first book about Findhorn; see Paul Hawken, *The Magic of Findhorn* (New York: Harper & Row, 1975).

9. Author interview with Stephen Humphrey, Gainesville, FL, June 2003. For a history of conservation biology, see Curt Meine, Michael Soulé, and Reed F. Noss, "A Mission-Driven Discipline: The Growth of Conservation Biology," *Conservation Biology* 20 (2006): 631–51.

10. Soulé organized the society's first conference in 1978 and subsequently published an anthology heralding the discipline, Michael Soulé and Bruce A. Wilcox, eds., *Conservation Biology: An Evolutionary-Ecological Perspective* (Sunderland, MA: Sinauer, 1980).

11. David Ehrenfeld, *The Arrogance of Humanism* (Oxford: Oxford University Press, 1978), 269. Ed Grumbine is another conservation biologist who has written about his spiritual connections to nature and affinity for deep ecology, including his participation in the Council of All Beings; see R. Edward Grumbine, *Ghost Bears: Exploring the Biodiversity Crisis* (Washington, DC: Island Press, 1992), 230–36.

12. Author interviews with Michael Soulé, near Tucson, AZ, 26 February 1993; and by telephone, 15 July 1997.

13. He did so even in academic publications; see Reed F. Noss and Allen Y. Cooperrider, *Saving Nature's Legacy: Protecting and Restoring Biodiversity* (Washington, DC: Island Press, 1994), 21–24. For similar dynamics among restoration ecologists, see William R. Jordan III, *The Sunflower Forest: Ecological Restoration and the New Communion with Nature* (Berkeley: University of California Press, 2003).

14. Richard Dawkins, *The God Delusion* (New York: Houghton Mifflin, 2006), 9.

15. Ibid., 11.

16. Carl Sagan, *Pale Blue Dot: A Vision of the Human Future in Space* (New York: Random House, 1994), 52, quoted in Dawkins, *God Delusion,* 12. Sagan (1934–1996) was best known for the thirteen-part public television series *Cosmos,* first broadcast in 1980 in the United States and subsequently in dozens of countries worldwide. His novel *Contact* (New York: Simon and Shuster, 1985) and the movie it became (Warner Bros., 1997) exemplify Gaian Naturalism.

17. Dawkins, *God Delusion,* 12.

18. Ibid., 13 ("failure to distinguish" and on Goodenough), 19 (on atheists).

19. All quotations attributed to the World Pantheist Movement website were accessed in February 2006 at www.pantheism.net.

20. Quoted in Dawkins, *God Delusion,* 15. Dawkins's final Einstein quotation on this page was "The idea of a personal God is quite alien to me and seems even naïve."

21. Suzuki, *Sacred Balance,* 239–40.

22. Joseph Wood Krutch, ed., *Great American Nature Writing* (New York: Sloane, 1950).

23. Joseph Wood Krutch, "A Kind of Pantheism," *Saturday Review,* 10 June 1950, 7, 8 (respectively).

24. Krutch also noted that for Thoreau and subsequent nature writers empathy came in part from seeing themselves as "in the same boat" as other creatures, adding that "it would be absurd . . . to suggest" Thoreau was the first with such an attitude. Quite right: both Wallace and Darwin expressed similar sentiments. See Krutch, "A Kind of Pantheism," 8.

25. Ibid., 8 and 32 (quotes in preceding paragraph), 33–34 (block quote; my emphasis).

26. Joseph Wood Krutch, *The Voice of the Desert* (New York: William Sloane Associates, 1954), 221–22, see also 219. Close reading of *Desert Solitaire* and *The Voice of the Desert* shows the profound influence Krutch had on Abbey.

27. Ernest Callenbach, *Ecotopia* (New York: Bantam, 1975). See also Ernest Callenbach, "Ecotopian Reflections," in *Encyclopedia of Religion and Nature,* ed. Taylor, 566–68, and the cross-references listed there for its influence.

28. Starhawk, *The Spiral Dance: A Rebirth of the Ancient Religion of the Great Goddess* (San Francisco: Harper & Row, 1979), or the tenth and twentieth anniversary editions.

29. Jone Salomonsen, "Starhawk," in *Encyclopedia of Religion and Nature,* ed. Taylor, 1595. See also Jone Salomonsen, *Enchanted Feminism: Ritual, Gender and Divinity among the Reclaiming Witches of San Francisco* (London: Routledge, 2002).

30. For example, Starhawk, *The Fifth Sacred Thing* (New York: Doubleday, 1993).

31. Demonstrating its ongoing popularity, Adler's book has gone through at least five editions. The earliest and latest are *Drawing Down the Moon: Witches, Druids, Goddess-Worshippers, and Other Pagans in America Today* (New York: Viking Press, 1979); and *Drawing Down the Moon: Witches, Druids, Goddess-Worshippers, and Other Pagans in America,* rev. and updated ed. (New York: Penguin, 2006). It was from Adler in a July 2008 e-mail that I learned Starhawk's book was published on the very same day as Adler's. The scholarship on contemporary Paganism, and from scholarly pagans, continues to grow; see Michael York, *The Emerging Network: A Sociology of the New Age and Neo-Pagan Movements* (Lanham, MD: Rowman & Littlefield, 1995); Graham Harvey and Charlotte Hardman, eds., *Paganism Today* (New York: Thor-

sons/HarperCollins, 1996); Graham Harvey, *Contemporary Paganism: Listening People, Speaking Earth* (New York: New York University Press, 1997); Helen A. Berger, *A Community of Witches: Contemporary Neo-Paganism and Witchcraft in the United States* (Columbia: University of South Carolina Press, 1999); Wendy Griffin, *Daughters of the Goddess: Studies of Healing, Identity, and Empowerment* (Walnut Creek, CA: AltaMira, 2000); Sarah Pike, *Earthly Bodies, Magical Selves: Contemporary Pagans and the Search for Community* (Berkeley: University of California Press, 2000); Sarah Pike, *New Age and Neopagan Religions in America* (New York: Columbia University Press, 2004); and Michael York, *Pagan Theology* (New York: New York University Press, 2004).

32. Alice Walker, *The Color Purple: A Novel* (New York: Harcourt Brace Jovanovich, 1982). The film did not win any Academy Awards.

33. Alice Walker, *Anything We Love Can Be Saved: A Writer's Activism* (New York: Random House 1997), 3, 9. The long title of the book's lead essay was telling, "The Only Reason You Want to Go to Heaven Is That You Have Been Driven Out of Your Mind (Off Your Land and Out of Your Lover's Arms): Clear Seeing Inherited Religion and Reclaiming the Pagan Self" (3–27).

34. Walker, *Anything We Love,* 20–21, 25 (respectively).

35. Alice Walker, *Living by the Word: Selected Writings, 1973–1987* (San Diego: Harcourt Brace Jovanovich, 1988), 3–8, 139–42.

36. Alice Walker, *The Same River Twice: Honoring the Difficult; A Meditation on Life, Spirit, Art, and the Making of the Film, the Color Purple, Ten Years Later* (New York: Scribner, 1996), 25, 42–43.

37. Quoted in Donna Haisty Winchell, *Alice Walker* (New York: Twayne, 1992), 133.

38. Pike, *New Age and Neopagan Religions in America,* 155.

39. James Redfield, *The Celestine Prophecy* (New York: Warner, 1993); James Redfield, *The Tenth Insight* (New York: Warner, 1996); and James Redfield, *The Secret of Shambhala: In Search of the Eleventh Insight* (New York: Warner, 1999).

40. Redfield, *Tenth Insight,* 80, 208 (respectively).

41. Ibid., 224 (this quote), 227 (next quote).

42. Associates of Marianne Williamson, one of the best-known New Age writers, told me in 2007 that she has become a democracy and environmental activist while retaining her overall New Age message, which is exemplified in *A Return to Love: Reflections on the Principles of a Course in Miracles* (New York: HarperCollins, 1992).

43. I have written extensively about such bricolage, especially in Bron Taylor, "Earth and Nature-Based Spirituality (Part I): From Deep Ecology to Radical Environmentalism," *Religion* 31, no. 2 (2001): 175–93; Bron Taylor, "Earth and Nature-Based Spirituality (Part II): From Deep Ecology and Bioregionalism to Scientific Paganism and the New Age," *Religion* 31, no. 3 (2001), 225–45; and Bron Taylor, "Diggers, Wolves, Ents, Elves and Expanding Universes: Bricolage, Religion, and Violence from Earth First! and the Earth Liberation Front to the Antiglobalization Resistance," in *The Cultic Milieu: Oppositional Subcultures in an Age of Globalization,* ed. Jeffrey Kaplan and Heléne Lööw (Walnut Creek,

CA: AltaMira, 2002), 26–74. To use Redfield as an example of such mutual influence, he has become actively engaged in a number of environmental causes, working with the Washington, DC–based environmental group Save America's Forests, and has participated in the Global Renaissance Alliance (GRA), a New Age organization devoted to peace and positive social change.

44. The inattention to music in this book is remedied at www.brontaylor.com.

45. Photographs of this artwork are also at www.brontaylor.com. Bernard Zaleha alerted me to this exhibit, located in Terminal T.

46. Most famously, in Ansel Adams, *Yosemite and the Range of Light* (Boston: New York Graphic Society, 1979).

47. Stephen Fox, *The American Conservation Movement: John Muir and His Legacy* (Madison: University of Wisconsin Press, 1981), 274.

48. Linda Graber, *Wilderness as Sacred Space* (Washington, DC: Association of American Geographers, 1976).

49. Garry Suttle, "Adams, Ansel," in *Encyclopedia of Religion and Nature,* ed. Taylor, 15.

50. Matthew Glass, "National Parks and Monuments," in *Encyclopedia of Religion and Nature,* ed. Taylor, esp. 1154. For such dynamics during the formative years at Yellowstone and Yosemite national parks, see John Sears, *Sacred Places: American Tourist Attractions in the Nineteenth Century* (New York: Oxford University Press, 1989), 122–81.

51. Kerry Mitchell, "Managing Spirituality: Public Religion and National Parks," *Journal for the Study of Religion, Nature and Culture* 1, no. 4 (2007): 431–49.

52. The gallery seeks to promote "an ethic to respect the landscape"; see "Our History," www.anseladams.com/content/customer_service/history.html, and also the links to Adams's photography on the site.

53. One scholar who has written about such things is J. Ronald Engel. See his "Biosphere Reserves and World Heritage Sites," in *Encyclopedia of Religion and Nature,* ed. Taylor, 192–94; and "Renewing the Bond of Mankind and Nature: Biosphere Reserves as Sacred Space," *Orion* 4, no. 3 (1985): 52–63. See also Dave Harmon and Allen D. Putney, eds., *The Full Value of Parks: From Economics to the Intangible* (Lanham, MD: Rowman & Littlefield, 2003).

54. On Brower's first ascents, see Fox, *American Conservation,* 276.

55. David Ross Brower, *Let the Mountains Talk, Let the Rivers Run: Prescriptions for Our Planet* (New York: HarperCollins, 1995), 176.

56. On their meeting, see Fox, *American Conservation,* 275.

57. For the point about arts, especially poetry, see Gavin Van Horn and Brent Blackwelder, "Brower, David," in *Encyclopedia of Religion and Nature,* ed. Taylor, 225. I am not saying Brower used the term *mountain music,* but I think this is an appropriate metaphor for his sensory experience in nature and his sense of the sacred that flowed from it. For his Naturalistic Animism, see David Ross Brower and Steve Chapple, *Let the Mountains Talk, Let the Rivers Run: A Call to Save the Earth* (Gabriola Island, BC: New Society, 2000), esp. 5, 139; for his spirituality of belonging, grounded in the evolutionary story, see

196. From an interview Brower gave shortly before his death in 2000, one can see his Earth mysticism and a kind of Gaian spirituality. In response to the interviewer's comment about how important it is "to allow people to see, hear, feel, smell, taste, touch the place so they will learn to love it," Brower said, "That's why we have our six senses. We're supposed to use them all and maybe some others that I haven't counted. We have that ability. And, I think that we just have to listen to the Earth, to look at the Earth to read it, and certainly to get the aromas." Ron Good, "Interview with David Brower," 27 May 2000, Hetch Hetchy Valley, www.hetchhetchy.org/brower_interview_5_27_00.html.

58. Ansel Adams and Nancy Newhall, *This Is the American Earth* (San Francisco: Sierra Club, 1960); Eliot Porter and David Ross Brower, *The Place No One Knew: Glen Canyon on the Colorado* (San Francisco: Sierra Club, 1963).

59. Unsurprisingly, the prose came from many already discussed, for example, Thoreau, Muir, Burroughs, Leopold, Krutch, Einstein, Stegner, Brower, and Abbey. Several Loren Eiseley quotations illustrate the tone: "If there is magic on this planet, it is contained in the water" (44). "I know that the word 'miraculous' is regarded dubiously in scientific circles because of past quarrels with theologians. . . . We forget that nature itself is one vast miracle" (140). "One must seek . . . a natural revelation" (142). All are from Eliot Porter and David Ross Brower, *The Place No One Knew: Glen Canyon on the Colorado,* commemorative ed. (San Francisco: Sierra Club, 2000).

60. Porter and Brower, *Place No One Knew,* commemorative ed. The edition was produced with support and new material from the Glen Canyon Institute, which among other things is working to decommission the Glen Canyon Dam; see www.glencanyon.org.

61. David Ross Brower, Ansel Adams, and Robinson Jeffers, *Not Man Apart: Lines from Robinson Jeffers* (San Francisco: Sierra Club, 1965). For a more recent example of the genre, mixing Muir and Adams, see John Thaxton, ed., *The American Wilderness: Essays by John Muir; Photographs by Ansel Adams* (New York: Barnes and Noble, 1993).

62. For the full poem online, with pertinent additional material, see nature photographer Bill Curtsinger's website, www.billcurtsingerphoto.com/page24jeffers.html. The poem is also available in Robinson Jeffers, *The Collected Poetry of Robinson Jeffers,* ed. Tim Hunt (Stanford, CA: Stanford University Press, 1988). In a 1951 statement, Jeffers expressed ambivalence about humanistic philosophy, urging a nature-based parareligion as an alternative, a sense of belonging to nature "which can be a sort of worship." Robinson Jeffers, *The Wild God of the World: An Anthology of Robinson Jeffers,* ed. Albert Gelpi (Stanford, CA: Stanford University Press, 2003), 201.

63. The advertisement's heading read, "Should we also flood the Sistine Chapel so tourists can get nearer the ceiling?" See David Ross Brower, *For Earth's Sake: The Life and Times of David Brower* (Salt Lake City, UT: Peregrine Smith Books, 1990), 368, 343–70.

64. Bill Devall, ed., *Clearcut: The Tragedy of Industrial Forestry* (San Francisco: Sierra Club Books and Earth Island Press, 1994). This effort was funded

primarily by Douglas Tompkins, a mountaineer and entrepreneur who converted to deep ecology, dropped out of the business world, and became an environmental activist and philanthropist.

65. Frans Lanting, *Eye to Eye: Intimate Encounters with the Animal World* (Köln, Germany: Taschen, 1997).

66. Selma Lagerlöf, *The Wonderful Adventures of Nils* (New York: Pantheon, 1947 [1907]).

67. Lanting, *Eye to Eye,* 14 (first two quotes), 15 (last two quotes).

68. The foundation draws on the cosmology of the indigenous people in the region to promote its mission to "integrate biocultural conservation with social well being at the ends of the Earth." Omora Foundation, www.cabodehornos.org. Also see the special issue of *Environmental Ethics* 30, no. 3 (2008): 225–336, about the Omora Ethnobotanical Park biocultural approach.

69. Ricardo Rozzi et al., *Multi-Ethnic Bird Guide of the Austral Temperate Forests of South America,* trans. Christopher Anderson (Punta Arenas, Chile: Fantástico Sur-Universidad de Magallanes, 2003), 25.

70. Ibid., 25 ("birds were humans"), 27 (the next two quotes), 28 ("not separate from nature").

71. According to Rozzi, "Lichens are symbiotic associations of a fungus and a photosynthetic partner (an alga or cyanobacterium). The fungus provides a habitat for the alga, which produces food for the lichen from sunlight." Personal communication, July 2008.

72. Author Skype interview with Ximena Arango, 29 June 2008.

73. World Commission on Environment and Development, *Our Common Future* (Paris: United Nations World Commission on Environment and Development, 1987), 87. The full passage was: "However, the case for the conservation of nature should not rest only with development goals. It is part of our moral obligation to other living beings and future generations." I am grateful to Steven C. Rockefeller for drawing my attention to this passage in a 31 July 2007 e-mail. He added, "This statement is consistent with the ethical outlook in the World Conservation Strategy issued by IUCN [International Union for the Conservation of Nature] in 1982 and the World Charter for Nature adopted by the UN in 1982."

74. See the UNESCO website, http://portal.unesco.org/en/ev.php-URL_ID=3328&URL_DO=DO_TOPIC&URL_SECTION=201.html (accessed June 2008; no longer available).

75. UNESCO, *Man Belongs to the Earth: International Cooperation in Environmental Research* (Paris: UNESCO-MAB, 1988), 8 (both quotes).

76. Ibid., 10.

77. Ibid., 9, 12, 142.

78. Ibid., 10.

79. Mikhail Gorbachev, "Nature Is My God," *Resurgence: An International Forum for Ecological and Spiritual Thinking* 184, no. 184 (September/October 1997), 15. Alexander Likhotal, the president of Green Cross International and a close associate of Gorbachev's, reviewed the current manuscript and stressed

that Gorbachev is "a complete atheist." Likhotal added that Gorbachev does have a deep affection and connection to nature, which began when he was young, growing up close to nature in agricultural settings. Likhotal also said that in 2001 Gorbachev sent the Earth Charter to the pope at the Vatican and received a response that was receptive to the initiative. When I receive a copy of this response, I will make it available at www.brontaylor.com.

80. For background, see Steven C. Rockefeller, "Earth Charter," in *Encyclopedia of Religion and Nature,* ed. Taylor, 516–18; and also the Earth Charter Initiative website, www.earthcharter.org.

81. See the documentary *Grizzly Man* (2005), directed by the German director Werner Herzog, which was initially aired on the Discovery Channel.

82. In a survey released in June 2008 by the Pew Survey Research Center about the religious beliefs of Americans, "*7% did not express belief in God and an additional 25%,* who did express such a belief, *thought of 'God' as an impersonal force.*" This is certainly not an orthodox, Abrahamic understanding of God, but it is one that seems amenable to a naturalistic understanding of the sacrality of nature and nature's laws. "U.S. Religious Landscape Survey," http://religions.pewforum.org/reports (my emphasis).

83. Early in the nineteenth century Alexis de Tocqueville, the great French observer of democracy in the United States, made a number of points that anticipated the kind of criticisms leveled against dark green religion that are summarized in this section (i.e., about its globalization and dangers). The Roman Catholic thinker, distressed by some of what he saw in democratic revolutions, asserted that "pantheism has made great progress" in Europe and America. He then linked this to democracy's egalitarian tendencies, which he thought eroded respect for individuals and a proper appreciation of "man's greatness." Tocqueville concluded, "Of all the different philosophical systems used to explain the universe . . . pantheism is one of those most fitted to seduce the mind in Democratic ages. All those who still appreciate the true nature of man's greatness should combine in the struggle against it." Alexis de Tocqueville, *Democracy in America,* 2 vols., trans. George Lawrence. (New York: Anchor, 1969 [1835/1840]), 452 (first quote), 453 (next two quotes). Many contemporary Christians echo his sentiments. For a typical example written by a conservative evangelical Christian, see Samantha Smith, *Goddess Earth: Exposing the Pagan Agenda of the Environmental Movement* (Lafayette, LA: Huntington House, 1994). See also these two journal issues of the Spiritual Counterfeits Project: "Gaia: A Religion of the Earth," *SCP Journal* 16, no. 1 (1991); and "The Way of Ecology: Remaking Man in the Earth's Image," *SCP Journal* 17, no. 3 (1992); as well as the associated website at www.scp-inc.org.

Donald Worster, who drew my attention to the Tocqueville passage in his biography of John Muir, commented there: "As Tocqueville perceived, democracy was in love with nature, and nature was the natural and logical religion of democracy." In this biography, Worster argued that for Muir and his progeny, generally speaking, nature religion and liberal democracy have been in a mutually supportive and reinforcing relationship: "The modern love of nature began as an integral part of the great modern movement toward freedom and social equality, which has led to the pulling down of so many oppressive hierarchies that once plagued the world. . . . All those efforts at nature preservation. . . . flow out of the worldview of liberal democracy. Modern societies have not only sought to preserve Nature in all of her forms but also to open those preserved places to any and all human beings, regardless of class or ethnicity, far more so than our universities, country clubs, or gated communities. In that preservation effort they have acknowledged a moral obligation beyond the human species." If this eminent historian's conclusion is correct, and I believe it is, then concern about nature religion harboring totalitarian impulses is overwrought. See Donald Worster, *A Passion for Nature: The Life of John Muir* (Oxford: Oxford University Press, 2008), 9, 465 (respectively), and see also 9–10, 464–66.

84. For an exception that proves the rule, see Mark I. Wallace, *Finding God in the Singing River: Christianity, Spirit, Nature* (Minneapolis, MN: Augsburg Fortress, 2005).

85. A good example is Lee Penn's online article, "The Earth Charter—Agenda for Totalitarianism," which was posted in 2001 and appears at http://fatima.freehosting.net/Articles/Art4.htm. See also Lee Penn, *False Dawn: The United Religions Initiative, Globalism, and the Quest for a One-World Religion* (Hillsdale, NY: Sophia Perennis, 2004).

86. See, for example, the right-wing website, www.discoverthenetworks.org, which seeks to uncover a variety of nefarious environmentalist and left-wing conspiracies, including those that threaten the national sovereignty of the United States and that seek the destruction of industrial civilization.

87. The higher moral priority given to human life is usually based on peoples' supposed spiritual, moral, or cognitive superiority (or on more than one of these).

Chapter 8

1. Al Gore, *Earth in the Balance: Ecology and the Human Spirit* (Boston: Houghton Mifflin, 1992), 269.

2. Ibid., 12, and see 12–14 for the broader discussion.

3. Ibid., 246 (first two quotes), 265 (third quote). For the influence of Thomas Berry and Gore's view that a new story is needed and that Christian interpretations need correction, see 218.

4. For the entire text, see the Gaia Foundation website, www.gaiafoundation.org/about/history.php. Van der Post at least implicitly criticized Europeans for repressing the wildness of Africa and her nature-connected peoples. A friend of Carl Jung, he also significantly influenced Prince Charles and his conservationist worldview; see Robert Hinshaw, "van der Post, Sir Laurens," in *Encyclopedia of Religion and Nature*, ed. Taylor, 1690–91. See also the anonymously written biography, "Laurens van der Post (1906–1996)," www.kirjasto.sci.fi/laurens.htm, which comments that "in van der Post's works, Africa

emerged as a place where one could experience something of the oneness of being."

5. Ernest Friedrich Schumacher, *Small Is Beautiful: Economics As If People Mattered* (New York: Harper & Row, 1973). Schumacher published another seminal and influential contribution to dark green religion in 1966, an essay titled "Buddhist Economics," which was subsequently republished many times and is readily available in *Toward a Steady-State Economy,* ed. Herman E. Daly (San Francisco: W. H. Freeman, 1973). For a biography of Schumacher by the editor of *Resurgence,* see Satish Kumar, "Schumacher, Ernest Friedrich," in *Encyclopedia of Religion and Nature,* ed. Taylor, 1491–92. Goldsmith has expressed affinity for deep ecology, including in Edward Goldsmith, *The Way: An Ecological World-View,* rev, and enlarged ed. (Athens: University of Georgia Press, 1998 [1992]).

6. See the Goldman Environmental Prize website, www.goldmanprize.org.

7. See Goodall's website, www.janegoodall.org. On the Mbuti (now the preferred term to Pygmies among most scholars), see Justin Kenrick, "Pygmies (Mbuti Foragers) and Bila Farmers of the Ituri Forest (Democratic Republic of the Congo)," in *Encyclopedia of Religion and Nature,* ed. Taylor, 1316–18.

8. Goodall's talk was on 26 August 2002; a postlecture interview I had with her there led to the in-depth interview drawn on in chapter 2.

9. One mark of Vandana Shiva's prominence within the dark green religious milieu is that David Suzuki considered her one of the world's leading scientist-activists and quoted a number of dark green statements she has made; see David Suzuki, *The Sacred Balance: Rediscovering Our Place in Nature* (Vancouver, BC: Greystone; Seattle: Mountaineers Books, 1999 [1997]), esp. 232–35. For Shiva's most important book, see *Staying Alive: Women, Ecology, and Development* (London: Zed, 1989).

10. Soon after the conference, McGlade became executive director of the European Environment Agency in Copenhagen, taking a leave from University College of London.

11. Rory Spowers, *Rising Tides: A History of the Environmental Revolution and Visions for an Ecological Age* (Edinburgh: Canongate, 2002). For Huxley on Leibniz, see Aldous Huxley, *The Perennial Philosophy* (New York: Harper & Row, 1945), vii.

12. About Girardet, see "Council Members," at the Schumacher UK website, www.schumacher.org.uk/council.htm; and see the home page for the history of what was initially called the Schumacher Society. His book is also replete with themes characteristic of dark green religion; see Herbert Girardet, *Earthrise: Halting the Destruction, Healing the World* (London: Paladin/HarperCollins, 1992), 232–35.

13. In an interview, Tompkins said that reading Bill Devall and George Sessions, *Deep Ecology: Living as If Nature Mattered* (Salt Lake City, UT: Peregrine Smith, 1985), was an "epiphany"; see "Doug Tompkins Interview," *Wild Duck Review* 2, no. 6 (1996): 14–17. Tompkins called David Brower his "environmental hero" and Robinson Jeffers his "poet hero" in Lucy Knight, "Profile: Douglas

Tompkins," *New Statesman,* January 25, 2007, www.newstatesman.com/environment/2007/01/douglas-tompkins-chile-land.

14. And see Cormac Cullinan's *Wild Law: A Manifesto for Earth Justice* (Totnes, U.K.: Green, 2003).

15. For the Global Community Foundation's mission, see http://globalcommunity.org. An online version of the "Walk through Time" is at the foundation website, http://globalcommunity.org/wtt/walk_menu/index.html.

16. Although he was lucid and easy to understand, Tiango's English grammar was imperfect, so I corrected a few words without in any way changing his meaning.

17. Mburu, who was a part of our conversation, later wrote in a similar way to Tiango in Gathuru Mburu, "Kenya Greenbelt Movement," in *Encyclopedia of Religion and Nature,* ed. Taylor, 957–61. In 2009, Mburu was the African Biodiversity Network's general coordinator. See www.africanbiodiversity.org.

18. The idea of spirituality as the fourth pillar of sustainability is a central assertion in Andres Edwards, *The Sustainability Revolution: Portrait of a Paradigm Shift* (Gabriola, BC: New Society, 2005).

19. David Chappell, "Soka Gakkai and the Earth Charter," in *Encyclopedia of Religion and Nature,* ed. Taylor, 1581–82.

20. Steven C. Rockefeller and Earth Charter Steering Committee, "The Earth Charter at the Johannesburg Summit: A Report Prepared by the Earth Charter Steering Committee and International Secretariat," Earth Charter in Action, November 2002. This report was available in May 2008 at the Earth Charter USA website, but was subsequently moved to www.earthcharterinaction.org/resources/files/2002%2011%20WSSD%20Report.doc.

21. About the Ark of Hope, its pilgrimages, and pictures, see http://arkofhope.org.

22. Mbeki also lamented behavior "that has pity neither for beautiful nature nor for living human beings." For the complete text, see "Address at the Welcome Ceremony of the World Summit on Sustainable Development, 25 August 2002," Department of Foreign Affairs, Republic of South Africa, www.dfa.gov.za/docs/speeches/2002/mbek0825.htm.

23. From Mbeki's 1 September 2002 speech at the Cradle of Humanity, posted at Department of Foreign Affairs, Republic of South Africa, www.dfa.gov.za/docs/wssd029g.htm (accessed June 2003; no longer available).

24. Author discussion with Steven C. Rockefeller, 26 August 2002, after the celebration of the Earth Charter ay the IUCN venue.

25. The report noted, "In earlier UN declarations and treaties, there are references to nature, the earth, and ecosystems, but in the Johannesburg Declaration one finds . . . the first reference to the 'community of life' in a UN international law document." Rockefeller and committee, "Earth Charter at the Johannesburg Summit," 2 (my emphasis). Those speaking in favor of the charter stressed its emphasis on protecting both cultural and biological diversity; see 5–6, 9–10.

26. William Ophuls, *Ecology and the Politics of Scarcity: Prologue to a Political Theory of the Steady State* (San Francisco: W. H. Freeman, 1977), 232–38.

Daniel Deudney first discussed terrapolitan earth religion in "Global Village Sovereignty: Intergenerational Sovereign Publics, Federal-Republican Earth Constitutions, and Planetary Identities," in *The Greening of Sovereignty in World Politics,* ed. Karen Litfin (Cambridge, MA: MIT Press, 1998), 299–325. Deudney wrote provocatively about civic or Gaian Earth Religion in two earlier articles. See "In Search of Gaian Politics: Earth Religion's Challenge to Modern Western Civilization," in *Ecological Resistance Movements: The Global Emergence of Radical and Popular Environmentalism,* ed. Bron Taylor (Albany: State University of New York Press, 1995), 282–99; and "Ground Identity: Nature, Place, and Space in Nationalism," in *The Return of Culture and Identity in IR Theory,* ed. Yosef Lapid and Friedrich Kratochwil (Boulder, CO: Lynne Rienner, 1996), 129–45.

27. Robert Bellah, "Civil Religion in America," *Daedalus* 96 (1967): 1–21; Robert Bellah, *The Broken Covenant: American Civil Religion in Time of Trial* (New York: Seabury, 1975); and Wilbur Zelinsky, *Nation into State: The Shifting Symbolic Foundations of American Nationalism* (Chapel Hill: University of North Carolina Press, 1988).

28. Deudney, "Global Village," 313. He continued that this is "a sentiment dubbed *geopiety* by John Kirtland Wright and *topophilia* by Yi-Fu Tuan" (313). Other typical characteristics of national identities, Deudney said, are "an ethnonational identity as member of a group based upon shared attributes . . . and identity based upon membership in a particular political community or political regime, which gives rise to a regime patriotism" (313).

29. Deudney, "Gaian Politics," 289–90.

30. Deudney, "Ground Identity," 144.

31. This is not to say that every cultural form is valuable: certainly many cultural beliefs and practices are sharply criticized by those within the environmentalist milieu.

32. Deudney, "Ground Identity," 130.

33. Author Skype interview with Ximena Arango, 29 June 2008.

34. Deudney, "Global Village," 299.

35. Ibid., 303, 304, 311, see also 312.

36. Ibid., 317. The entire page on which this quotation appeared is revealing and shows that Deudney would, in the terms of this study, be a Gaian Naturalist: "A major limitation of the great premodern theological cosmologies is that modern natural science has undermined their credibility." He also wrote here that "a striking feature of Gaian Earth religion as a spiritual and moral system is its ability to make at least a prima facie claim to being compatible with the important natural science of ecology. Gaia is the most salient metaphorical structure spanning the divide between ecological science and Earth identity narratives." Deudney then discussed Lovelock's theory and quoted one of his most religion-sympathetic statements: "Thinking of the Earth as alive makes it seem, on happy days, in the right places, as if the whole planet were celebrating a sacred ceremony. Being on the Earth brings that same special feeling of comfort that attaches to the celebration of any religion when it is seemly and when one is fit to receive" (317).

37. Ibid., 317 ("Earth religion"), 307 ("Unlike restraint"), 312 ("Such an Earth" and "establish a system").

38. Ibid., 318, 312 (respectively).

39. Deudney, "Gaian Politics," 293.

40. I argued similarly in Bron Taylor, "Deep Ecology and Its Social Philosophy: A Critique," in *Beneath the Surface: Critical Essays on Deep Ecology,* ed. Eric Katz, Andrew Light, and David Rothenberg (Cambridge, MA: MIT Press, 2000), 269–99.

Chapter 9

1. For extensive references to these evolutionary explanations for religion, see the additional notes online at www.brontaylor.com.

2. Lance H. Gunderson and C. S. Holling, *Panarchy: Understanding Transformations in Systems of Humans and Nature* (Washington, DC: Island Press, 2002), 111.

3. Thomas Kuhn, *The Structure of Scientific Revolutions* (Chicago: University of Chicago Press, 1962).

4. As Fikret Berkes has argued, "the experience of a resource crisis is not only a major, but a *necessary* ingredient of social learning." Fikret Berkes, *Sacred Ecology: Traditional Ecological Knowledge and Resource Management* (Philadelphia: Taylor and Francis, 1999), 160.

5. Steven C. Rockefeller, "Crafting Principles for the Earth Charter," in *A Voice for Earth: American Writers Respond to the Earth Charter,* ed. Peter Corcoran and James Wohlpart (Athens: University of Georgia Press, 2008), 3–23. I completed my analysis before this article was published. I highly recommend it as a nuanced insider's account of the process, which reflects a kind of terrapolitan process at work. Especially interesting were Rockefeller's observations that the idea of intrinsic value was clearly in the 1982 United Nations World Charter for Nature (12); Buddhist philosophers objected to the "intrinsic value" trope but were contented with expressing the idea with other words (12–14); concerns and debates surfaced about whether to refer to "our planetary home" as Earth, the Earth, or the earth, and concerns about pantheism/paganism led to changes, including the deletion of a reference to "Mother Earth" desired by indigenous peoples and that was included in an early draft (7–9); and that care was taken to avoid language that could be understood as an endorsement of abortion. Rockefeller also stated that, although criticisms that environmentalists deify "the planet and [promote] pantheism and Earth worship are for the most part without justification, the drafting committee had to keep controversies of this nature in mind" (7).

6. For the entire text, see Center for Respect of Life and the Environment (CRLE), "The Earth Charter: Benchmark Draft," Special Issue, *Earth Ethics* 8, nos. 2–3 (1997): 1–23; or in the *Dark Green Religion* section at www.brontaylor.com, where I have posted a version downloaded from the Earth Charter site

on 26 June 2000. The final version is available at the Earth Charter website, www.earthcharter.org.

7. Berry's influence was, with little doubt, in part because a number of the people involved in the Earth Charter initiative had been profoundly influenced by him, including Mary Evelyn Tucker and John Grim (mentioned previously), who have been among the most influential scholars promoting religious environmentalism globally, in no small measure through their central role in orchestrating conferences and books devoted to the world's major religious traditions and ecology (see the volumes on Buddhism, Christianity, Confucianism, Daoism, Hinduism, indigenous traditions, Jainism, Judaism, Islam, and Shinto in the Religions of the World and Ecology series, published by Harvard University Press between 1997 and 2004). For more on this academic discipline and Tucker's and Grim's important roles in it, see also Bron Taylor, "Religious Studies and Environmental Concern," in *Encyclopedia of Religion and Nature,* ed. Taylor, 1373–79. Not incidentally, Berry's muse was Pierre Teilhard de Chardin (who ran afoul of the Church for writings that many considered pantheistic), and both Tucker and Grim have also been longtime leaders in the American Teilhard Association. See Tucker's biography of Teilhard, "Teilhard de Chardin, Pierre," in *Encyclopedia of Religion and Nature,* ed. Taylor, 1627–29; and the association's website,www.teilharddechardin.org/association.html.

8. I downloaded the second benchmark draft from the Earth Charter's official website in 1999, but it was no longer available there in July 2008; I did find it at *One Country: The Online Newsletter of the Bahá'í International Community,* www.onecountry.org/e112/ecbench2.htm.

9. See Thomas Sieger Derr, "The Earth Charter and the United Nations," *Religion & Liberty* 11, no. 2 (1001): 5–8, www.acton.org/publications/randl/rl_article_377.php. *Religion & Liberty* is the newsletter of the Action Institute for the Study of Religion and Liberty.

10. Derr was incorrect, however, in his assertion that United Nations documents eschew biocentric language, as noted previously.

11. Derr, "Earth Charter," 7, quoting the Earth Charter's conclusion.

12. Ibid., 8. See also the critics of the charter discussed in chapter 7.

13. Jonathan Benthall, *Returning to Religion: Why a Secular Age Is Haunted by Faith* (London: I. B. Tauris, 2008), 139 (both quotes).

14. See the "Spirituality" section in chapter 1 for details on Proctor's study.

15. For a Jewish example, see Manfred Gerstenfeld, "Paganism—a Jewish Perspective," in *Encyclopedia of Religion and Nature,* ed. Taylor, 1244–47.

16. James Lovelock, *Gaia: A New Look at Life on Earth,* rev. ed. (Oxford: Oxford University Press, 1995 [1979]), 133 (all but last quote), 134 (last quote).

17. Ibid., 136. Lovelock here quoted a Paganism-friendly Wordsworth sonnet.

18. Ibid., xiv.

19. See the entries (and references) devoted to the "world religions" in Bron Taylor, *Encyclopedia of Religion and Nature,* 2 vols. (London: Continuum International, 2005).

20. Malcolm Gladwell, *The Tipping Point: How Little Things Can Make a Big Difference* (Boston: Little, Brown, 2000), 30–88 (for the "law of the few").

21. Ibid., 89–132 (for Gladwell's "stickiness factor").

22. Ibid., 133–92 ("power of Context/Environment"), 259 ("Tipping points are a reaffirmation").

23. Fritjof Capra, *The Turning Point: Science, Society, and the Rising Culture* (New York: Simon and Schuster, 1982); David Korten, *The Great Turning: From Empire to Earth Community* (San Francisco: Kumarian Press, 2006).

24. Bron Taylor, "Hundredth Monkey and Monkeys in the Field," in *Encyclopedia of Religion and Nature,* ed. Taylor, 802–5.

25. For the term *cultural creatives,* see Paul H. Ray and Sherry Ruth Anderson, *The Cultural Creatives: How 50 Million People Are Changing the World* (New York: Harmony Books, 2000). Like other social scientists cited previously, they contend that a growing segment of the North America public has rejected traditional religion in favor of a spiritual life that eschews materialism and promotes progressive political and environmental causes.

26. One of the most prolific environmental/sustainability studies scholars is David Orr, who I will mention only to note his affinity with dark green religion. He has said that "it is no accident that connectedness is central to the meaning of both the Greek root word for ecology, *oikos,* and the Latin root word for religion, *religio.*" Quoted in Marci Janas, "Ancestry and Influence: A Portrait of David Orr," *Oberlin Online,* www.oberlin.edu/news-info/98sep/orr_profile.html.

27. Donald Worster, *Nature's Economy: A History of Ecological Ideas,* second ed. (Cambridge: Cambridge University Press, 1994 [1977]), 334 (previous quote), 335 (block quote).

28. Ibid., 338 (this and previous quotes).

29. In his biography of John Muir, *A Passion for Nature: The Life of John Muir* (Oxford: Oxford University Press, 2008), which was published after I initially submitted this manuscript, Worster offered a similar, sympathetic portrayal of this influential early proponent of (dark green) nature religion. He concluded that for Muir and his progeny, nature is "granted a higher emotional, spiritual, and aesthetic value—a value in itself" (466). Worster left open the question of whether the human species will ever demonstrate the "reverence, restraint, generosity [and] vision" (466) needed to build the green societies that are "the ultimate destination of the conservation (or environmental) movement that Muir helped found" (465). Worster saw too many obstacles to have confidence in this regard. So do I, but the contemporary evidence mustered in the present study suggests that, as unlikely as such a possibility might be, such a green transformation may not be impossible.

30. J. Baird Callicott, *Earth's Insights: A Survey of Ecological Ethics from the Mediterranean Basin to the Australian Outback* (Berkeley: University of California Press, 1994). See also J. Baird Callicott, *In Defense of the Land Ethic: Essays in Environmental Philosophy* (Albany: State University of New York Press, 1989).

31. J. Baird Callicott, "Natural History as Natural Religion," in *Encyclopedia of Religion and Nature,* ed. Taylor, 1169.

32. J. Baird Callicott, "Environmental Philosophy Is Environmental Activism: The Most Radical and Effective Kind," in *Environmental Philosophy and Environmental Activism,* ed. Don E. Marietta Jr. and Lester Embree (Lanham, MD: Rowman & Littlefield, 1995), 19–35.

33. Neil Evernden, *The Social Creation of Nature* (Baltimore, MD: John Hopkins University Press, 1992).

34. The article first appeared in the *New York Times Sunday Magazine* (giving it broad exposure) and then in William Cronon, "The Trouble with Wilderness; or, Getting Back to the Wrong Nature," in *Uncommon Ground: Toward Reinventing Nature,* ed. William Cronon (New York: Norton, 1995), 69–90.

35. For the vitriolic debate that followed, see the first volume and issue of *Environmental History* (1996), which reprinted Cronon's article alongside critiques by prominent conservation historians.

36. William Cronon, "The Trouble with Wilderness: A Response," *Environmental History* 1, no. 1 (1996): 56, 57.

37. For all quotes from this website, see "Think Gaia: For Life and the Earth," Sanyo Electric Company, www.sanyo.com/thinkgaia.

38. Paul Hawken, *The Magic of Findhorn* (New York: Harper & Row, 1975).

39. See Paul Hawken, Amory Lovins, and L. Hunter Lovins, *Natural Capitalism: Creating the Next Industrial Revolution.* (Boston: Little, Brown and Co., 1999).

40. Paul Hawken, *Blessed Unrest: How the Largest Movement in the World Came into Being, and Why No One Saw It Coming* (New York: Viking, 2007), 12, 4.

41. Ibid., 186, 184 (respectively), see also 189–90.

42. The Parliament of World Religions, which formed in 1988, seeks "to cultivate harmony among the world's religions and spiritual communities" and to promote "a just, peaceful and sustainable world." See "About Us" at www.parliamentofreligions.org.

43. Roger S. Gottlieb, *A Greener Faith: Religious Environmentalism and Our Planet's Future* (Oxford: Oxford University Press, 2006); Roger S. Gottlieb, ed., *This Sacred Earth: Religion, Nature, Environment* (New York: Routledge, 1996); Laurel Kearns and Catherine Keller, *Ecospirit: Religions and Philosophies for the Earth* (New York: Fordham University Press, 2007); and the journals *Worldviews* and *Ecotheology.*

44. Here quoting the Parliament of World Religions 2009 meeting theme, "A World of Difference: Hearing Each Other, Healing the Earth."

45. An excellent, pertinent book in this regard, which focuses on deep ecology, one form of dark green religion, is Michael E. Zimmerman, *Contesting Earth's Future: Radical Ecology and Postmodernity* (Berkeley: University of California Press, 1994); or a kindred argument in Michael E. Zimmerman, "Ecofascism," in *Encyclopedia of Religion and Nature,* ed. Taylor, 531–32.

46. Sam Harris, *The End of Faith: Religion, Terror, and the Future of Reason* (New York: Norton, 2004); Dennett, *Breaking the Spell: Religion as a Natural*

Phenomenon (New York: Viking, 2006); Dawkins, *The God Delusion* (New York: Houghton Mifflin, 2006); Christopher Hitchens, *God Is Not Great: How Religion Poisons Everything* (New York: Twelve, 2007).

47. I have written extensively about these movements and whether they have used or might use small- or large-scale violence to achieve their objectives. I believe these movements are rarely violent both because of factors external to them (the perceived and real power of the state) but more importantly because of specific beliefs central to their worldviews. I do not minimize the difficulty philosophers have long identified of defending individual persons believed to have moral value against the desires and preferences of majorities in ethical systems that weigh consequences or that consider the well-being of some, designated whole, to trump individual preferences or needs. I simply do not think there is much evidence of the feared despotism of teleological and holistic ethics when it comes to ecological ethics. See Bron Taylor, "Religion, Violence, and Radical Environmentalism: From Earth First! to the Unabomber to the Earth Liberation Front," *Terrorism and Political Violence* 10, no. 4 (1998): 10–42; Bron Taylor, "Green Apocalypticism: Understanding Disaster in the Radical Environmental Worldview," *Society and Natural Resources* 12, no. 4 (1999): 10–42; Bron Taylor, "Threat Assessments and Radical Environmentalism," *Terrorism and Political Violence* 15, no. 4 (2004): 172–83; and Bron Taylor, "Revisiting Ecoterrorism," in *Religionen Im Konflikt,* ed. Vasilios N. Makrides and Jörg Rüpke (Münster, Germany: Aschendorff, 2004), 237–48.

48. This was the thesis of Donella H. Meadows, et. al., *Limits to Growth: A Report for the Club of Rome's Project on the Predicament of Mankind* (New York: Universe, 1972). This controversial study appears to be vindicated by accumulating empirical data, which is analyzed in Graham M. Turner, "A Comparison of the *Limits to Growth* with 30 Years of Reality," *Global Environmental Change* 18 (2008): 397–411. Also especially illuminating are Peter M. Vitousek, Paul R. Ehrlich, Anne H. Ehrlich, and Pamela A. Matson, "Human Appropriation of the Products of Photosynthesis," *Bioscience* 36 (June 1986): 368–73; Peter M. Vitousek, Jane Lubchenco Mooney, and Jerry M. Melillo, "Human Domination of Ecosystems," *Science* 277, no. 5325 (1997): 494–99; Helmut Haberl et al., "Quantifying and Mapping the Human Appropriation of Net Primary Production in Earth's Terrestrial Ecosystems," *Proceedings of the National Academy of Sciences* 104, no. 31 (2007): 12492–97.

49. William Catton, *Overshoot: The Ecological Basis of Revolutionary Change* (Urban: University of Illinois Press, 1980); Garrett Hardin, *Living within Limits* (New York: Oxford University Press, 1993).

50. This passage is from Loren Eiseley's beautiful, wise, and sometimes melancholy memoir, *All the Strange Hours* (Lincoln: University of Nebraska Press, 2000 [1975]), 242. Eiseley (1907–1977) was an anthropologist and naturalist whose wide-ranging books and essays express reverence for life and its mysteries. He came to his perspective in no small part through scientific inquiry. A strong believer in evolution, he nevertheless averred that science was unable to

fully explain the beauty, value, and mystery of life. See also "The Flow of the River," in Loren Eiseley, *The Immense Journey: An Imaginative Naturalist Explores the Mysteries of Man and Nature* (New York: Vintage, 1959 [1946]), 27; and Loren Eiseley, *The Unexpected Universe* (New York: Harcourt, 1972), which includes "The Star Thrower" (67–92), his best-known essay and probably the best place to start when reading his work. His *Star Thrower* (New York: Harcourt/ Harvest, 1979) reprints this essay (169–85) and many others, including "Science and the Sense of the Holy" (186–201).

51. See, for example, Charles Alexander Eastman, *The Soul of the Indian* (Boston: Houghton Mifflin, 1911).

52. Rachel Carson, *Lost Woods: The Discovered Writing of Rachel Carson*, ed. Linda Lear (Boston: Beacon Press, 1998), 159. In the same 1954 talk, Carson expressed more dark green spirituality: "I am not afraid of being thought a sentimentalist when I stand here tonight and tell you that I believe natural beauty has a necessary place in the spiritual development of any individual or any society. I believe that whenever we destroy beauty . . . we have retarded some part of man's spiritual growth. I believe this affinity of the human spirit for the earth and its beauties is deeply and logically rooted. . . . Our origins are of the earth. And so there is in us a deeply seated response to the natural universe."

53. I agree with Edward Abbey, who urged people to dispense with metaphysical speculation. For me, such musing is a terrible waste of perfectly good time. I concede, however, through my argument about this with Michael York, that for some it can be an interesting hobby and that, maybe someday, something will come of it. With Eiseley, however, I rather more expect the answers to nagging questions about the existence of the universe and its meaning will remain beyond our grasp.

54. On 15 February, I was driving a small rental truck through rural Wisconsin, just four days after the death of my mother. Her meager belongings were in the back and the copyedited manuscript of this book, which I received the morning she died, sat beside me. As I drove through the region of the state near where my immigrant ancestors established homesteads, I listened to a radio essay by Diane Roberts, a writer and English professor. She was pondering the 150th anniversary of Darwin's *Origin of Species* and the subsequent religious controversies. Her essay was a clear reflection of a naturalistic, evolutionary, dark green religion, evidence that such religion was gaining cultural currency, and a reminder that that for many the more naturalistic forms of dark green religion are more compelling and plausible than the world's long-standing religious traditions. "Does accepting our place in the animal kingdom make us any less miraculous?" she rhetorically asked, offering as her answer: "The human brain evolved to remember the past. We can imagine the future. . . . We can delight in the stars of the night sky and know that we are made of the same stuff as they are. We are part of nature—we lose nothing by admitting it." Diane Roberts, "Taking Darwin Personally," National Public Radio, *Weekend Edition Sunday,* 15 February 2009, www.npr.org/templates/story/story.php?storyId=100731606.

Appendix

1. Henry David Thoreau, “Walking,” *Atlantic Monthly* (June 1862): 657–74, www.theatlantic.com/doc/186206/thoreau-walking. The essay also appears in many Thoreau anthologies, including one edited and with an introduction by Joseph Wood Krutch; see Henry David Thoreau, *Thoreau: Walden and Other Writings,* ed. Joseph Wood Krutch (New York: Bantam, 1965).

2. Henry David Thoreau, *Henry David Thoreau: Collected Essays and Poems,* ed. Elizabeth Hall Witherell (New York: Library of America/Penguin, 2001), 225–55, 444–67, and 468–501 (respectively).

3. Henry David Thoreau, *Faith in a Seed: The Dispersion of Seeds and Other Late Natural History Writings,* ed. Bradley P. Dean (Washington, D.C.: Island Press, 1993), 177–203; Henry David Thoreau, *Wild Fruits: Thoreau's Rediscovered Last Manuscript,* ed. Bradley P. Dean (New York: Norton, 1999).

4. Henry David Thoreau, *Henry David Thoreau: A Week on the Concord and Merrimack Rivers [1849]; Walden, or Life in the Woods [1854]; the Maine Woods [1864]; Cape Cod [1865],* with notes by Robert F. Sayer (New York: Library of America/Penguin, 1985).The three parts of *The Maine Woods* are “Ktaadn” (593–655), “Chesuncook” (656–712), and “The Allegash and East Branch” (713–822). “Ktaadn” is Thoreau's spelling of the mountain in Maine, otherwise spelled variously.

5. Henry David Thoreau, *The Annotated Walden: Walden; or Life in the Woods, together with Civil Disobedience,* edited by Philip Van Doren Stern (New York: Barnes and Noble, 1970 [1854]).

6. Thoreau, *Annotated Walden,* 155 (subsequent page citations are in the text).

7. Thoreau, “Walking,” in *Essays and Poems,* 240–41 (subsequent page citations are in the text).

8. Thoreau, *Annotated Walden,* 339.

9. Thoreau, “Walking,” in *Essays and Poems,* 239.

10. Thoreau, *Annotated Walden,* 323.

11. Thoreau, *Essays and Poems,* 491.

12. Thoreau, *Annotated Walden,* 426 (subsequent page citations are in the text).

13. Thoreau, *Essays and Poems,* 487–88.

14. Thoreau, *Henry David Thoreau: A Week on the Concord . . . ,* 684–85 (subsequent page citations are in the text). For the entire text of *The Maine Woods,* see 589–845.

15. Thoreau, “Walking,” in *Essays and Poems,* 233 (subsequent page citations are in the text).

16. Thoreau, *Annotated Walden,* 270 (subsequent page citations are in the text).

17. Thoreau, *Annotated Walden,* 152 (subsequent page citations are in the text).

18. Thoreau, “Walking,” in *Essays and Poems,* 250 (subsequent page citations are in the text).

19. Thoreau, *Annotated Walden,* 206–7 (subsequent page citations are in the text).

20. Thoreau, "Walking," in *Essays and Poems,* 242 (subsequent page citations are in the text).

21. Thoreau, "Huckleberries," in *Essays and Poems,* 493 (subsequent page citations are in the text).

22. Thoreau, "Walking," in *Essays and Poems,* 225; see also the first paragraph of "Walking.".

23. Thoreau, *Annotated Walden,* 339 (subsequent page citations are in the text).

24. Thoreau, *Henry David Thoreau: A Week on the Concord . . . ,* 653–54.

25. Thoreau, *Annotated Walden,* 151 (subsequent page citations are in the text).

26. Thoreau, "Huckleberries," in *Essays and Poems,* 501.

27. Thoreau, "Life without Principle," in *Essays and Poems,* 365; see 348–66 for the entire essay.

28. Thoreau, *Henry David Thoreau: A Week on the Concord . . . ,* 645–46 (subsequent page citations are in the text).

Bibliography

Abbey, Edward. *Abbey's Road*. New York: Plume, 1991.

———. "A Response to Schmookler on Anarchy." *Earth First!* 6, no. 7 (1986): 22.

———. *Desert Solitaire*. Tucson: University of Arizona Press, 1988 [1968].

———. *Down the River.* New York: Plume 1991 [1982]

———. *The Journey Home: Some Words in Defense of the American West.* New York: Dutton, 1977.

———. *The Monkey Wrench Gang*. New York: Avon, 1975.

Abram, David. "The Ecology of Magic." *Orion* 10, no. 3 (Summer 1991): 28–34.

———. "Merleau-Ponty and the Voice of the Earth." *Environmental Ethics* 10 (1988): 101–20.

———. "The Perceptual Implications of Gaia." *The Ecologist* 15, no. 3 (1985): 96–103. Reprinted in *ReVision* 9, no. 2 (1987): 9–15.

———. *Spell of the Sensuous: Perception and Language in a More-Than-Human World*. New York: Pantheon, 1996.

Adams, Ansel. *Yosemite and the Range of Light*. Boston: New York Graphic Society, 1979.

Adams, Ansel, and Nancy Newhall. *This Is the American Earth*. San Francisco: Sierra Club, 1960.

Adler, Margot. *Drawing Down the Moon: Witches, Druids, Goddess-Worshippers, and Other Pagans in America*. Rev. and updated ed. New York: Penguin, 2006.

———. *Drawing Down the Moon: Witches, Druids, Goddess-Worshippers, and Other Pagans in America Today.* New York: Viking, 1979.

Albanese, Catherine L. *Nature Religion in America: From the Algonkian Indians to the New Age*. Chicago: University of Chicago Press, 1990.

Alston, William P. "Religion." In *Encyclopedia of Philosophy*, edited by Paul Edwards, 140–45. New York: Macmillan and the Free Press, 1967.

Anderson, William. *Green Man: The Archetype of Our Oneness with the Earth.* San Francisco: HarperCollins, 1990.

Anonymous. "Haole Go Home." In *Zero Break: An Illustrated Collection of Surf Writing, 1777–2004,* edited by Matt Warshaw, 312. Orlando, FL: Harcourt Books, 2004.

Arnold, Ron. *Ecoterror: The Violent Agenda to Save Nature—the World of the Unabomber.* Bellevue, WA: Free Enterprise, 1997.

Attenborough, David. *The Life of Mammals.* Princeton, NJ: Princeton University Press, 2002.

Bailey, Edward I. *Implicit Religion in Contemporary Society.* Leuven, Belgium: Peeters, 1997.

Bainbridge, William. "After the New Age." *Journal for the Scientific Study of Religion* 43 (2004): 381–94.

Bandow, Doug. *Ecoterrorism: The Dangerous Fringe of the Environmental Movement.* Backgrounder No. 764. Washington, DC: Heritage Foundation, 1990.

Barlow, Connie. "The Epic of Evolution: Religious and Cultural Interpretations of Modern Scientific Cosmology." *Science and Spirit,* February 1998. www.science-spirit.org/article_detail.php?article_id=31.

Barnes, James. "Dieback: A Vision of Darkness." *Earth First!* 17, no. 8 (1997): 3, 13.

Bekoff, Marc. *The Emotional Lives of Animals.* Novato, CA: New World Library, 2007.

———. *Minding Animals: Awareness, Emotions, and Heart.* Oxford: Oxford University Press, 2002.

———, ed. *The Smile of a Dolphin: Remarkable Accounts of Animal Emotions.* New York: Random House/Discovery, 2000.

Bekoff, Marc, Colin Allen, and Gordon Burghardt, eds. *The Cognitive Animal: Empirical and Theoretical Perspectives on Animal Cognition.* Cambridge, MA: MIT Press, 2002.

Bellah, Robert. *The Broken Covenant: American Civil Religion in Time of Trial.* New York: Seabury, 1975.

———. "Civil Religion in America." *Daedalus* 96 (1967): 1–21.

Benthall, Jonathan. *Returning to Religion: Why a Secular Age Is Haunted by Faith.* London: I. B. Tauris, 2008.

Bentley, Peter, and Philip J. Hughes. *Australian Life and the Christian Faith: Facts and Figures.* Melbourne, Australia: Christian Research Association, 1998.

Berger, Helen A. *A Community of Witches: Contemporary Neo-Paganism and Witchcraft in the United States.* Columbia: University of South Carolina Press, 1999.

Berkes, Fikret. *Sacred Ecology: Traditional Ecological Knowledge and Resource Management.* Philadelphia: Taylor and Francis, 1999.

———. *Sacred Ecology: Traditional Ecological Knowledge and Resource Management.* 2nd ed. New York: Routledge, 2008.

Berry, Thomas. *The Dream of the Earth*. San Francisco: Sierra Club Books, 1988.

———. *Evening Thoughts*. San Francisco: Sierra Club Books, 2006.

———. *The Great Work*. New York: Bell Tower, 1999.

Bird-David, Nurit. "'Animism' Revisited: Personhood, Environment, and Relational Epistemology." *Current Anthropology* 40 (1999): 567–91.

Blea, Chim [Dave Foreman]. "The Heritage of Western Civilization." *Earth First! Newsletter* 2, no. 5 (1982): 6.

Bradley, Marion Zimmer. *The Mists of Avalon*. New York: Knopf, 1983.

Bramwell, Anna. *Blood and Soil: Walter Darré and Hitler's Green Party*. Buckinghamshire, U.K.: Kensal, 1985.

———. *Ecology in the 20th Century: A History*. New Haven, CT: Yale University Press, 1989.

Brower, David Ross. *For Earth's Sake: The Life and Times of David Brower*. Salt Lake City, UT: Peregrine Smith Books, 1990.

———. *Let the Mountains Talk, Let the Rivers Run: Prescriptions for Our Planet*. New York: HarperCollins, 1995.

Brower, David Ross, Ansel Adams, and Robinson Jeffers. *Not Man Apart; Lines from Robinson Jeffers*. San Francisco: Sierra Club, 1965.

Brower, David Ross, and Steve Chapple. *Let the Mountains Talk, Let the Rivers Run: A Call to Save the Earth*. Gabriola Island, BC: New Society, 2000.

Bruun, Ole, and Arne Kalland. *Asian Perceptions of Nature: A Critical Approach*. London: Curzon, 1995.

Buell, Lawrence. *The Environmental Imagination: Thoreau, Nature Writing, and the Formation of American Culture*. Cambridge, MA: Belknap Press of Harvard University Press, 1996.

Burke, Edmund. *Philosophical Enquiry into the Origin of Our Ideas of the Sublime and Beautiful*. Edited by Adam Phillips. Oxford: Oxford World Classics, 1990 [1757].

Burnham, Philip. *Indian Country, God's Country: Native Americans and the National Parks*. Washington, DC: Island Press, 2000.

Burroughs, John. *In the Light of Day: Religious Discussions and Criticisms from a Naturalist's Point of View*. Boston: Houghton Mifflin, Riverside Press, 1900.

———. *Time and Change*. Amsterdam: Fredonia, 2001 [1912].

Callenbach, Ernest. *Ecotopia*. New York: Bantam, 1975.

———. "Ecotopian Reflections." In *Encyclopedia of Religion and Nature*, edited by Taylor, 566–68.

Callicott, J. Baird. *Earth's Insights: A Survey of Ecological Ethics from the Mediterranean Basin to the Australian Outback*. Berkeley: University of California Press, 1994.

———. "Environmental Philosophy Is Environmental Activism: The Most Radical and Effective Kind." In *Environmental Philosophy and Environmental Activism*, edited by Don E. Marietta Jr. and Lester Embree, 19–35. Lanham, MD: Rowman & Littlefield, 1995.

———. *In Defense of the Land Ethic: Essays in Environmental Philosophy.* Albany: State University of New York Press, 1989.

———. "Natural History as Natural Religion." In *Encyclopedia of Religion and Nature,* edited by Taylor, 1164–69.

Campbell, Colin. "The Cult, the Cultic Milieu and Secularization." *A Sociological Yearbook of Religion in Britain* 5 (1972): 119–36.

———. "The Cult, the Cultic Milieu and Secularization." In *The Cultic Milieu: Oppositional Subcultures in an Age of Globalization,* edited by Jeffrey Kaplan and Heléne Lööw, 12–25. Walnut Creek, CA: AltaMira, 2002.

Capra, Fritjof. *The Turning Point: Science, Society, and the Rising Culture.* New York: Simon and Schuster, 1982.

Carroll, Peter N. *Puritanism and the Wilderness: The Intellectual Significance of the New England Frontier, 1620–1700.* New York: Columbia University Press, 1969.

Carson, Rachel. *The Edge of the Sea.* Boston: Houghton Mifflin, 1955.

———. *Lost Woods: The Discovered Writing of Rachel Carson.* Edited by Linda Lear. Boston: Beacon, 1998.

———. *The Sea around Us.* New York: Oxford University Press, 1950.

———. *The Sense of Wonder.* New York: Harper & Row, 1965 [first published as an essay with a different title, 1956].

———. *Under the Sea Wind.* New York: Dutton, 1941.

Cartwright, Richard Austin. *Baptized into Wilderness: A Christian Perspective on John Muir.* Louisville, KY: John Knox Press, 1987.

Caruso, Mandy. "Healing Waters." *Surfer's Path,* no. 50 (2005): 124–29.

Catton, William. *Overshoot: The Ecological Basis of Revolutionary Change.* Urbana: University of Illinois Press, 1980.

Chadwick, Douglas. *Yellowstone to Yukon.* National Geographic Destinations. Washington, DC: National Geographic Society, 2000.

Chappell, David. "Soka Gakkai and the Earth Charter." In *Encyclopedia of Religion and Nature,* edited by Taylor, 1581–82.

Chidester, David. "Animism." In *Encyclopedia of Religion and Nature,* edited by Taylor, 78–81.

———. *Authentic Fakes: Religion and Popular American Culture.* Berkeley: University of California Press, 2005.

———. "Rituals of Exclusion and the Jonestown Dead." *Journal of the American Academy of Religion* 56, no. 4 (1988): 681–702.

Churchill, Ward. "Pacifism as Pathology" [article and graphic]. *Live Wild or Die,* no. 5 (1994): 15.

Cohen, Michael P. *The Pathless Way: John Muir and American Wilderness.* Madison: University of Wisconsin Press, 1984.

Colburn, Bolton, Ben Finney, Tyler Stallings, C. R. Stecyk, Deanne Stillman, and Tom Wolfe. *Surf Culture: The Art History of Surfing.* Corte Madera, CA: Ginko, 2002.

Cooper, Susan Fenimore. *Rural Hours.* New York: Putnam, 1850.

Corrington, Robert S. *Nature and Spirit: An Essay in Ecstatic Naturalism.* New York: Fordham University Press, 1992.

———. *Nature's Religion*. Lanham, MD: Rowman & Littlefield, 1997.

Center for Respect of Life and the Environment (CRLE). "The Earth Charter: Benchmark Draft." Special issue, *Earth Ethics* 8, nos. 2–3 (1997): 1–23.

Cronon, William. "The Trouble with Wilderness; or, Getting Back to the Wrong Nature." In *Uncommon Ground: Toward Reinventing Nature*, edited by William Cronon, 69–90. New York: Norton, 1995.

———. "The Trouble with Wilderness: A Response." *Environmental History* 1, no. 1 (1996): 47–57.

Csikszentmihalyi, Mihaly. *Flow: The Psychology of Optimal Experience*. San Francisco: Harper & Row, 1990.

Cullinan, Cormac. *Wild Law: A Manifesto for Earth Justice*. Totnes, U.K.: Green, 2003.

Custer, Charlie. "Speaking for the Trees." *Independent (Southern Humboldt News, Garberville, CA)*, 1998, 8.

Darwin, Charles. *On the Origin of Species* [1859] *and the Voyage of the Beagle* [1839]. With an introduction by Richard Dawkins. New York: Knopf, 2003.

Dawkins, Richard. *The God Delusion*. New York: Houghton Mifflin, 2006.

Dennett, Daniel C. *Breaking the Spell: Religion as a Natural Phenomenon*. New York: Viking, 2006.

Derr, Thomas Sieger. "The Earth Charter and the United Nations." *Religion & Liberty* 11, no. 2 (1001): 5–8. www.acton.org/publications/randl/rl_article_377.php.

Deudney, Daniel. "Global Village Sovereignty: Intergenerational Sovereign Publics, Federal-Republican Earth Constitutions, and Planetary Identities." In *The Greening of Sovereignty in World Politics*, edited by Karen Litfin, 299–325. Cambridge, MA: MIT Press, 1998.

———. "Ground Identity: Nature, Place, and Space in Nationalism." In *The Return of Culture and Identity in IR Theory*, edited by Yosef Lapid and Friedrich Kratochwil, 129–45. Boulder, CO: Lynne Rienner, 1996.

———. "In Search of Gaian Politics: Earth Religion's Challenge to Modern Western Civilization." In *Ecological Resistance Movements: The Global Emergence of Radical and Popular Environmentalism*, edited by Bron Taylor, 282–99. Albany: State University of New York Press, 1995.

Devall, Bill, ed. *Clearcut: The Tragedy of Industrial Forestry*. San Francisco: Sierra Club Books and Earth Island Press, 1994.

Devall, Bill, and George Sessions. *Deep Ecology: Living as If Nature Mattered*. Salt Lake City, UT: Peregrine Smith, 1985.

Diamond, Jared. *Collapse: How Societies Choose to Fail or Succeed*. New York: Viking, 2005.

———. *Guns, Germs, and Steel: The Fates of Human Societies*. New York: Norton, 1997.

Dowd, Michael. *Thank God for Evolution*. New York: Plume, 2009.

Eastman, Charles Alexander. *The Soul of the Indian*. Boston: Houghton Mifflin, 1911.

Edwards, Andres. *The Sustainability Revolution: Portrait of a Paradigm Shift*. Gabriola, BC: New Society, 2005.

Ehrenfeld, David. *The Arrogance of Humanism.* Oxford: Oxford University Press, 1978.

Ehrlich, Paul R. *The Machinery of Nature.* New York: Simon and Schuster, 1986.

Eiseley, Loren. *All the Strange Hours.* Lincoln: University of Nebraska Press, 2000 [1975].

———. *The Immense Journey: An Imaginative Naturalist Explores the Mysteries of Man and Nature.* New York: Vintage, 1959 [1946].

———. *The Star Thrower.* New York: Harcourt/Harvest, 1979.

———. *The Unexpected Universe.* New York: Harcourt, 1972.

Emerson, Ralph Waldo. *Ralph Waldo Emerson: Essays and Lectures.* New York: Library of America/Penguin, 1983.

Engel, J. Ronald. "Biosphere Reserves and World Heritage Sites." In *Encyclopedia of Religion and Nature,* edited by Taylor, 192–94.

———. "Renewing the Bond of Mankind and Nature: Biosphere Reserves as Sacred Space." *Orion* 4, no. 3 (1985): 52–63.

Evernden, Neil. *The Social Creation of Nature.* Baltimore, MD: John Hopkins University Press, 1992.

Feest, Christian F. "Pride and Prejudice: The Pocahontas Myth and Pamunkeyin." In *The Invented Indian,* edited by James A. Clifton, 49–70. New Brunswick, NJ: Transaction, 1990.

Feil, Ernst. *On the Concept of Religion.* Binghamton, U.K.: Global Publications, 2000.

Finney, Ben R., and James D. Houston. *Surfing: A History of the Ancient Hawaiian Sport.* Rev. ed. San Francisco: Pomegranate Art Books, 1996 [1966].

Ford, Nick, and David Brown. *Surfing and Social Theory: Experience, Embodiment, and Narrative of the Dream Glide.* London: Routledge, 2006.

Foreman, Dave. *Confessions of an Eco-Warrior.* New York: Harmony Books, 1991.

Foreman, Dave, and Bill Haywood, eds. *Ecodefense: A Field Guide to Monkeywrenching.* 2nd ed. Tucson, AZ: Ned Ludd, 1987 [1985].

Fournlander, Abraham, comp. *Fournlander's Collection of Hawaiian Antiquities and Folklore.* Memoirs of the Bernice P. Bishop Museum 4–6. Edited by Thomas G. Thrum. Honolulu: Bishop Museum Press, 1916–17.

Fouts, Roger. *Next of Kin: My Conversations with Chimpanzees.* New York: Avon, 1997.

Fox, Stephen. *The American Conservation Movement: John Muir and His Legacy.* Madison: University of Wisconsin Press, 1981.

Frazer, Sir James George. *Worship of Nature.* Whitefish, MT: Kessinger, 1975.

Fuller, Robert C. *Spiritual but Not Religious: Understanding Unchurched America.* Oxford: Oxford University Press, 2001.

Furtwangler, Albert. *Answering Chief Seattle.* Seattle: University of Washington Press, 1997.

Gardner, Gary T. *Inspiring Progress: Religion's Contributions to Sustainable Development.* New York: Norton, 2006.

Gatta, John. *Making Nature Sacred: Literature, Religion, and Environment in America from the Puritans to the Present.* Oxford: Oxford University Press, 2004.

Gerstenfeld, Manfred. "Paganism—a Jewish Perspective." In *Encyclopedia of Religion and Nature,* edited by Taylor, 1244–47.

Gibson, James J. *The Perception of the Visual World.* Boston: Houghton Mifflin, 1950.

———. *The Senses Considered as Perceptual Systems.* Boston: Houghton Mifflin, 1966.

Girardet, Herbert. *Earthrise: Halting the Destruction, Healing the World.* London: Paladin/HarperCollins, 1992.

Glacken, Clarence. *Traces on the Rhodian Shore: Nature and Culture in Western Thought from Ancient Times to the End of the Eighteenth Century.* Berkeley: University of California Press, 1967.

Gladwell, Malcolm. *The Tipping Point: How Little Things Can Make a Big Difference.* Boston: Little, Brown, 2000.

Glass, Matthew. "National Parks and Monuments." In *Encyclopedia of Religion and Nature,* edited by Taylor, 1152–58.

Glendon, Keith. "Chad Compton: The Comeback Kid." *Carbon* 2, no. 1 (2005): 70–75.

Globus, Robin, and Bron Taylor. "Environmental Millennialism." In *Oxford Handbook on Millennialism,* edited by Catherine Wessinger. Oxford: Oxford University Press, forthcoming.

Goldsmith, Edward. *The Way: An Ecological World-View.* Rev. and enlarged ed. Athens: University of Georgia Press, 1998 [1992].

Goodall, Jane. *40 Years at Gombe.* New York: Stewart, Tabori & Chang, 2000.

———. "Primate Spirituality." In *Encyclopedia of Religion and Nature,* edited by Taylor, 1303–6.

———. *Reason for Hope: A Spiritual Journey.* New York: Time Warner Books, 1999.

Goodall, Jane, and Marc Bekoff. *The Ten Trusts: What We Must Do to Care for the Animals We Love.* San Francisco: Harper San Francisco, 2003.

Gorbachev, Mikhail. "Nature Is My God." *Resurgence: An International Forum for Ecological and Spiritual Thinking,* no. 184 (September/October 1997): 14–15.

Gore, Al. *Earth in the Balance: Ecology and the Human Spirit.* Boston: Houghton Mifflin, 1992.

Gottlieb, Roger S. *A Greener Faith: Religious Environmentalism and Our Planet's Future.* Oxford: Oxford University Press, 2006.

———, ed. *This Sacred Earth: Religion, Nature, Environment.* New York: Routledge, 1996.

Gould, Rebecca Kneale. *At Home in Nature: Modern Homesteading and Spiritual Practice in America.* Berkeley: University of California Press, 2005.

———. "Back to the Land Movements." In *Encyclopedia of Religion and Nature,* edited by Taylor, 148–51.

———. "Thoreau, Henry David." In *Encyclopedia of Religion and Nature,* edited by Taylor, 1634–36.

Graber, Linda. *Wilderness as Sacred Space.* Washington, DC: Association of American Geographers, 1976.

Griffin, Donald R. *Animal Minds: Beyond Cognition to Consciousness.* New ed. Chicago: University of Chicago Press, 2001 [1992].

Griffin, Wendy. *Daughters of the Goddess: Studies of Healing, Identity, and Empowerment.* Walnut Creek, CA: AltaMira, 2000.

Grumbine, R. Edward. *Ghost Bears: Exploring the Biodiversity Crisis.* Washington, DC: Island Press, 1992.

Gunderson, Lance H., and C. S. Holling. *Panarchy: Understanding Transformations in Systems of Humans and Nature.* Washington, DC: Island Press, 2002.

Haberl, Helmut, K. Heinz Erb, Fridolin Krausmann, Veronika Gaube, Alberte Bondeau, Christoph Plutzar, Simone Gingrich, Wolfgangand Lucht, and Marina Fischer-Kowalski. "Quantifying and Mapping the Human Appropriation of Net Primary Production in Earth's Terrestrial Ecosystems." *Proceedings of the National Academy of Sciences* 104, no. 31 (2007): 12492–97.

Haeckel, Ernst Heinrich Philipp August. *Generelle morphologie der organismen: Allgemeine grundzüge der organischen formen-wissenschaft, mechanisch begründet durch die von Charles Darwin reformirte descendenztheorie.* 2 vols. Berlin: De Gruyter, 1988 [1866].

———. *Monism as Connecting Religion and Science: The Confession of Faith of a Man of Science.* Translated by J. Gilchrist. London: A. and C. Black, 1894.

———. *The Riddle of the Universe at the Close of the Nineteenth Century.* Translated by Joseph McCabe and Philip Lamantia. New York: Harper & Brothers, 1900.

———. *The Wonders of Life: A Popular Study of Biological Philosophy.* Translated by Joseph McCabe. New York: Harper, 1905.

Hall, David, ed. *Lived Religion in America: Toward a History of Practice.* Princeton, NJ: Princeton University Press, 1997.

Hardin, Garrett. *Living within Limits.* New York: Oxford University Press, 1993.

Harding, Walter. *The Days of Henry Thoreau: A Biography.* New York: Knopf, 1965.

Harmon, Dave, and Allen D. Putney, eds. *The Full Value of Parks: From Economics to the Intangible.* Lanham, MD: Rowman & Littlefield, 2003.

Harris, Sam. *The End of Faith: Religion, Terror, and the Future of Reason.* New York: Norton, 2004.

Harvey, Graham. *Animism.* New York: Columbia University Press, 2006.

———. "Animism—a Contemporary Perspective." In *Encyclopedia of Religion and Nature,* edited by Taylor, 81–83.

———. *Contemporary Paganism: Listening People, Speaking Earth.* New York: New York University Press, 1997.

Harvey, Graham, and Charlotte Hardman, eds. *Paganism Today.* New York: Thorsons/HarperCollins, 1996.

Hawken, Paul. *Blessed Unrest: How the Largest Movement in the World Came into Being, and Why No One Saw It Coming.* New York: Viking, 2007.

———. *The Magic of Findhorn.* New York: Harper & Row, 1975.

———. Hawken, Paul, Amory Lovins, and L. Hunter Lovins, *Natural Capitalism: Creating the Next Industrial Revolution.* Boston: Little, Brown and Co., 1999).

Heelas, Paul, Linda Woodhead, Benjamin Steel, Bronislaw Szerszynski, and Karin Tusting. *The Spiritual Revolution: Why Religion Is Giving Way to Spirituality.* Malden, MA: Blackwell, 2005.

Heinlein, Robert A. *Stranger in a Strange Land.* New York: G. P. Putnam, 1961.

Hening, Glen. "Mati Waiya: A Chumash Way of Thinking." In *Groundswell Society Annual Publication,* 3rd ed., by Glen Hening and contributors, 44–55. Oxnard, CA: Groundswell Society, 2001. www.groundswellsociety.org/publications/ThirdEdition/index.cfm.

Hening, Glen, and contributors. "Interview with Marilyn Edwards, Publisher, *Wahine* Magazine." In *Groundswell Society Annual Publication,* 3rd ed., 10–25. Oxnard, CA: Groundswell Society, 2001. www.groundswellsociety.org/publications/ThirdEdition/index.cfm.

Hening, Glenn, and Bron Taylor. "Surfing." In *Encyclopedia of Religion and Nature,* edited by Taylor, 1607–12.

Hessel, Dieter T., and Rosemary Radford Ruether. *Christianity and Ecology: Seeking the Well-Being of Earth and Humans.* Religions of the World and Ecology, edited by Mary Evelyn Tucker and John Grim, Cambridge, MA: Harvard University Press, 2000.

Hill, Julia Butterfly. *The Legacy of Luna.* San Francisco: Harper, 2000.

Hinshaw, Robert. "van der Post, Sir Laurens." In *Encyclopedia of Religion and Nature,* edited by Taylor, 1690–91.

Hitchens, Christopher. *God Is Not Great: How Religion Poisons Everything.* New York: Twelve, 2007.

Holmes, Steven J. "Muir, John." In *Encyclopedia of Religion and Nature,* edited by Taylor, 1126–27.

———. *The Young John Muir: An Environmental Biography.* Madison: University of Wisconsin Press, 1999.

Holt, Lawrence. *Wild by Law: The Rise of Environmentalism and the Creation of the Wilderness Act.* DVD. Directed by Lawrence Holt and Diane Garey. Originally aired on PBS's *American Experience* series, 1992.

Hornborg, Alf. "Knowledge of Persons, Knowledge of Things: Animism, Fetishism, and Objectivism as Strategies of Knowing (or Not Knowing) the World." *Ethnos* 71, no. 1 (2006): 1–12.

Hume, Lynne. "Paganism in Australia." In *Encyclopedia of Religion and Nature,* edited by Taylor, 1243–44.

Hunter, Robert. *Warriors of the Rainbow: A Chronicle of the Greenpeace Movement.* New York: Holt, Rinehart & Winston, 1979.

Hutton, Ronald. *The Triumph of the Moon: A History of Modern Pagan Witchcraft.* Oxford: Oxford University Press, 2000.

Huxley, Aldous. *The Perennial Philosophy.* New York: Harper & Row, 1945.

Ingram, David. *Green Screen: Environmentalism and Hollywood Cinema, Representing American Culture.* Exeter: University of Exeter Press, 2000.

Irwin, Terri. *Steve and Me.* New York: Simon Spotlight Entertainment, 2007.

Jacoby, Karl. *Crimes against Nature: Squatters, Poachers, Thieves, and the Hidden History of American Conservation.* Berkeley: University of California Press, 2001.

Jeffers, Robinson. "The Answer." In *The Collected Poetry of Robinson Jeffers,* edited by Tim Hunt. Stanford, CA: Stanford University Press, 1988.

———, ed. *The Wild God of the World: An Anthology of Robinson Jeffers.* Edited by Albert Gelpi. Stanford, CA: Stanford University Press, 2003.

Jensen, Derrick. *Endgame.* Vol. 1, *Resistance.* New York: Seven Stories, 2006.

———. *Endgame.* Vol. 2, *The Problem of Civilization.* New York: Seven Stories, 2006.

———. *A Language Older Than Words.* New York: Context, 2000.

———. *Listening to the Land: Conversations about Nature, Culture, and Eros.* New York: Sierra Club Books, 1995.

Johnson, Greg. "Rock Climbing." In *Encyclopedia of Religion and Nature,* edited by Taylor, 1398–400.

Jordan, William R., III. *The Sunflower Forest: Ecological Restoration and the New Communion with Nature.* Berkeley: University of California Press, 2003.

Kampion, Drew. *The Book of Waves: Form and Beauty on the Ocean.* Santa Barbara: Arpel Graphics/Surfer Publications, 1989.

———. *Stoked!: A History of Surf Culture.* Salt Lake City, UT: Gibbs Smith, 2003.

———. *The Way of the Surfer.* New York: Harry N. Abrams, 2003.

Kant, Immanuel. *Observations on the Feeling of the Beautiful and Sublime.* 2nd paperback ed. Berkeley, California: University of California Press, 2003 [1764].

Kearns, Laurel, and Catherine Keller. *Ecospirit: Religions and Philosophies for the Earth.* New York: Fordham University Press, 2007.

Keller, Robert H., and Michael F. Turek. *American Indians and National Parks.* Tucson: University of Arizona Press, 1998.

Kellert, Stephen R. *Kinship to Mastery: Biophilia in Human Evolution and Development.* Washington, DC: Island Press, 1997.

Kellert, Stephen R., and Edward O. Wilson, eds. *The Biophilia Hypothesis.* Washington, DC: Island Press, 1993.

Kenrick, Justin. "Pygmies (Mbuti Foragers) and Bila Farmers of the Ituri Forest (Democratic Republic of the Congo)." In *Encyclopedia of Religion and Nature,* edited by Taylor, 1316–18.

Kerouac, Jack. *Dharma Bums.* Cutchogue, NY: Buccaneer, 1958.

King, Anna S. "Spirituality: Transformation and Metamorphosis." *Religion* 26 (1996): 343–51.

Knight, Lucy. "Profile: Douglas Tompkins." *New Statesman,* 25 January 2007. www.newstatesman.com/environment/2007/01/douglas-tompkins-chile-land.

Kome, Penney, and Patrick Crean. *Peace, a Dream Unfolding.* San Francisco: Sierra Club Books, 1986.

Korten, David. *The Great Turning: From Empire to Earth Community.* San Francisco: Kumarian Press, 2006.

Kotler, Steven. *West of Jesus: Surfing, Science, and the Origins of Belief.* New York: Bloomsbury, 2006.

Krutch, Joseph Wood, ed. *Great American Nature Writing.* New York: Sloane, 1950.

———. "A Kind of Pantheism." *Saturday Review,* 10 June 1950, 7–8, 30–34.

———. *The Voice of the Desert.* New York: William Sloane Associates, 1954.

Kuhn, Thomas. *The Structure of Scientific Revolutions.* Chicago: University of Chicago Press, 1962.

Kumar, Satish. "Schumacher, Ernest Friedrich." In *Encyclopedia of Religion and Nature,* edited by Taylor, 1491–92.

Lagerlöf, Selma. *The Wonderful Adventures of Nils.* New York: Pantheon, 1947 [1907].

Langton, Katherine. "Findhorn Foundation/Community (Scotland)." In *Encyclopedia of Religion and Nature,* edited by Taylor, 658–60.

Lansing, J. Stephen. *Priests and Programmers: Technologies of Power in the Engineered Landscape of Bali.* Princeton, NJ: Princeton University Press, 1991.

Lanting, Frans. *Eye to Eye: Intimate Encounters with the Animal World.* Köln, Germany: Taschen, 1997.

Lee, David Webster. *Nature's Palette: The Science of Plant Color.* Chicago: University of Chicago Press, 2007.

Leopold, Aldo. *A Sand County Almanac: With Essays on Conservation from Round River.* New York: Sierra Club and Ballantine Books, 1986 [1949].

Leopold, Aldo, Susan L. Flader, and J. Baird Callicott. *The River of the Mother of God and Other Essays by Aldo Leopold.* Madison: University of Wisconsin Press, 1991.

Lopez, Barry. "The Language of Animals." *Wild Earth* 8, no. 2 (1998): inside front cover, 2–6.

———. "The Language of Animals." In *Wild Earth,* edited by Tom Butler, 296–305. Minneapolis, MN: Milkweed, 2002.

Lorbiecki, Marybeth. *Aldo Leopold: A Fierce Green Fire.* Oxford: Oxford University Press, 1996.

Lovelock, James. *The Ages of Gaia: A Biography of Our Living Earth.* New York: Norton, 1988.

———. *Gaia: A New Look at Life on Earth.* Rev. ed. Oxford: Oxford University Press, 1995 [1979].

———. "Gaian Pilgrimage." In *Encyclopedia of Religion and Nature,* edited by Taylor, 683–85.

———. *The Revenge of Gaia: Earth's Climate Crisis and the Fate of Humanity.* New York: Basic Books, 2006.

Lubbock, John. *The Origin of Civilization and the Primitive Condition of Man.* London: Longmans, Green, 1889.

Lynch, Gary, and Malcolm Gault-Williams. *Tom Blake: The Uncommon Journey of a Pioneer Waterman.* Corona Del Mar, CA: Croul Family Foundation, 2001.

Lyons, Dana. *The Tree.* Bellevue, WA: Illumination Arts Publishing, 2002.

———. "Tree Music." In *Encyclopedia of Religion and Nature,* edited by Taylor, 1656.

Mackert, Steffen. *Surf: A Visual Exploration of Surfing.* Edited by Robert Klantan. Berlin: Die Gestalen Verlag, 2005.

Macy, Joanna. "Council of All Beings." In *Encyclopedia of Religion and Nature,* edited by Taylor, 425–29.

Marcus, Ben. *Surfing and the Meaning of Life.* St. Paul, MN: Voyageur Press, 2006.

Marty, Martin. *A Nation of Behavers.* Chicago: University of Chicago Press, 1976.

Marx, Leo. *The Machine in the Garden: Technology and the Pastoral Ideal in America.* New York: Oxford University Press, 1964.

Masson, Jeffrey Moussaieff, and Susan McCarthy. *When Elephants Weep: The Emotional Lives of Animals.* New York: Delta/Random House, 1996.

Mazzeo, Tilar J. "Romanticism—American." In *Encyclopedia of Religion and Nature,* edited by Taylor, 1424–26.

Mburu, Gathuru. "Kenya Greenbelt Movement." In *Encyclopedia of Religion and Nature,* edited by Taylor, 957–61.

McGinnis, Michael Vincent, ed. *Bioregionalism.* New York: Routledge, 1999.

McGloin, Colleen. "Surfing Nation(S)—Surfing County(S)." PhD diss., University of Wollongong, Australia, 2005. www.library.uow.edu.au/adt-NWU/public/adt-NWU20060206.143742/index.html.

McIntyre, Rick, ed. *War against the Wolf: America's Campaign to Exterminate the Wolf.* Osceola, WI: Voyageur Press, 1995.

Meadows, Donella H., et. al. *The Limits to Growth: A Report for the Club of Rome's Project on the Predicament of Mankind.* New York: Universe, 1972.

Meine, Curt. *Aldo Leopold: His Life and Work.* Madison: University of Wisconsin Press, 1988.

———. "Leopold, Aldo." In *Encyclopedia of Religion and Nature,* edited by Taylor, 1005–8.

Meine, Curt, Michael Soulé, and Reed F. Noss. "A Mission-Driven Discipline: The Growth of Conservation Biology." *Conservation Biology* 20 (2006): 631–51.

Melekian, Brad. "Is God a Goofyfoot: If So, Surfing May Be the Next World Religion." *Surfer* 46, no. 3 (March 2005). www.surfermag.com/magazine/archivedissues/godgoofy/index.html.

Mendieta, Eduardo. "Casas, Bartolomé de las." In *Encyclopedia of Religion and Nature,* edited by Taylor, 271–72.

Merchant, Carolyn. *Ecological Revolutions: Nature, Gender, and Science in New England*. Chapel Hill: University of North Carolina Press, 1989.

Merleau-Ponty, Maurice. *The Phenomenology of Perception*. Translated by Colin Smith. London: Routledge & Kegan Paul, 1962.

Mies, Maria, and Vandana Shiva. *Ecofeminism*. London: Zed, 1993.

Miller, Perry. *Errand into the Wilderness*. Cambridge, MA: Harvard University Press, 1986 [1956].

Mitchell, Kerry. "Managing Spirituality: Public Religion and National Parks." *Journal for the Study of Religion, Nature and Culture* 1, no. 4 (2007): 431–49.

Mollison, Bill. *Introduction to Permaculture*. Tyalgum, Australia: Tagari, 1991.

Moriarity, Jay, and Chris Gallagher. *The Ultimate Guide to Surfing*. London: Lyons, 2001.

Muir, John. "Cedar Keys" [1916]. In *Muir: Nature Writings*, edited by Cronon, 818–27.

———. *The Mountains of California* [1894]. In *Muir: Nature Writings*, edited by Cronon, 311–547.

———. *Muir: Nature Writings*. Edited by William Cronon. New York: Library of America, 1997.

———. *My First Summer in the Sierra*. New York: Houghton Mifflin, 1911.

———. *My First Summer in the Sierra* [1911]. In *Muir: Nature Writings*, edited by Cronon, 147–309.

———. *A Thousand Mile Walk to the Gulf*. Edited by William Bade. New York: Houghton Mifflin, 1916.

———. "Wild Wool" [1875]. In *Muir: Nature Writings*, edited by Cronon, 598–606.

Müller, Friedrich Max. *Natural Religion*. Whitefish, MT: Kessinger, 2004 [1889].

Nabhan, Gary Paul. "Cultural Parallax in Viewing North American Habitats." In *Reinventing Nature? Responses to Postmodern Deconstruction*, edited by Michael Soulé and Gary Lease, 87–101. Washington, DC: Island Press, 1995.

———. *Enduring Seeds: Native American Agriculture and Wild Plant Conservation*. San Francisco: North Point, 1989.

———. "The Far Outside." In *Place of the Wild: A Wildlands Anthology*, edited by David Clarke Burks, 19–27. Washington, DC: Island Press, 1994.

Naess, Arne. "The Shallow and the Deep, Long-Range Ecology Movement: A Summary." *Inquiry* 16 (1973): 95–100.

Nash, James. "Christianity(9)—Christianity's Ecological Reformation." In *Encyclopedia of Religion and Nature*, edited by Taylor, 372–75.

Nash, Roderick Frazier. *The Rights of Nature: A History of Environmental Ethics*. Madison: University of Wisconsin Press, 1989.

———. *Wilderness and the American Mind*. 4th ed. New Haven, CT: Yale University Press, 2001 [1967].

Noll, Richard. "Haeckel, Ernst." In *Encyclopedia of Religion and Nature*, edited by Taylor, 735–36.

Norton, Bryan G. *Sustainability: A Philosophy of Adaptive Ecosystem Management.* Chicago: University of Chicago Press, 2005.

Noss, Reed F., and Allen Y. Cooperrider. *Saving Nature's Legacy: Protecting and Restoring Biodiversity.* Washington, DC: Island Press, 1994.

Odum, Howard T., and Elisabeth C. Odum. *A Prosperous Way Down: Principles and Policies.* Boulder: University of Colorado Press, 2001.

Oelschlaeger, Max. *The Idea of Wilderness: From Prehistory to the Age of Ecology.* New Haven, CT: Yale University Press, 1991.

Ophuls, William. *Ecology and the Politics of Scarcity: Prologue to a Political Theory of the Steady State.* San Francisco: W. H. Freeman, 1977.

Otto, Rudolf. *The Idea of the Holy.* 2nd ed. Oxford: Oxford University Press, 1950 [1923].

Pajama. "Bombthrowing: A Brief Treatise." *Wild Rockies Review* 6, no. 1 (1993): 9.

Pakenham, Thomas. *The Remarkable Baobab.* London: Weidenfeld & Nicolson, 2004.

Palmer, Martin, with Victoria Finlay. *Faith in Conservation: New Approaches to Religions and the Environment.* Washington, DC: World Bank, 2003.

Payne, Katy. *Silent Thunder: In the Presence of Elephants.* New York: Penguin, 1999.

Pecotic, David. "Ouspensky, Pyotr Demianovich." In *Encyclopedia of Religion and Nature,* edited by Taylor, 1225–27.

Penn, Lee. *False Dawn: The United Religions Initiative, Globalism, and the Quest for a One-World Religion.* Hillsdale, NY: Sophia Perennis, 2004.

Pepperberg, Irene M. *The Alex Studies: Cognitive and Communicative Abilities of Grey Parrots.* Cambridge, MA: Harvard University Press, 1999.

Pike, Sarah. *Earthly Bodies, Magical Selves: Contemporary Pagans and the Search for Community.* Berkeley: University of California Press, 2000.

———. *New Age and Neopagan Religions in America.* New York: Columbia University Press, 2004.

Plumwood, Val. "Being Prey." *Terra Nova* 1, no. 3 (1996): 33–44. A version is also at http://valplumwood.com/2008/03/08/being-prey.

Porter, Eliot, and David Ross Brower. *The Place No One Knew: Glen Canyon on the Colorado.* San Francisco: Sierra Club, 1963.

———. *The Place No One Knew: Glen Canyon on the Colorado.* Commemorative ed. San Francisco: Sierra Club, 2000.

Price, Joseph L. "Naturalistic Recreations." In *Spirituality and the Secular Quest,* edited by Peter Higbie Van Ness, 414–44. New York: Crossroad, 1996.

Proctor, James D. "Religion as Trust in Authority: Theocracy and Ecology in the United States." *Annals of the Association of American Geographers* 96, no. 1 (2006): 188–96.

Quammen, David. *Song of the Dodo: Island Biogeography in an Age of Extinctions.* New York: Scribner, 1996.

Quinn, Daniel. "Animism—Humanity's Original Religious Worldview." In *Encyclopedia of Religion and Nature,* edited by Taylor, 83–91.

———. *Ishmael: A Novel.* New York: Turner/Bantam, 1992.

———. *The Story of B.* New York: Bantam, 1996.

Ray, Paul H., and Sherry Ruth Anderson. *The Cultural Creatives: How 50 Million People Are Changing the World.* New York: Harmony Books, 2000.

Redfield, James. *The Celestine Prophecy.* New York: Warner, 1993.

———. *The Secret of Shambhala: In Search of the Eleventh Insight.* New York: Warner, 1999.

———. *The Tenth Insight.* New York: Warner, 1996.

Redfield, James, Michael Murphy, and Sylvia Timbers, eds. *God and the Evolving Universe: The Next Step in Personal Evolution.* New York: Tarcher/Putnam, 2002.

Reichel-Dolmatoff, Gerardo. *Amazonian Cosmos.* Chicago: University of Chicago Press, 1971.

———. "Cosmology as Ecological Analysis: A View from the Rainforest." *Man* 2, no. 3 (1976): 307–18.

———. *The Forest Within: The Worldview of the Tukano Amazonian Indians.* Totnes, U.K.: Themis-Green Books, 1996.

Robinson, David M. *Natural Life: Thoreau's Worldly Transcendentalism.* Ithaca, NY: Cornell University Press, 2004.

Rockefeller, Steven C. "Crafting Principles for the Earth Charter." In *A Voice for Earth: American Writers Respond to the Earth Charter,* edited by Peter Blaze Corcoran and James Wohlpart, 3–23. Athens: University of Georgia Press, 2008.

———. "Earth Charter." In *Encyclopedia of Religion and Nature,* edited by Taylor, 516–18.

Rockefeller, Steven C., and Earth Charter Steering Committee. "The Earth Charter at the Johannesburg Summit: A Report Prepared by the Earth Charter Steering Committee and International Secretariat." Earth Charter in Action, November 2002. www.earthcharterinaction.org/resources/files/2002%2011%20WSSD%20Report.doc.

Rogers, William C. [Avalon], ed. *Mountains and Rivers Compel Me: A Deep Ecology Reader for Forest Activists.* William C. Rogers, ca. 1995.

Roof, Wade Clark. *A Generation of Seekers.* San Francisco: Harper, 1993.

Roszak, Theodore. *The Voice of the Earth: An Exploration of Ecopsychology.* New York: Touchstone, 1992.

Rousseau, Jean-Jacques. *Discourse on the Arts and Sciences (First Discourse) and Polemics.* Lebanon, NH: Dartmouth College Press, 1992 [1750].

———. *A Discourse upon the Original Foundation of the Inequality among Mankind.* London: R. and J. Dodsley, 1761 [1755].

———. *Julie, or the New Heloise.* Lebanon, NH: Dartmouth College Press, 1997 [1761].

———. *Reveries of a Solitary Walker.* London: Penguin, 2004 [1782].

———. *The Social Contract.* New York: Penguin, 2006 [1762].

Rozzi, Ricardo, Francisca Massardo, Christopher Anderson, Steven McGehee, George Clark, Guillermo Egli, Eduardo Ramilo, Ursula Calderón, Cristina

Calderón, Lorenzo Aillapan, and Cristina Zárraga. *Multi-Ethnic Bird Guide of the Austral Temperate Forests of South America*. Translated by Christopher Anderson. Punta Arenas, Chile: Fantástico Sur-Universidad de Magallanes, 2003.

Rue, Loyal. *Everybody's Story: Wising up to the Epic of Evolution*. Albany: State University of New York Press, 2000.

Russell, Dick. *Eye of the Whale*. Washington, DC: Island Press, 2004.

Sagan, Carl. *Pale Blue Dot: A Vision of the Human Future in Space*. New York: Random House, 1994.

Saler, Benson. *Conceptualizing Religion: Immanent Anthropologists, Transcendent Natives, and Unbounded Categories*. Leiden, The Netherlands: Brill, 1993.

Salomonsen, Jone. *Enchanted Feminism: Ritual, Gender and Divinity among the Reclaiming Witches of San Francisco*. London: Routledge, 2002.

———. "Starhawk." In *Encyclopedia of Religion and Nature*, edited by Taylor, 1595–96.

Sanford, Whitney. "Pinned on Karma Rock: Whitewater Kayaking as Religious Experience." *Journal of the American Academy of Religion* 75, no. 4 (2007): 875–95.

Schultz, P. Wesley, Chris Shriver, Jennifer J. Tabanico, and Azar M. Khazian. "Implicit Connections with Nature." *Journal of Environmental Psychology* 24 (2004): 31–42.

Schulz, Florian. *Yellowstone to Yukon: Freedom to Roam; A Photographic Journey*. Seattle: Mountaineers Books, 2005.

Schumacher, Ernest Friedrich. "Buddhist Economics." In *Toward a Steady-State Economy*, edited by Herman E. Daly, 231–39. San Francisco: W. H. Freeman, 1973.

———. *Small Is Beautiful: Economics As If People Mattered*. New York: Harper & Row, 1973.

Sears, John. *Sacred Places: American Tourist Attractions in the Nineteenth Century*. New York: Oxford University Press, 1989.

Seed, John. "Anthropocentrism." *Earth First!* 3, no. 6 (1983): 15.

———. "Re-Earthing." In *Encyclopedia of Religion and Nature*, edited by Taylor, 1354–58.

Seed, John, Joanna Macy, Pat Fleming, and Arne Naess. *Thinking Like a Mountain: Towards a Council of All Beings*. Philadelphia: New Society, 1988.

Sessions, George. "Spinoza and Jeffers on Man in Nature." *Inquiry* 20, no. 4 (1977): 481–528.

Sheldrake, Rupert, and Aimee Morgana. "Testing a Language—Using Parrot for Telepathy." *Journal of Scientific Exploration* 17, no. 4 (2003): 601–15.

Shepard, Paul. *Coming Home to the Pleistocene*. Washington, DC: Island Press, 1998.

Shiva, Vandana. *Biopiracy the Plunder of Nature and Knowledge*. Boston: South End Press, 1997.

———. *Staying Alive: Women, Ecology, and Development*. London: Zed, 1989.

Smith, Jonathan Z. "Religion, Religions, Religious." In *Critical Terms for Religious Studies,* edited by Mark C. Taylor, 269–84. Chicago: University of Chicago Press, 1998.

Smith, Samantha. *Goddess Earth: Exposing the Pagan Agenda of the Environmental Movement.* Lafayette, LA: Huntington House, 1994.

Snyder, Gary. *The Old Ways.* San Francisco: City Lights, 1977.

———. *The Practice of the Wild.* San Francisco: North Point, 1990.

———. *The Real Work: Interviews and Talks 1964–1976.* New York: New Directions, 1980.

———. *Turtle Island.* New York: New Directions, 1969.

Snyder, Samuel S. "New Streams of Religion: Fly Fishing as a Lived, Religion of Nature." *Journal of the American Academy of Religion* 75, no. 4 (2007): 896–922.

Soulé, Michael, and Bruce A. Wilcox, eds. *Conservation Biology: An Evolutionary-Ecological Perspective.* Sunderland, MA: Sinauer, 1980.

Southwold, Martin. "Buddhism and the Definition of Religion." *Man* 13 (1978): 362–79.

Spence, Mark David. *Dispossessing the Wilderness: Indian Removal and the Making of the National Parks.* Oxford: Oxford University Press, 1999.

Spiritual Counterfeits Project. "Gaia: A Religion of the Earth." *SCP Journal* 16, no. 1 (1991).

———. "The Way of Ecology: Remaking Man in the Earth's Image." *SCP Journal* 17, no. 3 (1992).

Spiro, Melford. "Religion: Problems of Definition and Explanation." In *Anthropological Approaches to the Study of Religion,* edited by Michael Banton, 85–126. London: Tavistock, 1966.

Spowers, Rory. *Rising Tides: A History of the Environmental Revolution and Visions for an Ecological Age.* Edinburgh: Canongate, 2002.

Starhawk. *The Fifth Sacred Thing.* New York: Doubleday, 1993.

———. *The Spiral Dance: A Rebirth of the Ancient Religion of the Great Goddess.* San Francisco: Harper & Row, 1979.

Stoddard, Tom. "How Far Should We Go?" *Earth First!* 9, no. 2 (1988): 27.

Stone, Christopher D. *Should Trees Have Standing?* Los Altos, CA: William Kaufmann, 1974.

———. "Should Trees Have Standing? Toward Legal Rights for Natural Objects." *So. California Law Review* 45 (Spring 1972): 450–501.

Stuckrad, Kocku von. "Discursive Study of Religion: From States of the Mind to Communication and Action." *Method & Theory in the Study of Religion* 15 (2003): 255–71.

———. "Mountaineering." In *Encyclopedia of Religion and Nature,* edited by Taylor, 1119–20.

Sullivan, Lawrence. "Worship of Nature." In *Encyclopedia of Religion,* edited by Mircea Eliade, 324–28. New York: Macmillan, 1987.

Suttle, Garry. "Adams, Ansel." In *Encyclopedia of Religion and Nature,* edited by Taylor, 14–16.

Suzuki, David. *The Sacred Balance: Rediscovering Our Place in Nature.* Vancouver, BC: Greystone; Seattle: Mountaineers Books, 1999 [1997].

Suzuki, David, and Peter Knudtson. *Wisdom of the Elders: Honoring Sacred Native Visions of Nature.* New York: Bantam, 1992.

Swanwick, Howard. "Afterthought." *Drift* 1, no. 3 (2007): 148.

Swimme, Brian, and Thomas Berry. *The Universe Story: From the Primordial Flaring Forth to the Ecozoic Era; A Celebration of the Unfolding of the Cosmos.* San Francisco: HarperCollins, 1992.

Takacs, David. *The Idea of Biodiversity: Philosophies of Paradise.* Baltimore, MD: John Hopkins University Press, 1996.

Taylor, Bron. "Aquatic Nature Religion." *Journal of the American Academy of Religion* 75, no. 4 (2007): 863–74.

———. "Bioregionalism and the North American Bioregional Congress." In *Encyclopedia of Religion and Nature,* edited by Taylor, 190–2.

———. "Bioregionalism: An Ethics of Loyalty to Place." *Landscape Journal* 19, nos. 1–2 (2000): 50–72.

———. "Conservation Biology," in *Encyclopedia of Religion and Nature,* edited by Taylor, 415–18.

———. "Death and Afterlife in Jeffers and Abbey." In *Encyclopedia of Religion and Nature,* edited by Taylor, 455–56.

———. "Deep Ecology and Its Social Philosophy: A Critique." In *Beneath the Surface: Critical Essays on Deep Ecology,* edited by Eric Katz, Andrew Light and David Rothenberg, 269–99. Cambridge, MA: MIT Press, 2000.

———. "Diggers, Wolves, Ents, Elves and Expanding Universes: Bricolage, Religion, and Violence from Earth First! and the Earth Liberation Front to the Antiglobalization Resistance." In *The Cultic Milieu: Oppositional Subcultures in an Age of Globalization,* edited by Jeffrey Kaplan and Heléne Lööw, 26–74. Walnut Creek, CA: AltaMira, 2002.

———. "Disney Worlds at War." In *Encyclopedia of Religion and Nature,* edited by Taylor, 489–93.

———. "Earth and Nature-Based Spirituality (Part I): From Deep Ecology to Radical Environmentalism." *Religion* 31, no. 2 (2001): 175–93.

———. "Earth and Nature-Based Spirituality (Part II): From Deep Ecology and Bioregionalism to Scientific Paganism and the New Age." *Religion* 31, no. 3 (2001): 225–45.

———. "Earthen Spirituality or Cultural Genocide: Radical Environmentalism's Appropriation of Native American Spirituality." *Religion* 17, no. 2 (1997): 183–215.

———. "Earth First! Fights Back." *Terra Nova* 2, no. 2 (Spring 1997): 29–43.

———. "Earth First!'s Religious Radicalism." In *Ecological Prospects: Scientific, Religious, and Aesthetic Perspectives,* edited by Christopher Key Chapple, 185–209. Albany: State University of New York Press, 1994.

———. "Ecology and Nature Religions." In *Encyclopedia of Religion,* edited by Lindsay Jones, 2661–66. New York: Macmillan, 2005.

———. *Encyclopedia of Religion and Nature.* 2 vols. London: Continuum International, 2005.

———. "Evoking the Ecological Self: Art as Resistance to the War on Nature." *Peace Review* 5, no. 2 (1993): 225–30.

———. "Exploring Religion, Nature, and Culture." *Journal for the Study of Religion, Nature and Culture* 1, no. 1 (2007): 5–24.

———. "Green Apocalypticism: Understanding Disaster in the Radical Environmental Worldview." *Society and Natural Resources* 12, no. 4 (1999): 377–86.

———. "Hundredth Monkey and Monkeys in the Field." In *Encyclopedia of Religion and Nature,* edited by Taylor, 802–5.

———. "Religion, Violence, and Radical Environmentalism: From Earth First! to the Unabomber to the Earth Liberation Front." *Terrorism and Political Violence* 10, no. 4 (1998): 10–42.

———. "Religion and Environmentalism in America and Beyond." In *The Oxford Handbook of Religion and Ecology,* edited by Roger S. Gottlieb, 588–612. Oxford: Oxford University Press, 2006.

———. "The Religion and Politics of Earth First!" *The Ecologist* 21, no. 6 (November/December 1991): 258–66.

———. "Religious Studies and Environmental Concern." In *Encyclopedia of Religion and Nature,* edited by Taylor, 1373–79.

———. "Resacralizing Earth: Pagan Environmentalism and the Restoration of Turtle Island." In *American Sacred Space,* edited by David Chidester and Edward T. Linenthal, 97–151. Bloomington: Indiana University Press, 1995.

———. "Revisiting Ecoterrorism." In *Religionen Im Konflikt,* edited by Vasilios N. Makrides and Jörg Rüpke, 237–48. Münster, Germany: Aschendorff, 2004.

———. "Sea Spirituality, Surfing, and Aquatic Nature Religion." In *Deep Blue: Critical Reflections on Nature, Religion and Water,* edited by Sylvie Shaw and Andrew Francis, 213–33. London: Equinox, 2008.

———. "Snyder, Gary—and the Invention of Bioregional Spirituality and Politics." In *Encyclopedia of Religion and Nature,* edited by Taylor, 1562–67.

———. "Surfing into Spirituality, and a New, Aquatic Nature Religion." *Journal of the American Academy of Religion* 75, no. 4 (2007): 923–51.

———. "Threat Assessments and Radical Environmentalism." *Terrorism and Political Violence* 15, no. 4 (2004): 172–83.

———. "The Tributaries of Radical Environmentalism." *Journal of Radicalism* 2, no. 1 (2008): 27–61.

———. *Wild Fruits: Thoreau's Rediscovered Last Manuscript.* Edited by Bradley P. Dean. New York: Norton, 1999.

Taylor, Bron, and Gavin Van Horn. "Nature Religion and Environmentalism in North America." In *Faith in America,* vol. 3, *Personal Spirituality Today,* edited by Charles H. Lippy, 165–90. Westport, CT: Praeger, 2006.

Taylor, Bron, and Joseph Dylan Witt. "Nature in New and Alternative Religions in America in America: Cases from Radical Environmentalism to Adventure Sports." In *New and Alternative Religions in the United States,* edited by W. Michael Ashcraft and Eugene V. Gallagher, 253–72. Westport, CT: Greenwood, 2006.

Taylor, Laurie. "Interview: Watching David Attenborough." *New Humanist* 123, no. 1 (2008). http://newhumanist.org.uk/1673.

Teilhard de Chardin, Pierre. *The Phenomenon of Man.* New York: Harper, 1976 [1959].

Thaxton, John, ed. *The American Wilderness: Essays by John Muir; Photographs by Ansel Adams.* New York: Barnes and Noble, 1993.

Thayer, Robert L. *Lifeplace: Bioregional Thought and Practice.* Berkeley: University of California Press, 2003.

Thomas, Nick C. "Steiner, Rudolf—and Anthroposophy." In *Encyclopedia of Religion and Nature,* edited by Taylor, 1596–97.

Thoreau, Henry David. *The Annotated Walden: Walden; or Life in the Woods, together with Civil Disobedience.* Edited by Philip Van Doren Stern. New York: Barnes and Noble, 1970 [1854].

———. *Faith in a Seed: The Dispersion of Seeds and Other Late Natural History Writings.* Edited by Bradley P. Dean. Washington, DC: Island Press, 1993.

———. *Henry David Thoreau: A Week on the Concord and Merrimack Rivers [1849]; Walden, or Life in the Woods [1854]; the Maine Woods [1864]; Cape Cod [1865].* New York: Library of America/Penguin, 1985.

———. *Henry David Thoreau: Collected Essays and Poems.* Edited by Elizabeth Hall Witherell. New York: Library of America/Penguin, 2001.

———. *Thoreau: Walden and Other Writings.* Edited by Joseph Wood Krutch. New York: Bantam, 1965.

———. "Walking." In *Walden and Other Writings.* New York: Random House, 1981 [1862].

———. *Wild Fruits: Thoreau's Rediscovered Last Manuscript.* Edited by Bradley P. Dean. New York: Norton, 1999.

Tocqueville, Alexis de. *Democracy in America.* New York: Harper & Row, 1966 [2 vols., 1835, 1840].

Tompkins, Douglas. "Doug Tompkins Interview." *Wild Duck Review* 2, no. 6 (1996): 14–17.

Tuan, Yi-Fu. "Discrepancies between Environmental Attitude and Behaviour: Examples from Europe and China." *Canadian Geographer* 12 (1968): 176–91.

Tucker, Mary Evelyn. "Teilhard de Chardin, Pierre." In *Encyclopedia of Religion and Nature,* edited by Taylor, 1627–29.

———. *Worldly Wonder: Religions Enter Their Ecological Phase.* LaSalle, IL: Open Court, 2003.

Turner, Graham M. "A Comparison of the *Limits to Growth* with 30 Years of Reality." *Global Environmental Change* 18 (2008): 397–411.

Turner, Victor. *The Ritual Process.* London: Routledge, 1969.

Tylor, Edward Burnett. *Primitive Culture: Researches into the Development of Mythology, Philosophy, Religion, Art and Custom.* London: J. Murray, 1871.

UNESCO. *Man Belongs to the Earth: International Cooperation in Environmental Research.* Paris: UNESCO-MAB, 1988.

van der Merwe, Chris. *Deep Ecology Elephant Programme (the Deep Guide).* Pretoria, South Africa: First Light Adventure, 1999.

Van Horn, Gavin, and Brent Blackwelder. "Brower, David." In *Encyclopedia of Religion and Nature,* edited by Taylor, 225–26.

Van Ness, Peter Higbie. *Spirituality, Diversion, and Decadence: The Contemporary Predicament.* Albany: State University of New York Press, 1992.

Victorin-Vangerud, Nancy M. "The Sacred Edge: Women, Sea and Spirit." *Sea Changes: The Journal of Women Scholars of Religion and Theology* 1 (2001). www.wsrt.net.au/seachanges/volume1/index.shtml.

Vitousek, Peter M., Paul R. Ehrlich, Anne H. Ehrlich, and Pamela A. Matson. "Human Appropriation of the Products of Photosynthesis." *Bioscience* 36 (June 1986): 368–73.

Vitousek, Peter M., Jane Lubchenco Mooney, and Jerry M. Melillo. "Human Domination of Ecosystems." *Science* 277, no. 5325 (1997): 494–99.

Walker, Alice. *Anything We Love Can Be Saved: A Writer's Activism.* New York: Random House 1997.

———. *The Color Purple: A Novel.* New York: Harcourt Brace Jovanovich, 1982.

———. *Living by the Word: Selected Writings, 1973–1987.* San Diego: Harcourt Brace Jovanovich, 1988.

———. *The Same River Twice: Honoring the Difficult; A Meditation on Life, Spirit, Art, and the Making of the Film, the Color Purple, Ten Years Later.* New York: Scribner, 1996.

Walker, Matt. "Keeping the Faith: Surfing Is Officially a Religion. So, What Now?" *Surfing,* July 2008, 126–33.

Wallace, Alfred Russel. *The Malay Archipelago, the Land of the Orang-Utan and the Bird of Paradise: A Narrative of Travel, with Studies of Man and Nature.* London: Macmillan, 1869.

Wallace, Mark I. *Finding God in the Singing River: Christianity, Spirit, Nature.* Minneapolis, MN: Augsburg Fortress, 2005.

Warshaw, Matt. *Above the Roar: 50 Surfer Interviews.* Santa Cruz, CA: Waterhouse, 1997.

———. *The Encyclopedia of Surfing.* New York: Harcourt, 2003.

———. "Religion and Surfing." In *The Encyclopedia of Surfing,* edited by Matt Warshaw, 499. New York: Harcourt, 2003.

———. *Surf Movie Tonight!: Surf Movie Poster Art, 1957–2004.* San Francisco: Chronicle Books, 2005.

———, ed. *Zero Break: An Illustrated Collection of Surf Writing, 1777–2004.* Orlando, FL: Harcourt Books, 2004.

Washington, E. F. "The Council Fire" [graphic]. *Entmoot!: The Washington Earth First! Newsletter* (Spring 1994): 3.

Watson, Paul. "Biocentric Religion, A Call for." In *Encyclopedia of Religion and Nature,* edited by Taylor, 176–79.

———. *Ocean Warrior: My Battle to End the Illegal Slaughter on the High Seas.* Toronto: Key Porter, 1994.

———. "An Open Letter to Norwegians." *Sea Shepherd Log* (1st Quarter 1993): 5, 8, 11, 12.

———. *Seal Wars: Twenty-Five Years on the Front Lines with the Harp Seals.* Buffalo, NY: Firefly Books, 2002.

Watts, Steven. *The Magic Kingdom: Walt Disney and the American Way of Life.* Columbia: University of Missouri Press, 2001.

White, Lynn. "The Historical Roots of Our Ecologic Crisis." *Science* 155 (1967): 1203–7.

Whitley, David. *The Idea of Nature in Disney Animation.* Aldershot, Hampshire, U.K.: Ashgate, 2008.

Whitman, Walt. *Leaves of Grass.* 150th Anniversary ed. Oxford: Oxford University Press, 2005 [1855].

Willers, Bill, ed. *Learning to Listen to the Land.* Washington, DC: Island Press, 1991.

Williams, J. "A Study of the Influence of Surfing and Surf Culture on the Identity of Its Participants, inside the Case Study of Surf Tourism in Newquay." Bachelor's thesis in geography, University of Exeter, 2002.

Williamson, Marianne. *A Return to Love: Reflections on the Principles of a Course in Miracles.* New York: HarperCollins, 1992.

Willoya, William, and Vinson Brown. *Warriors of the Rainbow: Strange and Prophetic Indian Dreams.* Healdsburg, CA: Naturegraph, 1962.

Wilson, Edward Osborne. *Biophilia: The Human Bond with Other Species.* Cambridge, MA: Harvard University Press, 1984.

———. *On Human Nature.* Cambridge, MA: Harvard University Press, 2004 [1978].

Winchell, Donna Haisty. *Alice Walker.* New York: Twayne, 1992.

Wittgenstein, Ludwig. *Philosophical Investigations.* Malden, MA: Blackwell, 2001 [1953].

World Commission on Environment and Development. *Our Common Future.* Paris: United Nations World Commission on Environment and Development, 1987.

Worster, Donald. *Nature's Economy: A History of Ecological Ideas.* 2nd ed. Cambridge: Cambridge University Press, 1994 [1977].

———. *A Passion for Nature: The Life of John Muir.* Oxford: Oxford University Press, 2008.

York, Michael. *The Emerging Network: A Sociology of the New Age and Neo-Pagan Movements.* Lanham, MD: Rowman & Littlefield, 1995.

———. *Pagan Theology.* New York: New York University Press, 2004.

Young, Nat. *A History of Surfing.* Sidney, Australia: Palm Beach Press, 1983.

———, ed. *Surf Rage.* Angorie, NSW, Australia: Palm Beach Press/Nymboida Press, 2000.

Zaleha, Daniel Bernard. "The Only Paradise We Ever Need: An Investigation into Pantheism's Sacred Geography in the Writings of Edward Abbey, Thomas Berry, and Matthew Fox, and a Preliminary Survey of Signs of Emerging Pantheism in American Culture." Master's thesis, University of Florida, 2008.

Zelinsky, Wilbur. *Nation into State: The Shifting Symbolic Foundations of American Nationalism.* Chapel Hill: University of North Carolina Press, 1988.

Zerzan, John, ed. *Against Civilization: Readings and Reflections.* 2nd ed., Los Angeles: Feral House, 2005.

———. *Elements of Refusal.* Seattle: Left Bank Books, 1988.

———. *Future Primitive.* Columbia, MO: C.A.L. Press, 1994.

Zimmerman, Michael E. *Contesting Earth's Future: Radical Ecology and Postmodernity.* Berkeley: University of California Press, 1994.

———. "Ecofascism." In *Encyclopedia of Religion and Nature,* edited by Taylor, 531–32.

Zinnbauer, Brian J., Kenneth I. Pargament, and others. "Religion and Spirituality: Unfuzzying the Fuzzy." *Journal for the Scientific Study of Religion* 36, no. 4 (1997): 549–64.

Index